The Rule of Law in Crisis and Conflict Grey Zones

This book responds to ongoing calls for clarification and consensus regarding the meaning, scope and interplay of humanitarian law and human rights law in the 'grey zones' of unconventional operational environments such as counterterrorism and counterinsurgency operations. It contributes to the debate in this area by developing objective criteria for determining where the shift from the legal framework of law enforcement to that of non-international armed conflict occurs in relation to targeting law and weaponry law; by developing improved objective criteria for determining what constitutes direct participation in hostilities and *de facto* membership in an organised armed group; by taking stock of how existing targeting and weaponry rules are being applied to unconventional conflicts within civilian populated areas by key state players as well as by international and regional human rights mechanisms; by arguing for the progressive realisation of targeting and weaponry law so that they are more fitting for operational environments that are increasingly urbanised and civilianised; by seeking to understand how global networked connectivity may affect our understanding of the operational theatre of war and the geographical reach of the legal framework of non-international armed conflict.

Michael John-Hopkins has worked with the United Nations ICTY, the UK Refugee Council and a private legal practice in France. He has also worked as a Tutor in Law at Aberystwyth University and is currently a Senior Lecturer in Law at Oxford Brookes University, UK. He teaches tort law, land law, human rights law and humanitarian law.

The Rule of Law in Crisis and Conflict Grey Zones

Regulating the Use of Force in a Global Information Environment

Michael John-Hopkins

Routledge
Taylor & Francis Group
LONDON AND NEW YORK

First published 2017
by Routledge
2 Park Square, Milton Park, Abingdon, Oxfordshire OX14 4RN
711 Third Avenue, New York, NY 10017

Routledge is an imprint of the Taylor & Francis Group, an informa business

First issued in paperback 2018

British Library Cataloguing in Publication Data
A catalogue record for this book is available from the British Library

Library of Congress Cataloging in Publication Data
Names: John-Hopkins, Michael, author.
Title: The rule of law in crisis and conflict grey zones : regulating the use of force in a global information environment / Michael John-Hopkins.
Description: Abingdon, Oxon, [UK] ; New York : Routledge, 2017. | Includes bibliographical references and index.
Identifiers: LCCN 2016032757| ISBN 9781472486950 (hardback) | ISBN 9781351996747 (adobe reader) | ISBN 9781351996730 (epub3) | ISBN 9781351996723 (mobipocket)
Subjects: LCSH: War (International law) | Aggression (International law) | Humanitarian law. | Human rights. | War victims—Civil rights. | Terrorism—Prevention—Law and legislation. | Counterinsurgency.
Classification: LCC KZ6355 .J64 2017 | DDC 341.6/3—dc23
LC record available at https://lccn.loc.gov/2016032757

ISBN: 978-1-4724-8695-0 (hbk)
ISBN: 978-0-367-02510-6 (pbk)

Typeset in Galliard
by Apex CoVantage, LLC

For Ma and Pa.

Contents

Preface and acknowledgments

'. . . the progress of civilization should have the effect of alleviating as much as possible the calamities of war. . .'[1]

'Rules developed against the background of a reality which has changed must take on dynamic interpretation which adapts them, in the framework of accepted interpretational rules, to the new reality.'[2]

* * *

After reading Antonio Cassese's *The Human Dimension of International Law* I sought to further his analysis of the law relating to the conduct of hostilities by examining the social, legal and doctrinal conditions that have emerged within our contemporary global security environment, particularly during the course of the last decade of the twentieth century and the first decade of the twenty-first. I felt inspired by what I would describe as Cassese's visionary, cosmopolitan and policy-oriented approach to international law and have been keen to emulate this in my own way:

> While most existing textbooks or treatises take a strictly legal approach, I have attempted not to look at international legal institutions as abstract entities 'petrified' in time and space. I believe that it is misleading to consider international law as a piece of reality cut off from its historical, political, and ideological context. To grasp international law in all its ramifications, one ought to look at it as a set of continuously changing elements of a whole. I have therefore tried to combine the strictly legal method with the historical and sociological approach, to expound the *dynamic* of international law: in particular, to illustrate the tension between traditional law, firmly grounded

1 Declaration of St. Petersburg of 1868.

2 *Public Committee Against Torture v The Government of Israel* Israel, Supreme Court, Judgment of 14 December 2006, HCJ 769/02, 28 per Justice Barak.

> in the rock of State sovereignty, and the new or nascent law, often soft and hazy as a cloud, but inspired with new, community values.[3]

I have also sought to further one of the themes presented by Professor Christopher Harding et al. in *Renegotiating Westphalia: Essays and Commentary on the European and Conceptual Foundations of Modern International Law*, namely examining the extent to which international organisations can contribute to the progressive realisation of international law.

I hope this work will be of interest to teachers, students and practitioners (legal and military) in the field of international law and relations as well as military and strategic studies.

* * *

I am deeply thankful to Pa, and especially Ma, for all of their support and assistance in helping me to write this book. I am most grateful to Professor Christopher Harding and Professor Ryszard Piotrowicz for their valuable time and their constructive comments. I would also like to thank Dr Marco Odello for hosting troublesome PhD students at 'Chez Marco' on innumerable occasions, for tolerating and humouring the debates that would frequently break out in the dining room or the kitchen and for offering valuable insights during the quieter moments. I am grateful for the assistance that the Department of Law and Criminology at Aberystwyth University offered me and also for the excellent research assistance and support programmes offered to junior research staff at Oxford Brookes University. I am grateful for having wonderful friends such as Shea Esterling, Matthew Cawte, Bec Corn, Tom Jackson, Sundeep Rana, Tom Cummins, Alberica Bazzoni, Tecla Castella and especially Rosie Atherton, who have kept my spirits high and my mind broad. I am also deeply grateful to all of my colleagues at Oxford Brookes University who have been so supportive in the development of my teaching and research. In particular, I would like to thank Professor Peter Edge, Dr Shirley Shipman and Dr Dawn Sedman for their valuable guidance and support.

Michael John-Hopkins, Oxford, Summer 2016

3 Antonio Cassese, *International Law* (2nd edn Oxford University Press, 2005) Preface.

Table of international treaties, statutes and protocols

Declaration Renouncing the Use, in Time of War, of Explosive Projectiles Under 400 Grammes Weight. Saint Petersburg, 29 November–11 December 1868 (St Petersberg Declaration)

Convention (II) with Respect to the Laws and Customs of War on Land and its annex: Regulations concerning the Laws and Customs of War on Land. The Hague, 29 July 1899

Convention (IV) respecting the Laws and Customs of War on Land and its annex: Regulations concerning the Laws and Customs of War on Land. The Hague, 18 October 1907

Protocol for the Prohibition of the Use of Asphyxiating, Poisonous or Other Gases, and of Bacteriological Methods of Warfare. Geneva, 17 June 1925 (Geneva Gas Protocol)

United Nations, Charter of the United Nations, 24 October 1945, 1 UNTS XVI

United Nations, Statute of the International Court of Justice, 18 April 1946

Inter-American Commission on Human Rights (IACHR), American Declaration of the Rights and Duties of Man, 2 May 1948

Geneva Convention (III) relative to the Treatment of Prisoners of War. Geneva, 12 August 1949

Geneva Convention (IV) relative to the Protection of Civilian Persons in Time of War. Geneva, 12 August 1949

Council of Europe, European Convention for the Protection of Human Rights and Fundamental Freedoms, as amended by Protocols Nos 11 and 14, 4 November 1950, entry into force 3 September 1953

Optional Protocol to the International Covenant on Civil and Political Rights, December 16 1966, 999 UN.S 302

Organization of American States (OAS), American Convention on Human Rights, "Pact of San Jose", Costa Rica, 22 November 1969, entry into force 18 July 1978

International Covenant on Civil and Political Rights adopted and opened for signature, ratification and accession by General Assembly resolution 2200A (XXI) of 16 December 1966 entry into force 23 March 1976, in accordance with Article 49

Convention on the Prohibition of the Development, Production and Stockpiling of Bacteriological (Biological) and Toxin Weapons and on their Destruction. Opened for Signature at London, Moscow and Washington. 10 April 1972

Protocol Additional to the Geneva Conventions of 12 August 1949, and relating to the Protection of Victims of International Armed Conflicts (Protocol I), 8 June 1977

Protocol Additional to the Geneva Conventions of 12 August 1949, and relating to the Protection of Victims of Non-International Armed Conflicts (Protocol II), 8 June 1977

Convention on Prohibitions or Restrictions on the Use of Certain Conventional Weapons Which May be Deemed to be Excessively Injurious or to Have Indiscriminate Effects. Geneva, 10 October 1980

Vienna Convention on the Law of Treaties, 1155 U.N.T.S. 331, 8 I.L.M. 679, entered into force Jan 27, 1980

Protocol on Non-Detectable Fragments (Protocol I). Geneva, 10 October 1980

Protocol on Prohibitions or Restrictions on the Use of Mines, Booby-Traps and Other Devices. Geneva, 10 October 1980 (CCW Protocol II)

Protocol on Prohibitions or Restrictions on the Use of Incendiary Weapons (CCW Protocol III). Geneva, 10 October 1980

Convention on the Prohibition of the Development, Production, Stockpiling and use of Chemical Weapons and on their Destruction, Paris 13 January 1993

Statute of the International Criminal Tribunal for Rwanda, Security Council resolution 955, 8 November 1994

Convention on the Prohibition of the Use, Stockpiling, Production and Transfer of Anti-Personnel Mines and on their Destruction, 18 September 1997 ('Ottawa Convention')

UN General Assembly, Rome Statute of the International Criminal Court (last amended 2010), 17 July 1998

Optional Protocol to CAT of 18 December 2002, UN Doc A/RES/57/199

Protocol on Explosive Remnants of War (Protocol V to the 1980 CCW Convention), 28 November 2003

Convention on Cluster Munitions, 30 May 2008

Updated Statute of the International Criminal Tribunal for the Former Yugoslavia adopted 25 May 1993 by UNSC Resolution 827 (September 2009)

Figures

Table

Abbreviations

ACHR	American Convention on Human Rights
API	Protocol I Additional to the Geneva Conventions of 1949
APII	Protocol II Additional to the Geneva Conventions of 1949
CA3	Common Article 3 to the Geneva Conventions of 1949
CCM	Convention on Cluster Munitions
CCW	Convention on Prohibitions or Restrictions on the use of Certain Conventional Weapons
CWC	Chemical Weapons Convention
COIN	Counterinsurgency
Daesh/Da'Esh	Dawlat al-Islamiyah f'al-Iraq wa al-Sham
ECHR	European Convention on Human Rights
ECtHR	European Court of Human Rights
IHRL	International Human Rights Law
ICL	International Criminal Law
ICRC	International Committee of the Red Cross
IRC	Information Related Capabilities
ICTY	International Criminal Tribunal for the Former Yugoslavia
ICTR	International Criminal Tribunal for Rwanda
ISAF	International Security Assistance Force (Afghanistan)
ISIS	Islamic State of Iraq and Syria
ISIL	Islamic State of Iraq and the Levant
ISR	Information, Surveillance and Reconnaissance
IHL	International Humanitarian Law
LOAC	Law of Armed Conflict
MOUT	Military Operations on Urban Terrain
NIAC	Non-international Armed Conflict
NLW	NonLethal Weapon(s)
FM	Field Manual
RCA	Riot Control Agents
UN	United Nations
UK	United Kingdom
UKHOL	UK House of Lords
UKSC	UK Supreme Court

Introduction

Avoiding the strategic costs of civilian harm through the effective use of force

Heightened standards to promote the effective use of force

Taking stock of contemporary developments

Uncertainty and controversy not only surround the classification of situations of crisis and conflict, but also the meaning, scope and interplay of humanitarian law and human rights law in situations of irregular armed conflict and other situations of violence, and in turn the legal frameworks with which to assess the lawfulness and legitimacy of targeted killings. For example, in 2016 the Parliamentary Joint Committee on Human Rights alerted the United Kingdom (UK) government that it must clarify the legal justifications for its policy on the use of lethal force and urged the UK government to take the lead in developing an international consensus about how international frameworks apply to the use of lethal force abroad, particularly in counterterrorism operations outside the context of an armed conflict, both multilaterally and within the context of the UN Human Rights Council and the Council of Europe. The UK House of Commons Defence Committee also raised concerns about the lack of clarity and certainty that arise out of the tension and overlap between IHL/LOAC and human rights law, as well as the 'judicialisation of war'. Furthermore, the Defence Committee stressed that unless government policy, as determined by Parliament, military doctrine and legal principles, are clarified, then uncertainty for military personnel and claimants will continue to grow, and it urged a strategic plan to address these issues. Accordingly, this book sets out a provocative discussion that attempts to provide further clarification vis-à-vis what targeting and weaponry rules apply to the use of force in unconventional and irregular situations of violence and how to coordinate the application of these two very different legal frameworks. It argues for the progressive realisation of targeting and weaponry law so that they are more fitting for urbanised and civilianised operational environments. In particular, it focuses on the following interrelated issues: developing objective criteria for determining where the shift from a law-and-order paradigm to an armed conflict occurs in relation to targeting law (in particular, targeting by status) and weaponry law; developing improved objective criteria for determining civilian direct participation in hostilities and de facto membership in an organised armed group; and taking stock of how existing targeting and weaponry rules are being applied to unconventional conflicts within civilian populated areas by key state players, as well as by international and regional human rights mechanisms. This discussion seeks to contribute to ongoing debates within future strategic defence and security reviews about the extent to which we should expect legal scrutiny and cases to be brought under human rights law and the threshold from which this may be regarded as infeasible and an impediment to operational effectiveness.

In 2016 David Kilcullen argued that conventional military approaches adopted since 9/11 have turned out to be 'a strategic failure' and 'represent nothing less than the collapse of Western counterterrorism strategy'. Kilcullen suggests that this has cost us our 'strategic freedom of action and eroded the legitimacy of a cause that, at the outset, enjoyed huge global support'. According to Kilcullen, 'we're worse off today than before 9/11, with a stronger and more motivated, more dangerous enemy than before 9/11' and that 'with so much . . . happening simultaneously, in so many places . . . leaders are struggling to decide what to do and in what order'.[1] The main threats that Western democracies now have to struggle to contend with are organized crime, home-grown terrorism with links to foreign groups, the return of foreign fighters from wars in Africa and the Middle East, the rise of ISIS and its incendiary effect on global terrorism and conventional conflicts in the Middle East that are spilling over neighbouring regions.[2] The simultaneous convergence of these challenges, of crime and war, and the blurred distinction between the two is having a devastating effect on international peace and security and poses exceptional challenges to law enforcement. It risks turning our conceptions of peace, normality, democracy and the rule of law into a 'grey zone' wherein the cascade of human rights and civil liberties allows state strategy to become increasingly militarised and brutal, in particular, with secret 'kill lists' and extrajudicial or targeted killings (the intentional and premeditated killing of individuals by the police or armed forces of a state) without any due process or legal scrutiny. This discussion forms part of a civil society effort to influence progressively our notions of what constitutes appropriate responses to an extremely complex and dangerous security environment, wherein states themselves struggle to manage population growth, migration, civic control and order in the face of dissident and marginalised groups, as well as overlapping and transnational criminal groups. To paraphrase Georges Clemenceau and David Kilcullen, war is too important for the generals, and peace is too important for the politicians. The exceptions that have been made to human rights and the rule of law have not brought us greater security or contributed to an enduring peace.

Indeed, the controversies and alleged abuses surrounding state responses to contemporary conflict situations suggest that there are many gaps and uncertainties

1 David Kilcullen, *Blood Year: Islamic State and the Failures of the War on Terror* (Hurst & Company, London, 2016) 198.

2 Ibid., 202.

in the legal protection of civilians. Therefore, an account is needed of the regulatory framework relating to the conduct of hostilities, that is to say, targeting and weaponry law, which analyses structural, institutional and contextual features and then proposes a series of reforms in order to ensure that the use of military or police force is effective in achieving its own ends. The contributions put forward in this discussion draw from a rich stream of progressive jurisprudence, military doctrine and scholastic argument that seeks to enhance human security in contemporary hostilities through what may be described as the population-centric legal regulation of means and methods of force. This study comes to fruition at an opportune moment. That is to say, it is part of a new discourse that is beginning to emerge following just over a decade's worth of full-spectrum conflicts, such as counterinsurgencies, during which key players in these conflicts have themselves admitted that important lessons learnt from the major conflicts of the preceding twentieth century were somehow forgotten or flouted.

Putting this study into context, a contributor to this study suggested that these lessons forged out of twentieth- and twenty-first-century warfare became wise policy which crystallised into general and indeterminate standards, such as those set out in the four Geneva Conventions of 1949 and their two Additional Protocols of 1977. In 1949 the International Committee of the Red Cross (ICRC) sought to extend the four Geneva Conventions to all forms of armed conflict, both international and non-international. At the time such proposals were rejected by states that focused on establishing rules for protecting people who are not taking part in hostilities of an international character. The exception to this was Common Article 3 which sets out minimum standards in non-international armed conflicts. During the Diplomatic Conference on the Reaffirmation and Development of International Humanitarian Law applicable to Armed Conflict of 1974–1977 the ICRC again attempted to develop the protections available in non-international armed conflicts, but its proposals were rejected and deleted from the final texts of Additional Protocol I, which deals with international armed conflicts and which is much more expansive than Additional Protocol II, which deals with non-international armed conflicts. The proceedings of the Diplomatic Conference indicate that states resisted attempts to introduce Hague law provisions, which relate to the conduct of hostilities, into non-international armed conflicts, but were willing to allow more extensive Geneva law provisions on the protection of victims of war, albeit at a higher threshold than that which applies to Common Article 3. Since then the ICRC has sought to eliminate this threshold in practice, in particular through identifying rules of customary international humanitarian law. Indeed, since the 1990s everything has changed with developments in the fields of human rights law and especially international criminal law. Significantly, the International Criminal Tribunal for the Former Yugoslavia (ICTY) extended Hague law into non-international armed conflicts as a matter of customary law, and the ICRC Customary International Law Study also sought to remove the differences between the law relating to international and non-international armed conflict. In these ways, the boundary between international and non-international armed conflict became less important, and the focus was instead on identifying the point at which international humanitarian law begins to apply, or, in other words, on identifying a factual state of armed conflict. Given the indeterminacy between a state of emergency and a state of non-international armed conflict, the overlap with human rights law made this increasingly important, particularly on the issue of the use of force where human rights law seems to conflict with humanitarian law, particularly in relation to the 'permissions' granted under Hague law, such as status-based targeting (as compared to threat-based) with seemingly different interpretations of the meaning of the 'right to life'. There are growing disagreements between humanitarian law and human rights law proponents about how to regulate what often seems to be a 'grey area' of legal regulation, namely unconventional conflicts and the frequent use of lethal force abroad in the context of targeted killings or small-scale military operations. For example, a number of books on the topics of targeted killings and counterinsurgency such as *Counterinsurgency Law* by William Banks et al. (Oxford University Press, 2013), *Targeted Killings* by Finklestein et al. (Oxford University Press, 2012) and *International Law and the Classification of Conflicts* by Wilmshurst et al. (Oxford University Press, 2012) reveal diverging approaches, particularly between human rights law and military scholars, as well as in broad-brush proposals for reform. This study seeks to examine this legal grey area, to build on existing proposals and to provide ways forward for further consensus building and reform.

Indeed, the time is ripe to take stock of the military doctrine as well as the normative and institutional innovations that we have witnessed during the course of the beginning of the twenty-first century. Although an implication of this is that some issues raised in this discussion are not new, Chapter 1 suggests that existing legal frameworks are increasingly being challenged as trends such as urbanisation, global connectivity and population growth have become more acute and greater in extent. Furthermore, in the contemporary world we can observe great advances in military and communications technology combined with a proliferation of small arms and explosive weaponry. This means that the traditional battlefield has become more complex and 'civilianised', or, in other words, since 1977 there has been 'a continuous shift in the conduct of hostilities into civilian population centres' and this 'has led to an increasing intermingling of civilians with armed actors and has facilitated their involvement in activities more closely related to military operations'.[3] This has made it increasingly challenging to apply the conventional military doctrine and humanitarian law frameworks of this era, together with more recent legal and policy-based law enforcement frameworks based on human rights standards, to the complex factual situations of contemporary conflict where the discussion between crime and war is blurred, especially in the context of terrorism. On the issue of terrorism, these two models are traditionally seen as being in tension. The

3 Françoise Hampson, 'Direct Participation in Hostilities and the Interoperability of the Law of Armed Conflict and Human Rights Law', in Raul Pedrozo and Daria Wollschlaeger (eds), *International Law Studies* (Vol. 87, US Naval War College, 2011) 198.

basic law enforcement approach to terrorism would be through the criminal justice system, with suspected or actual terrorists being arrested and prosecuted on criminal charges with their attendant due process and habeas corpus rights. Under such a model, the use of lethal force may only be used where absolutely necessary – that is, in response to an individual who poses a direct and immediate lethal threat and there are no other ways to mitigate this threat. The basic LOAC approach to terrorism would be that it represents a form of violence that is too intense and the adversary is too organized to be amenable to law enforcement approaches, and thus the response should be military in nature – that is, lethal force can be used as a method of first resort where an individual is viewed as being a military threat by way of being a combatant, a civilian directly participating in hostilities or a member of a nonstate–organised armed group, even if they do not pose an immediate lethal threat.

This tension calls into question whether existing standards and approaches are fit for purpose in the sense that it is difficult to know what rules to apply to contemporary situations of violence and then to identify what those general rules actually mean in practice. This is particularly so with regard to non-international armed conflicts, which constitute a major focus of this study, because, as noted by Pejic, the typology of this general form of armed conflict has evolved to become more varied and complex in practice.[4] Indeed, although Haines stated that 'there is nothing new about irregularity in war . . . the British experienced it during the Boer War and Lawrence demonstrated its effectiveness in relation to the Arab Revolt which he described in Seven Pillars of Wisdom'[5], there is nevertheless recognition that irregular or unconventional wars constitute the 'messy end of the spectrum of contemporary hostilities' because their complexity makes them a challenge to understand and classify for the purposes of applying international humanitarian law and/or human rights law. In particular, this is because in any one operational theatre there may be a diverse mix of actors and armed 'interactions' between these actors, not to mention the diverse and highly subjective labels that are attached by the actors themselves as well as third parties, for example, guerrillas, terrorists, insurgents, criminals, unlawful combatants and so on. The chairperson of the UK Parliamentary Joint Committee on Human Rights stated in its 2016 report that 'we find ourselves today in a new situation for which our long established legal frameworks were not designed' in that

> [t]he line between war . . . and . . . terrorism has been blurred by two developments: rapid technological advance, including drone technology . . . and . . . the steady rise of non-state armed groups such as ISIL/Da'esh with

---

4 Jelena Pejic, 'The Protective Scope of Common Article 3: More than Meets the Eye' (2001) 93 (881) *International Review of the Red Cross* 189.

5 Steven Haines, 'The Nature of War and the Character of Contemporary Armed Conflict', in Elizabeth Wilmshurst (ed.), *International Law and the Classification of Conflicts* (OUP, 2012) 20.

> the intent and capability to carry out terrorist attacks globally and aspirations without territorial limit.[6]

In this sense, we face distinct contemporary challenges in relation to clear legal ordering in that humanitarian law and human rights law have to deal with these 'messy' situations.[7] In particular, in such increasingly complex and civilianised contemporary 'battle-spaces', Haines notes that 'those doing the fighting will find it difficult to distinguish between those fighting on the opposing side and those who are not fighting at all . . . and those who are only directly participating in hostilities intermittently'.[8]

This process of stock taking requires, it is argued, a bold normative and regulatory audit of what can be described as Hague principles – that is, the branch of IHL that generally seeks to fix 'the technical limits at which the necessities of war ought to yield to the requirements of humanity',[9] and ensure that innocent civilians are kept outside of hostilities as far as possible and also that they enjoy general protection from danger arising from hostilities.[10] Accordingly, this discussion aims to develop the notion that humanitarian interests are vital components of the pragmatic doctrines of military advantage and necessity, rather than being obstacles or a counterweight to them.

The greater coincidence of military and humanitarian considerations in the context of contemporary conflicts has led to important changes in what may be viewed as state practice, and with this comes normative evolution. One of the most significant features of contemporary military doctrine is the adoption and priority given to population-centric approaches, that is methods that aim to understand the political, social and economic environment in which operations occur, as well as the dynamic that sustains ongoing fighting; procedures, protocols and policy that aim to mitigate civilian harm and to connect the raised standards of civilian protection in contemporary operational theatres to the wider strategic picture of achieving politically durable military victories rather

6 UK House of Lords & House of Commons Joint Committee on Human Rights, 'The Government's Policy on the Use of Drones for Targeted Killing' (Second Report of Session 2015–2016) (House of Lords and House of Commons Paper, 10 May 2016) 1.25 and 1.26.

7 Steven Haines, 'The Nature of War and the Character of Contemporary Armed Conflict', in Elizabeth Wilmshurst (ed.), *International Law and the Classification of Conflicts* (OUP, 2012) 21–29.

8 Ibid., 30.

9 Declaration Renouncing the Use, in Time of War, of Explosive Projectiles Under 400 Grammes Weight. Saint Petersburg, 29 November/11 December 1868 (St Petersburg Declaration); Convention (II) with Respect to the Laws and Customs of War on Land and its annex: Regulations concerning the Laws and Customs of War on Land. The Hague, 29 July 1899; Convention (IV) respecting the Laws and Customs of War on Land and its annex: Regulations concerning the Laws and Customs of War on Land. The Hague, 18 October 1907.

10 Y Sandoz, C Swinarski, and B Zimmermann (eds), *Commentary on the Additional Protocols of 8 June 1977 to the Geneva Conventions of 12 August 1949* (ICRC/Martinus Nijhoff, Geneva, 1987) 1923 and 1935.

than causing a situation to escalate and making the return to peace unnecessarily difficult.

Such contemporary doctrinal shifts embody and reflect the population-centric approaches advanced by international civil society actors, which include UN treaty and charter mechanisms, regional human rights mechanisms and even nongovernmental organisations. These actors also prioritise human rights, the rule of law and civic security, or, in other words, a presumptive human rights–oriented approach to the use of force through the law enforcement model.

The dynamic nature of our contemporary international legal order provides fertile ground for novel and progressive legal protection of individuals and groups. Existing norms relating to the regulation of means and methods may be viewed as undergoing a process of transformation that can be described as 'population-centric', whereby greater weight is being ascribed to humanitarian considerations by both state and nonstate civil society actors in the process of *ex ante* and *ex post facto* determinations on the permissibility and legitimacy of utilising certain means and methods of force. Emerging doctrinal and jurisprudential shifts in this regard represent a departure from the classic conception of international humanitarian law being state-centred and applying equally to both parties to a conflict. Furthermore, they suggest that an appropriate balancing of military and humanitarian considerations in the context of asymmetric urban conflicts is to be achieved through higher standards of reasonableness. Reasonableness in this regard equates with the minimum and 'economical' use of force. Whilst taking on board the spectrum of scholarly discourse that characterises such state-led developments as mere policy, this study begs to differ and aims to set the scene for a fuller as well as more open and progressive debate concerning the normative implications of over a decade's worth of state practice in full-spectrum operations, counterinsurgency campaigns and a range of low-intensity conflicts. Thus, although it may be regarded as having its basis in the concordance of self-interest and wise policy of states, it may be suggested that higher standards of reasonableness should continue to crystallise into customary and treaty-based norms of targeting and weaponry law.

In short, there are signs that the strategic imperatives of key players in contemporary conflict situations have led to a greater coincidence of military and humanitarian interests, and, it is suggested, this feeds into normative development. Put another way, contemporary strategic imperatives allow for a progressive reconceptualisation of humanitarian law (that is, the development of more protective interpretations of existing standards) in the field of unconventional conflicts, and this mirrors the approach taken by domestic courts as well as regional and international human rights mechanisms. This shift is emerging as a practical and increasingly normative response to the material dynamics and exigencies of contemporary full-spectrum operations involving the use of force. That is to say, a population-centric approach is emerging from the strategic synthesis of the legal frameworks which have developed in response to the atrocities that have occurred over the course of the twentieth and twenty-first centuries. In particular, in the contemporary world there has been a prevalence of unconventional, as opposed to conventional, conflicts. Unconventional conflicts have a number of distinct traits: they are urban, they are asymmetric, they are non-international in character, they involve state and nonstate actors operating within and across state territorial boundaries, they are endemic and they are protracted. Additionally, for the purposes of legal regulation, they are a challenge to characterise. This is due to the mixed and fluid nature of contemporary full-spectrum conflicts that, by definition, have involved entangled threads of law enforcement, combat operations and military operations other than war, such as counterinsurgency operations.

The international humanitarian and human rights norms protective of human life in their substantive and procedural forms are therefore being appliqued to the fabric of unconventional and low-intensity conflict by state and nonstate human rights actors and, furthermore, this fabric is made from a complex weave of different threads. In part due to the extremely limited enforcement mechanisms of the IHL, which, for example, are characterised by the absence of individual complaints procedures as well as universal and compulsory enforcement mechanisms, individual recourse is now regularly being made to domestic courts as well as regional and United Nations human rights mechanisms. These actors are all playing a major role in applying not only human rights norms, but also norms of humanitarian law, in some cases expressly and in others implicitly. Whatever approach is taken by domestic, regional and international supervisory mechanisms, the very act of adjudicating or responding to 'grey area' hostilities involves explicit or implicit substantive reconceptualisation of substantive and procedural protections which is tending towards greater legal protections.

Main lines of argument

Summary

One of the main consequences that can be observed from state and nonstate responses to the grey zone of contemporary full-spectrum operations is that international humanitarian law, or more specifically Hague law, on the conduct of hostilities is coming down (from its high threshold of applicability), and international human rights law (IHRL) that substantively and procedurally protects the right to life is coming up in situations that are objectively tantamount to armed conflict. As the boundaries between crime and war become blurred and as operations become increasingly militarised, it is increasingly unclear what legal framework and which supervisory institutions have jurisdiction to regulate and supervise the use of force, namely that of law enforcement or combat, as well as the form that regulation should take. Arguably, this process is creating novel strategic, doctrinal and normative adaptations, but also increases risks of civilian harm together with the counterproductive use of military force and operational and strategic failures associated with targeting and intelligence blunders.[11]

11 Christopher Rogers, Rachel Reid, and Chris Kolenda, The Strategic Costs of Civilian Harm – Applying Lessons from Afghanistan to Current and Future Conflicts (Report) (Open Society Foundations–Washington, DC, June 2016) 24 and 25.

A major advantage of this trend is that it can serve to redress the substantive and institutional indeterminacy and weaknesses of IHL (that is, it is unclear what the rules mean in practice, and the institutions for their enforcement are weak) which undermine its effectiveness in providing substantive and procedural safeguards to civilians in contemporary conflicts. Accordingly, this contribution will examine and extrapolate the approaches taken in international criminal law in order to ensure that the legal line between the paradigm of law enforcement and hostilities does not become too blurred, resulting in Hague law permissions on the use of force being employed too broadly and arbitrarily, that is, outside armed conflict.

Grey area conflicts that are subject to mixed legal regulation and supervision represent a challenge for clear and consistent legal ordering. Additionally, this phenomenon creates a host of protection issues of a legal nature that this study aims to address.[12] In particular, as IHL and IHRL norms and mechanisms converge in the same operational theatres, there is an inevitable cross-fertilisation of substantive and procedural approaches.

Challenges for the protection of civilians in contemporary hostilities

The main challenges to the protection of civilians during the course of unconventional conflicts represent an opportunity for the progressive reconceptualisation (that is, the development of more protective interpretations of existing standards) and sequenced application of existing normative frameworks vis-à-vis targeting and weaponry law. With regard to the concept of 'sequencing', this study aims to clarify where the shift from a law-and-order paradigm to an armed conflict occurs in relation to targeting law (in particular, targeting by status) and weaponry law in order to clarify the conditions under which individuals can be lawfully killed, for example, in the context of targeted killings such as drone strikes. This is vital to ensure that individuals are not arbitrarily deprived of their right to life, as, according to some, targeted killings dangerously resemble unjustified homicide by the state or mandatory death sentences.[13] For example, in its 2016 report, the Parliamentary Joint Committee on Human Rights warned the UK government that it urgently needs to clarify the law on targeted killings[14] – that is, whether targeted killings are based upon self-defence within the framework of law enforcement outside of an armed conflict or the targeting of military

12 Giossi Caverzasio (ed.), 'Strengthening Protection in War: A Search for Professional Standards' (Summary of Discussions among Human Rights and Humanitarian Organizations at ICRC Workshops from 1996–2000) (International Committee of the Red Cross, Geneva, 2001). The concept of protection that will be applied throughout the course of this study is defined as : '. . . all activities aimed at ensuring full respect for the rights of the individual in accordance with the letter and the spirit of the relevant bodies of law, ie human rights law, international humanitarian law . . .'

13 Claire Finkelstein, Jens David Ohlin, and Andrew Altman, *Targeted Killings: Law and Morality in an Asymmetrical World* (Oxford University Press, 2012) 7.

14 UK House of Lords & House of Commons Joint Committee on Human Rights, above n 6, 7.

objectives within the framework of an armed conflict, since the UK government has to date presented an unclear and contradictory approach towards this issue. The committee further urged the UK government to take the lead in developing an international consensus about how international frameworks apply to the use of lethal force, particularly in counterterrorism operations outside the context of an armed conflict, both multilaterally and within the context of the UN Human Rights Council and the Council of Europe. The committee stressed the need for the UK government to be more explicit in setting out the legal basis for its policy of using lethal force abroad and stressed that it is vital that the legal line between the law enforcement framework and the law of armed conflict framework does not become blurred. The UK House of Commons Defence Committee raised concern that the tension and overlap between IHL/LOAC and HRL has resulted in a lack of certainty and clarity for the Ministry of Defence and the armed forces, as well as the 'judicialisation of war', in particular, with regard to the extraterritorial application of the ECHR to allow claims in the UK courts from foreign nationals.[15] Recent contributions to academic discourse, such as those mentioned earlier by Banks's et al., Finklestein et al. and Wilmshurst et al., have offered valuable legal analyses and proposals on how existing international legal frameworks should apply to the use of force both inside and outside the context of armed conflict. Banks et al. and Finkelstein et al. also highlight the uncertainties regarding what constitutes a sufficient link between an individual who is targeted and the organisation that poses a threat in the context of armed hostilities, as well as uncertainties surrounding the threshold criteria for the applicability of humanitarian law: this study aims to build on and develop the discourse in this area. With regard to 'reconceptualisation', Chapters 3 through 8 of this study set out to redress the substantive indeterminacies of IHL, or, in other words, it aims to clarify the meaning and scope of a range of IHL-targeting norms and how these can become generally interoperable with human rights norms on the use of force. The three main normative indeterminacies to be discussed relate to individual status determination, contextual status determination and targeting and weaponry law. In short, this discussion concerns three general issues that are relevant to contemporary situations of conflict and other situations of violence: first, this contribution explores the rules and guidelines for the classification of conflicts and aims to further elucidate the fuzzy boundaries between internal disturbances and tensions and Common Article 3 and then between Common Article 3 and APII non-international armed conflicts and whether those borderlines are currently drawn in the right place; second, this contribution discusses where the shift from a law-and-order paradigm to an armed conflict paradigm (in particular, vis-à-vis targeting by status) in relation to targeting should currently occur. In this regard, the discussion aims to address what is regarded to be a fundamental

15 UK House of Commons Defence Committee, 'UK Armed Forces Personnel and the Legal Framework for Future Operations' (Twelfth Report of Session 2013–4) (House of Commons, 2 April 2013) 4, 23, 24, 130.

question concerning the interoperability of human rights and humanitarian law on the use of force: namely, when does a situation become such that it exceeds the capacity of law enforcement mechanisms and thus may become subject to the paradigm of hostilities, or, in other words, how can we identify situations that exceed the capacity of the law enforcement model to make individualized threat assessments and use law enforcement techniques? This contribution queries whether the paradigm of law enforcement is practicable and to be expected in what have been referred to as 'low intensity' CA3 non-international armed conflicts. This study takes issue with this notion and proposes a model based on international criminal law (ICL) jurisprudence that can serve to guide the escalation and sequencing of force in a clear and pragmatic fashion so as to be of use to primary duty bearers as well protection actors who have developed doctrines and standards to this effect. In relation to this, this contribution aims to elucidate further the parameters of civilian immunity from attack, particularly in relation to the concepts of civilian direct participation in hostilities and, more importantly, individual membership in an organised armed group by exercising a continuous combat function, through reference to international criminal law notions of accessorial liability and coperpetration; third, this discussion aims to identify trends, possibilities and opportunities for the progressive development of existing standards concerning targeting and weaponry law (for example, clarifying the parameters of civilian loss of immunity from attack, distinction, precautions, proportionality, explosive weaponry in urban areas and 'nonlethal' weaponry). In relation to this, due to the limited enforcement mechanisms of IHL as well as the gaps associated with IHL enforcement mechanisms, recourse is now being made to a range of international and regional human rights bodies that are increasingly being called upon to gather facts and evaluate claims of alleged violations of human rights law as well as humanitarian law in a range of conflict situations, as well as other situations of violence not amounting to armed conflict. In this context, a range of human rights mechanisms is playing an important role in supervising, monitoring, fact finding and even adjudicating on alleged violations of human rights law and/or humanitarian law arising out of contemporary operational theatres of conflict. In so doing, they can be seen to be having a positive impact upon the meaning, scope and interoperability of human rights law and humanitarian law norms, such as those on the use of force, which is the focus of this study, not issues such as detention or economic, social or cultural rights, which also constitute other important areas of convergence and interoperability.

The parameters of civilian immunity from attack and individual status determination

As alluded to earlier, not only is it a challenge to classify situations as non-international in character, but within this general category of armed conflict, it may, by current standards, be extremely challenging to draw a clear distinction between loss of civilian immunity from attack on the basis of direct participation in hostilities and general loss of immunity from attack on the basis of a 'continuous combat function' which equates with de facto membership of an organised armed group. It is not only the case that the norms governing the parameters of immunity from attack are unclear, but in relation to the latter category (that is, membership), it is unclear at what threshold status-based targeting should apply in the complex environment of non-international armed conflicts, as well as its meaning and scope in practice. It is generally unclear who can be lawfully attacked in the complex operational environment of contemporary hostilities where conflicts are often fought 'amongst the people' or concentrations of civilians in urban areas.[16] The status and protection of 'irregulars' are unclear, and greater clarity is needed in this regard from both military and humanitarian points of view. Irregulars are key players in contemporary 'unconventional' conflicts even though they do not belong to a regularly constituted or conventional army. Such irregulars may be labelled in various ways as 'terrorists', 'guerrillas', 'insurgents' 'unlawful combatants', 'unprivileged combatants' or 'criminals'. The Hague Conventions and the Geneva Conventions of 1949 provide that certain 'irregulars' such as militias, volunteer corps and organised resistance movements 'belonging to a Party to the conflict' may be considered lawful 'combatants' entitled to prisoner of war status providing that they meet four criteria set out in Article 4 of the third Geneva Convention: namely that they are (a) commanded by a person responsible for his subordinates, (b) they wear a fixed distinctive sign recognisable at a distance, (c) they carry their arms openly and (d) they conduct their operations in accordance with the laws and customs of war.

Due to a recognition that because of 'the nature of hostilities', certain irregulars 'cannot so distinguish' themselves, and in order further to 'promote the protection of the civilian population from the effects of hostilities', Article 44 of Additional Protocol I (API) provides that combatant status, as defined under Article 43 API (that is, those who are members of the armed forces of a party to a conflict, under a command responsible to that party and subject to an internal disciplinary system), shall be retained by those who carry arms openly 'during each military engagement' and 'during such time as he is visible to the adversary while he is engaged in a military deployment preceding the launching of an attack in which he is to participate'. Because a similar provision is not included in Additional Protocol II, there is no combatant status in situations of non-international armed conflict and so no incentive for 'irregulars' or 'fighters' to distinguish themselves clearly from the civilian population.

More fundamentally, in asymmetric conflicts where an irregular force is faced with militarily superior adversaries which they simply cannot confront in conventional terms, they adopt unconventional tactics such as 'concealment warfare' amongst the civilian population in order to confer tactical, operational and, ultimately, strategic advantages. The dynamics of asymmetric hostilities are highly detrimental to civilian populations in that it is a challenge to discriminate

16 Rupert Smith, *The Utility of Force: The Art of War in the Modern World* (Allen Lane, London, 2006).

between objects of lawful attack from objects of protection because the prevailing objective criteria are indeterminate and thus of very little assistance in penetrating the unconventional operational environment.

Chapters 4 and 5 of this study will attempt to clarify and elucidate what it means to participate directly in hostilities and, more importantly, membership in an organised armed group, on the basis that the consequences that flow from individual status determination are constrained. This reconceptualisation is intended to assist primary duty bearers in making lawful and strategically effective targeting decisions in the complex operational environment of unconventional and full-spectrum conflicts.

Contextual status determination

The term 'contextual status determination' is used as a shorthand way of describing the process by which a situation of violence is evaluated for legal purposes vis-à-vis the use of force. This has two distinct approaches: first, in order to determine what legal framework is applicable generally to a situation; and, second, to determine the legal framework applicable to a specific incident.[17] The prevailing objective criteria for contextual status determination are unclear, and this represents a major obstacle to the application of the most apposite legal framework in both a strategic and humanitarian sense. Furthermore, the complexities of contemporary 'grey area' operational environments make unclear and contentious the identification of situations to which the permissive targeting and weaponry norms of IHL apply. Again, this study aims to clarify where the shift from a law-and-order paradigm to an armed conflict occurs in relation to targeting law (in particular, targeting by status) and weaponry law. It is suggested that such a clarification is important given that it is primary duty bearers – that is, states – who have a broad margin of discretion to self-classify according to their own political and strategic exigencies. The presumption is that states are best placed to do this. However, in practice, primary duty bearers may often need guidance and support in identifying and applying the most appropriate legal framework. Using states' political and strategic exigencies as a starting point in order to apply force that is operationally and strategically effective, a clearer and more detailed objective classification scheme is required so as to apply a minimum and economy of force. Although Hampson (p. 9) argues that 'there is no general, top-down principle which can be applied to establish if an issue should be handled in one way or another' and that 'the answers vary not only in relation to the issue involved but also in relation to other variables', such as whether or not a state has derogated from its human rights obligations or recognised the applicability of humanitarian law, it is suggested that improved objective classification schemes in relation to

17 Françoise Hampson, 'The Relationship between International Humanitarian Law and Human Rights Law', in Scott Sheeran and Sir Nigel Rodley (eds), *The Routledge Handbook of International Human Rights Law* (Routledge, 2013) 209.

basic CA3 non-international armed conflicts can assist with the identification of those situations where a presumptive human rights–oriented approach is apposite because it is feasible.[18]

Indeterminate and permissive standards of targeting and weaponry law and weak IHL supervision and enforcement mechanisms

Conventional IHL norms are permissive because of the historic will of major military powers following the Second World War. However, in the context of asymmetric urban conflicts, targeting and weaponry norms under IHL are arguably too permissive. It is suggested that key states in contemporary conflicts have recognised this and have accordingly adopted more restrictive rules of engagement vis-à-vis targeting and weaponry in practice so as not to undermine the strategically effective use of force. Account needs to be taken of the legally relevant practice of major military powers in their military manuals, operational manuals and rules of engagement, which are adopting greater restrictions on how hostilities can be conducted than those otherwise permitted under IHL.

Indeed, our post-1949 normative landscape has become more diverse and nuanced. Although this means that it is more complex, it also means that it allows for flexible and accurate normative adaptation, as well as the progressive interpretation of existing standards. Arguably, the law should be adaptive so that it can respond to the danger of existing standards not being suited to the protection needs of civilians caught up in fighting in contemporary operational theatres. However, from the point of view of states, there is the danger of doctrine and policy being seen as legal obligation and thus becoming customary law, and, as can be seen from the US Law of War Manual of 2015, many heightened standards and principles are couched as policy. The development of heightened standards in this area is the result of a constant struggle to codify the expectations of civil society. Although states may often resist this, in the past twenty years we have also increasingly seen states rely on their compliance with heightened legal and policy standards to legitimise and promote the strategic goals behind the use of force.

Given the fluid material conditions of contemporary operational environments, improved objective classification allows for the coordination and sequencing of legal frameworks and institutions within a single, but multifaceted, multidimensional and perhaps also a multigenerational, operational environment. Thus although IHRL should apply as far as possible, the progressive interpretation of

18 Françoise Hampson and Noam Lubell, 'Hassan v. United Kingdom, 29750/09, Intervention submitted by Professor Francoise Hampson & Professor Noam Lubell of The Human Rights Centre, University Of Essex' in Françoise Hampson and Noam Lubell. Georgia v. Russia (II) 38263/08, Amicus Curiae Brief submitted by Professor Francoise Hampson and Professor Noam Lubell of the Human Rights Centre, University Of Essex, 26.

conventional norms of IHL is necessary because conventional interpretations of general IHL principles are at odds with contemporary military or humanitarian considerations vis-à-vis the use of force in areas with a high density of civilians and civilian objects. This is particularly so with regard to conventional targeting and weaponry law, which can give undue weight to military considerations in the standard IHL analysis. Thus the scales of justice within a 'civilianised' operational theatre may actually allow for an unbalanced or skewed analysis, which can justify widespread 'collateral' damage and loss without necessarily conferring any strategic military advantage.[19]

The scales of justice are further skewed by the lack of effective monitoring, adjudication and enforcement of IHL. For example, the system of 'protecting powers' is not being used or is not relevant to many contemporary conflicts. Also, the International Humanitarian Fact-Finding Commission, a treaty body established pursuant to Article 90 API, has never been used. In view of the institutional weaknesses of the existing protection architecture of IHL, international and regional human rights mechanisms have stepped into the breach and have responded to protection needs of civilians and civilian populations in contemporary hostilities by carrying out a range of activities such as fact finding and adjudication as well as initiating domestic and international legal processes that lead to accountability and compensation for victims. In many ways, this contemporary process allows for the progressive interpretation and coordination of existing IHL and IHRL standards, and account should be taken of it so as to further the coincidence of military and humanitarian considerations by filling the gaps in the existing conventional protection architecture. Thus, the validity of progressive interpretation is increased where it is premised on the underlying strategic goals of states as well as the imperatives of international civil society.

Our international 'landscape' lacks a formal central authority and mechanisms for developing and coordinating protection. Rather, the pluralism and cosmopolitanism that characterises our contemporary normative and operational environment permits a principled reconceptualisation and restructuring of IHRL and IHL to suit the protection needs of civilians and civilian populations in contemporary conflicts, as well as to formally guide primary duty bearers when making strategically, operationally and tactically effective decisions with regard to targeting and weaponry.

Overview of discussion

Whereas Wilmshurst notes that the main problem in contemporary armed conflicts concerns implementation – in particular, by state and nonstate groups failing to follow the applicable rules of international humanitarian law – the focus of this

19 Chris af Jochnick and Roger Normand, 'The Legitimization of Violence 1: A Critical History of the Laws of War' (1994) 35 (1) *Harvard Journal of International Law*.

discussion is not implementation.[20] Rather, given the difficulties and uncertainties surrounding the classification of conflicts, as well as the scope, meaning and interplay of the frameworks of humanitarian law and human rights law applicable to diverse situations of armed conflict and other situations of violence, the objective is to develop a provocative and original argument for a radical reconceptualisation and restructuring of legal frameworks relative to the use of force, namely targeting and weaponry law. Thus it seeks to develop and encourage improvements in the existing legal frameworks, rather than identifying ways of promoting their implementation vis-à-vis state and nonstate actors. Nevertheless, this discussion does set out policy-based and practical arguments that aim further to encourage implementation of existing legal standards on the part of states, and so for reasons of focus, this discussion takes a state-centric view. This is because states play a primary role in the classification of situations of violence and are usually best placed to determine the appropriate legal framework that should be applied. Accurate classification in accordance with the guidelines discussed in Chapter 3 can thus ensure that human rights standards relative to the use of force therefore apply as far as possible, and this may play a major role in preventing the escalation of crisis or emergency situations into that of armed conflict. Broadly speaking, lines of empirical, theoretical and normative analysis and argument have been organised into the following clusters.

Chapter 1 of the study outlines contemporary protection issues and seeks to identify key problems, trends and challenges. In other words, it aims to conduct an enquiry into the general nature and characteristics of contemporary hostilities, which, it is suggested, are mostly non-international in character (that is, between state and nonstate actors or just between nonstate actors). The materials that will be used in carrying out this enquiry are the military manuals of key state players in contemporary conflicts of this nature (this study does not examine whether there are 'manuals' produced by nonstate actors). Military manuals are used because they constitute good evidence of state practice in an operational environment that is dangerous and challenging to investigate and may also be regarded as primary sources or first-hand accounts of the material conditions of contemporary conflicts that need to be accommodated by military forces at tactical, operational and strategic levels of command. In particular, before carrying out analysis from a legal perspective in relation to whether the existing legal frameworks are fit for contemporary purposes and, if not, how they can be reinterpreted towards this objective, this part of the discussion aims to consider how contemporary situations of crisis and conflict are viewed by primary duty bearers (that is, the state armed forces of key players in these situations) whose job it is to identify, analyse and respond to threats in a complex operational environment, which is made even more complex due to the array of legal, policy and doctrinal considerations in play. Accordingly, Chapter 1 explores developments in contemporary military

20 Elizabeth Wilmshurst, 'Conclusions', in Elizabeth Wilmshurst (ed.), *International Law and the Classification of Conflicts* (OUP, 2012) 492.

doctrine and identifies trends in contemporary situations of violence. It suggests that the most prevalent forms of conflict, namely non-international (NIAC) or less-than-non-international (less-than-NIAC) armed conflicts are, in fact, more likely to be perceived as a 'grey area' of legal regulation. Chapter 3 takes issue with the contention that Common Article 3 NIACs can be regarded as a 'less-than-NIAC' situation to which the paradigm of law enforcement applies.

Chapter 2 discusses whether existing standards for the legal regulation of means and methods of force are fit for purpose and fit for contemporary contexts, and also explores the core substantive and procedural weaknesses of the current system of humanitarian protection. It briefly examines evolutive approaches to the formation and interpretation of targeting and weaponry law and policy that are particular to international humanitarian law.

Chapters 3 through 8 proceed to identify and discuss a range of substantive, procedural and institutional solutions to contemporary protection issues. Chapter 3 sets out improved criteria for categorising situations of violence. Chapters 4 and 5 set out improved criteria for assessing whether an individual is directly participating in hostilities or is a member of an organised armed group, and these criteria borrow from international criminal law models of accessorial liability and coperpetration.

Chapters 6 and 7, respectively, discuss how treaty-based and customary targeting and weaponry law and policy have been progressively interpreted and developed to suit the challenges to military operations in civilianised and urbanised operational theatres. It examines how doctrine and policy are the core of the operation of legal norms, and especially the notion of military necessity and military advantage. In this regard, it is suggested that population-centric approaches that impose heightened restrictions on the use of force have been imposed by states in order to avoid the strategic costs of misidentification of civilians as fighters, as well as incidental harm and collateral damage that is seen as being excessive according to contemporary standards. The use of force abroad in counterinsurgency or counterterror operations – for example, in the context of occupation or targeted killings executed by remotely piloted air systems or special operations forces – has served to blur the line between counterterrorism law enforcement and the waging of war. Building on Chapter 3, which aims to make a clearer distinction between zones of law enforcement and zones of law of armed combat, Chapter 8 discusses developments with regard to the extraterritorial effect of human rights restrictions and obligations, and examines potential modalities for the parallel application of human rights law and international humanitarian law in order to ensure that adequate substantive and procedural safeguards are in place in order to regulate the use of force adequately, particularly when it comes to targeted or extrajudicial killing.

Overall, this study questions whether treaty-based humanitarian law, which was primarily designed for interstate conflicts and, to a limited degree, classic civil wars, is fit for purpose in the context of contemporary conflicts of asymmetric and irregular warfare involving organised armed groups, with diffuse organisational structures, who conduct protracted and opportunistic attacks. In so doing, it attempts to clarify the meaning and scope of this branch of public international law, as well as its interoperability with human rights law in relation to the use of force. The other areas of potential interoperability, such as detention, are not the focus of this study. Furthermore, the section entitled 'War and peace in the information environment' in Chapter 3 represents one of the first to attempts to lay the ground work for assessing the effect that information communications technology is having on the organisational structures, functions and behaviour of armed groups and in turn our understanding of the operational theatre of war to which the law of armed conflict applies.

1 The contemporary theatre of operations

The 'Medusa effect': the dynamics, context and strategy of contemporary responses to crises and conflicts[1]

Chapter 1 carries out a survey of the material conditions of contemporary conflicts in order to identify key trends that are pertinent to normative analysis and reconceptualisation. It examines the dynamics of the largely asymmetric power relations of contemporary conflicts which have led to conflicts becoming increasingly unconventional and irregular in nature and urban in context. The unconventional tactics employed mean that conflicts and confrontations tend to be continuous in duration and mixed or hybrid in character.[2] This means that within a single operational theatre, there may be different types of armed confrontation reaching the threshold of an armed conflict of an international and/or non-international character. Further complicating this is violence that may be associated with terrorism, uprisings, organised crime, public disorder or petty crime that does not reach the threshold of an armed conflict or which is connected with surrounding hostilities.

Broadly speaking, the operational environment can thus constitute a regulatory grey area, given that it may require a mix of combat, law enforcement and humanitarian activities. In this sense, there is a full spectrum or continuum of violence ranging from petty crime to armed hostilities between states or between states and organized armed groups. An appraisal of violence within the contemporary operational environment as protracted, civilianised, full spectrum, transnational and globally connected in turn requires a reappraisal of a conventional classification scheme that is merely structured to distinguish between war and peace. In this way, what is needed from both a military and legal point of view is an enhanced schematic framework that can recognise that in any one civilianised

---

1 Bryan Prior, 'U.S. Counterinsurgency: A Historic Plan under a New Guise' (2009) 29 (2) *SAIS Review of International Affairs* 87–91: 'There are undoubtedly side-effects when such bombings entail collateral damage and lead to a medusa effect: creating new insurgents in place of old ones'.

2 Rupert Smith, *The Utility of Force: The Art of War in the Modern World* (Allen Lane, London, 2006) 371.

operational theatre, there may be a range of activities, confrontations and conflicts that call for a range of responses, and thus different regulatory and supervisory frameworks.

Furthermore, any contemporary classification scheme ought to be sensitive to the information environment, which is defined as 'the aggregate of individuals, organisations, and systems that collect, process, disseminate, or act on information',[3] as well as a group's information-related capabilities (IRCs), which are defined as 'tools, techniques, or activities using data, information, or knowledge to create effects and operationally desirable conditions within the informational, physical and cognitive dimensions of the information environment'.[4] Counterinsurgency doctrine defines the information dimension as 'the place where information is collected, processed, stored, disseminated, displayed, and protected'; the physical dimension as comprising 'systems, human beings (including decision makers, leaders, and military forces), and supporting infrastructure that enable individuals and organisations to create effects, conduct operations across air, land, maritime, space and cyberspace domains across multiple domains'; and the cognitive dimension as comprising 'the mind of the decision maker or specific audience and is the dimension where people think, perceive, visualize, and decide'.[5]

The importance of this is that legal and military doctrine must keep up with the means and ends with which IRCs are increasingly being used to produce effects within the physical domain in particular. For example, advanced wired and wireless information technology is used to foster global networked connectivity in order to gain strategic, operational and tactical advantages and effects, namely, influencing international, national, regional and local audiences in near real time, anonymously and/or securely. Global networked connectivity brings countries, groups and people around the world closer together. It has a stimulating effect on crises and conflicts in that it provides for the freer flow of weaponry, information and finances for groups and individuals, and it allows them to have wider strategic and operational effects than in the past.[6]

Understanding the nature, scope, characteristics and effects of individuals, organisations and systems that collect, process, disseminate or act on information is essential in order to assess whether or not there is a state of armed internal conflict in existence. In other words, it is now essential to gain a clear understanding of a transnational information environment so as to identify adaptive and

3 US Joint Chiefs of Staff, Information Operations, Joint Publication 3–13 (27 November 2012 Incorporating Change 1, 20 November 2014).

4 Ibid.

5 US Department of the Army (Training and Doctrine Command) Counterinsurgency (COIN) Field Manual (FM) 3–24 and Fleet Marine Force Manual (FMFM) 3–24 (Final Draft) (Headquarters, Department of the Army, Washington, DC & Marine Corps Combat Development Command, Department of the Navy, Headquarters, United States Marine Corps, Washington, DC, 16 June 2006) 2–34.

6 Ibid., 2–5.

unconventional methods of command and control and assess whether a group's organisational, fighting and logistical abilities mean that it has the ability for protracted military operations in such a way that exceeds the capacity of law enforcement agencies to respond.[7] Furthermore, in an unconventional environment it is a major challenge to establish a nexus between an individual and any surrounding hostilities, either on the basis of their direct participation in hostilities or their membership in an organised armed group, in order to categorise them as a lethal threat. Where an individual does not constitute a direct and immediate lethal threat, recourse will have to be made to the information and cognitive dimensions in order to ascertain their intentions and motivations, as, more often than not, this will be the decisive issue when it comes to targeting on the basis of status and ensuring that it is done legitimately and lawfully.

A corollary of sounder legal ordering is enhanced substantive and procedural protection. Therefore, a clearer schematic framework is needed to regulate the use of force in 'grey area' operational theatres, as such situations pose a major threat to civilians, particularly when conventional military means and methods are employed within a civilianised and urbanised battle space. Military doctrine and sociopolitical analysis lay the foundations for a more nuanced classification scheme that promotes descriptively accurate and modulated status determination. This approach can ensure that IHL is kept at a relatively high threshold of applicability and is not normalised in terms of being brought down into situations of social crisis or public emergency too readily, that is, outside situations of armed conflict. It would also help governments to clarify and justify, for example, why the legal paradigm of humanitarian law in armed conflict, rather than the legal paradigm of human rights in law enforcement, applies to a use of lethal force abroad. In its 2016 Report, the UK Parliamentary Joint Committee on Human Rights stated that the legal line between counterterrorism law enforcement and the waging of war by military means risks becoming blurred and stated that urgent clarification is needed, particularly about how the international legal frameworks apply to the use of lethal force abroad in counterterrorism operations outside armed conflict. It went on to state that it is imperative that the UK government acknowledge that where it takes a life when there is no armed conflict, the higher standards laid down in the human rights law have to be met, and that it is only where the taking of life is in an armed conflict that the lower standards of the law of war apply. This is to ensure that operations resulting in the use of lethal force outside of armed conflict are planned and controlled in a way that minimises the risk of loss of life.[8]

Chapter 1 examines how the material conditions of contemporary confrontations and conflicts have informed and affected contemporary military

7 Ibid., 2–33 and 2–34.

8 UK House of Lords & House of Commons Joint Committee on Human Rights, 'The Government's Policy on the Use of Drones for Targeted Killing' (Second Report of Session 2015–2016) (House of Lords and House of Commons Paper, 10 May 2016).

doctrine and practice. In turn, Chapter 1 also lays the foundations for suggesting that contemporary military doctrine and sociopolitical analysis pave the way for progressive normative reconceptualisation and restructuring in a number of respects: first, in terms of the sequencing of law enforcement and combat activities along a continuum of force and, as a corollary of this, the sequencing of the legal paradigm of law enforcement and the legal paradigm of hostilities; second, in terms of developing clearer objective criteria for individual and contextual status determination; and third, in terms of the progressive realisation and sequencing of targeting and weaponry norms so as to correlate and guide the force continuum with the violence continuum within a full-spectrum operational environment. Better objective criteria for sequencing are used to assist with marking the point at which the law enforcement paradigm is no longer practicable as the violence has reached the threshold of an armed conflict. In this regard, sequencing means shifting from the law enforcement framework to the framework of hostilities in relation to targeting and weaponry law. It is suggested that unless we set out and consistently apply clear objective criteria that set the threshold for the applicability of Hague NIAC rules at a high level, then there is the risk that within the operational and normative uncertainties of contemporary operational environments, IHL may be 'coming down' from its high threshold of applicability and IHRL may be 'coming up'. This is a major protection issue, because, if the threshold of NIAC rules is not kept at an appropriately high level, then there is increased scope for the unwarranted legitimisation of targeted killings and use of high-intensity means and methods of conventional military force across a range of low-intensity hostilities. In this regard, the Parliamentary Joint Committee for Human Rights urged the UK government to clarify the legal basis of its policy of targeted killings, for example, in Syria and Libya. This is important in an international context where states such as the United Kingdom, Russia, United States and Israel appear to rely increasingly on targeted killing as a method of law enforcement, war and self-defence, and so the parameters and bases of justifiable targeted killings need to be clarified.

Former Special Rapporteur on extrajudicial, summary or arbitrary executions, Philip Alston, defined targeted killing as

> the intentional, premeditated and deliberate use of lethal force, by States or their agents acting under colour of law, or by an organized armed group in armed conflict, against a specific individual who is not in the physical custody of the perpetrator.[9]

9 UNGA (Human Rights Council) 'Report of the Special Rapporteur on Extrajudicial, Summary or Arbitrary Executions, Philip Alston, Addendum, Study on Targeted Killings' (28 May 2010) UN Doc. A/HRC/14/24/Add. 6, 1.

In other words, unlike combatants or soldiers who are targeted on the basis of their identifiable status, individuals are named or identified in advance and killed as a first port of call, that is, without first attempting to arrest and prosecute them on criminal charges. Targeted killings may be executed by remotely piloted aircraft systems, aircraft, helicopters or special forces on the ground. Targeted killings are problematic for the following reasons.

First, individuals are usually identified in advance and their names are placed on secret 'kill lists'. More often than not, this involves detailed operational and tactical planning as well as the ability to remotely observe and track individuals over hours or days in real time. Targeting decisions will often be made jointly at high levels of military and political leadership on the basis of human and signals intelligence.[10] This suggests that permissive targeting rules needed for operational effectiveness in the fog of war do not have as much purchase as they may have done in the nineteenth and twentieth centuries. Indeed, according to John Nagl, a former counterinsurgency advisor to a former commander of forces in Afghanistan and former director of the CIA,

> [W]e've gotten far, far better at correlating human intelligence and signals intelligence to paint a very tight coherent picture of who the enemy is and where the enemy hangs his hat . . . we've gotten better at using precision firepower to give those people very, very bad days.[11]

It is unlikely that the criteria for being included on such 'kill lists', if there are any, will be made public and subject to review. For example, the US Joint Special Operations Command uses a kill list called the Joint Prioritized Effects List, which is classified. This lack of fair notice does not enable individuals to know exactly what conduct will lead to what is effectively an extrajudicial death sentence being imposed by the military and/or executive branch of government. The potential for arbitrariness is all the more serious in an operational environment that is increasingly civilianised and networked. Targeted killings to date indicate that there is the danger that the criteria for being placed on kill lists – again if there are any – may be construed in an overly broad fashion, that is to encompass those who play indirect and support roles as opposed to directly engaging in combat against the military forces of a state, or even those who incite, encourage or glorify acts of violence. For example, Anwar Al-Aulaqi was placed on the US Treasury Department's Specially Designated Global Terrorist List for 'providing financial, material

---

10 US Joint Chiefs of Staff, Close Air Support, Joint Publication 3–09.3 (25 November 2014); US Joint Chiefs of Staff, above n 3; US Joint Chiefs of Staff, Joint Targeting, Joint Publication 3–60 (31 January 2013); US Joint Chiefs of Staff, Joint Communications System, Joint Publication 6–0 (10 June 2015).

11 Claire Finkelstein, Jens David Ohlin, and Andrew Altman, *Targeted Killings: Law and Morality in an Asymmetrical World* (Oxford University Press, 2012), Ch. 13, 354.

or technological support for . . . terrorism', particularly in relation to his role in disseminating propaganda, recruiting and training persons engaged in jihad.[12] Individuals may not be entirely aware that their conduct is viewed as contributing to harm. Furthermore, in the context of targeted killings, more often than not, individuals will not have been charged with any crime or have had any evidence presented against them prior to being placed on a kill list and subjected to the use of lethal force. More often than not, individuals will not have been notified that they are on a kill list and will have no opportunity to challenge this and demonstrate their innocence or challenge the criteria used, as well as not having the opportunity to surrender. This increases the chance of mistakes and erroneous decision making. Although not affording fighters (frequently referred to as combatants in military doctrine) the opportunity to surrender by giving warnings may be necessary to confer the military advantage of surprise and initiative when facing intense hostilities, it cannot be said that this justification is applicable outside of this context. Tesón criticises targeted killing on the basis that the state cannot unilaterally repeal the strict moral code and legal restrictions on state killing by just declaring war on terrorists or the persons it intends to kill. Tesón argues that this is dangerous and open to abuse, as it may constitute law-of-war permissions outside of a 'war zone' (for example, in not attempting an arrest or giving an individual the opportunity to surrender) and that states can simply declare war on members of a group who share some arbitrary and potentially overinclusive characteristic, compile a list and start to kill them, for example, 'mafiosi', 'sexual predators', 'terrorists', 'subversives' and so on. The risk of abuse posed by status-based targeted killing (for example, the US Treasury Department's Office of Foreign Assets Control 'Specially Designated Global Terrorist List') cautions against abandoning the strict prohibition on deliberate killing.[13] The UN Counter-Terrorism Committee has also noted that the principle of legality requires that acts constituting criminal conduct be clearly codified in law so as to give notice to potential wrongdoers and to ensure that criminal sanctions are not imposed arbitrarily or retroactively. Definitions of terrorist acts that are broad or vague pose a risk of misuse, such as the expression of controversial views or nonviolent criticism of a government.[14] Guiora discusses the importance and sets out some of the substance of criteria-based reasoning rather than the intuitionism and discretion of military commanders in targeted killing decisions. However, it is suggested that the discussion is in want of more detail on the fundamental issues of when an individual can be a legitimate target on the basis of their direct participation in hostilities or membership of an organised armed group and what constitutes the threshold of an armed conflict for the purposes of applying status-based targeting.[15] Rather than acting as an obstacle

---

12 *Al-Aulaqi v. Obama*, US District Court for District of Columbia, case number 10–1469 (JDB), 7 December 2010, 5.

13 Finkelstein, Ohlin, and Altman, above n 11, 423.

14 United Nations Counter Terrorism Committee, Technical Guide to the Implementation of Security Council Resolution 1373 of 2001 (2009) (counterterrorism Committee Executive Directorate).

15 Finkelstein, Ohlin, and Altman, above n 11, 304.

to effective operational decision making, Guiora argues that a clear criteria-based analysis can actually enhance it by promoting 'the correct identification and targeting of a legitimate target',[16] and is feasible in those situations where forces have the initiative and may be proactive – that is, where they are not confronting the need to react instinctually to a stark life-and-death dilemma.[17] Guiora also argues that an absence of clear process and criteria is 'profoundly dangerous' as it allows decision makers to act primarily on their subjective perceptions without taking into consideration all relevant information and broader considerations such as the nature of the threat, the degree of the danger, the strength of the intelligence and the reliability of the sources of intelligence.[18]

Second, individuals may be targeted in situations where they are not engaged in active hostilities or where they do not represent a concrete, specific and imminent threat to life or physical safety. Furthermore, targeting on the basis of a particular designation risks basing the use of force on an individual's propensity to commit future acts of violence or direct support, and this may or may not be based on their previous conduct. In this way, a targeted killing may not be entirely defensive as individuals need not represent a direct and imminent threat, and furthermore, targeted killings risk being illegitimately retributive, as individuals may be arbitrarily deprived of their right to life without due process of law. This facet of status-based targeting may be viewed as being justified in a situation of hostilities where due process of law is not practicable, namely because an individual is deemed to be a threat on account of their being sufficiently linked to the collective threat posed by an armed group that is engaged in ongoing hostilities. However, targeted killings risk applying law-of-war permissions to individuals outside a situation of hostilities – that is, where individuals do not constitute a threat qua directly participating in hostilities or qua members of an organised armed group because the objective conditions for these two phenomena are not in existence. An increased criminal threat – for example, terrorism or organised crime, is not per se sufficient for the state to make this shift into law-of-war permissions. For this we need an enemy that is organised militarily, for individuals to be satisfactorily incorporated into that organisation and for intense collective violence to be actuated. An individual-level threat or a threat from a diffuse network of individuals may not be sufficient to represent a strategic military threat or a threat to national security that is beyond the capacity of intelligence-led law enforcement responses. The restrictions on targeted killings should therefore be set out primarily in clearer guidelines for evaluating a state of affairs in terms of the intensity of the violence and the organisational capabilities of an armed group, as well as an individual's status and threat in terms of their link to an organised armed group or hostilities. As will be discussed later, these guidelines should take into account the fact that the nature of the threat may be protracted, diffuse and

16 Ibid., 310.
17 Ibid., 309.
18 Ibid., 310.

adaptive in nature. Ohlin suggests a number of linking principles in general terms such as direct participation in hostilities, military membership, cobelligerency, control, complicity and conspiracy. This is important as Ohlin also recognises the import of criminal law principles to target analysis as having 'intuitive appeal' that is 'undeniable' and that 'at first glance the only difference between the classical criminal law situation and the situation of a national armed struggle is the size of the collective endeavour' but that 'the other side of the equation – the individual as well as his relationship to the collective remains the same'. This discussion will build on Ohlin's work by offering a more detailed set of guidelines for linking individuals with organised armed groups and understanding what it means to participate in hostilities, as well as by suggesting that approaches based on complicity and conspiracy have import to questions of target analysis.[19]

Third, individuals may reside outside a 'war zone', and there may be reasonable ways of responding to the purported lethal threat they represent other than the use of lethal force – for example, by arrest and prosecution if they are within the jurisdiction of a state, or by arrest, extradition and prosecution if they are within the jurisdiction of a foreign state. In this regard, there is the issue that states may be resorting to lethal force on the basis of purported justifications that would not be legally or politically acceptable within their own jurisdiction. Additionally, states may frequently argue that such killings may not be subjected to political review or judicial scrutiny, as this would impede operational effectiveness in a conflict situation and is accordingly a 'nonjusticiable' military or political issue, and therefore not within the subject matter jurisdiction of ordinary civilian justice through criminal, civil, administrative or human rights courts. Finklestein argues that this is deeply problematic in that all states need to do is perform an act of combat against an individual in order to justify the resort to status-based targeting under the law-of-war paradigm. In Finkelstein's words, 'it seems that we can bootstrap our way up into establishing the legitimacy of our own wrongful acts of targeting by engaging in illegal-targeting-turned-legal by its own existence'.[20] This point that Finklestein makes highlights the incongruence and circularity of the reasoning that is now all too frequently being employed by states and which is made easier through lack of clarity about what constitutes a non-international armed conflict. Again, clearer context-bound threshold criteria for an armed conflict are needed in order to circumscribe such justifications for targeted killing. In this respect, Tesón suggests that one way of identifying a situation of armed conflict is through a 'geographical institutional criterion'. Namely a war-time setting is one where the ordinary tools of law enforcement cannot operate because 'rival political groups' are making 'opposing claims' to 'political supremacy', or because there are 'no claims to political supremacy whatsoever', or because 'law and order have broken down because of war, revolution or anarchy'.[21] Although this

19 Ibid., 65 and 76.
20 Ibid., 169.
21 Ibid., 420.

analysis provides a useful inroad into resolving this problem, it does not provide us with more detailed and objective guidelines, which are arguably much needed given that lawlessness may often be a matter of perception. Indeed, Tesón's main conclusion is that 'many settings where terrorists operate defy classification' and so 'all one can say is this: if the magnitude of the threat is sufficiently generalized to resemble an insurrection where the only plausible response is to use the armed forces, then the war paradigm will apply and targeted killings' may be justified, but not 'if the threat can be contained by law enforcement officials'.[22]

Given the complex factors involved in assessing the legitimacy of targeted killing, there is wide scope for mistakes to be made. McMahan argues that retributory and defensive justifications for targeted killing policies are insufficient to justify the risks that they impose on innocent people, such as the risk of misidentifying the intended victim and the risk of harming or killing innocent bystanders as a side effect.[23] If we are to accept targeted killing as a general policy, then avoidance of mistakes requires accurate and credible intelligence as to the identity, motivations and conduct of individuals. Mistaking or misidentifying civilians as fighters has been deemed to be the primary cause of civilian harm in Afghanistan, and such erroneous determinations were at times based on faulty assumptions about civilian behaviour – that is targeteers making 'positive identification errors' whereby they erroneously presume civilian behaviour to be hostile or suspicious or having differing interpretations of what it means directly to participate in hostilities or be a member of an organized armed group.[24] In unconventional conflicts, legitimacy and the effective use of force require an accurate and credible assessment of and response to intelligence that probes the social dynamic which sustains ongoing fighting. Without this, there is the danger that targeted killings could cause a relatively calm situation to escalate and become far more dangerous, or that targeted killings could be based on manipulation or intelligence failures, for example, being used by one faction against another as part of a vendetta or dispute.[25]

Rather, on such fundamental issues as the right to life and distinction, our approach to normativity should be expanded so that military doctrine that is effectively put on an institutional footing or which is expressed in mandatory and imperative terms can assist us with the interpretation of existing norms. In other words, doctrine and practice can be viewed as elucidating existing norms

---

22 Ibid., 421.

23 Ibid., 135 and 136.

24 Christopher Rogers, Rachel Reid, and Chris Kolenda, The Strategic Costs of Civilian Harm – Applying Lessons from Afghanistan to Current and Future Conflicts (Report) (Open Society Foundations–Washington, DC, June 2016) 19.

25 Ibid., 18, 19, 22, 23. See also, Akbar Ahmed's, *The Thistle and the Drone: How America's War on Terror Became a Global War on Tribal Islam* (EDS Publications Ltd., 30 March 2013) and Matthew Hoh's 2009 resignation from his post as a Political Officer in the US Foreign Service and Senior Civilian Representative for the US Government in the Zabul Province of Afghanistan. http://www.washingtonpost.com/wp-srv/hp/ssi/wpc/ResignationLetter.pdf?sid=ST2009102603447 and http://www.washingtonpost.com/wp-dyn/content/article/2009/10/26/AR2009102603394.html.

regulating the means and methods of force. For example, the United States Department of the Army Field Manual 3–24, arguably the most developed and sophisticated military manual on counterinsurgency, states that its main *raison d'être* is to 'institutionalize Army and Marine Corps knowledge of this longstanding form of conflict'.[26] An important reason for institutionalising doctrine and practice – or, in other words, putting it on a more obligatory and imperative footing – is so that lessons learned from experiences in contemporary conflicts are not forgotten and that the use of force to achieve strategic goals is not undermined. Manuals therefore serve *inter alia* to guide the effective and legitimate use of force in on-going and future operations[27] and may also serve to guide the interpretation of general standards of military law set out in military manuals and IHL.

Such a reflexive relationship between normativity and practice is advantageous in that a greater coincidence of military and humanitarian considerations promotes the strategically effective use of force. The effective use of force has been described as that which provides 'sustained improvements in objective and subjective indicators of security'.[28] Contemporary military doctrine can ensure that norms are relevant to the world in which we live in terms of reflecting strategic and operational imperatives rather than their being merely a product of conventional inter-state conflicts that are rarely seen in contemporary international relations. Such a bottom-up approach to normativity is fundamental to IHL, which makes it a cutting-edge field of public international law, but one that is necessary, given that fundamental interests of the international community are at stake.

The contemporary milieu as reflected in military manuals and sociopolitical studies

In the early nineteenth century, Clausewitz observed that

> our wars are made up of a number of great and small simultaneous or consecutive combats, and this severance of the activity into so many separate actions is owing to the great multiplicity of the relations out of which war arises with us.[29]

---

26 US Department of the Army (Training and Doctrine Command) *Counterinsurgency* (COIN) Field Manual (FM) 3–24 and Marine Corps War fighting Publication (MCWP) 3–33.5 (Headquarters, Department of the Army, Washington, DC & Marine Corps Combat Development Command, Department of the Navy, Headquarters, United States Marine Corps, Washington, DC, 15 December 2006) Introduction.

27 US Department of Army (Training and Doctrine Command) *Stability Operations*, Field Manual (FM) 3–07 (Headquarters, Department of the Army, Washington, DC, 6 October 2008) Foreword.

28 Small Arms Survey, *Urban Landscapes of Violence* (Small Arms Survey, 2007) 181.

29 Carl von Clausewitz, *On War* (Wordsworth Classics of World Literature, 1997) 204.

More recently, social anthropologist Dennis Rogers has suggested that our contemporary milieu is mainly afflicted by what he describes as 'civic', as opposed to 'civil' or 'sovereign', conflicts. Rogers defines classic 'sovereign conflicts' as 'conflicts between states' and classic 'civil conflicts' as 'conflicts over the state between the state and one or more groups within a society'. 'Civic conflicts', on the other hand, do not necessarily involve the state and are not necessarily political in their orientation, but may involve conflicts between groups which have different levels of organisation, capabilities and motivations.[30] Only recently has military doctrine truly caught up with and embodied these conceptions of the milieu of conflict in order to fill the 'doctrinal gap' that emerged in the face of the challenges posed by the full-spectrum hostilities of the first decade of the twenty-first century.[31]

The fresh doctrine and practice to have emerged out of these conflicts is set out in a range of military handbooks, operational field manuals and operational law by key players in these conflicts, namely the United States and the United Kingdom. In contrast with codes of military justice which set out the military law applicable to various branches of a state's armed forces, military manuals, operational field manuals and rules of engagement are significant as they may reflect domestic, foreign and international law as well as military doctrine, practice and policy relevant to the circumstances of a particular operation or operational environment – for example, unconventional engagements as part of counterinsurgency operations or small wars.[32] Accordingly, they may constitute important evidence of how states implement their obligations under humanitarian law. The military doctrine and practice contained in military manuals and operational field manuals is therefore integral to the effective organisation and functioning of armed forces as it sets out a common approach and conceptual framework for carrying out operations. It embodies contemporary experiences so that important lessons are not lost, and in some countries failure to comply with military manuals or operational field manuals may constitute an offence in itself. In contrast with military law set out in codes such as the United States Uniform Code of Military Justice and the UK Armed Forces Act 2006 which have legal standing and are enforceable by military courts, military doctrine and practice relate to maximising the utility of 'principles, tactics, techniques, and procedures applicable worldwide' in a range of contemporary conflicts.[33]

It is important to understand and analyse military doctrine, as it embodies lessons learned from historical and contemporary conflicts. In other words, the uncertain and ambiguous conditions of contemporary conflicts involving insurgencies, non-international armed conflicts and international organised crime can be seen to have led to a paradigm shift in military doctrine and practice,

---

30 International Committee of the Red Cross, 'Interview with Dennis Rogers' (2010) 92 (878) *International Review of the Red Cross* 315–316. Mary Kaldor, *Global Civil Society: An Answer to War* (Polity, 2003).

31 See above n 3, Foreword.

32 Ibid.

33 Ibid. See also US FM 3–07 above n 27, Foreword.

and thus in the response to contemporary confrontations and conflicts. Military field manuals are analysed in order to penetrate what major armed forces perceive to be the conditions but, most importantly, the restrictions necessary for the achievement of strategic objectives. Furthermore, operational and field manuals indicate how military doctrine accommodates what is perceived to be the ambiguous and uncertain material conditions, or the grey areas, of contemporary conflicts.[34] Essentially, operational and field manuals indicate that states themselves have chosen to restrict the usage of means and methods of force in excess of the restrictions imposed by conventional interpretations of a free-standing body of IHL. This marks fertile ground into which existing legal frameworks relative to means and methods of force can expand and develop through a process of normative accommodation, reconceptualisation and restructuring.

This is not to suggest a new form of legal regulation, but rather a reconceptualised approach to the substance and legal ordering of existing IHL and IHRL, which reflects the fact that this is essentially already occurring in practice, as states themselves respond to the complex conditions of contemporary conflicts.[35] It is not only contemporary operational and field manuals, but also sociological and demographic studies which offer accounts and analyses of the contemporary milieu, conditions and forms of agency, action and organisation of confrontations and conflicts that are more penetrating, and thus more adequate than a conventional normative account. These accounts can and should, therefore, serve to elucidate legal discourse so that it is more relevant to our contemporary milieu and constitutes a more effective guide vis-à-vis the legitimate use of force.

Demographic studies on urbanisation and urban violence are useful in mapping out and categorising various types of violence within urban areas and correlating this with a range of appropriate policy responses manifest at tactical, operational and strategic levels of the use of force. Furthermore, such insights promote the coordination and sequencing of law enforcement and military responses to a range of urban confrontations and conflicts so as to avoid undermining the desired end state of the rule of law and civic security.[36]

This chapter focuses mainly on US and UK military doctrine as these states arguably have had the most experience in restoring and maintaining civil security as part of stabilisation and counterinsurgency operations in the aftermath of conventional conflicts, and the doctrinal response to this is both significant

34 US Department of Army (Training and Doctrine Command) *Operations*, Field Manual (FM) 100–5 (Headquarters, Department of the Army, Washington, DC, 14 June 1993) Ch. 1.

35 FM 3–24, above n 7, 316.

36 Alexandre Vautravers, 'Military Operations in Urban Areas' (2010) 92 (878) *International Review of the Red Cross* 437; Marion Harfoff-Tavel, 'Violence and Humanitarian Action in Urban Areas: New Challenges, New Approaches' (2010) 92 (878) *International Review of the Red Cross* 329, 334, 350. Small Arms Survey, above n 28, 181.

and potentially transformative. Although US and UK military doctrine is, strictly speaking, relevant to their own experiences in performing stability and counter-insurgency operations, particularly in urban areas, as Dale Stephens argues, this experience and associated doctrinal development is, nevertheless, shared by many modern militaries, particularly those that have formed part of contemporary UN-backed peacekeeping forces in conflict and postconflict operational environments around the world.[37] Accordingly, doctrinal and tactical law enforcement responses in a range of contemporary peacekeeping and stability operations are not significantly dissimilar.[38]

Urbanisation and the continuum of urban violence and urban conflict

Urbanisation

Operational and field manuals as well as sociological and anthropological studies suggest that during the late twentieth and early twenty-first centuries there has been an explosion in the size of urban populations and urbanised terrain[39] coupled with a general shift or transition of conflicts to urbanised terrain and that this represents a major threat to human safety and security.[40] Projections are that in the future the world will be more urbanised and populated.

Demographic studies have highlighted the growing urbanisation and urban population growth in developed but particularly in developing countries. For example, in 1950 only 86 cities had a population of more than 1 million, whereas by 2002 that number had risen to approximately 400.[41] A 2003 UN-Habitat Working Paper indicates that in many conflict-afflicted countries a significant percentage of the urban population lives in slum conditions, characterised by "overcrowding, poor or informal housing, inadequate access to safe water and sanitation, and insecurity of tenure".[42] The United Nations' Report on World Urbanisation Prospects indicates that, globally, 'more people live in urban areas

---

37 Dale Stephens, 'Military Involvement in Law Enforcement' (2010) 92 (878) *International Review of the Red Cross* 453, 459.

38 Ibid., 460.

39 Alexandre Vautravers, see above n 36, 439.

40 United Nations Human Settlements Programme (UN-Habitat) *Global Reports on Human Settlements 2007: Enhancing Urban Safety and Security* (UN-Habitat, 2007) 4, 7–8, 51.

41 UN Department for Economic and Social Affairs (Population Division), *World Urbanisation Prospects: 2001 Revision* (New York, 2002); Mike Davies, *Planet of the Slums* (Verso, 2007) 1–3; See Alexandre Vautravers, above n 36, 438; See Small Arms Survey, above n 28, 162.

42 Mike Davies, Ibid., 23; United Nations Human Settlements Programme (UN-Habitat), *The Challenge of the Slums: Global Report on Human Settlements 2003* (UN-Habitat, London, 2003) 3; United Nations Human Settlements Programme (UN-Habitat) Slums of the World: The Face of Urban Poverty in the New Millennium? Working Paper (UN-Habitat, 2003) Annex 3.

than in rural areas, with 54 per cent of the world's population residing in urban areas in 2014'. In terms of increased urbanisation the report estimates that

> in 1950, 30 per cent of the world's population was urban, and by 2050, 66 per cent of the world's population is projected to be urban . . . the urban population of the world has grown rapidly since 1950, from 746 million to 3.9 billion in 2014.[43]

The US military estimates that the global population will increase by approximately 1.2 billion by 2025 with more than a billion new people living in urban areas. By 2050 it is anticipated that 60 per cent of the world's population will live in urban areas. Furthermore, the US military anticipates that the rapid growth of urban areas, particularly in the Middle East, Africa and South Central Asia, combined with increased resource scarcity and inequality enhances the possibility of insurgencies in highly populated developing countries whose governments lack the capacity to provide effective governance, including security and the rule of law.[44]

Given the scale and magnitude of urbanised terrain as well as the concentration of civilian populations affected by chronic confrontations and conflicts, civilian populations are highly vulnerable in the face of the physical consequences of conflict – that is, damaged or destroyed infrastructure as well as the social consequences of conflict – that is, a breakdown in law and order and effective governance leading to new forms of violence and conflict.[45] In its report to Congress entitled "Conduct of the Persian Gulf War", the US Department of Defense stated that "to engage in military operations in urban terrain" is "a form of fighting that is costly to attacker, defender, innocent civilians, and civilian objects".[46] This notion is supported by Herold's finding that the majority of civilian deaths that occurred in the 2001 US military operations in Afghanistan were recorded in areas of high population density.[47] This assertion is also reflected in military doctrine on military operations on urban terrain which advises that military operations in urban areas are high risk, time consuming, challenging and so, primarily, such areas should be isolated and bypassed unless this is unavoidable.[48]

43 United Nations, Department of Economic and Social Affairs, Population Division (2014). World Urbanisation Prospects: The 2014 Revision, Highlights (ST/ESA/SER.A/352).

44 USFM 3–24, above n 5, 2–3.

45 See UN-Habitat, above n 40, 8, 23.

46 US Department of Defense, 'Report to Congress on the conduct of the Persian Gulf War' (1992) 3 *ILM* 721.

47 Marc W Herold (ed.), A Dossier on Civilian Victims of the United States' Aerial Bombing of Afghanistan: A Comprehensive Accounting (Report) (March 2002) Appendix 5: 'The Spatial Distribution of Afghan Civilian Casualties Caused by the US Air War, 7 October–6 December <http://cursor.org/stories/appendix5.htm> and <http://pubpages.unh.edu/~mwherold/dossier.htm> accessed 1 October 2013.

48 US Department of Army (Training and Doctrine Command) *Military Operations in Urbanized Terrain* (MOUT), Field Manual (FM) 90–10 (Headquarters, Department of the Army, Washington, DC, 15 August 1979) Ch. 1.

Indeed, the risks that urban warfare poses to civilians have led to specialised doctrine regulating 'military operations on urban terrain' (MOUT), which is said to comprise all military 'actions planned and conducted on a topographical complex and its adjacent terrain where manmade construction is the dominant feature'. It includes 'combat in cities, which is that portion of MOUT involving house-to-house and street-by-street fighting in towns and cities'.[49] It also includes combat in built-up areas which comprises a 'concentration of structures, facilities, and populations, such as villages, cities, and towns that form the economic and cultural focus for the surrounding area'. Built-up areas include villages with populations of up to 3,000, towns and small cities (comprising populations of up to 100,000) and large cities with a high degree of urban sprawl. The makeup and layout of built-up areas will often comprise a city centre, commercial area and core residential area as well as outlying residential and industrial areas.[50]

The urbanised environment is described in military doctrine as a 'three dimensional', or, more appropriately, multidimensional, urban 'battle space' that comprises aerial, terrestrial and subterranean levels.[51] This physical environment is ideal for cover and concealment.[52] According to MOUT doctrine, before proceeding with the use of force, it is crucial for armed forces to gather intelligence vis-à-vis the varied infrastructure and terrain as well as patterns and locations of civilian use of and settlement in urban areas.[53] Furthermore, forces must be trained to understand the effects of different weapons in an urbanised terrain that may contain a

49 US Marine Corps, Military Operations on Urbanized Terrain (MOUT), Marine Corps War fighting Publication 3–35.3 (Department of the Navy, Headquarters United States Marine Corps Washington, DC, 26 April 1998) 1003.

50 Ibid.

51 Ibid.: The terrestrial level or approach includes the building level which often comprises multi-storey buildings that provide warring parties with cover and concealment from attack. Buildings are advantageous points for sniper, antitank and antiair attack, which conversely turns their location into military objectives. It also comprises the street level through which parties to a conflict or law enforcement bodies can manoeuvre and engage. The subterranean level or approach will often comprise sewage systems and tunnels and are also advantageous features for concealment and a range of attacks such as ambushes and may be integral to the logistics of transporting military resources and personnel. The aerial level or approach may be used by forces equipped with aviation assets to attack military objectives at building or street level. Generally speaking, air assets are vulnerable to attack in urban areas due to the many concealed apertures from which attacks can be launched. Furthermore, the fields of vision may be obstructed or obscured by buildings or other constructions at the terrestrial level.

52 See US FM 3–24, above n 3, Appendix B-2.

53 See US FM 90–10, above n 48, Ch. 1. For example, in old towns and cities, there is likely to be a high density of thick masonry buildings that are not arranged according to a modern grid structure. Modern urbanised terrain is likely to comprise large areas of residential sprawl that contain dwellings of various sizes and constructed out of highly penetrable and structurally weak materials. In larger towns and cities in developed and developing countries, there is likely to be a high frequency of high-rise buildings in the centre as well as industrial areas on the periphery.

concentration of civilians.[54] Accordingly, close regard must be had to the effects that particular types of weaponry will have in the urban environment.[55] In particular, given the weakness and penetrability of construction materials used in much residential, commercial and industrial infrastructure in modern urbanised terrain, the appropriateness of the use of the penetrative, kinetic, blast and fragmentary effect of conventional small arms and explosive ordnance has to be considered carefully.[56]

Not only that, an example of contemporary doctrine states that military leaders '*must consider* not only the [first-order], desired effects of a munition or action but also possible second- and third-order effects – including undesired ones' [emphasis added] when making *ex ante* proportionality assessments of what means and methods to employ so as to minimise collateral damage.[57] In this regard, military doctrine recognises that the use of conventional area weapons and indirect fire should be avoided in urban areas where military objectives exist in close proximity to civilians.[58] MOUT doctrine expresses recognition that there ought to be greater restrictions on the use of conventional military force in urbanised terrain, particularly where there is a degree of civil stability. This is so as not to undermine strategic objectives by causing an escalation in hostilities[59] through the use of 'brutish' levels of force.[60] This may occur where the population is antagonised and alienated, and also where domestic and international public support for the use of force is lost due to the high level of civilian incidental loss and collateral damage.[61] This has led to what has been described in doctrine as the paradox of diminishing returns on the use of force, whereby 'the more force is used, the less effective it is'.[62] The underlying rationale of this principle of diminishing returns is that the application of conventional force in urban areas is more likely to result in mistaken attacks and collateral damage. Although this may be permissible under traditional or 'classic' interpretations of the loose and free-standing principles of IHL, military doctrine regards it as essentially counterproductive. It is proposed that this state of affairs means that the time is ripe for normative reconceptualisation and restructuring.

'Brutish' levels of force may undermine the legitimacy of the use of force and can lead to the creation or escalation of an insurgency. Accordingly, the use of substantial conventional force in urban areas can be counterproductive[63] and, as discussed later, this has led to a doctrinal reconceptualisation of the core principles

54 US FM 3–24, above n 5, 7–36.
55 MCWP 3–35.3, above n 49, Appendix B.
56 Alexandre Vautravers, above n 36, 447.
57 USFM 3–24, above n 5, 7–36.
58 Ibid.
59 Ibid., 7–37.
60 US Department of Army (Training and Doctrine Command) *Civil Disturbance Operations*, Field Manual (FM) 3–19.15 (Headquarters, Department of the Army Washington, DC, 18 April 2005) 1–1 to 1–6.
61 MCWP 3–35.3, above n 49, 7201. US FM 90–10, above n 48, Ch. 1.
62 USFM 3–24, above n 5, 1–150.
63 Ibid.

of proportionality and distinction which, it is suggested, have potential normative consequences. Furthermore, MOUT doctrine demands a high level of situational awareness in order to adapt tactics and weaponry to the particular urban milieu, to promote force protection and survival, as well as to minimise the effects of hostilities on civilian populations and civilian infrastructure though accurate and proportionate targeting decisions.[64] The conflict in Chechnya demonstrated that the Russian armed forces had inadequate knowledge of the structure and layout of the urban terrain, and this prevented them from carrying out successful military operations.[65]

The continuum of urban violence and conflict

Particularly in the urban milieu, the boundaries between urban violence and urban conflict, as well as participation in these forms of collective violence, are often blurred and thus unclear. Urban confrontations and conflicts may be situated in conflict and postconflict environments, such as in Iraq, Afghanistan and Somalia, where armed conflict has caused a collapse of governance. In these situations, this has created insurgencies and power vacuums that were filled with intercommunal violence as different groups vie with each other for forms of political, territorial and economic control.[66]

Urban violence can also be found within states which are not officially at war, such as Mexico, where there is more of a blurred boundary between forms of criminal and political violence. In any case, these general categories of violence are most often interconnected, particularly in terms of kidnappings, murders, robberies and trafficking carried out by paramilitary organisations. In such circumstances, it is difficult to find distinctions between forms of organised criminality and low-intensity armed conflicts.[67] Conflicts taking place in this milieu tend to be unconventional and irregular in character and are mixed up with other forms of urban violence. Insurgencies and stability operations, for example, overlap with armed conflicts of an international and non-international character. Mixed and overlapping forms of violence may also be a major concern during the ending of active hostilities.[68]

It is a major challenge to distinguish military objectives from objects of protection and then to apply the appropriate level of force in response in situations where there is a broad continuum or spectrum of violence (see Figure 1.1).[69] At the lower end of the 'violence continuum' are forms of 'social' violence within the family and community such as domestic violence and sexual abuse, as well as everyday gratuitous and routine violence and confrontations. Moving up, the next category is that of socioeconomic violence that involves low-level gang

64 US FM 90–10, above n 48; MCWP 3.35–3, above n 25.
65 Alexandre Vautravers, above n 36, 441.
66 Small Arms Survey, above n 28, 161.
67 Ibid., 173–176.
68 USFM 3–24, above n 5, D-11.
69 UN-Habitat, above n 40, 8.

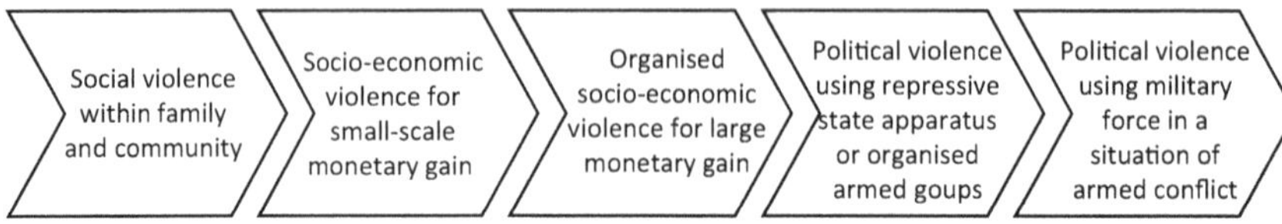

Figure 1.1 The continuum of violence.

Source: UN-Habitat 2007.

violence taking forms such as petty theft and robbery as well as riots and affray. Above this come forms of economic violence that are more organised than the preceding category, and this form of violence may be institutionalised. Organised criminal activity that falls into this category takes forms such as kidnapping and armed robbery as well as trafficking of weapons, persons and drugs. Violence above this may be categorised as institutional violence perpetrated by the state or informal vigilante groups. Examples of violence here may include extrajudicial killings. The last category comprises political violence carried out by the state or even nonstate–organised armed groups, which can take a variety of forms such as insurgencies, armed conflicts, extrajudicial killings and terrorist acts.[70] The UN-Habitat report thus sets out an analytical framework termed the 'violence continuum'[71] which can be visualised as follows:

This framework is useful for understanding the context of urban confrontations and conflicts, as well as the appropriate strategic and normative responses, but it does not offer further clarity vis-à-vis the point at which the law enforcement paradigm is to be considered no longer practicable. However, this analytical framework may be used to undergird both normative and doctrinal classification schemes so that the application of force and regulatory oversight can be sequenced in an apposite fashion, particularly within the mixed and full-spectrum operational environments. Ideally, sequencing in this fashion is predicated on an intelligence-led and evidence-based approach more in keeping with the paradigm of law enforcement than that of combat.

The impact of urbanisation on asymmetrical and low-intensity conflicts

Dynamics of asymmetric urban armed conflicts

When military asymmetry combines with urbanisation, the result is asymmetric urban warfare in which militarily weak parties do not directly engage militarily

70 Ibid., 8, 51 figures 1.1 and 3.1.

71 Ibid., 8, figure 1.1.

strong adversaries by using the conventional means and methods typical of interstate wars, but rather unconventional or asymmetric tactics.[72] Vautravers notes that in the mid-twentieth century, most hostilities in urban areas were seen as states responding to emergency situations in order to maintain law and order, whereas from the late twentieth century onwards, urban areas have increasingly become the sites of armed conflicts.[73] Modern conflicts in Vietnam, Chechnya, Gaza, the West Bank, Afghanistan and Iraq are prime examples of this type of conflict, characterised by a major imbalance *ab initio* of the opposing armed forces' military capabilities. The overarching trend identified in military doctrine is that today's wars are 'wars amongst the people', and that despite their particular features, they nevertheless embody standard themes as well as tactical and operational features.[74] In such conflicts, militarily strong parties may apply direct offensive strategies, using conventional means and methods of warfare such as infantry, armour and airpower to capture, destroy or neutralise military objectives and thus destroy the opponent's physical capacity to resist.[75] They may also apply indirect offensive strategies such as "barbarism", a term that Arreguín-Toft defines as the deliberate and systematic harm of civilians in order to destroy a weaker opponent's will and capacity to fight; examples he gives of this include the bombing of civilian infrastructure, as well as the internment in concentration camps, murder, torture and rape of civilians.[76]

The conditions of asymmetric conflict affect the tactics, organisation and, in some cases, strategy of a weaker party. For militarily weak parties, defeat would invariably be the outcome of fighting on the stronger party's conventional terms, for instance, on the open battlefield.[77] They may therefore employ indirect offensive and defensive strategies such as guerrilla warfare, concealing themselves among supportive civilian populations in cities, towns and villages which provide cover for them to launch attacks and protection from counterattack without them being identified and engaged by a militarily superior opponent on conventional terms.[78] Generally speaking, insurgent groups usually follow one or a combination of conspiratorial, militaristic, urban and protracted approaches. A conspiratorial approach is one where generally there is an absence of open violence and propaganda. Militaristic approaches tend to comprise a leadership, political

72 US FM 3-24, above n 5, Introduction.

73 Alexandre Vautravers, above n 36, 439. Examples include Lebanon, Beirut and Grenada in 1982–1983, Panama in 1989, Mogadishu in 1993, Bosnia, Croatia and Kosovo from 1993–1999, Chechnya in 1994–1996 and then 1999–2000, Iraq since 2003, Lebanon in 2006, Gaza in 2009, Libya in 2011 and the conflict in Syria in 2012 which is on-going at the time of writing.

74 US FM 3-24, above n 5, Foreword.

75 Ivan Arreguín-Toft, *How the Weak Win Wars: A Theory of Asymmetric Conflict* (Cambridge University Press, 2008) 4.

76 Ibid., 31–32, 34, 43.

77 Ibid., 34 and 204–205.

78 Ibid., 33. British Army, *Countering Insurgency*, Field Manual Volume 1 Part 10 (Army Code 71876, October 2009) 1-1.

cadre and fighters (usually referred to as 'combatants' in military doctrine) but limited, if any, mass popular support. Urban approaches tend to utilise a cellular organisational structure concealed within urban areas which enables attacks and harassment of opposing forces and terrorist attacks upon civilians. The use of a clandestine cellular structure will often prevent any mass-based support and so this approach is reliant on a greater proportion of fighters. Protracted and popular wars are those which enjoy widespread support from the population and there is frequent resort to conventional combat and information campaigns.[79]

Armed groups are unlikely to start with an organisation which is capable of mounting sustained and concerted operations. This is usually something that is built up to as a conflict escalates from internal tensions and disturbances to what may be described as a non-international armed conflict. As will be discussed in Chapter 3, this would tend to suggest that in the early stages of internal tensions and disturbances where armed groups are insufficiently organised to undermine the capacity of law enforcement bodies to respond, then the paradigm of law enforcement should apply. However, once a sufficient level of organisation has been reached and the intensity of the violence escalates into a non-international armed conflict, then the dynamics of asymmetric conflict may foster greater fragmentation of organised armed groups that further increases the range of violence and thus operational challenges in full-spectrum conflicts such as individual and situational threat evaluation and status determination. Thus at the outset of an armed conflict there will be an organised armed group that has an organisational structure enabling it to carry out sustained and coordinated attacks, but this opens them up more to surveillance and attack by their militarily stronger adversary. In this case, the impact of successful military and law enforcement operations can serve to fragment armed groups into smaller, more autonomous and clandestine groups that adopt unconventional and irregular individual and small-group-level tactics in order to promote their survivability.[80] Conflicts involving fragmented and low-network-density groups are thus challenging, if not impossible, to deal with in purely conventional military terms and are a common progression from successful military engagement with highly organised and structured armed groups with a high network density.[81]

The organisation and approach of insurgent groups, as well as their military capabilities and motivations, will, to a great, extent have an impact on the tactics they employ.[82] Accordingly, a typical asymmetric strategy is attrition, whereby low-intensity and sporadic attacks are launched over a long period.[83] The strategic

79 US FM 3–24, above n 5, 3–116 & Table 3–6.

80 Ibid., B-35.

81 Ibid.

82 Ibid., 3–120.

83 British Army COIN FM, above n 78, 1–1; US FM 3–24, above n 5, 1–28, 3–101, 3–120, Table 3–7: Common asymmetric tactics include Ambushing counterinsurgent forces; Assassinating opposing political and military leaders; Attacking opposing forces using a different types of explosive violence such as improvised explosive devices, suicide bombers, car bombs;

logic behind this is that it is hard for the constituted government or occupying power to sustain the financial and political cost of a high military and police security presence for any long period.[84] As will be discussed in Chapter 3, from a practical point of view, it thus becomes a challenge to determine whether acts of violence are isolated or whether they are connected to wider protracted hostilities. Furthermore, it is a challenge to identify those activities which form an integral part of the organised violence that forms part of the surrounding hostilities. A clearer schema for individual and situational status determination is thus necessary to promote clearer legal ordering, and as a corollary of this, substantive and institutional protection. In any case, the dynamics of asymmetric warfare will generally result in a broad continuum of violence, most of which may be in a grey area of legal regulation where it is unclear whether the threshold for the existence of an armed conflict has been reached. As will be discussed later, this calls for an intelligence-led approach that can objectively modulate and sequence the use of force to the situation or prevailing conditions.

Low-intensity conflicts: a grey area of legal regulation

The dynamics of asymmetric conflict as described earlier lead to what can be described as low-intensity conflicts that represent a grey area for legal regulation. Low-intensity hostilities are recognised by the US military as being a key feature of contemporary conflicts and are defined as being protracted 'political-military' confrontations between states and armed groups that persist below and sometimes at the threshold of conventional conflict.[85] As indicated in Figure 1.2, this grey area of military operations other than war may comprise counterinsurgency and counterterrorist operations.

Van Creveld has suggested that future 'wars' will be 'overwhelmingly' low intensity in character. In this strategic environment, Van Creveld suggests that

> organisationally and in terms of the equipment at their disposal, the armed forces of the world will have to adjust themselves to this situation by changing their doctrine, doing away with much of their heavy equipment and becoming more like the police.[86]

Organizing mass demonstrations and inciting widespread violence; Raids and attacks on facilities in order to, for example, acquire resources and demonstrate the weaknesses of the government or occupying power.

84 US FM 3–24, above n 5, 1–10.

85 US Marine Corps, Military Police in Support of Marine Air-Ground Task Force, Marine Corps War fighting Publication (MCWP) 3–34.1 (Department of the Navy, Headquarters United States Marine Corps, Washington, DC, 13 October 2000).

86 M Van Creveld, 'Through a Glass, Darkly – Some Reflections on the Future of War' (2000) 53(4) *Naval War College Review* 26.

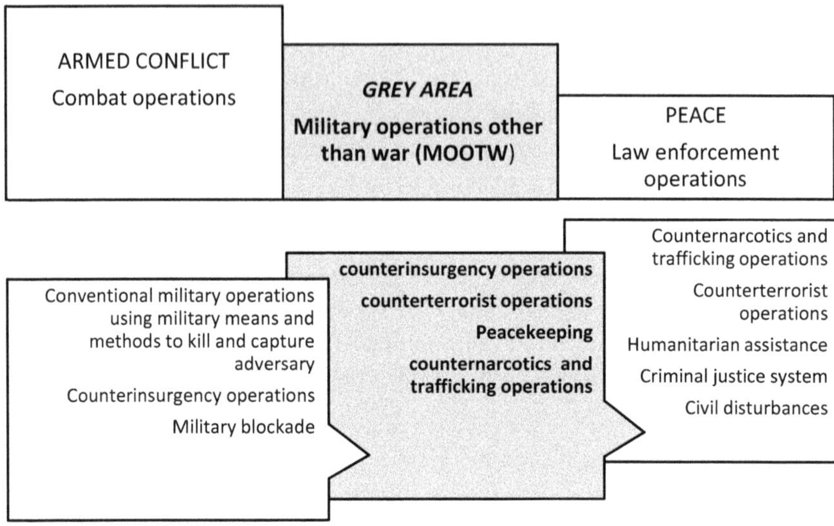

Figure 1.2 The 'grey zone' of military operations.

Source: Adapted from Figure 2–1 Stability in Full Spectrum Operations FM 3–07 2–15, 6 October 2008.

The elements and composition of asymmetric urban armed conflicts

Unconventional or asymmetric warfare 'amongst the people' means that civilians are affected to a greater degree, but also that there are increased pressures, incentives and threats to play a variety of direct and indirect supportive roles.[87] Military doctrine and, as will be discussed in Chapters 4 and 5, criminal law take a realistic and functional approach in recognising that armed groups engaging in hostilities are often highly networked and embedded within a supportive population and that this degree of networked connectivity, so to speak, makes it extremely difficult to distinguish between those who engage directly in combat activities, those who directly or indirectly support them and those who are neutral in the sense that their activities lack proximity or a nexus with surrounding

87 Michael Schmitt, 'Civilians at War: Deconstructing the 21st Century Battlefield' (Chatham House International Law Discussion Group, A summary of the Chatham House International Law discussion group meeting held on 1 November 2007).

hostilities.[88] This opens civilians up to great danger and thus constitutes a major protection issue.

Military doctrine has responded to this by advocating social network analysis that seeks to 'understand the social dynamic that sustains on-going fighting'.[89] Social network analysis thus seeks to describe and analyse how an armed group operates in terms of the roles and functions performed in an organisation and how these can overlap and change over time.[90] It also seeks to describe and analyse how armed groups operate within and exploit existing social, criminal and political structures and networks.[91] Furthermore, it seeks to describe and analyse how social, criminal and political structures and networks support and contribute to hostilities, for example, in terms of financial, material, logistical or intelligence support.[92] Indeed, it may be the case that criminal networks and insurgent groups are so highly interconnected that they can be construed as being functionally fused into a single organisation.[93]

Social network analysis thus advocates an intelligence-led and evidence-based approach to analysing threat levels and functional participation in hostilities that is predicated on accurate and reliable human and documentary intelligence in order to develop a 'clear appreciation of the essential nature and nuances of the conflict' as a basis for effective tactical, operational and strategic responses.[94] Indeed, there is evidence of a recognition that separating the 'reconcilable', that is 'nonlethal threats', from the 'irreconcilable', that is 'lethal threats', cannot be done merely through the application of the paradigm of hostilities, but rather requires 'engagement, population control measures, information operations and political activities' or, in other words, an intelligence-led law enforcement model which prioritises detailed and nuanced assessments of 'hostile' intent and actions whilst not obstructing the use of force in self-defence where necessary or indeed the application of conventional means and methods of force in accordance with the conditions prevailing at the time.[95]

This approach recognises that 'reconcilables' or the categories of 'nonlethal' actors referred to earlier should not be subject to lethal force as a method of first resort, but may be apprehended and used as 'part of the solution',[96] namely for intelligence and evidential purposes that assist with deescalation and conflict transformation, or, in any case, accurate targeting decisions and force protection. Thus a critical analytical approach to intelligence should be adopted when

88 US FM 3–24, above n 5, Appendix B – 54.
89 Ibid., Appendix B – 47.
90 Ibid., 1–307, 1–309.
91 Ibid., Appendix B – 47.
92 Ibid., 3–110, 3–111, Appendix B – 47.
93 Ibid., 3–110, 3–111.
94 Ibid., 1–125, 1–126.
95 Multi-National Force–Iraq (MNF-I), 'Guidelines' in Thomas Ricks (ed), *The Gamble* (Penguin Press, New York, 2009) Appendix D, 369.
96 Ibid.

involved in confrontations and conflicts amongst the people, particularly with regard to human intelligence from informants and detained criminal suspects as well as fighters. In particular, there is a need to verify, cross-reference and corroborate intelligence in order to ensure that mistakes are not made on the basis of information that is purposefully inaccurate or given with the hostile intention, for example, of leading forces into compromising situations such as ambushes, overreacting and causing collateral damage and settling private disputes or vendettas.[97]

The sociological and anthropological approaches of social network analysis is context specific in that it not only seeks to understand and respond to the deep and interconnected links within and between military, political and social organisations, but also the symbolic and functional practices and links between individuals that are specific to particular groups within contemporary forms of irregular activity[98] and insurgency which may reach the threshold of a non-international or internationalised armed conflict.[99]

Social network analysis can construe the ambit of civilian status narrowly by focusing target analysis and target acquisition on the 'internal support structure' of an organised armed group engaging in hostilities (see Figure 1.3). Thus in a purely functional sense the 'internal support structure' of an insurgency may be construed broadly[100] so as to comprise 'military and political leaders',[101] 'combatants',[102] 'auxiliaries',[103] a 'political or ideological cadre'[104] and a 'mass

97 US FM 3-24, above n 5, 3-134.

98 British Army COIN FM, above n 78: e.g., isolated terrorist acts, banditry, organised crime.

99 Ibid., 2-A-1 to 2-A-15: e.g., popular insurgencies, militia insurgencies, gang insurgencies, clan or tribal insurgencies, global insurgencies.

100 US FM 3-24, above n 5, 5-102.

101 British Army COIN FM, above n 78, 2-15; US FM 3-24, above n 5, 1-61. The role and attributes of military and political leaders are generally organising and planning at the strategic and operational levels. They provide the strategic direction and ideological impetus to the movement that underpins the activities of auxiliaries, the political cadre, combatants and the mass base of support.

102 British Army COIN FM, Ibid., 2-15; US FM 3-24, Ibid., 1-62. Combatants are the organised and armed groups that participate directly in hostilities and, in some cases, to provide security and control territory. They implement the overarching strategic aims through combat, recruitment and controlling the flow of resources necessary for combat activities.

103 British Army COIN FM, Ibid., 2-15; US FM 3-24, Ibid., 1-62. Auxiliaries have been defined as those 'active sympathisers' who play an active role in supporting combat activities rather than engaging directly in combat activities. Forms of support provided by auxiliaries may include collecting and transmitting intelligence; running safe houses; sending signals and warnings; and procuring, transporting and storing weapons, supplies and documents.

104 British Army COIN FM, Ibid., 2-15. US FM 3-24, Ibid., 1-65. The political or ideological cadre is not necessarily formally constituted, for example into a political party or extremist group, but in substance, its function is to assist with the organisation, planning and direction necessary for the implementation of the overarching political or ideological goals that stem from the leadership.

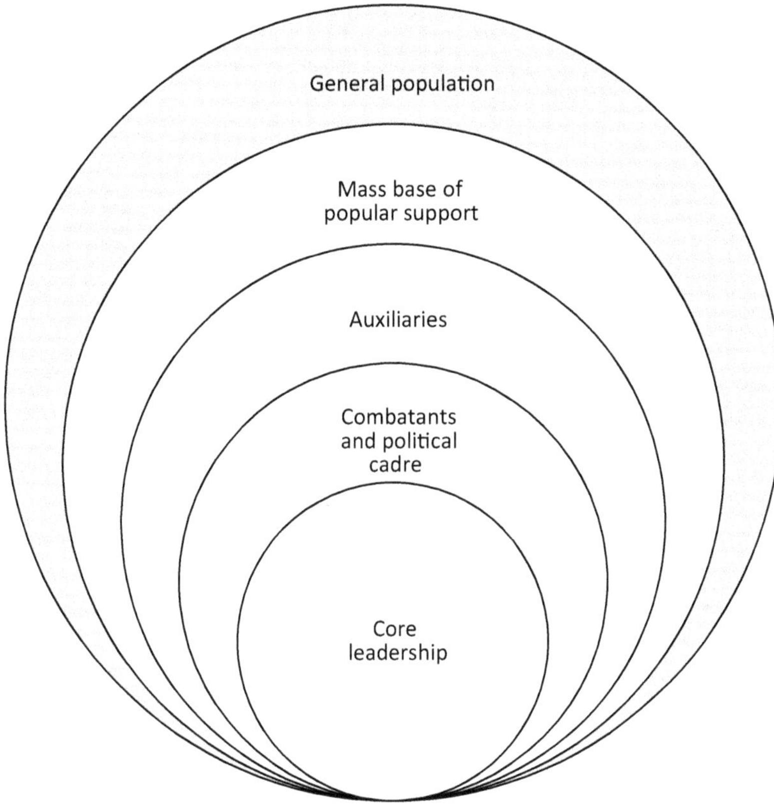

Figure 1.3 Core elements of an internal support structure.
Source: Adapted from British Army COIN FM 2009.[105]

base of popular support'.[106] As noted above, the use of the term 'combatants' in military doctrine is usually generic and is not necessarily used in a legal sense to denote those who are members of the armed forces under Additional Protocol I, or

105 Adapted from British Army COIN FM, Ibid., 2–16, figure 2–2.
106 British Army COIN FM, Ibid., 2–15. US FM 3-24, Ibid., 1–66. The base of popular support comprises those elements of the civilian population who do not remain neutral, but who play a general, clandestine and indirect role in supporting an insurgency or armed group in their activities. Rather than functioning as active auxiliaries, the base of popular support engages in normal everyday civilian activities, whilst at the same time providing general and occasional supportive functions, such as providing intelligence, concealment, funding and transport. Importantly, it is recognised that insurgencies involving clans or tribes have roles and functions that are difficult to define and are fluid, in that individuals have no formal status, but constantly move between combat, auxiliary and follower functions.

those who are entitled to prisoner of war status if captured under the Hague Regulations, but rather an individual who performs a fighting role within a nonstate–organised armed group. Accordingly, as indicated above, in this sense, this discussion generally uses the term 'fighter' for an individual who plays a continuous combat function in an armed group.

Given the potentially broad scope for target acquisition under this analysis, counterinsurgency doctrine makes a distinction between lethal and nonlethal human targets[107] and area targets[108] so that the strategic objectives undergirding the use of force are not undermined. Human targets that are defined as 'lethal' comprise the leaders and fighters within organised armed groups and may be subject to military operations to capture or kill. Human targets that are defined as 'nonlethal' comprise the political and ideological cadre, auxiliaries and the mass base of popular support. Given that their indirect supportive functions mean that they do not pose a direct and immediate lethal threat, they are to be engaged primarily by 'nonlethal' means and methods. As for area targets, areas of active and open combat, bases, safe houses, storage facilities, transport and smuggling routes may be targeted using conventional lethal means and methods of attack. Urban populated areas where fighters are based and operate or control may be engaged by either lethal or nonlethal means of attack. However, in populated areas where there is a measure of civil security, nonlethal means and methods of engagement are required.[109] This ties in with the doctrinal reconceptualisation of the core principles of proportionality and distinction that indicate doctrinal shifts towards more population-centric approaches to unconventional or asymmetric urban warfare.

For example, US counterinsurgency doctrine incorporates the conventional concept of proportionality that 'the anticipated loss of life and damage to property incidental to attacks must not be excessive in relation to the concrete and direct military advantage expected to be gained' (see Figure 1.4).[110] However, it goes on to state that this 'utilitarian' standard applies in 'conventional operations'.[111] In contrast, in unconventional or irregular warfare, soldiers/combatants must make 'positive commitments to [preserving non-combatant] lives by limiting the damage [that] they do'.[112] To this end, forces are required to go further and consider the relative importance of military objectives. Furthermore, regard should be had as to where and when it is best to pursue a target which takes into account the loss of civilian life and destruction of civilian property against the harm that an armed individual or group participating in hostilities could do if allowed to escape. Most significantly, however, the US COIN manual prescribes that '[i]f the target in question is *relatively inconsequential*, then proportionality *requires* combatants *to forego*

107 US FM 3–24, above n 5, Table 5–8.
108 Ibid.
109 Ibid., 5–103.
110 Ibid., 7–30.
111 Ibid., 7–32.
112 Ibid., 7–30.

Figure 1.4 Levels of force should be proportionate to the situational threat.

severe action, or *seek noncombative means of engagement*' [emphases added].[113] Moreover, counterinsurgency doctrine goes as far as to say that once 'conditions of civil security exist', forces '*may not* take any actions that might knowingly harm civilians' [emphasis added].[114] Furthermore, given the heightened risks to civilians in unconventional environments, counterinsurgency doctrine goes further by stating that, particularly in situations where 'civil security exists . . . [forces] *should pursue nonlethal means first, using lethal force only when necessary*' [emphasis added].[115]

Rather than restrict or limit the use of force, the increasing resort to nonlethal methods and the inclusion of nonlethal weapons within the arsenal of military forces is to increase their operational capabilities and thus their effectiveness across a range of operations such as controlling civil disturbances, antiterrorist operations, force protection and isolating hostile forces.[116] Some of the recognised advantages of using nonlethal weapons are that they limit the escalation of hostilities, can prevent or deter hostile acts, allow unconventional military action where conventional means and methods of force would not be appropriate and allow for a less problematic return to peace, as they are primarily intended to disable individuals and materiel rather than completely destroy them.[117]

113 Ibid., 7–32.
114 Ibid.
115 Ibid., 7–36.
116 MCWP 3–34, above n 85, Ch. 7.
117 Ibid.

Thus, although IHL rules of proportionality apply, we can nevertheless observe an important conceptual shift. Namely, rather than making a simple 'hostile' status determination and applying conventional military force to destroy a military objective as a method of first resort, US military doctrine appears to be incorporating an assessment of the level of threat posed by an individual or group. This assessment is then factored into a recalibrated contextual proportionality assessment that gives due, or even greater, weight to humanitarian considerations on the basis that they are a core aspect of military advantage rather than a separate and countervailing factor.[118] Also, this conceptualisation arguably links what may be referred to as an absolute necessity standard to the use of force where 'conditions of civil security exist' and thus promotes the resort to 'noncombative means of engagement'. As stated in the US Field Manual entitled 'Military Operations in Urbanized Terrain' and also the 'Small Wars Manual',

> [t]*he responsibility of officers* . . . and *the training necessary* are of a very different order from their responsibilities and training in ordinary military duties. Instead of striving to generate the maximum power with the forces available, the goal is to gain decisive results with the least application of force and the consequent minimum loss of life [emphasis added].

Similarly, the British army's doctrine of 'minimum force' goes well beyond standard notions of military necessity in that 'no more force must be used than is *absolutely necessary* and reasonable to achieve the immediate military aim' [emphasis added].[119]

Significantly, doctrinal shifts also indicate a shift towards strengthening the principle of distinction. In this regard, the conduct of hostilities may also be limited or 'complicated' by 'the requirement for positive target identification'.[120] This means that a member of a hostile force has to be positively identified or there have to be clear indications of hostile intent before the use of lethal force.[121]

---

118 Toni Pfanner, 'Editorial' (2010) 92 (878) *International Review of the Red Cross* 311–312.

119 MCWP 3–35.3, above n 49, 7101; US Marine Corps, Small Wars Manual Field Manual (FMFRP) 12–15 (Department of the Navy, Headquarters, United States Marine Corps, Washington, DC 22 December 1990); British COIN FM, 3–27.

120 MCWP 3–35.3, Ibid., 6102(b); See also, Center for Law and Military Operations, 'Legal Lessons Learned From Afghanistan and Iraq, Major Combat Operations: Volume I' (Report) (11 September 2001–1 May 2003) The Judge Advocate General's Legal Center & School, United States Army, Charlottesville, Virginia, 72, 98 <www.fas.org/irp/doddir/army/clamo-v1.pdf> accessed 1 October 2013; Center for Law and Military Operations, 'Legal Lessons Learned from Afghanistan and Iraq: Volume II, Full Spectrum Operations' (Report) (2 May 2003 to 28 June 2004) The Judge Advocate General's Legal Center & School, United States Army, Charlottesville, Virginia, 139 <www.fas.org/irp/doddir/army/clamo-v2.pdf> accessed 1 October 2013.

121 MCWP 3–35.3, Ibid., 6102(b). US FM 3–24, Appendix D-8.

Indeed, the US Department of Defense instruction on 'No-Strike and the Collateral Damage Estimation Methodology' goes as far as stating that

> [i]t is an inherent responsibility of all commanders, observers, air battle managers, weapons directors, attack controllers, weapons systems operators, intelligence analysts, and targeting personnel to . . . [e]stablish positive identification and to accurately locate targets consistent with current military objectives.

Furthermore, the instruction defines the requirement of positive identification as 'the reasonable certainty that a functionally and geospatially defined object of attack is a legitimate military target in accordance with the Law of War . . .'[122] Thus, there must be positive identification either of a hostile force or a hostile actor. Identification of a hostile actor is based on an individual's manifest hostile action – that is, the direct or indirect use of force – or hostile intent[123] – that is, the threat of imminent force.[124]

Contemporary military operations and their overriding political strategies

Levels of conflict, full-spectrum operations, the utility of force, and the full-spectrum force continuum

It is suggested that the continuum of violence framework ties in with what military doctrine refers to as levels of conflict. This is to say military and law enforcement involvement in conflicts and confrontations occurs at strategic, operational and tactical levels. This notion of 'levels of conflict' is discussed as it serves as an important conceptual tool for guiding and evaluating the consequences and thus the utility of force at each operational level, in this case within unconventional or asymmetrical conflicts. Actions taken at these different levels of involvement should be joined up and complementary, not only within but also across lines of

---

122 Chairman of the Joint Chiefs of Staff, *Instruction: No-Strike and The Collateral Damage Estimation Methodology* (13 February 2009) 15; Center for Law and Military Operations, above n 120.

123 Major Mark Martins, 'Rules of Engagement for Land Forces: A Matter of Training, Not Lawyering' (1994) 143 *Military Law Review* citing US Army Headquarters, 10th Mountain Division, Operations Plan for Restore Hope, Annex N, at para. 3b(cXl) (1993): 'Hostile intent is the threat of imminent use of force against United States Forces or other persons in those areas under the control of United States Forces. Factors you may consider include: (a) weapons: are they present? what types?; (b) size of opposing force; (c) if weapons are present, the manner in which they are being displayed; that is, are they being aimed? are the weapons part of a firing position?; (d) how did the opposing force respond to United States Forces?; (e) how does the opposing force act toward unarmed civilians?

124 Chairman of the Joint Chiefs of Staff, above n 98, 15. Center for Law and Military Operations, above n 120.

operations. Actions should be directed towards common strategic goals in a full-spectrum operational theatre that involves combat and military operations other than war and law enforcement operations.

Generally speaking, the respective goals of these three broad contextual categories are decisive military victory in armed conflict, preventing and deterring conflict and crime in military operations other than war and maintaining the rule of law.[125] Figure 1.2 illustrates the types of operations which may fall into each contextual category. It also suggests that combat operations, military operations other than war and law enforcement operations may exist simultaneously within a state, or more appropriately, within a single theatre of operations.[126] In this respect there is a degree of overlap in terms of the means and methods of force used. For instance, military police and law enforcement methods are considered important 'force multipliers' in full-spectrum operational theatres that contain offensive, defensive and stability operations. As the latter will often involve restoring and maintaining civic security as well as a civilian system based on the rule of law, law enforcement methods can provide and maintain security and control across a range of operational contexts, either exclusively or alongside combat operations.[127]

The 'levels of conflict' doctrine emphasises that there is a close relationship between the results emanating from the means and methods employed at the tactical and the operational levels of force and the achievement of overriding objectives at the strategic level.[128] Disconnect between these levels of conflict may mean that conventional tactical victories not only fail to achieve results at the strategic level, but may actually serve to worsen the strategic and operational environments by escalating conflict and degrading the institutions and infrastructure of civil society. Rather, coordination and integration of force are essential in order to ensure that the operational environment does not descend into a series of unconnected battles or even engagements.[129] Thus it is suggested that an integral aspect of modern military doctrine is the notion that across all types of operations, 'a return to the environment of peacetime is part of the desired strategic goal'.[130] Indeed, a common strategic goal in 'grey area' or low-intensity conflicts is to restore and maintain civic security, civilian administration and infrastructure, as well as humanitarian relief.[131]

In view of the financial and political costs of high-level and long-term military and police operations, strategic goals ought to be achieved with an economy of

125 US FM 3–07, above n 27, Figures 2–1, 2–15; MCWP 3–34.1, above n 85, figure 1–1.
126 US FM 3–07, Ibid., 2–19.
127 US FM 3–07, above n 27, 2–19. The concept of force multiplication refers to particular means or methods of force that contribute to the effectiveness, thus multiply, other means or methods of force.
128 FM 100–5, above n 34, Ch. 6.
129 Ibid.
130 Ibid., Ch. 2.
131 US FM 3–07, above n 27, Introduction.

force.[132] Economy of force means that the limited time, materiel and personnel have to be used in the most efficient and effective manner possible in order to achieve the desired strategic objectives, which in contemporary conflicts are military but, most importantly, political in nature.[133] This notion of economy of force can be seen to have a significant restraining effect on the use of force in unconventional conflicts in that the application of conventional means and methods of force in confrontations and conflicts amongst the people may mean that 'lives and resources may be wasted for no real gain'.[134] Economy of force is thus connected with the achievement of strategic objectives which are realised through their effective operationalisation and implementation at the operational and tactical levels through the economic employment of means and methods.

The US Department of Defense Law of War Manual recognises that during the 'fog of war' information is often limited, unreliable and uncertain because of the chaotic nature of combat and the opposing sides' efforts to deceive one another, for example, with regard to the numerical strength of the enemy, their equipment and capabilities, their command structure and their intentions. Recognition of the fog of war has a bearing on how principles such as military necessity are applied, particularly with regard to how military personnel are to assess information.[135] In view of US operational manuals, joint doctrine and rules of engagement, as well as modern information-related capabilities, this notion seems to be limited, if not outdated. Militarily superior sides to a conflict will often have the initiative. This means that they do not necessarily have to improvise in the 'fog of war', but rather decisions as to the effective use of force at all levels of conflict in terms of training, organisation, materiel and targeting can be made at the predeployment or preoperational stages or even as part of deliberate (planned targets) or dynamic (targets of opportunity) targeting processes.[136] In the context of contemporary asymmetric conflicts, very rarely, if ever, will militarily superior forces lose the initiative to such a degree that any form of predeployment or preoperational planning and operationalisation is an impossibility.[137] For example, in view of the operational challenges of conducting full-spectrum operations amongst a civilian population, current military doctrine requires soldiers to apply a broad-ranging skills set across a continuum of operations that vary in intensity, and so require the fluid application of military combat skills as well as nonmilitary policing skills in a single theatre of operations. This is because operational environments involving insurgencies 'frequently and rapidly [shift] from war fighting to policing and back again'.[138] Recent US Joint Targeting Doctrine on the joint targeting process generally requires detailed planning and assessment of the

132 US FM 3-24, above n 5, 1-10.
133 FM 100-5, above n 34, Ch. 2.
134 US FM 3-24, above n 5, 1-156.
135 US Department of Defence, *Law of War Manual* (12 June 2015), 1.4.2.2.
136 FM 100-5, above n 34, Ch. 6.
137 Ibid. JP 3-60, above n 10, II 28-33.
138 US FM 3-24, above n 5, Foreword, 7-26; British Army COIN FM, above n 78, 7-26.

target before the execution of deliberate operations. Generally, planning requires direct access to detailed information on the targets, together with analytical reasoning that links the target with a desired effect. Prior to an engagement, planning will also need to identify positively a target on the basis of observation and analysis of target characteristics, including visual recognition and electronic support systems, as well as to validate a target so as to ensure that planned targets will contribute to objectives, that targets are accurately located and to assess how planned actions will affect other friendly operations.[139] According to US Joint Targeting Doctrine, instead of responding to threats in the fog of war, targets may be planned, in which case they are known and identified and engagement actions may be scheduled against them for a specific time, or they may be planned without having a specific delivery time. In contrast, unplanned targets (including those placed on a target list but not selected for engagement, those nominated but not placed on the joint integrated prioritised target list or those not expected to be available for engagement within the target cycle) could be engaged using expedited procedures. Unanticipated targets are those not known or expected to be in the operational environment and therefore not included on a target list, and so the US Joint Targeting Doctrine requires that an evaluation be made of unanticipated targets so as to determine and satisfy engagement requirements. In addition, US Joint Doctrine on the targeting process indicates that the two general categories of targeting – deliberate, or planned targets, and dynamic, or targets of opportunity – do not generally take place in the fog of war, but as part of a rigorous joint targeting cycle. Deliberate targeting will often be a coordinated joint forces effort that is overseen by joint staff over a targeting cycle that lasts from between twenty-four to seventy-two hours. Dynamic targeting may employ expedited planning and engagement of targets that require more immediate responsiveness and usually occurs within a twenty-four-hour targeting cycle.[140] The core targeting steps that are applicable to time-sensitive targets are, first, using intelligence to find a target; second, using sensors to locate, identify and fix a target and assess time available for execution; third, using intelligence, surveillance and reconnaissance to maintain track of the target and update the time available; fourth, developing options for means and methods of engaging the target as well as carrying out target area and risk assessment before making a decision; fifth, ordering the engagement of the target and monitoring and managing the strike; and sixth, assessing the attack and reporting the results.[141] US Joint Doctrine states that these core aspects of deliberate and dynamic targeting may be possible for time-sensitive targets and that arrangements should include the rapid identification and communication capabilities for expedited decision making at subordinate levels of command and control.[142] US Joint Doctrine also

139 JP 3–60, above n 10, II-20, (g) (1)(2).
140 Ibid., Executive Summary.
141 Ibid., II-23.
142 Ibid., II-33.

suggests that although time-sensitive targets may be engaged with dynamic and expedited decision making, aspects of target analysis such as guidance, validation, prioritisation and assessment criteria can be accomplished during preoperational planning or deliberate targeting.[143] US Joint Doctrine refers to 'emerging targets' as those that meet the criteria to be regarded as potential targets and will normally require further ISR and/or analysis to develop, confirm and continue the targeting process.[144]

In the context of the modern unconventional operational environment, counterinsurgency and economy of force doctrine considers it 'imperative' that forces '[u]se the appropriate level of force'.[145] This approach admits the underlying principle of military necessity and self-defence which permit any degree of overwhelming force necessary to destroy the adversary or defend against legal attack. However, it recognises that this may be counterproductive, and so modifies doctrine to require that commanders use 'escalation of force', 'force continuum procedures' or the 'graduated use of force' in order to ensure that force is precisely measured to suit the particular level of threat posed in any given situation.[146] This approach becomes ever more necessary as full-scale combat deescalates, the spectrum of operations widens and the rule of law and civil security returns.[147] As will be discussed further in Chapter 3, progressive normative developments on situational status determination may guide the sequencing and regulation of the continuum of operations that range from policing and civil security operations to traditional combat operations as illustrated by Figure 1.5.

Indeed, it is instructive to see how the force continuum of full-spectrum operations correlates with, and can thus be used to respond to, the violence continuum discussed earlier and illustrated again in Figure 1.6.

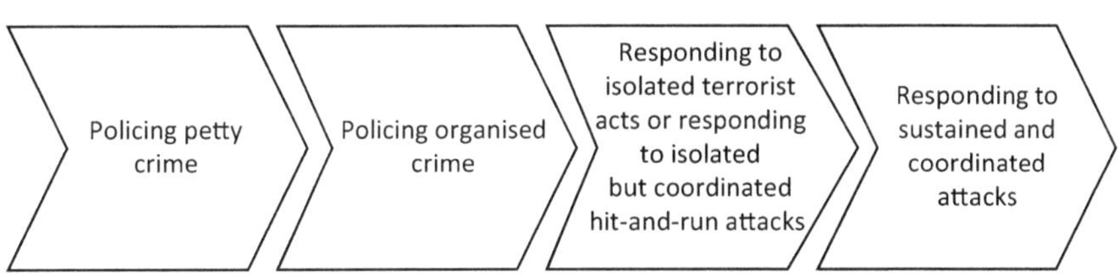

Figure 1.5 The continuum of force in full-spectrum operations.

Source: Adapted from US FM 3–24 2006.[148]

143 Ibid.
144 Ibid., II-23.
145 US FM 3–24, Ibid., 1–141.
146 US FM 3–24, Ibid.
147 US FM 3–24, Ibid., 1–142.
148 Adapted from US FM 3–24, Ibid., figures 5–1 and 5–2.

Figure 1.6 The continuum of violence.
Source: Adapted from UN-Habitat 2007.[149]

Given the broad continuum of violence prevalent in full-spectrum operational environments, military doctrine has recognised the need for a graduated response matrix to guide the application of the appropriate level of force.[150] The premise of this approach is that an immediate armed threat is indicative of a hostile act and a hostile intent, and so this approach proceeds to model out more clearly the various lethal and nonlethal responses to situations involving a range of armed and unarmed threats.[151] Graduated force doctrine requires an escalation of nonlethal measures before escalating to lethal force and also an escalation of lethal force per se.[152] Riot control agents are defined under Article 2(7) of the Chemical Weapons Convention as '[a]ny chemical [not prohibited under the CWC] which can produce rapidly in humans sensory irritation or disabling physical effects which disappear within a short time following termination of exposure'. It is important to note here that riot control agents may be regarded as so-called 'nonlethal' weapons, and although they are prohibited from being used as a method of warfare under the CWC, they may be used for law enforcement operations. The concepts of warfare and law enforcement operations are left undefined under the CWC, and so an attempt will be made in Chapter 7 to clarify the conditions under which the use of riot control agents may be regarded as permissible. In this regard, graduated response matrices for the escalation of nonlethal and lethal force can be expressed diagrammatically in Figures 1.7 through Figure 1.10.

The transition towards strategic goals in the 'three block battlefield'

This leads to the challenging operational environment of what has been described as the 'three block battlefield' which requires the 'continuous [and] simultaneous combinations of offensive, defensive, and stability tasks'. In this operational environment, no single type of response necessarily prevails or is more important than the others. Rather, the key to successful military operations is

149 UN-Habitat, above n 40, 8, figure 1.1.
150 US FM 3–19.15, above n 60, figure 2–1.
151 Ibid.
152 Ibid., 2–60.

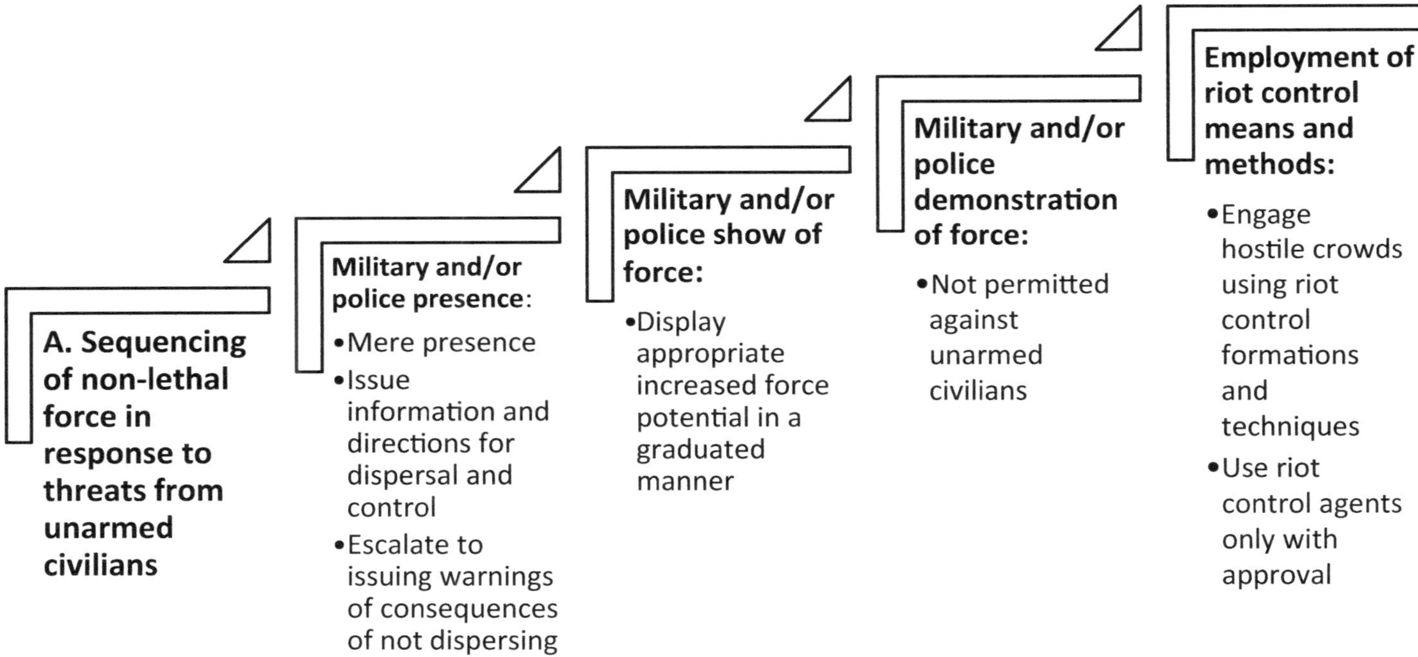

Figure 1.7 Sequencing of nonlethal force in response to threats from unarmed civilians.

Source: Adapted from US FM 3–19.15, 2–1 2005.

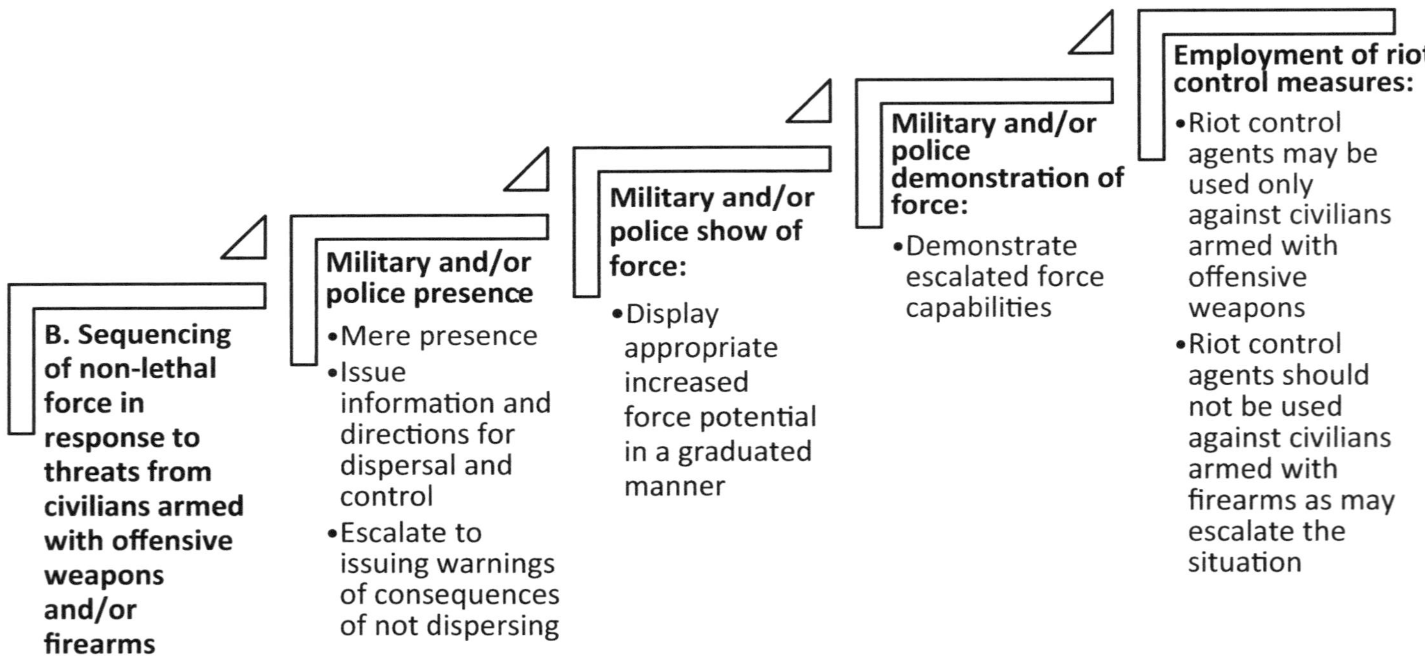

Figure 1.8 Sequencing of nonlethal force in response to threats from civilians armed with offensive weapons and/or firearms.

Source: Adapted from US FM 3–19.15, 2–1 2005.

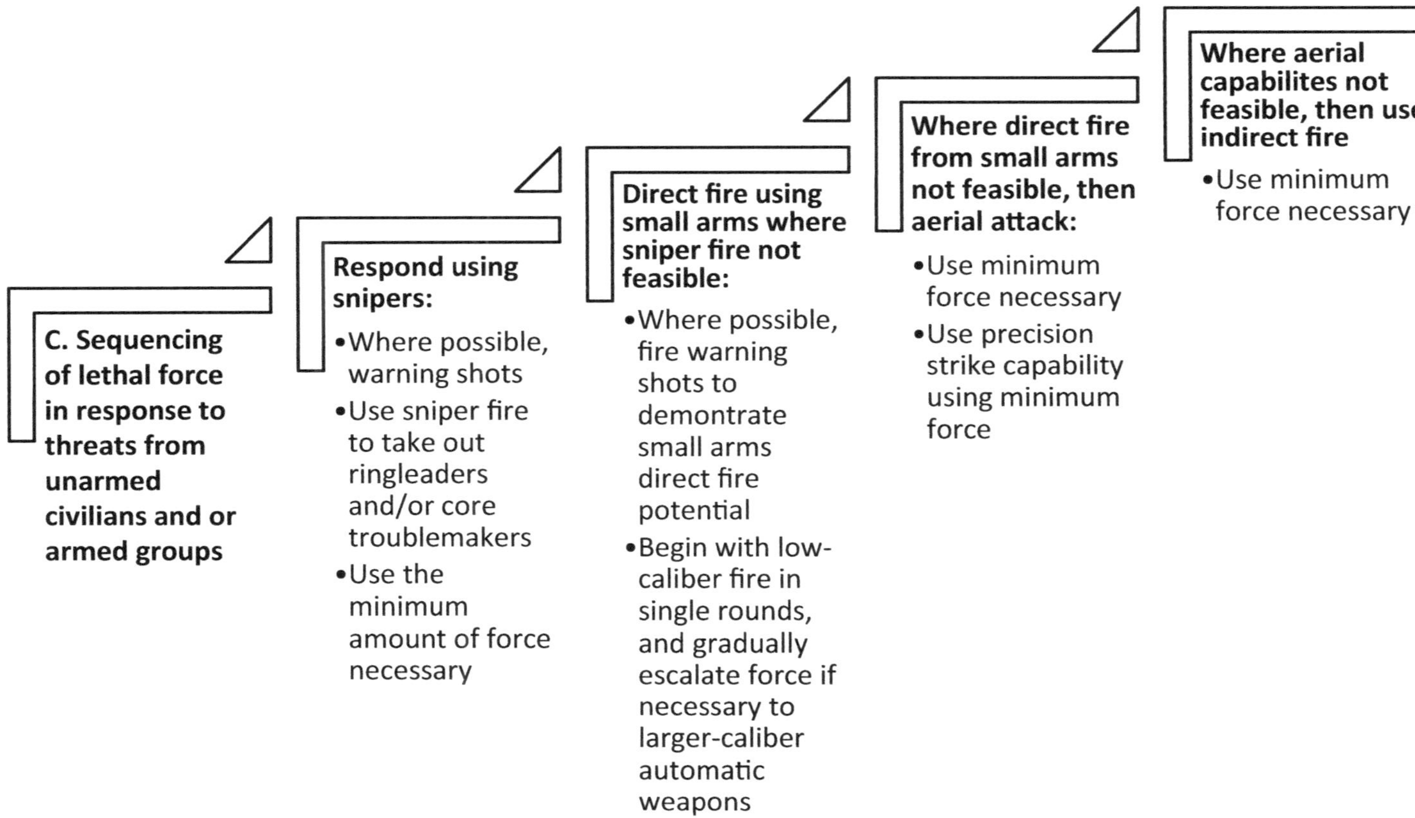

Figure 1.9 Sequencing of lethal force in response to threats from unarmed civilians and/or armed groups.

Source: Adapted from US FM 3–19.15, 2–1 2005.

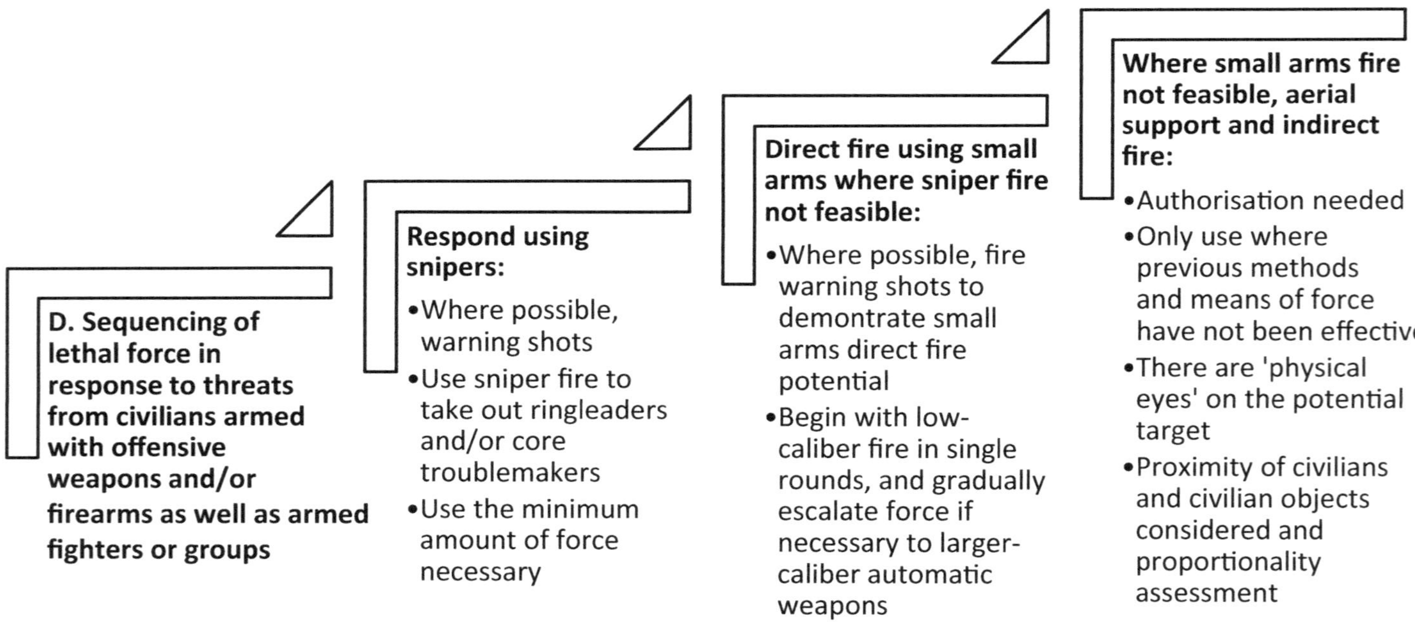

Figure 1.10 Sequencing of lethal force in response to threats from civilians armed with offensive weapons and/or firearms as well as armed fighters or groups.

Source: Adapted from US FM 3–19.15, 2–1 2005.

constantly to combine and adapt these elements together with their associated 'mutually supporting lethal and nonlethal capabilities' over space and time.[153] Thus, in a full-spectrum operational context, for force to be used effectively, it should be continuously modulated and sequenced to suit the particular type of violence or conditions prevailing at the time. For example, within conflict or, more pertinently, postconflict environments where conflict is deescalating such as situations of belligerent occupation, the military may have to assume or assist law enforcement functions in order to restore and maintain civil security so as to prevent the conflict reescalating or taking on new unconventional and irregular forms.[154] The main examples of contemporary military law enforcement operations with security responsibility are those carried out by UN-backed peacekeeping forces, as well as multilateral or unilateral stabilisation forces.[155] The danger is that Hague permissions on targeting 'creep' outside of situations of armed conflict, especially in situations where the violence is transnational and protracted in character.

A key principle of counterinsurgency operations is that application of conventional military force to unconventional conflicts may be counterproductive or of extremely low utility. Recent conflicts have seen counterinsurgent military forces being required 'to overcome their institutional inclination to wage conventional war against insurgents'[156] as it is recognised that this approach 'will almost always fail'.[157] Indeed, contemporary military doctrine itself recognizes that the application of conventional military force in asymmetric urban confrontations or conflicts that leads to extrajudicial killings or collateral damage may be both 'unjustified' and 'self-defeating' in terms of undermining the short- and long-term goals behind the use of force. In particular, military doctrine recognises that 'any human rights abuses . . . quickly become known throughout the local

153 US FM 3–24, above n 5, 1–105; US FM 3–07, above n 27, 2–1; US Department of Army (Training and Doctrine Command) *Operations*, Field Manual (FM) 3–0, C1 (Headquarters, Department of the Army, Washington, DC, 22 February 2011); MCWP 3–35.3, above n 49, 1008.

154 MCWP 3–35.3, Ibid., 6106.

155 Stephens, above n 37, 453 and 455. An example of peacekeeping forces is the United Nations Transitional Administration in East Timor (ENTAET) which was mandated to restore peace and security to postconflict East Timor. This UN-backed multinational peacekeeping force at once had to deal with a high-security threat as well as restoring a functioning host-nation criminal justice system. An example of unilateral and multilateral stabilisation and counterinsurgency operations following on from conventional armed conflicts were those in Iraq and Afghanistan where armed forces had to deal with operational environments of peace and combat as well as the grey areas in between. In these contexts stabilisation and counterinsurgency forces have been assuming law enforcement–type functions and rules of engagement whereby the use of conventional force is seen as unnecessary and counterproductive. Furthermore, adherence to the rule of international and domestic law and restrictive rules of engagement is viewed as one of the chief ways of ensuring legitimacy in the use of force and thus the achievement of strategic goals.

156 US FM 3–24, above n 5, 7–45.

157 Ibid., Introduction.

populace and eventually around the world'[158] and can be exploited for political effect.[159]

As it is recognised that this can lead to the escalation of a conflict, military doctrine promotes conflict transformation in order to 'reduce the means and motivations for violent conflict while developing more viable, peaceful alternatives for the competitive pursuit of political and socio-economic aspirations'.[160] In this way, in order to minimise the risk of the counterproductive application of force, US military doctrine has described the restoration and maintenance of civic security under the rule of law[161] as 'essential', and this requires that military commanders 'transition security activities from combat operations to law enforcement as quickly as feasible'.[162] Thus, in addition to combat lines of operation, law enforcement lines of operation are required to bring into effect a fair system of law, enforced by independent and impartial law enforcement agencies, courts and penal bodies[163] so as to 'protect the recognized rights of individuals'.[164] Furthermore, there ought to be a system for monitoring and enforcing human rights standards.[165] Acting in accordance with the rule of law serves as a basis for legitimising the use of appropriate force and thus promotes the transition towards strategic objectives.[166] Indeed, US military doctrine in particular suggests that although the presence of conventional lethal capabilities is necessary as a deterrent, nonlethal tactics and capabilities are nevertheless critical to success in contemporary full-spectrum conflicts and, what is more, become more of a possibility once a degree of civic security has been restored and there is both a greater strategic imperative and an operational feasibility for a broader range of graduated

158 Ibid., 1–131, 1–132, 1–133.

159 Ibid., 3–24, 3–103, 3–104.

160 US FM 3–07, above n 27, 1–23.

161 Ibid., 1–40 and 1–41. The rule of law is a civil system whereby 'all persons, institutions, and entities, public and private, including the state itself, are accountable to laws that are publicly promulgated, equally enforced, and independently adjudicated, and that are consistent with international human rights principles.'

162 US FM 3–24, above n 5, 1–131, 1–132, 1–133. A feature of the latter approach is that rather than viewing and treating fighters as 'insurgents', they are classified as 'criminals' and subjected to a criminal justice system that brings with it the benefit of due process. Accordingly, there is an emphasis on gathering evidence 'that may be required sometime later in a court of law' and also 'to counter insurgent propaganda'. Whilst being a benefit to an accused, it also serves to bring legitimacy to the host-nation government, occupying power or belligerent. Without such a doctrine of transition followed by a presumption in favour of the paradigm of law enforcement and criminal justice with its police forces, criminal courts and penal systems, within a civilianised and urbanised area of operations there is a high risk of the indiscriminate use of force, extrajudicial killings and punishments, such as detention, without trial.

163 Ibid., 5–7.

164 Ibid., 7–28.

165 US FM 3–07, above n 27, 2–30.

166 US FM 3–24, above n 5, 5–7.

force to be employed.[167] Arguably, this doctrine on law enforcement and human rights needs constantly to be borne in mind in the context of future US and UK Strategic Defence and Security Reviews, because, as seen from the UK House of Commons Defence Committee, there is the constant political pressure from military justice proponents within the government and armed forces to limit the legal scrutiny in coroners' courts, public inquiries and cases brought under human rights law on the premise that the 'judicialisation of war' impedes operational effectiveness.

Population-centric approach to contemporary conflicts

Although the objective of the use of military force is ultimately to dominate and prevail over the adversary, in the reality of the contemporary operational environment, this may only be achieved when it is connected to the introduction of law enforcement operations that are strategically oriented towards the establishment of the rule of law and a safe and secure environment for the local population.[168] Therefore, population-centric approaches constitute a mainstay of military doctrine aimed at promoting the legitimacy of the use of force and thus the legitimacy of a constituted government, occupying power, stabilisation forces or peacekeeping force.[169] This necessarily implies the growing prominence of human rights norms and accountability mechanisms in overseeing law enforcement approaches, as well as the importance of keeping strategic, operational and tactical responses within the bounds of the law enforcement paradigm as far as possible. Accordingly, the notion of legitimacy can be considered an important evaluative concept within military doctrine to ensure that the use of force is in line with the perceptions and expectations of the local population in terms of what is justified and acceptable.[170] In this regard, the use of force is legitimate when it is in accordance with human rights and humanitarian laws.[171]

Conclusions

In this chapter, it has been observed that asymmetric urban armed conflict exposes the militarily superior side's political vulnerabilities, for in the process of attacking

167 US FM 3–07, above n 27, 2–13 to 2–16.

168 Ibid., 1–83. US FM 3–24, above n 5, 1–3; British COIN FM, above n 54, Ch. 3; Stephens, above n 37, 459; David Kilcullen, *The Accidental Guerrilla: Fighting Small Wars in the Midst of a Big One* (Hurst & Company, London, 2009) 265.

169 Kilcullen, Ibid., 167: 'forces that are legitimate in local eyes, operate under the rule of law' and '[d]irect combat (not remote engagement by air or artillery) is essential, in order to minimize collateral noncombatant casualties, ensure flexible responses to complex ground environments . . .'

170 British COIN FM, above n 54, 1–13; US FM 3–07, above n 4, 1–28–1–34; US FM 100–05, above n 104, Ch. 13; Stephens, above n 37, 453.

171 US FM 3–07, Ibid., 1–29.

and counterattacking its weaker opponent, the militarily superior side will face a major challenge. On the one hand, it may perceive that full compliance with international humanitarian law lessens its ability quickly and decisively to achieve strategic objectives such as a ceasefire, surrender, regime change, restoration of international peace, security and the rule of law. On the other hand, it may find that in trying to achieve its strategic objectives, the presence of military objectives within densely populated urban areas makes it difficult to stay within lawful parameters. This is to the weaker side's strategic advantage, for it can then seek to exploit any direct or indirect attacks upon civilians through media coverage, well aware that the stronger side is subject to international and domestic political pressure to achieve a quick and decisive military victory at a minimum cost to human lives and material resources.

Clausewitz once stated that "war is a mere continuation of policy by other means".[172] This still holds true for contemporary armed conflicts, but with the added proviso that humanitarian law may serve as a continuation of war by other means. In other words, militarily stronger parties to a conflict can either adopt and employ IHL-compliant military strategies as a prerequisite for both military and political success or risk sacrificing "victory in peace for victory in war".[173] The latter has been described as a poor policy, because forms of direct or indirect "barbarism" generally promote and stimulate militarily weak adversaries rather than deter them.[174] Also, it results in protracted and costly conflicts that either do not attain the desired political objective, as in Vietnam, or are otherwise not conducive to a stable political outcome, as in Iraq and Afghanistan.[175]

These material dynamics of asymmetric or unconventional conflicts have affected contemporary military doctrine in major and seemingly counterintuitive ways.[176] The doctrinal shifts discussed here indicate what Stephens describes as 'an uneasy accommodation' whereby 'a means-end rationality [. . .] is constantly being weighed in determining the right policy response to a threat'.[177] In any case, these doctrinal shifts are an important reminder that general principles of IHL are coloured by policy considerations and are ultimately expressed through military doctrine and rules of engagement.

It is asserted that in the context of unconventional and full-spectrum conflicts, military and humanitarian considerations should not be regarded as

172 Clausewitz, above n 29, chs. 1 and 24.
173 Arreguín-Toft, above n 75, 225.
174 Ibid., 224.
175 Ibid., 213.
176 US FM 3–24, above n 5: This is reflected in a series of paradoxes that are said to reflect the challenges of responding to contemporary conflicts, first '[s]ometimes, the more you protect your force, the less secure you may be'; second, '[s]ome of the best weapons for counterinsurgents do not shoot'; third, '[s]ometimes, the more force is used, the less effective it is'; and fourth '[t]he more successful the counterinsurgency is, the less force can be used and the more risk must be accepted'.
177 Stephens, above n 37, 459.

countervailing considerations, but that contemporary doctrine has fostered their ever-increasing coincidence, indeed, to such an extent that humanitarian considerations are to be regarded as integral to the notion of military advantage. Put another way, according to contemporary military doctrine, 'the human dimension of war will be decisive in the campaigns and battles of the future'.[178] In this regard, contemporary doctrine reveals that greater consideration is being given to 'the social effect of legal interpretation' as a 'key indicator of both military success and legitimacy in guiding military decision-making'.[179] For example, British military doctrine states in imperative terms that in dealing with insurgencies 'the population is central to the outcome' and that the restoration of civic security is paramount.[180] Thus, the civilian population together with its legitimate interests and expectations is a centre of gravity or a key strategic priority towards which efforts have to be channelled.[181] This doctrinal shift highlights the complex milieu in which law, policy and doctrine operate to minimise the effects of force so as to ensure that its use is not counterproductive. This population-centric view of the use of force is based on the view that contemporary operations are military-political in nature and that 'political purpose has primacy [. . .] regardless of how violent the situation may be'.[182] Accordingly, intervention has to be multifaceted in the sense that military, security, political, developmental and diplomatic responses have to be applied simultaneously because 'there can be no such thing as a purely military solution to an insurgency because insurgency is not primarily a military activity'.[183] Although taking on board the spectrum of scholarly discourse (for example, Bellinger and Hayes) that characterises such state-led developments as mere policy, this discussion takes a very different stance and suggests that one of the effects of institutionalising doctrine and practice, or, in other words, putting it on a more obligatory and imperative footing, is that it may serve to guide the effective and legitimate use of force in on-going and future operations, and thus expectations that can serve to guide the interpretation of general legal standards set out in military manuals and general IHL. This discussion has attempted to make a contribution to academic discourse by highlighting the fact that because mainstream military doctrine has embraced what may be described as population-centric approaches at strategic, operational and tactical levels of force, this serves to contrast with the argumentative force of proponents who advocate adherence to conventional, positivistic and military justice approaches to the regulation of contemporary operational theatres in opposition to normative evolution that comes from greater civilian justice and oversight. Accordingly, this discussion aims to take issue with such approaches that make black-and-white binary distinctions between the paradigm of hostilities and the paradigm of law

178 US FM 100–05, above n 104, Ch. 14.
179 Stephens, above n 37, 455.
180 British COIN FM, above n 78, Section 5, 1–22.
181 Ibid., 1–23.
182 Ibid., 3.
183 Ibid., 1–23.

enforcement and also that make certain assumptions about the nature of 'the harsh realities of war'[184] and thus what can realistically be expected therein. For example, it is argued that military scholars such as Hansen[185] and Corn often strongly criticise the proposed complementary interrelationship between the paradigm of hostilities and law enforcement, or in other words, IHL and IHRL, by tending to assume that developments in this direction will inevitably result in negative consequences without providing any evidence or examples to this effect. For instance, Corn argues that the 'operationally inapposite' application of human rights instruments 'based on a perceived necessity to comply with human rights during armed conflict' will result in their 'routine disregard' and 'absolute resistance'.[186] Similarly, Hansen argues that normative progress needs to be 'halted' to prevent the 'emasculation of warfare' which 'will unnecessarily restrict warfighters to a point never envisioned by those who framed and ratified the major instruments designed to regulate warfare'.[187] Furthermore, Hansen suggests that progressive development will lead to 'overregulation of the battlefield' serving to 'prolong conflict rather than facilitate a quick end to wars'.[188] Similarly, the recent UK House of Commons Defence Select Committee's report expressed its concern that the requirement for full and detailed investigations over every death resulting from an armed conflict is putting a significant burden on the UK Ministry of Defence and the armed forces and seems to risk the 'judicialisation of war' which risks 'far bloodier engagements on the battlefields as commanders may take fewer risks with their own troops and make more use of close air support or remotely actioned weapons'.[189]

It is suggested that such assumptions do not give a full and fair account of the strategic and operational possibilities for responding to the current spectrum of challenges and trends, and in this regard there are no valid reasons why our policy should be dominated by an IHL/LOAC paradigm rather than a HRL paradigm. Such assumptions are not necessarily in keeping with material conditions of contemporary conflict and military doctrine, and so therefore should be treated with scepticism. This is because military operations may often occur outside of armed conflict, and seemingly violent situations or activities may have little or no connection with surrounding hostilities, especially in a transnational context. Accordingly, a multilateral criminal justice and human rights regulatory

---

184 Michelle Hansen, 'Preventing the Emasculation of Warfare: Halting the Expansion of Human Rights Law into Armed Conflict' (2007) 194 *Military Law Review* 8.

185 Ibid.

186 G Corn, 'Mixing Apples and Hand Grenades, the Logical Limit of Applying Human Rights Norms to Armed Conflict' (2010) 53 *International Humanitarian Legal Studies* 52–94, 55.

187 Hansen, above n 184, 8.

188 Ibid.

189 UK House of Commons Defence Committee, 'UK Armed Forces Personnel and the Legal Framework for Future Operations' (Twelfth Report of Session 2013–14) (House of Commons, 2 April 2013), 129.

framework may not only be regarded as having a broader field of practical application along the continuum of violence than many military justice proponents would care to accept, but also, as discussed earlier, may be regarded as being strategically desirable. Although the UK House of Commons Defence Committee noted a concern amongst armed forces personnel that 'they and their legitimate actions are frequently exposed to extensive legal scrutiny in coroners' courts, public inquiries and cases brought under human rights law', this is to assume that which ought to be established first: namely that their actions are legitimate and that this impedes operational effectiveness.[190]

In these ways, although such viewpoints may have validity vis-à-vis conventional engagements of the past, present and future, they may be criticised for their limited conception of contemporary conflict, normativity and regulation. What such analyses lack is a constructive sense that contemporary material conditions are making the complementary application of the paradigms of hostilities and law enforcement increasingly workable and desirable. Furthermore, they fail to consider that progressive doctrinal and normative developments may not be regarded by key war-fighting states as unduly restrictive or impractical, but rather as integral to the achievements of their strategic objectives in using force.[191] Indeed, contemporary counterinsurgency strategy indicates that the operational rules have become increasingly restrictive to protect civilians in order to contribute to the achievement of the goals underlying the use of force.

Accordingly, it is suggested that as part of future strategic defence and security reviews, states should look strategically at developing the legal frameworks for future conflicts in view of the whole spectrum of military operations and violence that they may face, as well as the issue that the widespread and unregulated application of Hague permissions on means and methods of force, particularly in the context of extrajudicial/targeted killings, do not necessarily contribute to the legitimate or effective use of force. Chapter 3 aims to set out more clearly the extent to which we should expect legal scrutiny and more cases brought under human rights law and the threshold from which this may be regarded as unfeasible and an impediment to operational effectiveness. Kilcullen, a leading authority on counterterrorism and counterinsurgency theory and practice, suggests that the conventional military approaches to the 'grey area between war and peace' over the past fifteen years have been misguided and have failed to bring about viable political outcomes. Rather, he suggests that there is a limited role for military force in the face of the complex and dynamic threat of terrorism and that democracies must respond through political leadership, law enforcement and public engagement in order to bring about enduring and stable peace.[192]

---

190 Ibid., 11.

191 Ibid. Indeed, it is suggested that Hansen's claim that 'excessive humanisation might exceed the limits acceptable to armed forces, and provoke their resistance, and thus erode the credibility of those rules' is not one that is reflected in contemporary military doctrine itself.

192 David Kilcullen, *Blood Year: Islamic State and the Failures of the War on Terror* (Hurst & Company, London, 2016), 203 and 230.

The outcome of this discussion is that it is possible to suggest that the doctrinal and normative milieu that has emerged makes it possible progressively to reconceptualise and restructure existing norms so as to promote the effective use of force in terms of achieving strategic goals. As discussed, this is ultimately predicated on maximising human security, particularly in the urban spaces of contemporary conflict. According to this rationale, strategy and human security are effectively synonymous, and this is reflected in contemporary doctrine and jurisprudence vis-à-vis the use of force. Contemporary military doctrine relative to contemporary full-spectrum operations thus reveals limitations placed on the use of means and methods of force, which may be in excess of that permitted under conventional IHL. It supports Provost's observation that there has been a 'progressive rejection of military necessity as a valid justification for disregarding humanitarian law over the course of the last century' and that this 'can also be linked to the development of individual human rights'.[193]

This chapter concludes by suggesting that policy and doctrinal considerations are central to the operation of IHL in practice and thus should be taken into consideration when it comes to the continuous evolution of this field of public international law. In other words, the point that is foreshadowed here is that interpretative approaches to the substance and ordering of humanitarian law and human rights law should not be insulated from the strategic policy considerations that are being implemented in practice.[194] To this end, the relevant contemporary practice discussed here indicates that in spite of the loose norms under IHL, there has been a policy-based shift towards population-centric approaches to the use of force in unconventional confrontations and conflicts amongst concentrations of civilians. As the previous discussion indicates that population-centric policy considerations are being 'institutionalised' within relevant military doctrine, then according to methodologically liberal policy-oriented approaches to normativity that are plausible within this field of public international law, they may be regarded as entering into and progressing along a normative continuum.

In addition to the examples of population-centric doctrine discussed earlier, this chapter finishes with an example of progressive norms being institutionalised within military doctrine at the international level, namely, the Tactical Directive issued in 2009 by the commander of NATO's International Security Assistance Force, General Stanley McChrystal, which was designed to provide 'guidance and intent for the employment of force in support of ISAF operations'.[195] Although most of the Tactical Directive was classified on grounds of force protection, excerpts of it were made public in order to ensure 'a broader awareness of the intent and scope of . . . guidance to . . . forces'.[196] In relation to levels of force, the

---

193 René Provost, *International Human Rights and Humanitarian Law* (Cambridge University Press, 2002) 41.

194 Stephens, above n 37, 85–118.

195 NATO/International Security Assistance Force, 'Tactical Directive' (6 July 2009).

196 Ibid.

Tactical Directive stated that the 'strategic goal is to defeat the insurgency' and, in this context, 'there is a struggle for the support and will of the population'. Accordingly, the Tactical Directive provides that '[g]aining and maintaining that support must be our overriding operational imperative – and the ultimate objective of every action'. To this end, the Tactical Directive stated that military victory is not based 'on the number . . . we kill, but instead on our ability to separate insurgents from the centre of gravity – the people'. Accordingly, 'that means that we must respect and protect the population from coercion and violence and operate in a manner which will win their support'. In this regard, the Tactical Directive noted that this type of unconventional operational environment 'is different from conventional combat' and that 'traditional measures' could lead to 'the trap of winning tactical victories – but suffering strategic defeats – by causing excessive damage'. The Tactical Directive framed this as a 'legal . . . moral [and] overarching operational issue' which requires 'carefully controlled and disciplined employment of force'. In particular, the Tactical Directive stated that leaders at all levels are expected 'to scrutinize and limit the use of force like close air support against residential compounds and other locations likely to produce civilian casualties'.

Rather than a straight balance of military and humanitarian considerations, the Tactical Directive is indicative of the doctrinal trend of integrating humanitarian considerations within military-strategic objectives. The Tactical Directive states that '[c]ommanders must weigh the gain of using [close air support] against the cost of civilian casualties, which in the long run make mission success more difficult and turn the . . . people against us'. Although not prescribing 'the appropriate use of force for every condition that a complex battlefield will produce', the Tactical Directive required forces to 'internalize and operate in accordance with . . . a cultural shift within our forces' that must be 'clearly communicated and continually reinforced'. For example, 'the use of air-to-ground munitions and indirect fire against residential compounds is only authorized under very limited and prescribed conditions'. The specific circumstances where such acts would be authorised were not declassified due to operational security.[197]

As such doctrine becomes widespread and consistent, Stephens observes that over time, the force of arguments that seek to make a distinction between law and policy are weakened in the face of 'consistent policy preferences' that shift our 'logic of appropriateness' and that leads to the internalisation of 'socialized norms of behaviour within military circles'.[198] This then operates to impose greater restraints on military considerations, or military discretion, in order to achieve strategic outcomes by assigning more weight to humanitarian considerations in order to redress the imbalance that would otherwise ensue in contemporary

197 Ibid.

198 Dale Stephens, 'Blurring the Lines: The Interpretation, Discourse and Application of the Law of Armed Conflict' (2009) 12 *Yearbook of International Humanitarian Law* 85–118, 90.

asymmetric operations. Moreover, this raises the interpretative possibility that population-centric policy 'may transform into soft legal norms and eventually crystallize into hard rules'.[199]

The UK House of Commons Defence Committee and the Joint Committee on Human Rights have both suggested that there is an urgent need to reappraise and address in a strategic way the legal regulation of the conduct of military operations so as to provide greater clarity and certainty in identifying the boundaries between different levels and types of violence. Whereas within the UK government, the Joint Committee on Human Rights is concerned about the emergence of an unclear, unarticulated and unregulated policy of targeted killing, the Defence Committee is concerned that civilian oversight and regulation are putting an excessive burden upon the Ministry of Defence and the armed forces. Rather than trying to ensure, in absolute terms, that IHL/LOAC has primacy over HRL, or vice-versa, it is suggested that the justiciability of the use of force in general, and targeted killings in particular, is a nuanced and context-specific question which raises the following legal questions that will be dealt with in Chapters 3 through 8. First, is it possible that human rights and humanitarian law standards on the use of force can be applied in the same operational theatre, and, if so, how are they interoperable in practice? Where can we draw the line and say that law enforcement operations and thus the paradigm of human rights is no longer practicable? Second, are higher standards of reasonableness required or becoming expected vis-à-vis targeting and weaponry law in the context of military operations in civilianised and urbanised terrain? If so, how are these becoming manifest? Third, given that the theatre of operations is becoming increasingly civilianised, in that there is not only greater intermingling between civilians and combatants and fighters, but civilians may also be playing a range of indirect supportive roles in hostilities, where should the parameters of civilian loss of immunity be set?

---

199 Ibid., 87, 90, 108. Dieter Fleck, 'International Accountability for Violations of the Ius in Bello: The Impact of the ICRC Study on Customary International Humanitarian Law' (2006) 11(2) *Journal of Conflict & Security Law* 179–199.

2 A general critique of IHL targeting and weaponry norms and institutions

Introduction

As highlighted in Chapter 1, the contemporary operational environment may in part be characterised as a 'grey area', not only for operational and doctrinal purposes, but also for normative purposes. This grey area may comprise activities that constitute a response to a state of emergency or exceptional law enforcement measures, namely military operations that do not amount to an armed conflict, but which, as indicated by Chapter 1, may be performed simultaneously with military operations that form part of a wider armed conflict.

Chapter 2 proposes that the conventional protection architecture relative to the use of force is not entirely fit for the contemporary context of full-spectrum operations. In the context of contemporary military operations, there is the risk that increasing numbers of civilians are being brought within the scope of the paradigm of armed conflict rather than law enforcement, particularly as warfare becomes increasingly civilianised and urbanised. Furthermore, it is proposed that unless we set out and consistently apply clear objective criteria that set the threshold for the applicability of Hague NIAC rules at a high level, then there is the risk that within the operational and normative uncertainties of contemporary operational environments, IHL may be 'coming down' from its high threshold of applicability and IHRL may be 'coming up'. A major protection issue, therefore, concerns the potential for the increasing legitimisation of extrajudicial killing, or murder, across a range of low-intensity hostilities where the distinction between armed conflict and military operations other than armed conflict may often be blurred.

It is suggested that this is an outcome of the structural weaknesses in the norms and institutions of IHL. Initiatives such as the Turku Declaration on 'Minimum Humanitarian Standards' demonstrates a recognition amongst international experts that 'human rights and humanitarian norms applicable in armed conflicts do not adequately protect human beings in situations of internal violence, disturbances, tensions and public emergency'.[1] In relation to targeting and weaponry

1 Turku Declaration of Minimum Humanitarian Standards, adopted on 2 December 1990 by an expert meeting convened from 30 November to 2 December 1990 at the Abo Akademi University Institute for Human Rights in Turku, Finland.

law under IHL, it will be suggested that the general and open-textured principles of IHL – namely proportionality, precaution, distinction and military advantage – are too indeterminate and too broad to constitute clear and adequate guidelines on operational and strategic decision making. Furthermore, IHL does not clearly spell out what constitutes a non-international armed conflict or even a conflict zone. In relation to weaponry law, a major protection issue is that in the absence of weapon-specific prohibitions, principles of IHL do not generally prohibit the means of warfare that cause the most harm to civilians in contemporary conflicts. Furthermore, there is wide scope for the harm caused by conventional means and methods of warfare to be justified under the general principles of IHL.

In response to the various structural weaknesses, international and regional human rights mechanisms have been attempting to fill these 'protection gaps' through a variety of forms of political and legal intervention. This is having the effect of creating a progressive body of jurisprudence as well as 'authoritative pronouncements' that may be just as significant as norms that have the status of 'law'.

It is suggested that the interpretation of legal frameworks relevant to the contemporary full-spectrum operational environment has been affected by a modern normative landscape which has become increasingly pluralistic and cosmopolitan since the foundational IHL Conventions came into effect following the Second World War. Within our evolving international civil society, 'inter-governmental' and 'supranational' civil society actors are playing a varied and controversial role in the application of IHL, IHRL and ICL to contemporary situations of crisis and conflict. Actors include UN treaty bodies, international criminal tribunals and regional human rights courts. The application of various legal frameworks to the vicissitudes of full-spectrum operations necessarily involves interpretation and ordering of existing standards. This represents an opportunity for the progressive realisation of existing standards so that they are relevant to the strategic and humanitarian considerations of contemporary international society. However, it also raises major protection issues that require a discussion of the capacity and competence of human rights actors to become involved in situations of crisis through their various fact-finding, monitoring and adjudicatory activities. Although this issue of developing common standards to increase the credibility and legitimacy of the pronouncements of UN and regional human rights bodies is beyond the scope of the present discussion, it is suggested that developments such as the *Siracusa Guidelines for International, Regional and National Fact-Finding Bodies* of 2013, the ICRC's *Professional Standards for Protection Work Carried Out by Humanitarian and Human Rights Actors in Armed Conflict and Other Situations of Violence* of 2013 and even the ICTY's *Manual on Developed Practices* (2009) provide valuable policy and practice guidance.

General critique of targeting and weaponry norms and institutions under IHL

Introduction

Treaty-based law takes a bifurcated approach to legal regulation by setting out different rules depending on whether or not a conflict is international or non-international in character. These rules fall within two distinct categories: namely, those rules relating to the conduct of hostilities, otherwise known as Hague law, and those rules that relate to the treatment and conditions of persons who have protected status under IHL, otherwise known as Geneva law. Hampson notes that Hague law is primarily a set of considerations outlined in general principles such as proportionality and distinction. These general targeting principles are directed to guide the decision making of military operators acting under battlefield conditions.[2] In contrast, Hampson suggests that Geneva law 'is focused on the actual or potential victim rather than the perpetrator' and that '[m]any, but by no means all, of the issues that it addresses arise away from the immediate field of battle'.[3]

This section sets out to focus on the adequacy of treaty-based Hague law for contemporary conflict situations. The issue of thresholds for the applicability of Hague and Geneva law are touched on only very briefly in Chapter 2. The notion of normative effectiveness is understood to be the existence of comprehensive, clear and detailed legal frameworks that provide a sufficient degree of protection as well as adequate guidance on the use of means and methods of force. One of the main structural indeterminacies affecting the effective operation of IHL concerns the open-textured and indeterminate character of rules on targeting set out in Additional Protocol I (API), Additional Protocol II (APII) and Common Article 3 (CA3) to the Geneva Conventions of 1949, which means that they provide weak *ex post facto* substantive protection to civilians.

Furthermore, the general prohibitions contained within API have circumscribed subject matter jurisdiction and applicability. They apply to international armed conflicts but not non-international armed conflicts to which APII and CA3 to the Geneva Convention apply. In comparison with API, APII does not contain general rules relating to proportionality and precaution in attack. In this way, APII has been described as 'legal ectoplasm' as these omissions mean that the text is 'devoid of any real humanitarian substance and mandatory character'.[4] In this sense, it is suggested that in comparison with the IHL applicable to international armed conflicts, APII contains very weak, or, as alluded to earlier vis-à-vis 'legal ectoplasm', virtually nonexistent Hague rules on the conduct of hostilities. CA3 contains very basic minimum rules applicable in conflicts not of an international character, and it is generally contended that it does not contain any Hague rules on the conduct of hostilities per se, and so beyond the rudimentary protections that it offers, CA3 non-international armed conflict 'falls into an unregulated IHL space'.[5] Hampson notes that in comparison with the rules relative to inter-

2 Françoise Hampson, 'Direct Participation in Hostilities and the Interoperability of the Law of Armed Conflict and Human Rights Law', in Raul Pedrozo and Daria Wollschlaeger (eds), *International Law Studies* (Vol. 87, US Naval War College, 2011) 193.

3 Ibid.

4 Antonio Cassese, *The Human Dimension of International Law* (Oxford University Press, 2008) 247.

5 Jelena Pejic, 'The Protective Scope of Common Article 3: More than Meets the Eye' (2001) 93 (881) *International Review of the Red Cross* 190.

national armed conflicts, the rules relating to the grounds for detention and the status of members of organised armed groups in non-international armed conflicts are comparatively nonexistent.[6]

Thus, as will be argued in Chapters 3 and 6, to assert that prohibitive and permissive customary Hague rules can only apply where the threshold of an APII NIAC has been reached on the basis that the only reference to NIAC Hague-type rules is found in APII as opposed to CA3 is to overstate the Hague law content of APII and to overgeneralise the scope of its threshold criteria to include customary Hague law in an unwarranted fashion. Weaponry law in the form of specific weapons' prohibitions may have limited subject matter jurisdiction, meaning that they may not prohibit new modalities of a particular category of weapon. Nevertheless, as will be discussed in Chapters 6 and 7, contemporary weaponry law is important as certain weapon-specific treaties expressly apply to both IACs and NIACs.

The rationale of the following discussion and critique of treaty-based IHL is to stress the importance of progressively developing customary IHL and applying it to urban armed conflicts *ab initio*, namely, once the threshold of a CA3 armed conflict has been reached according to the *Boškoski* indicative guidelines. As will also be discussed later, this may be applied alongside a human rights–oriented law enforcement model that may apply in parts of a territory where violence does not reach this threshold, and this model may be escalated where necessary.[7] In turn, Chapter 3 will set out in more detail the proposed guidelines to lend rigour and clarity to the parallel applicability and sequenced application of HRL and IHL in the context of unconventional and full-spectrum operational environments.[8]

Targeting law norms

Article 48[9] of API sets out the general rule on distinction, which acts as a basis for the rules prohibiting indiscriminate[10] and disproportionate attacks, as well as

6 Françoise Hampson, above n 2, 195.

7 Lindsay Moir, *The Law of Internal Armed Conflict* (Cambridge University Press, 2002) 51.

8 Naz Modirzadeh, 'The Dark Sides of Convergence: A Pro-Civilian Critique of the Extraterritorial Application of Human Rights Law in Armed Conflict' in Raul Pedrozo (ed.), *The War in Iraq: A Legal Analysis* (International Law Studies Series, Vol. 86, US Naval War College, 2010) 335 and 386.

9 Protocol Additional to the Geneva Conventions of 12 August 1949, and relating to the Protection of Victims of International Armed Conflicts (Protocol I), 8 June 1977 ("API") Article 48 provides that '[i]n order to ensure respect for and protection of the civilian population and civilian objects, the Parties to the conflict shall at all times distinguish between the civilian population and combatants and between civilian objects and military objectives and accordingly shall direct their operations only against military objectives'.

10 Article 51 paragraph (4) of API prohibits 'indiscriminate attacks' and defines them in the following terms: (a) those which are not directed at a specific military objective; (b) those which employ a method or means of combat which cannot be directed at a specific military objective; (c) those which employ a method or means of combat the effects of which cannot

the rules requiring precaution in attack. Article 52 paragraph (2) defines civilian objects in the negative by stating that only military objectives may be attacked. The term 'military objectives' is defined broadly as 'those objects which by their nature, location, purpose or use make an effective contribution to military action and whose total or partial destruction, capture or neutralization, in the circumstances ruling at the time, offers a definite military advantage'. The broad scope of this definition gives parties to a conflict broad discretion when it comes to targeting, particularly with regard to dual-use objects that have both civilian and military functions. As for civilians themselves, Article 51(3) provides, in equally broad terms, that civilians are immune from attack 'unless and for such time as they take a direct part in hostilities'.

By prohibiting 'indiscriminate attacks', the chapeau and subparagraph (a) of Article 51 paragraph (4) have the character of targeting law. Subparagraphs (b) and (c) of Article 51 paragraph (4) seemingly not only have the character of targeting law, but also contain the traits of weaponry law in that they respectively appear to prohibit 'means . . . of combat which cannot be directed at a specific military objective' and 'means of combat the effects of which cannot be limited as required by the Protocol'.

However, these general prohibitions cannot be described as weaponry law proper, as they do not expressly prohibit any weapon or category of weapon *per se*. Rather, they frame the prohibitions in terms of their general prohibited effects or general characteristics, which are to be assessed *ex post facto* and on a case-by-case basis.[11] This argument is made even though, *prima facie*, Article 51 paragraph (4) subparagraphs (b) and (c) appear to prohibit weapons that 'by their nature' are incapable of discrimination or limitation and are thus 'blind'. In other words, they release forces and effects which cannot be contained. A key illustration of this point is the issue of nuclear weapons that are defined in Protocol III to the Modified Brussels Treaty of 1954 as weapons which are 'by explosion or other uncontrolled nuclear transformation of nuclear fuel or by radioactivity of nuclear fuel or radioactive isotopes, capable of mass destruction, mass injury or mass poisoning'. Nevertheless, Article 51 paragraph (4) does not apply to nuclear weapons, despite this international recognition that by their very nature they release blind and uncontrollable forces.[12]

---

be limited as required by this Protocol; and consequently, in each such case, are of a nature to strike military objectives and civilians or civilian objects without distinction.

11 Cassese, above n 4, 218; Convention (IV) respecting the Laws and Customs of War on Land and its annex: Regulations concerning the Laws and Customs of War on Land. The Hague, 18 October 1907, Article 23 [Hague Regulations]: 'In addition to the prohibitions provided by special Conventions, it is especially forbidden (a) To employ poison or poisoned weapons; (b) To kill or wound treacherously individuals belonging to the hostile nation or army; (c) To kill or wound an enemy who, having laid down his arms, or having no longer means of defence, has surrendered at discretion; (d) To declare that no quarter will be given; (e) To employ arms, projectiles, or material calculated to cause unnecessary suffering'.

12 Statement (a) made by the UK on ratification of AP1 on 28 January 1998: 'It continues to be the understanding of the United Kingdom that the rules introduced by the Protocol

Despite the inconsistencies that may result from targeting and weaponry norms operating within the strategic context of international relations, the approach of applying general rules and prohibitions may be considered advantageous. This is because they may cover new as well as existing forms of weaponry that have the prohibited characteristics or effects without having to formulate specific prohibitions through the multilateral treaty process.[13] Furthermore, they can serve as benchmark standards with which to review new forms of weaponry and generate the political will to enact specific weapons' prohibitions through the multilateral treaty process.

However, these provisions do not constitute a clear and specific guide as to what exactly is prohibited and under what circumstances. This leaves open the possibility for divergent and, in some cases, seemingly contentious and counter-intuitive interpretations as to whether particular weapons fall within the ambit of general prohibitions.[14] This can be understood in the sense that the application of general rules requires a general balancing of humanitarian and military considerations. Accordingly, the effectiveness of a weapon in obtaining a desired military advantage will usually be a decisive factor in determining whether or not a particular weapon is covered by a general prohibition. States will usually vigorously resist the application of general prohibitions to weapons that have a high degree of utility.[15] Cassese noted that no agreement has emerged on the prohibition of particular weapons based on general provisions alone and that in the absence of an applicable treaty ban, general provisions do not amount to a per se prohibition of any particular weapon.[16] As will be further discussed in

---

apply exclusively to conventional weapons without prejudice to any other rules of international law applicable to other types of weapons. In particular, the rules so introduced do not have any effect on and do not regulate or prohibit the use of nuclear weapons' <www.icrc.org/applic/ihl/ihl.nsf/Notification.xsp?action=openDocument&documentId=0A9E03F0F2EE757CC1256402003FB6D2> accessed 1 October 2013; Diplomatic Conference on the Reaffirmation and Development of International Humanitarian Law Applicable in Armed Conflicts (Conférence diplomatique sur la réaffirmation et le développement du droit international humanitaire applicable dans les conflits armés) (CDDH), 1974–1977, CDDH Official Records Volumes I–VI, this limitation is not merely confined to nuclear weapons, as can be seen from the UK's interpretation of Article 51 paragraph (4) at the CDDH: '[T]he definition of indiscriminate attacks given in that paragraph was not intended to mean that there were means of combat the use of which would constitute an indiscriminate attack in all circumstances'. Similarly the US signed Protocol I subject to the declaration that: 'The rules established by Protocol I were not intended to have any effect on and do not regulate or prohibit the use of nuclear weapons'.

13 Cassese, above n 4, 221.

14 Hague Regulations, above n 22, Article 2: '[b]elligerents have not got an unlimited right as to the choice of means of injuring an enemy'. Similarly Article 35 of API provides that 'in any armed conflict, the right of the parties to the conflict to choose methods or means of warfare is not unlimited'.

15 Cassese, above n 4, 222 and 235 (Cassese suggests that this phenomenon was evident during Diplomatic Conferences leading the Additional Protocols to the Geneva Conventions).

16 Ibid., 188.

Chapter 7, this is problematic given that most of the damage and loss caused to civilians and civilian objects in contemporary urban conflicts stem from the use of conventional explosive weapons.

The main protective thrust lies in Article 51 paragraph (5) in that it provides an example of what constitutes an 'indiscriminate attack' and sets out the rule on proportionality in attack.[17] However, Article 51 (4) and (5) (b) grants states a broad margin of discretion in that the proportionality standard is premised on the subjective appreciation of the military advantage expected and the level of collateral damage anticipated from an attack.[18] In this way military commanders must desist from carrying out attacks, which, according to their own knowledge, foresight or attitudes, 'may' cause what they deem to be 'excessive' damage to civilians and that damage or loss is disproportionate to their own valuation of what they anticipate to be a military advantage.[19] The issue with this formulation of the proportionality rule is that it comes down to examining these 'subjective interpretations' of a belligerent's state of mind rather than applying an objective standard, that is that 'the actual incidental damage to civilians must not be out of proportion to the military advantage actually gained'.[20] Under the conditions of armed conflict, the inscrutable nature of any such subjective interpretation, as well as the preeminence given to it, weighs the *ex post facto* application of the proportionality rule in favour of the decision maker rather than civilians and civilian objects.[21]

The substantive protection offered by Article 51 paragraph (5) subparagraph (b) has been weakened by the broad interpretations given to the element of 'concrete and direct military advantage'. For example, the United Kingdom's interpretation states that the '"military advantage anticipated" from an attack was intended to refer to the advantage anticipated from the attack as a whole and not only from isolated or particular parts of the attack'.[22] By allowing a belligerent to assign a larger value to an attack in the aggregate, only then to balance it against separate and smaller units of incidental loss or damage may serve to discount collateral damage in aggregate, resulting in a potentially unbalanced proportionality analysis which stems from the structure of the rule itself. Moreover, the rule requires a balancing of dissimilar military and humanitarian considerations. In this respect, the subjective focus of the rule allows belligerents to ascribe larger

---

17 Namely, *inter alia*, the following types of attacks are to be considered indiscriminate: '(a) an attack by bombardment by any methods or means which treats as a single military objective a number of clearly separated and distinct military objectives located in a city, town, village or other area containing a similar concentration of civilians or civilian objects; and (b) an attack which may be expected to cause incidental loss of civilian life, injury to civilians, damage to civilian objects, or a combination thereof, which would be excessive in relation to the concrete and direct military advantage anticipated'.

18 Cassese, above n 4, 230.

19 Ibid., 187.

20 Ibid.

21 Ibid.

22 Ibid., 230.

values to military considerations than to humanitarian ones, making it easier for them to exonerate themselves in the face of widespread incidental loss or damage.

Article 57 (1) imposes a general precautionary requirement that 'constant care shall be taken to spare the civilian population, civilians and civilian objects', and Article 57(2) delineates the nature of the 'constant care' that 'those who plan or decide upon an attack' shall take.[23] The provisions of Article 57 grant states a broad margin of appreciation and are open to varying subjective interpretations that weaken the protective strength of this norm for the purposes of objective *ex post facto* review of the use of force. For example, the United Kingdom entered a reservation to Article 57 (2) to the effect that it 'understands the term "feasible" as used in the Protocol to mean that which is practicable or practicably possible, taking into account all circumstances ruling at the time, including humanitarian and military considerations'.[24]

Weaponry law

In contrast to the general provisions of targeting law, states have also adopted particular treaty-based rules and developed customary rules prohibiting the use of specific weapons in recognition of their indiscriminate effects on civilians and combatants alike.[25] However, Cassese notes that states have historically only proved willing to adopt specific prohibitions of weapons that lack military utility or decisiveness.[26] Specific bans may be framed by identifying the primary effects,

---

23 Article 57(2) of API: 'those who plan or decide and attack' shall: (i) do everything feasible to verify that the objectives to be attacked are neither civilians nor civilian objects and are not subject to special protection but are military objectives within the meaning of paragraph (2) of Article 52 and that it is not prohibited by the provisions of this Protocol to attack them; (ii) take all feasible precautions in the choice of means and methods of attack with a view to avoiding, and in any event minimizing, incidental loss or civilian life, injury to civilians and damage to civilian objects; (iii) refrain from deciding to launch any attack which may be expected to cause incidental loss of civilian life, injury to civilians, damage to civilian objects, or a combination thereof, which would be excessive in relation to the concrete and direct military advantage anticipated.

24 Protocol Additional to the Geneva Conventions of 12 August 1949, and relating to the Protection of Victims of International Armed Conflicts (Protocol I), 8 June 1977. United Kingdom, Reservation.

25 Cassese, above n 4, 218. For example, the Conventional Weapons Convention of 1980 is an important advance as it established an international forum to address concerns over contentious conventional means of warfare and which can draft and adopt legally binding protocols prohibiting or restricting the use of specific weapons. However, one of the main obstacles to achieving this is that the Conventional Weapons Convention requires consensus before protocols can be adopted. Another important contemporary development has been the Chemical Weapons Convention of 1993 in that it adopted an absolute ban on such weapons and established a verification to ensure elimination and compliance.

26 Ibid., 235; Convention (II) with Respect to the Laws and Customs of War on Land and its annex: Regulations concerning the Laws and Customs of War on Land. The Hague, 29 July 1899: Contracting Parties were 'to abstain from the use of projectiles the sole object of which is the diffusion of asphyxiating or deleterious gases'. Also prohibited were 'the

objective characteristics or technical specifications of weapons[27] so as to clearly identify which weapon or category of weapons are covered by the prohibition[28] or, in the words of the Saint Petersburg Declaration, to fix 'the technical limits at which the necessities of war ought to yield to the requirements of humanity'.[29] Weaponry treaties serve to prohibit specific weapons in certain, if not all, circumstances, whereas under general prohibitions there may be room to argue that the prohibited effects have not occurred or have occurred but not to the requisite degree under the circumstances.[30] However, once a weapon has been prohibited on the basis of objectively defined primary effects, objective characteristics or technical specifications, states may nevertheless proceed to alter the characteristics or the primary use of any particular weapon and then argue that there is no technical breach of the relevant provisions of the prohibition.[31] In this way, Paust observed that 'since we cannot always predict context and technological change, the effort to ban specific weapons is an effort geared to the past'.[32]

A major challenge with regard to specific prohibitions on weaponry is that agreements will usually lag behind and thus fail to cover technological or technical developments in weaponry. Indeed, as stated at the diplomatic conference leading the Additional Protocols to the Geneva Conventions of 1949, a major challenge in weaponry law is that 'even assuming that it is possible to arrive at the enactment of specific bans, such bans could be easily dodged by manufacturing new and even more inhumane weapons'.[33] Accordingly, the states agreed at the diplomatic conference to address this challenge partly by enacting Article 36, which obliges states to review their own developments in conventional weaponry

discharge of projectiles from balloons', 'bullets which expand or flatten easily in the human body' and 'poison and poisoned weapons'.

27 Declaration Renouncing the Use, in Time of War, of Explosive Projectiles Under 400 Grammes Weight. Saint Petersburg, 29 November/11 December 1868 (St Petersburg Declaration), which prohibited 'the use, in time of war, of explosive projectiles under 400 grams'; The Convention on the Prohibition of the Development, Production and Stockpiling of Bacteriological (Biological) and Toxin Weapons and on Their Destruction 1972: introduced an arms control regime to prohibit their production, retention, stockpiling and acquisition. However, this lacks an effective verification and compliance regime.

28 Cassese, above n 4, 225.

29 St Petersburg Declaration, above n 27, Preamble.

30 Cassese, above n 4, 225.

31 Ibid., 226; Hague Regulations, above n 22, prohibited 'the use of projectiles the sole object of which is the diffusion of asphyxiating or deleterious gases'. However, in World War I, belligerents circumvented this by releasing poisonous gases from stationary cylinders or employing projectiles that diffused gas but had primary blast or fragmentation effects. Protocol for the Prohibition of the Use of Asphyxiating, Poisonous or Other Gases, and of Bacteriological Methods of Warfare, Geneva, 17 June 1925 (Geneva Gas Protocol): prohibited the use in war of 'asphyxiating, poisonous or other gases, all analogous liquids, materials or devices [and] bacteriological [weapons]'.

32 Jordan Paust, 'Remarks on Human Rights and Armed Conflicts' (1973) *Proceedings of the 67th Annual Meeting of the American Society of International Law* 163.

33 CDDH/SR, above n 1 2, 3–27.

and to assess their new weapons' technologies in the light of humanitarian principles in order to ensure that states do not develop weapons that circumvent existing prohibitions.[34] The obligation is thus merely to establish domestic review procedures. Article 36 does not oblige states to disclose any information about weapons under development or review, and so there is no possibility of external review or scrutiny. Furthermore, Article 36 does not set out mechanisms for censure or sanction in cases of failure to establish domestic review procedures.

Limitations on locus standi and institutional weaknesses of IHL

In short, a key institutional weakness of IHL is the general absence of universal and compulsory mechanisms to monitor and enforce IHL, as well as the absence of an individual complaints procedure for victims. Under IHL, individuals have no right directly to seek compensation for violations of the laws and customs of wars against states, but rather this has to be done on their behalf by their own state. However, Article 75 of the ICC Statute allows for victims of war crimes to request reparations, including restitution, compensation and rehabilitation.[35]

The four Geneva Conventions of 1949 and their two Additional Protocols of 1977 lack compulsory and universal monitoring, enforcement and adjudicatory mechanisms,[36] and so it is primarily states that have the duty to respect and ensure the adherence of IHL through its application, enforcement and interpretation in good faith.[37] Furthermore, the International Humanitarian Fact-Finding Commission

34 Ibid.; Article 36 of API provides that: 'in the study, development, acquisition, or adoption of a new weapon, means or method of warfare, a High Contracting Party is under an obligation to determine whether its employment would, under some or all circumstances, be prohibited by this Protocol of by any other rule of international law applicable to the High Contracting Party'.

35 Jean S Pictet (ed.), *Geneva Convention relative to the Protection of Civilian Persons in Time of War* (International Committee of the Red Cross, Geneva, 1958) (Commentary IV) 211 and 603. Rather, the Commentary to Geneva Conventions provides that '[t]he Convention does not give individual men and women the right to claim compensation. The State is answerable to another contracting state and not to the individual . . . It is inconceivable, at least as the law stands today, that claimants should be able to bring a direct action for damages against the State in whose service the person committing the breach was working'.

36 David Weissbrodt, 'The Role of the Human Rights Committee in Interpreting and Developing Humanitarian Law' (2010) 31(4) *University of Pennsylvania Journal of International Law* 1185; Kristen Boon, 'Legislative Reform in Post-Conflict Zones: Jus Post Bellum and the Contemporary Occupant's Law-Making Powers' (2005) 50 *McGill Law Journal* 285, 305.

37 Weissbrodt, Ibid., 1188; Philip Alston, Jason Morgan-Foster, and William Abresch, 'The Competence of the UN Human Rights Council and its Special Procedures in Relation to Armed Conflicts: Extrajudicial Executions in the "War on Terror"' (2008) 19(1) *The European Journal of International Law* 183–209, 183, 185; Geneva Conventions (I)–(IV) of 1949, common Article 1; Article 1 of API & APII. The ICRC itself may offer its services to parties to an armed conflict, which may, *inter alia*, include monitoring and the issuing of confidential reports encouraging compliance, but it is not itself an adjudicative body that can

established pursuant to Article 90 of API of 1977 has to date never been called upon to perform its function of enquiring into allegations of grave breaches or serious violations of the Geneva Conventions or API.[38] API only applies in international armed conflicts, and in that respect the commission's fact-finding competence is limited and renders it largely irrelevant vis-à-vis the more common scourge of non-international armed conflicts; however, the commission has declared itself also competent to deal with situations of NIAC and, furthermore, to handle IHL as a whole.[39] Again, this indicates that states and organized armed groups may not consent to any form of external scrutiny in the form of IHL mechanisms in particular.[40] Therefore, a major obstacle within the current international system to achieving even a basic level of human rights and humanitarian protection is the lack of political will of states to use and cooperate with international monitoring and accountability mechanisms, but also it can be seen as being related to the lack of effectiveness on the part of existing IHL mechanisms.[41] According to Article 90 of API, the competence of the Humanitarian Fact-Finding Commission is *prima facie* restricted to enquiring into alleged grave breaches or other serious violations of the Geneva Conventions or API.[42] According to Article 90, '[i]n other situations, the Commission shall institute an enquiry at the request of a Party to the conflict only with the consent of the other Party or Parties concerned'. The commission has therefore demonstrated a willingness to investigate violations alleged to have occurred in the context of non-international

---

issue authoritative interpretations of IHL in order to promote clarity and thus greater protection conferred in law. Furthermore, the system envisaged under the Geneva Conventions whereby parties to an armed conflict can consent to the appointment of a third country to act in the capacity of a protecting power in order to supervise and monitor compliance with IHL also is not being used in contemporary conflicts.

38 Frits Kalshoven, 'The International Humanitarian Fact-Finding Commission: A Sleeping Beauty?' (2002) 4 *Humanitäres Völkerrecht* 213, 215; Konstantin Meljnik and Stefan Weiss, 'Conference Report – 30 Years Additional Protocols to the 1949 Geneva Conventions: Past, Present and Future, 18th Conference of the Legal Advisors to the German Army and of the Representatives of the German Red Cross' (2008) 9 *German Law Journal* 1355, 1360.

39 Kalshoven, Ibid., 213, 215, 214.

40 Dapo Akande and Hannah Tonkin, 'International Commissions of Inquiry: A New Form of Adjudication?' (2012) *EJIL: Talk!* <www.ejiltalk.org/international-commissions-of-inquiry-a-new-form-of-adjudication/> accessed 1 October 2013: For example, The International Commission of Inquiry on Syria and the UN Fact-Finding Commission for Gaza were both refused entry by Syria and Israel, respectively. ICRC, Improving Compliance with International Humanitarian Law ICRC Expert Seminars Report prepared by the International Committee of the Red Cross Geneva, October 2003.

41 Philip Leach, 'The Chechen Conflict: Analysing the Oversight of the European Court of Human Rights' (2008) 6 *European Human Rights Law Review* 732; International Committee of the Red Cross, 'Improving Compliance with International Humanitarian Law' (ICRC Expert Seminars Report prepared by the International Committee of the Red Cross) (Geneva, October 2003).

42 J Ashley Roach, 'The International Fact-Finding Commission, Article 90 of Protocol I Additional to the 1949 Geneva Conventions' (1991) 31 (281) *International Review of the Red Cross* 167–189, 167.

armed conflict provided that the parties involved consented. Therefore, this is problematic as during the conflict in the former Republic of Yugoslavia, the parties to the conflict did not consent to their complaints being referred to the independent fact-finding commission despite the constant advice from the ICRC. Thus where there are gaps in the system of monitoring, it cannot effectively respond to the protection needs of individuals and civilian populations and so, in the case of the former Republic of Yugoslavia, the UN Security Council had to intervene in order to set up mechanisms to establish the facts and to respond to alleged serious violations of the laws and customs of war.[43]

Despite the purported political independence and impartiality of the Humanitarian Fact-Finding Commission, it has generally lacked the political support and mandate to pursue its supervisory functions. Instead, it has been overshadowed by UN mechanisms in particular, which have had to intervene and essentially carry out its functions. In other words, in addition to inquiries and criminal prosecutions of war crimes at the domestic level, the UN and regional mechanisms for collective security and human rights may, in a variety of ways, be viewed as expanding their activities to cover the administration of IHL in the process of pursuing their various human rights mandates.[44] Accordingly, as noted by Kellenberger, international and regional human rights mechanisms outside the IHL framework are being used to monitor and adjudicate the use of force in conflicts primarily *because* they do not have the procedural obstacle of having to obtain the consent of parties to a conflict.[45] This signals a growing recognition on the part of international civil society that states' lack of commitment to enforcement of IHL and HRL can be tackled by a variety of what may be regarded as unconventional mechanisms for providing legal oversight in situations of conflict.[46]

Conventional gaps in the protection architecture can be seen to be creating the need for unconventional responses. Furthermore, this is to suggest that the supervisory 'protection architecture'[47] has evolved and is evolving in a way that

43 Kalshoven, above no. 39, 213, 215, 215.

44 Kalshoven, above no. 39, 213, 215, 215: for example, in Chechnya and Afghanistan; Erich Kussbach, 'The International Humanitarian Fact-Finding Commission' (1994) 43 (1) *The International and Comparative Law Quarterly* 174–185, 183; *Prosecutor v Rajić* (Rule 61 Decision) ICTY-95-12-R61 (13 September 1996).

45 Strengthening legal protection for victims of armed conflicts: The ICRC Study on the Current State of International Humanitarian Law, Address by J Kellenberger, ICRC President, 21 September 2010 in International Committee of the Red Cross, '31st International Conference of the Red Cross and Red Crescent: Strengthening Legal Protection for victims of armed conflicts' (Draft Resolution and Report) (ICRC, Geneva October 2011) EN 31IC/11/5.1.1, 2 & 6.

46 Patrizia Scannella and Peter Splinter, 'The United Nations Human Rights Council: A Promise to be Fulfilled' (2007) 7(1) *Human Rights Law Review* 42.

47 International Committee of the Red Cross, *Professional Standards for Protection Work Carried out by Humanitarian and Human Rights Actors in Armed Conflict and other Situations of Violence* (2nd edn ICRC, Geneva, 2013) 12.

corresponds to gaps in the existing system of legal protection.[48] Seen in this way, although the foundational conceptions of IHL were apolitical in the sense that the ideal enforcement mechanism was seen as being neutral, independent, impartial and essentially subservient to the 'Westphalian' system, it is arguable that, by and large, this attempt to separate the political aim of maintaining international peace and security from the nonpolitical humanitarian task of protecting civilians caught up in armed conflicts has not worked and so has had to be bolstered, rather than 'compromised' by legal imperatives and political exigencies.[49] It is suggested that this protection gap is being filled by a range of regional and international mechanisms that have a range of mandates, goals and capacities.

The framework of international protection in which these actors operate has evolved over time to become increasingly multifaceted and multilevelled, potentially within one single sphere of operations.[50] However, it is one that is ostensibly and justifiably being driven forward by politically motivated inter-governmental and supranational organizations. It is suggested that forms of monitoring, fact finding and adjudication are clear and established manifestations of 'protection' in that they are 'aimed at ensuring full respect for the rights of the individual in accordance with the letter and the spirit of the relevant bodies of law, ie human rights law, international humanitarian law . . .'[51] This will be seen to comprise international criminal tribunals as well as international and regional human rights mechanisms. Furthermore, the forms and functions of fact finding carried out by international and regional human rights mechanisms as well as international criminal tribunals represent a valuable opportunity to examine the substance and ordering of existing customary and treaty-based IHL and HRL standards in the complex factual circumstances of the unconventional and full-spectrum operational theatre of contemporary hostilities. Chapters 3 through 8 set out some proposals for a radical reconceptualisation and restructuring of legal frameworks relative to the use of force, namely classification of armed conflicts, the meaning of direct participation in hostilities, the meaning of membership in an organised armed group, targeting law and policy and weaponry law and policy.

The practical challenge of classifying armed hostilities

The discretion of military and political decision makers to classify an armed conflict as either international or non-international is limited by the ability of courts of law to make *ex post facto* determinations to this effect.[52] Nonetheless,

48 Kalshoven, above n 39, 213, 215.
49 Kussbach, above n 44, 183.
50 Weissbrodt, above n 36, 1185.
51 Giossi Caverzasio (ed.), 'Strengthening Protection in War: A Search for Professional Standards' (Summary of Discussions among Human Rights and Humanitarian Organizations at ICRC Workshops from 1996–2000) (International Committee of the Red Cross, Geneva, 2001).
52 *Prosecutor v Akayesu* (Trial Judgment) ICTR-96-4-T (2 September 1998) at 603.

in the absence of any capable and recognised determining body, such preliminary self-classification and self-regulation by parties to a conflict is unavoidable. Accordingly, it is suggested later that a wide range of international judicial and quasi-judicial bodies have a major role to play in using their fact-finding and supervisory capacities to make contemporaneous and *ex post facto* status determinations that can assist and even regulate primary duty bearers on the ground. Despite the increased contemporary prevalence of non-international armed conflicts in comparison with international armed conflicts, the threshold of applicability of treaty-based and customary IHL is set high in terms of the requisite levels of intensity and organisation.

The application of this binary classification system poses an acute practical challenge for decision makers on the ground, in that they may face complex factual situations that are oscillating, changing or mixed in character.[53] Indeed, as discussed in Chapter 1 and affirmed in the recent decision of the International Criminal Court in *Lubanga*, it is entirely plausible to conceive that 'conflicts taking place on a single territory at the same time may be of a different nature' and that 'international and non-international conflicts may coexist'.[54] Moreover, despite all the goodwill in the world, a major difficulty that will often arise for warring parties during the constraints of hostilities, especially during the initial and deescalation phases, is identifying where a given situation that may be in constant flux is to be placed on the sliding scale

53 *Prosecutor v Tadić* (Decision on the Defence Motion for Interlocutory Appeal on Jurisdiction) ICTY-94-1-AR72 (2 Oct 1995) at 72.

54 *Prosecutor v Lubanga* (Judgment pursuant to Article 74 of the Statute) ICC-01/04–01/06 (14 March 2012) at 540; *Nicaragua Case (Nicaragua v United States of America)* (Judgment) [1986] ICJ Rep 392 at 219: The International Court of Justice ("ICJ") acknowledged the principle of coexistence by finding that '[t]he conflict between the contras' forces and those of the Government of Nicaragua is an armed conflict which is "not of an international character". The acts of the contras towards the Nicaraguan Government are therefore governed by the law applicable to conflicts of that character; whereas the actions of the United States in and against Nicaragua fall under the legal rules relating to international conflicts. Because the minimum rules applicable to international and to non-international conflicts are identical, there is no need to address the question whether those actions must be looked at in the context of the rules which operate for the one or for the other category of conflict'; Chris De Cock, 'Counter-Insurgency Operations in Afghanistan. What about the '*Jus ad Bellum*' and the '*Jus in Bello*': Is the Law Still Accurate?' in M Schmitt et al. (eds.), *Yearbook of International Humanitarian Law* (Volume 13, T.M.C. ASSER Instituut, 2010) 127: 'in Afghanistan, [u]p until the take-over by the new Government of the Islamic Republic of Afghanistan there existed: An international armed conflict between the US (and allies) and the Taliban; A non-international armed conflict between the US (and allies) and Al Qaeda (Al Qaeda not *de facto* organ of the Taliban); An internationalized non-international armed conflict between the Northern Alliance and the Taliban. Today, the situation can be résumed as follows: An enforcement action (Chapter VII) between the ISAF and the insurgents, in which ISAF Forces are engaged therein as combatants; A non-international armed conflict between the OEF Forces and Al Qaeda; A non-international armed conflict between the ANSF and the insurgents; A law enforcement operation between the GIRoA and the drug traffickers'.

ranging from internal tensions and disturbances to internal and international armed conflicts.[55]

The grey areas of unconventional confrontations and conflicts are extremely difficult to classify according to the standard classification criteria, especially as law enforcement becomes an increasingly militarised phenomenon in the context of counterinsurgency and counterterrorism operations. In these contexts, it will often be a challenge to classify such operations on the spectrum of hostilities that range from internal tensions and disturbances, to non-international armed conflicts to which CA3 is applicable, and then to non-international armed conflicts to which APII is applicable. Nevertheless, this means that in the grey area of legal regulation, the paradigm of law enforcement provides a relevant and important legal framework for ensuring security and protection.

Fundamental standards of humanity – a panacea?

The challenges associated with contextual status determination create a major regulatory challenge in the sense that it is extremely difficult to know with certainty and clarity what legal frameworks apply to the use of force. In particular, an identified gap in protection is where the threshold of applicability of an armed conflict has not been reached but where a state declares a state of emergency derogating from certain of its human rights obligations.[56] As will be discussed later, this is not problematic given that the right to life, which has a major bearing on the use of force, is nonderogable and will apply despite the fact that states may use military force in such situations.[57] In spite of this, it has been suggested

55 Andrew J Carswell, 'Classifying the Conflict: A Soldier's Dilemma' (2009) 91 (873) *International Review of the Red Cross* 4.

56 ECOSOC (UNCHR) 'Report of the Sub-Commission on Prevention of Discrimination and Protection Of Minorities' (28 November 1995) UN Doc E/CN.4/1996/80, Annex. Declaration of Minimum Humanitarian Standards; Declaration of Minimum Humanitarian Standards, reprinted in Report of the Sub-Commission on Prevention of Discrimination and Protection of Minorities on its Forty-sixth Session, Commission on Human Rights, 51st Sess., Provisional Agenda Item 19, at 4, U.N. Doc. E/CN.4/1995/116 (1995) (Declaration of Turku); Asbjorn Eide, Allan Rosas, and Theodor Meron, 'Combating Lawlessness in Gray Zone Conflicts Through Minimum Humanitarian Standards' (1995) 89 (1) *The American Journal of International Law* 215–223; Theodor Meron and Allan Rosas, 'A Declaration of Minimum Humanitarian Standards' (1991) 85 *American Journal of International Law* 375 'the readers of this journal are familiar with the difficulties experienced in protecting human dignity in situations of internal violence that fall below the threshold of applicability of international humanitarian instruments but within the margin of public emergency . . . these difficulties are compounded by the inadequacy of the nonderogable provisions of human rights instruments, the weakness of international monitoring and control procedures, and the need to define the character of conflict situations'.

57 ECOSOC (UNCHR) 'Siracusa Principles on the Limitation and Derogation Provisions in the International Covenant on Civil and Political Rights' (24 September 1984) UN Doc ECOSOC E/CN.4/1985/4, at 69: '[n]o State, including those that are not parties to the Covenant, may suspend or violate, even in times of public emergency: (a) the right to life'.

that in situations of internal violence, IHL does not provide clear standards, and this has created the impetus for the identification of 'fundamental standards of humanity' in order to 'effectively address human rights abuses in situations of internal violence'[58] through the identification of 'common rules of human rights law and international humanitarian law that are applicable in all circumstances'.[59] The envisaged purport, therefore, of any such 'common framework of protection' is thus described as 'situations of internal violence'[60] where it is claimed that HRL suffers from inadequacies due to the 'possibility of derogation, the position of non-state armed groups vis-à-vis human rights obligations, and the lack of specificity of existing standards'.[61]

This initiative to establish 'common rules' was premised on the assertion that '[f]or too long, [IHL and IHRL] have operated in distinct spheres'.[62] However, it is contradictory in the sense that it envisages 'a fusion of rules' whilst at the same time recognising that 'particularly as regards the rules regulating international armed conflicts, or internal armed conflicts' then 'there are good reasons to maintain the distinctness' so as not to 'muddle existing mandates' or 'undermine existing rules'.[63] Accordingly, it is suggested that this initiative is unnecessary and flawed.

Rather than attempting to create a new set of common rules, it is suggested that clearer legal ordering can assist with the parallel and sequenced application of existing HRL and IHL standards and, furthermore, that there are legal and policy-based arguments for the progressive substantive elucidation of these complementary legal frameworks. This is to suggest that in full-spectrum operational

58 ECOSOC (UNCHR) 'Minimum Humanitarian Standards, Analytical Report of the Secretary General Submitted Pursuant to Commission on Human Rights Resolution 1997/21' (5 January 1998) UN Doc E/CN.4/1998/87 at 96.

59 Ibid.

60 UN Doc E/CN.4/1998/87, Ibid., 6, 57, 99.

61 Ibid., 6, 49, 57: The UN Commission on Human Rights, in its Analytical Report, suggested that this general expression 'internal violence' describes 'situations where fighting and conflict, of whatever intensity, is taking place inside countries, and without prejudice to any legal characterization of the fighting for the purposes of applying international humanitarian law'. See also Asbjorn Eide et al., above n 56, 215–223: They suggest that because IHL does not 'adequately protect human beings in situations of internal violence, ethnic, religious and national conflicts, disturbances or tensions, or public emergency', it is necessary 'to advance a declaration of minimum humanitarian standards'. Declaration of Minimum Humanitarian Standards, reprinted in Report of the Sub-Commission on Prevention of Discrimination and Protection of Minorities on its Forty-sixth Session, Commission on Human Rights, 51st Sess., Provisional Agenda Item 19, 4, UN Doc. E/CN.4/1995/116 (1995) (Declaration of Turku), Article 1: 'affirms minimum humanitarian standards which are applicable in all situations, including internal violence, disturbances, tensions, and public emergency, and which cannot be derogated from under any circumstances'; Turku Declaration of Minimum Humanitarian Standards, adopted on 2 December 1990 by an expert meeting convened from 30 November to 2 December 1990 at the Abo Akademi University Institute for Human Rights in Turku, Finland.

62 UN Doc E/CN.4/1998/87, above n 58, 99.

63 Ibid.

environments, existing international and regional HRL standards and oversight mechanisms are sufficient to regulate the use of force that is outside the conduct of hostilities without having to impose an additional layer of complexity.[64] In this regard, the vague and indeterminate terminology set out in the Turku Declaration on Minimum Humanitarian Standards does not clarify or substantively add anything practical towards our understanding of the modalities on the use of force,[65] particularly in times of derogation vis-à-vis the nonderogable right to life.[66] Indeed, to obtain clarification and guidance as to the meaning and scope of its 'common rules' would require a *renvoi* to the established standards and jurisprudence of IHL and HRL.[67]

In any case, the application of 'minimum' rules based on a fusion of IHL and HRL and which are applicable in all situations of internal violence is problematic vis-à-vis the right to life. To dispose of situational-status determination of violence and have 'fundamental standards of humanity . . . applicable at all times' in order 'to avoid lengthy debates on the definition of armed conflicts, the threshold of applicability of humanitarian law, and the legality under international law of derogations from human rights obligations' could serve to downgrade fundamentally existing protections, making exceptional standards the norm.[68] Rather, as will be discussed later, although the procedural aspect of the right to life under HRL may complement IHL protections, unnecessary substantive overlaps should

---

64 David Kretzmer, 'Rethinking Application of IHL in Non-International Armed Conflicts' (2009) 42 *Israel Law Review* 2.

65 Declaration of Turku, above n 56: Article 3(2)(a) prohibits violence to the life, health and physical or mental well-being of persons, in particular murder, torture, mutilation, rape, as well as cruel, inhuman or degrading treatment or punishment and other outrages upon personal dignity; Article 5(1) Attacks against persons not taking part in acts of violence shall be prohibited in all circumstances, (2) Whenever the use of force is unavoidable, it shall be in proportion to the seriousness of the offence or the objective to be achieved, (3) Weapons or other material or methods prohibited in international armed conflicts must not be employed in any circumstances; Article 8(1) Every human being has the inherent right to life. This right shall be protected by law. No one shall be arbitrarily deprived of his or her life.

66 This can be seen in relation to the terminology it adopts such as 'violence to life', 'arbitrarily deprived . . . of life', 'persons not taking part in acts of violence' and '[w]henever the use of force is unavoidable, it shall be in proportion to the seriousness of the offence or the objective to be achieved'.

67 For example, in relation to the legitimate 'objectives to be achieved' in the lawful use of lethal force, which in any case is entirely context dependent. The unqualified prohibition on 'violence to life' is a misnomer and does nothing to develop adequate and satisfactory minimum standards on the use of force. Neither FSH nor HRL is equipped to deal with identifying those persons 'taking part in violence', and for this recourse is needed not only to IHL. In any case, the issue of participation in hostilities under IHL is itself substantively indeterminate, and FSH does nothing to clarify this important issue that is of major significance to the adequate protection of individuals in contemporary situations of conflict and violence.

68 ECOSOC (UNCHR) 'Promotion and Protection of Human Rights: Fundamental Standards of Humanity' (Report of the Secretary-General submitted pursuant to Commission resolution 1998/29) (18 December 1998) UN Doc E/CN.4/1999/92, 3.

be avoided in order not to degrade human rights standards.[69] This ties in with the contemporary doctrinal requirement to restrain and minimise the application of the logic of conventional warfare to unconventional and irregular conflicts as far as possible.[70] By trying to identify minimum standards to address the issue of regulating 'irregulars' in contemporary crises and conflicts, the Fundamental Standards of Humanity initiative detracts from established international and domestic law enforcement and criminal justice mechanisms.

Customary IHL: its contemporary significance and its formation

According to the Nuremburg IMT, '[t]he laws of war were not only to be found in treaties' but also 'in the customs and practices of states which gradually obtained universal recognition . . . '[71] In this respect, customary IHL is of major contemporary significance in constituting a body of norms that can ensure there is adequate protection to civilians caught up in contemporary unconventional conflicts. Customary IHL provides protections where treaty-based IHL does not apply because of nonratification. In this way, API relative to international armed conflicts is not applicable to Israel or the United States in conflicts in the Middle East because these states have not ratified this protocol. Similarly, APII relative to non-international armed conflicts was not applicable in conflicts in Sri Lanka, Nepal or Sudan, again, because these states have not ratified this protocol.[72] Customary IHL is advantageous as it applies where a state has ratified a treaty which does not formally apply because the material conditions for its applicability have not met the requisite threshold. This is a critical issue in that unconventional conflicts may not reach the threshold for APII to become applicable. In contrast, as will be described later, customary IHL may apply at the lower armed conflict threshold for the purposes of CA3 in order to fill the gaps in protection. Unlike human rights law which relates primarily to the vertical relationship between a state and individuals within its territory or jurisdiction as opposed to the horizontal relationship between parties to an armed conflict, customary humanitarian law binds both state and nonstate parties to a non-international armed conflict, and, as stated earlier, it has universal applicability, unlike the obligations of states under international and regional human rights treaties which are not universally shared. In addition, it may be said that human rights standards on the use of force

69 Kellenberger, above n 45.

70 For an example see: Government of Israel, First Statement, 28 December 2000, para. 286, cited in Sharm el-Sheikh Fact-Finding Committee, Report (30 April 2001) ("Mitchel Report") <www.ucdenver.edu/academics/InternationalPrograms/CIBER/GlobalForum Reports/Documents/Mitchel_Report.pdf> accessed 1 October 2013.

71 Judgment of the International Military Tribunal for the Trial of German Major War Criminals, Nuremburg, 1 October 1946.

72 See ICRC Ratification table available at: <www.icrc.org/eng/resources/documents/misc/party_main_treaties.htm> accessed 1 October 2013.

(for example, absolute necessity, proportionality, and precautionary standards) are not designed to be put into practice in conflict situations.

In view of the substantive and institutional limitations and thus the protection gaps stemming from treaty-based IHL, the progressive utilisation and realisation of customary IHL represent an important and promising panacea for protecting fundamental values of the international community. Compared with the treaty law process, its inherent informality constitutes its main advantage in the sense that 'the degree of precision found in more formal processes of law-making is not to be expected' within the context of CIHL formation.[73] Although this creates a challenge in that the perceived standards and expectations of treaty law formation can cause 'interference' with the process of customary law formation,[74] this nevertheless presents an opportunity for its progressive reconceptualisation of existing standards of protection.

Article 38 of the Statute of the International Court of Justice states that the two main sources of international law are international conventions, whether general or particular, establishing rules expressly recognised by the consenting states and international custom, that comprise two elements: evidence of general practice, or what is sometimes still referred to as *usus*, and evidence that this general practice is accepted as law,[75] which is still commonly referred to as *opinio juris.*

Regarding the term of art 'general practice', in the *North Sea Continental Shelf Cases* of 1969, the ICJ stated that 'an indispensible requirement' for establishing an international customary rule is that 'State practice, including that of states whose interests are specially affected, should have been both extensive and virtually uniform in the sense of the provision invoked'.[76] The decision in *Nicaragua v United States* relaxed this standard in that for a rule to have customary status, it is not necessary that 'in the practice of states the application of the rules in question should have been perfect, in the sense that states should have refrained, with complete consistency,'[77] or that, 'the corresponding practice must be in absolute rigorous conformity with the rule'.[78] Rather, to establish a customary rule, it is sufficient that 'the conduct of states should, in general, be consistent with such rules, and that instances of state conduct inconsistent with a given rule should generally [be] treated as breaches of that rule, not as indications of the recognition

---

73 Committee on Formation of Customary (General) International Law, 'Final Report of the Committee: Statement of Principles Applicable to the Formation of General Customary International Law' in International Law Association Report of the Sixty-Third Conference (International Law Association, London 2000) (ILA) 2; Mendelson, 'The Formation of Customary International Law' (1998) 272 *Hague Academy of International Law, Collected Courses* 155–410, 172–176.

74 ILA, Ibid., 3.

75 United Nations, Statute of the International Court of Justice, 18 April 1946, Article 38(1)(b), ("ICJ Statute").

76 *Fisheries Jurisdiction Case (United Kingdom v Iceland)* (Judgment) [1973] ICJ Rep 3, 4 & 43: 'State practice must be common, consistent and concordant'.

77 *Nicaragua Case*, above n 54, 185.

78 Ibid.

of a new rule'.[79] Henckaerts argues that the general practice requirement does not imply a 'specific mathematical threshold for how extensive practice has to be'. Rather, 'the density of practice depends primarily on the subject matter' given that '[s]ome issues arise more than others and generate more practice'. Accordingly this mandates a 'differentiated approach' to the identification of customary rules.[80] Moreover, it is possible for a customary rule to be established within a short period as long as '[s]tate practice, including that of states whose interests are specially affected [is both] extensive and virtually uniform in the sense of the legal provision invoked'.[81] Again, this suggests that this question of the requisite density of state practice is to be considered a qualitative rather than a quantitative criterion, in that it need not necessarily be representative of the majority of states per se, but rather '[s]tates whose interests are specially affected'.[82] The implication of this is that it is not necessary to examine the practice of a representative sample of the world community of states in order to identify customary practices in the conduct of hostilities. Instead, if we can identify that states specially affected and involved in contemporary hostilities are adopting progressive population-centric approaches, then there is more of a basis for stating that these are 'crystallising' into customary norms.[83] This approach allows for key participants in contemporary asymmetric and full-spectrum crises and conflicts to play a special role in the process of customary law formation through 'verbal acts', which will now be discussed.

The ICJ's decision in the 1969 *North Sea Continental Shelf* case highlights that there is an unclear and subjective distinction between *usus* and *opinio juris* in that

> acts concerned [not only must] amount to a settled practice, but they must also be such, or be carried out in such a way, as to be evidence of a belief that this practice is rendered obligatory by the existence of a rule of law requiring it.[84]

This suggests that the nature and quality of acts may themselves evince an intent or motivation to conform to what amounts to a 'sense of legal duty' rather than 'considerations of courtesy, convenience or tradition'.[85] According to the International Law Association's survey of ICJ jurisprudence, both verbal and physical

79 Ibid.; See also ILA, above n 73, 22. Thus, as long as states do not attempt legally to justify physical acts that are inconsistent with verbal acts, it is still possible to find consistent practice for the purposes of customary law formation.

80 Jean-Marie Henckaerts, 'Customary International Humanitarian Law: A Response to US Comments' (2007) 89 (866) *International Review of the Red Cross* 473–488.

81 *North Sea Continental Shelf Cases (Federal Republic of Germany v Denmark; Federal Republic of Germany v Netherlands)* [1969] ICJ Rep 3, 71, 73, 74.

82 ILA, above n 73, 26.

83 Ibid.

84 *North Sea Continental Shelf Cases*, above n 81, 77.

85 Ibid.

acts can constitute state practice, and there is no inherent qualitative difference making one superior to the other. In fact, its survey indicated that verbal acts are more common forms of state practice. Common examples include

> diplomatic statements [such as] protests, policy statements, press releases, official manuals (eg on military law), instructions to armed forces, comments by governments on draft treaties, legislation, decisions of national courts and executive authorities, pleadings before international tribunals, statements in international organizations and the resolutions these bodies adopt.[86]

Therefore, such 'public verbal acts' may constitute good evidence as to what a state believes, or at least imply what a state believes so as to create legitimate expectations[87] in terms of its sense of fundamental values and strategic imperatives.

Accordingly, the formation of customary law is complex and may occur via a number of routes, which, it is suggested, have become increasingly liberalised. First, treaties may *crystallise* customary norms.[88] In other words, treaties can declare preexisting customary law,[89] or act as the impetus, model or 'material source' for subsequent establishment of a customary norm.[90] Where this occurs, treaty-based rules have a separate existence as customary rules.[91] Second, military manuals may provide important indications of state behaviour and *opinio juris.* The Trial Chamber in *Tadić* noted that

> it is difficult, if not impossible, to pinpoint the actual behaviour of the troops in the field' because 'not only is access to the theatre of military operations

86 ILA, above n 73, 14; *Lotus Case (France v Turkey)* [1927] PCIJ Rep Series A No 10, 23, 26–30; *Nottebohm Case (Lichtenstein v Guatemala)* (2nd Phase) [1955] ICJ Rep 4, 21–23; *Fisheries Jurisdiction Case*, above n 90, 24–26 and 55–58; *Nicaragua Case*, above n 54, 97–109; *Legality of the Threat or Use of Nuclear Weapons* (Advisory Opinion) [1996] ICJ Rep 226, 259–261; *Case Concerning the Gabcikovo-Nagymaros Project (Hungary v Slovakia)* (Judgment) [1997] ICJ Rep 7, 49, 54, 83, 85; ILC, 'Draft Articles on Responsibility of States for Internationally Wrongful Acts' (Report of the International Law Commission on the work of its Fifty-third session) (November 2001) Official Records of the General Assembly, Fifty-sixth session, Supplement No. 10 UN DocA/56/10, Ch. IV.E.1, Article 4.

87 ILA, above n 73, 14 and 17: State practice can also in some circumstances comprise the practice of the organs of which it is comprised, namely, the judicial, legislative and executive branches where they are acting within the scope of their powers.

88 *North Sea Continental Shelf Cases*, above n 81, 63: certain provisions of treaties may be 'regarded as reflecting, or as crystallizing, received or at least emergent rules of customary international law'.

89 Ibid., 61 and 63; *Fisheries Jurisdiction Cases*, above n 90, 22–23; *Continental Shelf Case (Tunisia v Libya)* (Judgment) [1981] ICJ Rep 3, 24. ILA, above n 73, 49.

90 ILA, above n 73, 43 and 50: The modes of 'crystallisation' are considered to be rare occurrences, and there is a presumption against such modes of formation; See also *Nicaragua* Case, above n 54, 177.

91 *Nicaragua Case*, Ibid.

> normally refused to independent observers [. . .] but information on the actual conduct of hostilities is withheld by the parties to the conflict.[92]

Therefore, 'on account of the "inherent nature" of armed conflict', and in order to ensure that fundamental norms of humanitarian protection apply, 'reliance must primarily be placed on such elements as official pronouncements of states, military manuals and judicial decisions'.[93] Third, although United Nations resolutions do not create new rules of customary law per se,[94] they may be regarded as express or implied 'legal pronouncements'[95] by states regarding their existing obligations or standards.[96] Fourth, according to Article 38(1) (d) of the Statute of the International Court of Justice, decisions of international courts and tribunals can constitute a subsidiary means for the interpretation of treaty-based and customary law. In other words, they may have weighty persuasive and precedential value as to the meaning and scope of the law.[97]

---

92 *Tadić* (Jurisdiction), above n 53, 99; Michael Byers, 'Custom, Power and the Power of Rules: Customary International Law from an Interdisciplinary Perspective' (1995) 119 *Michigan Journal of International Law* 109, 119.

93 Ibid.

94 United Nations Conference on International Organization, Documents (1945), III, 536–37, IX, 70 UN: According to the UN Charter and its *travaux préparatoires*, the GA can only issue non-binding recommendations. It does not have a mandate to issue legally binding resolutions and decisions or to enact rules of international law, as there was in 1945 no agreement that the GA can act as a 'world legislature'; United Nations, Charter of the United Nations, 24 October 1945, 1 UNTS XVI, Articles 13, 10, 11; Michael P Scharf, 'Seizing the "Grotian Moment": Accelerated Formation of Customary International Law in Times of Fundamental Change' (2010) 43 *Cornell International Law Journal* 439, 447; Gregory Kerwin, 'The Role of United Nations General Assembly Resolutions in Determining Principles of International Law in United States Courts' (1983) *Duke Law Journal* 876, 879; *South-West Africa Cases* (Advisory Opinion Concerning the Voting Procedure on Questions Relating to Reports and Petitions) [1955] ICJ Rep 67, 90 *per* Lauterpacht: '[t]he absence, in general, of full legal binding force in the Resolutions of the General Assembly is a proposition . . . fundamental and . . . rudimentary'.

95 ILA, above n 73, 56.

96 Ibid.; D.J. Harris, *Cases and Materials in International Law* (5th edn Sweet and Maxwell, 1998): Contrary to the previously mentioned argument put forward by Bellinger et al. on behalf of the US government (above n 112), in 1975, the US Department of State itself is on record as stating that GA resolutions can have significance with regard to the evidencing, establishment and evolution of customary law, although one needs to be highly cautious in this regard, particularly by examining the circumstances surrounding their adoption. Thus, according to the Department of State 'General Assembly resolutions are regarded as recommendations to Member States of the United Nations' and '[t]o the extent, which is exceptional, that such resolutions are meant to be declaratory of international law, are adopted with the support of all members, and are observed by the practice of states, such resolutions are evidence of customary international law on a particular subject matter'; See also *Siderman de Blake v Republic of Argentina*, 965 F2d 699, 719 (9th Cir. 1992) where it was ruled that 'a resolution of the General Assembly of the United Nations . . . is a powerful and authoritative statement of . . . customary international law'.

97 ILA, above n 73, 19; James Crawford, *The International Law Commission's Articles on State Responsibility: Texts and Commentaries* (Cambridge University Press, 2002).

The dual role for CIHL and IHRL

A discussion of the modified forms of the Martens Clause included within the preambles of API and APII is also necessary because its interpretation has a bearing on the applicability and relevance of customary IHL in contemporary unconventional conflicts, particularly those of a non-international character. This discussion provides a basis for its contribution to the discourse on the integration and sequencing of IHL and HRL.

This discussion is important as Abresch observes that treaty-based IHL 'leaves the planning and execution of attacks essentially unregulated in internal conflicts' as 'Protocol II provides only [at Article 13(1)] [t]he civilian population and individual civilians shall enjoy general protection against the dangers arising from military operations'.[98] Thus, the weakness with APII is that '[i]t does not include any provisions on indiscriminate attacks, proportionality in attack, and precautionary measures'. From his examination of the *travaux préparatoires*, he states that '[u]nfortunately, these omissions were not inadvertent' as proposals to include these types of regulations in APII were rejected by states' parties.[99] Accordingly, writers such as Bothe have stated that these omissions 'virtually invite' the conclusion that because these key legal protections have been intentionally included in the legal framework of International Armed Conflict (IAC) and intentionally excluded from the legal framework of Non-International Armed Conflict (NIAC), they therefore do not apply to NIAC.[100] Abresch himself concludes that 'Protocol II's text itself reflects a lack of consensus regarding any customary law on the conduct of hostilities in internal conflicts, and the value of law that is not accepted as such by states'.[101] In addition he concludes that the '*travaux préparatoires* inflict a heavy burden on anyone arguing for strong customary protections for civilians against the incidental effects of hostilities'.[102] This constitutes a major gap in protection for civilians in contemporary conflicts and is thus a major protection issue. As such, Abresch's argument will now be subject to critical assessment.

To assess the foundation for Abresch's first claim, we must look at the provisions of the APs, in particular Article 2 of API and the preamble of APII. Article 2 of API provides that

> [i]n cases not covered by this Protocol or by other international agreements, civilians and combatants remain under the protection and authority of the

---

98 William Abresch, 'A Human Rights Law of Internal Armed Conflict: The European Court of Human Rights in Chechnya' (2005) 16 (4) *The European Journal of International Law* 761.

99 Ibid.

100 Michael Bothe, *New Rules for Victims of Armed Conflicts: Commentary on the Two 1977 Protocols Additional to the Geneva Conventions of 1949* (Kluwer, 1982).

101 Abresch, above n 98.

102 Ibid.

> principles of international law derived from established custom, from the principles of humanity and from dictates of public conscience.[103]

In contrast, the preamble to APII provides that '[r]ecalling that, in cases not covered by the law in force, the human person remains under the protection of the principles of humanity and the dictates of the public conscience [. . .]'.

According to Abresch, the difference between these provisions is significant. In particular, the truncated or shortened version evident in the preamble and Article 13 of APII undermines claims that it can act as a 'gateway' for the application of 'established custom' requiring, for example, precautionary measures in attack, which are neither explicit nor implicit in the text of APII.[104] Furthermore, according to Abresch, '"the customary humanitarian law of internal armed conflicts" and "the human rights law of internal armed conflicts" are competing projects' for the legal regulation of contemporary hostilities.[105] Thus Abresch's contention is important in relation to the legal regulation of full-spectrum operational environments as it circumvents a discussion of the import of customary IHL and whether it complements HRL in an integrated and sequenced fashion. Rather, he suggests a different approach to the regulation of non-international armed conflicts, namely that the 'innovation [of IHRL] fills this gap in humanitarian law by beginning to develop a human rights law of the conduct of hostilities in internal armed conflicts'.[106] This is seen as an advantage because, in Abresch's opinion, human rights law mechanisms, the European Court of Human Rights (ECtHR) in particular, 'has developed a vigorous jurisprudence on the planning and execution of military operations in internal conflicts', and furthermore that 'the rules it has promulgated largely track those that humanitarian law provides for international conflicts'.[107] This raises contentious issues of whether HRL norms can be applied to the conduct of hostilities. It is submitted in brief that the process advocated by Abresch constitutes a cause for concern, as it lacks plausibility in that IHRL standards may not be regarded as being wholly suited to conflict situations. Their application may have the consequence of undermining the progressive development and enforcement of CIHL and IHRL. Furthermore, IHRL comes with its own substantive and institutional defects that render CIHL advantageous in comparison. Namely, CIHL applies to all parties to an armed conflict, including nonstate actors, as it provides for the individual penal responsibility for serious violations of the customs of war which can serve to have a deterrent effect, and customary law has a universal quality.

Again, Abresch proposes a 'human rights law of the conduct of hostilities in internal armed conflicts' on the basis of the previously mentioned lacunae in the

103 Ibid., 749.
104 Ibid., 762.
105 Ibid., 749.
106 Ibid., 748.
107 Ibid., 762.

preamble of APII. It is suggested that this proposal be *partially* rejected given that customary international law is a binding source of international law that is free standing and independent of international conventions – that is, it applies despite its omission from the preamble of APII. Moreover, as will be discussed in Chapter 3, customary and treaty-based IHL are designed for situations where human rights law cannot apply because the situation is such that it exceeds the capacity of law enforcement mechanisms to respond. Finally, his arguments do not take into account evolutive approaches to legal interpretation, as well as the issue that CIHL can be said to have developed since the drafting and adoption of the Geneva Conventions and their Additional Protocols, as evidenced by the ICRC CIHL study.

Returning to the former point, it is suggested that international customary law can apply to a situation independently of the legal obligations consented to by a state under an international convention.[108] For example, in *Nicaragua v United States*, the United States argued that the ICJ could not rule on an issue that arises concerning the nonuse of force and the nonuse of intervention in international affairs under Article 2 paragraph (4) of the United Nations Charter, because on ratifying the charter, the United States had entered a reservation precluding the subject-matter jurisdiction of the ICJ in this regard. The ICJ rejected this argument on the basis that

> [a]lthough the Court has no jurisdiction to determine whether the conduct of the United States constitutes a breach of those conventions, it can and must take them into account in ascertaining the content of the customary international law which the United States is also alleged to have infringed.[109]

Furthermore, the ICJ ruled that '[b]ound as it is by Article 38 . . . the Court may not disregard the essential role played by general practice'.[110] In other words, even though states may qualify and limit their legal obligations under international conventions, the fact remains that '[p]arties are bound by . . . rules as a matter of treaty law and of customary international law'[111] and so, regardless of the legal position adopted in international conventions, it cannot operate to preclude the applicability parallel norms of international customary law.[112] Moreover, the ICJ held that

> even if a treaty norm and a customary norm [. . .] were to have exactly the same content, this would not be a reason for the Court to take the view that

108 *Nicaragua Case*, above n 54, 183.
109 Ibid.
110 Ibid., 184.
111 Ibid., 185.
112 Ibid., 174–185.

> the operation of the treaty process must necessarily deprive the customary norm of its separate applicability.[113]

Crucial to the partial refutation of Abresch's argument is the court's ruling that the particular legal obligation adopted under an international convention cannot be interpreted 'as meaning that, once applicable to a given dispute, it would exclude the application of any rule of customary international law the content of which was the same as, or analogous to, that of the treaty-law rule [. . .]'. In this way, 'there are no grounds for holding that when customary international law is comprised of rules identical to those of treaty law, the latter "supervenes" the former, so that the customary international law has no further existence of its own'.[114] Essentially, the court found that 'customary international law continues to exist and to apply, separately from international treaty law, even where the two categories of law have an identical content'.[115] Additionally, according to the Advisory Opinion on Nuclear Weapons, 'a great many rules of humanitarian law applicable in armed conflict are so fundamental to the respect of the human person and "elementary considerations of humanity" . . . '[116] that they are 'to be observed by all states whether or not they have ratified the conventions that contain them, because they constitute intransgressible principles of international customary law'.[117] Thus according to the jurisprudence of the ICJ, the adoption of an international convention, in this case APII, relative to non-international armed conflicts does not serve to preclude the application of customary IHL.

In this sense, it is suggested that a better approach to the regulation of the grey area of full-spectrum operations is to sequence customary IHL and HRL with the continuum of violence and force according to classification criteria that are discussed in Chapter 3. In any case, it is suggested that treaty-based IHL foresees the sequenced and parallel application of IHL and HRL.[118] As there is no agreed limit vis-à-vis the threshold at which customary Hague law becomes applicable in the context of non-international armed conflicts (that is, CA3 or APII),[119] it is proposed in Chapter 3 that the CA3 threshold as set out in *Boškoski* marks the type of minimum conditions at which the law enforcement model may no longer

---

113 Ibid., 175.
114 Ibid., 177.
115 Ibid., 179.
116 *Nuclear Weapons* (Advisory Opinion), above n 86, 79.
117 Ibid.
118 API, Article 72: 'The provisions of this Section are additional to the rules concerning humanitarian protection of civilians and civilian objects in the power of a Party to the conflict contained in the Fourth Convention, particularly Parts I and III thereof, as well as to other applicable rules of international law relating to the protection of fundamental human rights during international armed conflict'. APII, Preamble: 'Recalling furthermore that international instruments relating to human rights offer a basic protection to the human person'.
119 Elizabeth Wilmshurst, 'Conclusions', in Elizabeth Wilmshurst (ed.), *International Law and the Classification of Conflicts* (OUP, 2012), 482.

be feasible and so justifies transition into the paradigm of hostilities wherein, notwithstanding the nonapplicability of APs I and II, customary IHL standards on the conduct of hostilities apply.

The practical utility of the *lex specialis* principle

The *lex specialis* principle is a long-standing general principle of international law. Its general function was described by Grotius as a means to determine 'what rules ought to be observed' in cases where there are two or more sets of applicable but opposing rules. Grotius asserted that in such cases, preference should be given to a special rule rather than a general rule because it 'approaches most nearly to the subject in hand'.[120] According to the International Law Commission, the *lex specialis* principle is a general and indeterminate principle of international law that does not have the effect of excluding the applicability of IHRL norms and mechanisms to situations of armed conflict, particularly where they are full spectrum in character. This section deals with the extent to which it can operate to resolve normative conflicts in contemporary full-spectrum conflicts and contribute to legal ordering or coordination between IHL and IHRL in the complex contemporary milieu. In particular, it will be suggested that this general interpretative principle is an insufficient tool for the legal ordering of IHL and IHRL due to the fact that IHL does not offer greater clarity or definitiveness, but rather loose and indeterminate provisions that have policy considerations at their core. Furthermore, the factual and conceptual complexities of contemporary armed conflict call into question the utility of simple and binary approaches to subject matter jurisdiction. Thus, in contemporary discourse it is not so simple to state that IHL is *lex specialis* to IHRL in situations of armed conflict. The notion that war is an exception to peace is an overly simplistic conception, and this suggests that our conceptual reasoning needs to become more refined and pragmatic than merely 'normal' and 'exceptional' determinations as a basis for subject matter jurisdiction.[121]

Because the *lex specialis* principle per se is insufficient to make such determinations, recourse is needed to relevant and contemporary doctrinal and legal developments in order to provide more guidance so that overly simplistic status determinations do not have the effect of justifying recourse to the exceptional normative framework of IHL, and also that the exceptional normative framework does

120 James Brown Scott (ed.), *Hugo Grotius, De Jure Belli ac Pacis*, (Clarendon Press, Oxford, 1925) 428; ILC, 'Report of the Study Group of the International Law Commission Finalized by Martti Koskenniemi: Fragmentation of International Law: Difficulties Arising from the Diversification and Expansion of International Law' (13 April 2006) General Assembly Official Records UN Doc A/CN4/L682; ILC, 'Fragmentation of International Law: Difficulties Arising from the Diversification and Expansion of International Law' (5 May–6 June and 7 July–8 August 2003) in *Report of the International Law Commission*, General Assembly Official Records, Fifty-eighth Session, UN Doc Supplement No 10 A/58/10, Chapter X 267, 60–63.

121 ILC., Ibid.

not become the norm in some situations. It is suggested that it is in states' best interests to take care and be thus obliged in this respect, as it not only promotes the effective use of force, but in turn may prevent negative publicity as well as serve to stop situations of armed violence from escalating out of control. This is not merely a matter of coordinating the normative frameworks of IHRL and IHL, but, in particular, it is suggested that the principle is an interpretative principle that may apply at the level of individual norms or provisions, such as the right to life, rather than legal frameworks as a whole.[122] This proposition is derived from the ICJ's Advisory Opinion on Nuclear Weapons which stated that the human right not to be arbitrarily deprived of one's life under the International Covenant on Civil and Political Rights (ICCPR) is nonderogable and, in principle, applies in the context of armed conflict.[123] However, this notion of what constitutes an arbitrary deprivation is to be assessed according to the standards of the *lex specialis* of IHL which regulates means and methods of force in situations that have reached the threshold of armed conflict.[124]

According to the ICJ's Advisory Opinion, the application of this general principle does not serve to displace one legal framework in favour of another *in toto*, and so the application of IHL does not automatically render HRL inapplicable.[125] Indeed, the International Law Commission's study on the *lex specialis* principle stated that although this principle 'works so as to justify recourse to an exception, what is being set aside does not vanish altogether' and furthermore that even though the court 'was careful to point out that human rights law continued to apply within armed conflict . . . [t]he exception – humanitarian law – only affected one (albeit important) aspect of it, namely the relative assessment of "arbitrariness"'. In this way, according to the ILC's reading of the ICJ's Advisory Opinion, '[t]he use of the *lex specialis* test did not intend to suggest that human rights were abolished in war'.[126] This reasoning was developed by the ICJ in its subsequent Advisory Opinion on the *Legal Consequences of the Construction of a Wall in the Occupied Palestinian Territory* where the court reaffirmed that 'the protection offered by human rights conventions does not cease in case of armed conflict, save through the effect of provisions for derogation'. Importantly, the court also noted that the relationship between IHL and IHRL may be complementary in that across different situations 'some rights may be exclusively matters of international humanitarian law; others may be exclusively matters of human rights law; yet others may be matters of both these branches of international law'.[127]

122 Ibid.

123 *Nuclear Weapons* (Advisory Opinion), above n 86, 25: 'the right not arbitrarily to be deprived of one's life applies also in hostilities'; Françoise Hampson, 'The Relationship between International Humanitarian Law and Human Rights Law From the Perspective of a Human Rights Treaty Body' (2008) 90 (871) *International Review of the Red Cross* 550.

124 Nuclear Weapons (Advisory Opinion), above n 86, 25.

125 Ibid., 42–46. See also Françoise Hampson, above n 2, 188.

126 ILC, 'Study on the Function and Scope of the *lex specialis* rule and the question of "self-contained regimes"' (7 May 2004) UN Doc ILC(LVI)/SG/FIL/CRD.1 and Add1, 76.

127 *Legal Consequences of the Construction of a Wall in the Occupied Palestinian Territory* (Advisory Opinion) 2004 ICJ Rep 136, 171, 106.

This reasoning was subsequently reaffirmed and applied by the court acting in its contentious rather than its advisory capacity in *Congo v Uganda* where violations of both IHL and IHRL were found in the context of an armed conflict,[128] thus giving a *res judicata* effect to this interpretation of the *lex specialis* principle which views IHL and IHRL as complementary.[129] In this case, the ICJ found that Uganda had violated Article 6 of the ICCPR *as well as* Articles 48, 51, 52, 57, 58 and 75 of API.[130] Reading the jurisprudence in this way suggests that regulating the use of force may be a matter for both IHL and IHRL. This interpretation has received endorsement amongst many other international[131] and regional[132] human rights mechanisms and has been seen as having achieved customary status.[133]

IHL and IHRL both regulate the use of lethal force and thus serve as mechanisms to assess the lawfulness of any consequent deprivation of life. Thus, it is

---

128 *Armed Activities on the Territory of the Congo (Democratic Republic of the Congo v. Uganda)* (Judgment) [2005] ICJ Rep 168, 216.

129 Philip Alston et al., above n 37, 194; ICJ Statute, above n 75, Articles 56, 59; *Factory at Chorzów (Germany v Poland)* (Judgment No. 11: Interpretation of Judgments No. 7 and 8) [1927] PCIJ Rep Series A No 13, 24: a decision shall have binding effect between the parties.

130 *DRC v Uganda*, above n 128, 345: 'Uganda [. . .] violated the following provisions of the international humanitarian law and international human rights law instruments, to which both Uganda and the DRC are parties: [. . .] International Covenant on Civil and Political Rights, Articles 6, paras 1, and 7; First Protocol Additional to the Geneva Conventions of 12 August 1949, Articles 48, 51, 52, 57, 58 and 75, paras 1 and 2 [. . .]' (para. 219); also at para. 220: 'Uganda is internationally responsible for violations of international human rights law and international humanitarian law committed by the UPDF and by its members in the territory of the DRC and for failing to comply with its obligations as an occupying Power in Ituri'.

131 Alston et al., above no 37, 194; UNGA Sixth Committee (60th Session) 'Report of the International Law Commission on the work of its fifty-seventh session' (2 May-3 June and 11 July-5 August 2005) Official Records of the General Assembly, UN Doc Supplement No 10 A/60/10, 172; ILC 'Second report on the effects of armed conflicts on treaties by Mr Ian Brownlie, Special Rapporteur' (16 June 2006) UN Doc A/CN.4/570, 30 & 41; UNHRC 'CCPR General Comment No. 29: Article 4: Derogations during a State of Emergency' (24 July 2001) UN Doc CCPR/C/21/Rev1/Add11, 3; UNHRC 'General Comment No 31 [80]: The nature of the general legal obligation imposed on States Parties to the Covenant' (26 May 2004) UN Doc. CCPR/C/21/Rev 1/Add.13, 11.

132 *Isayeva v Russia* (Application No 57950/00) ECHR 24 February 2005; *Isayeva, Yusupova and Bazayeva v Russia* (Application Nos 57947/00, 57948/00 and 57949/00) ECHR 6 July 2005; *Civil Liberties Organisation v Chad* (Decision 74/92) African Commission on Human and Peoples' Rights (11 October 1995), 22; *El Salvador, Case 6724, Loyola and Others* (Resolution No. 14/85 of 5 March 1985) Inter-American Commission on Human Rights Annual Report 1984–1985) Doc. OEA/Ser.L/V/II.66, Doc. 10 rev. 1 (1 October 1985), 1–2; *El Salvador, Case 10.190, José Ángel Alas Gómez*, (Resolution No. 6/92 of 4 February 1992) Inter-American Commission on Human Rights Annual Report 1992, Doc. OEA/Ser.L/V/II.81.rev. 1, Doc. 6 (14 February 1992), preamble and 1; *Juan Carlos Abella v Argentina* (Report No 55/97) Inter-American Commission on Human Rights, Case 11/137, OEA/ Ser L/V/II.98 (13 April 1998), 158.

133 Jean-Marie Henckaerts and Louise Doswald-Beck, *Customary International Humanitarian Law* (Volume 2: Practice, ICRC-Cambridge University Press, 2005) 940.

suggested that this raises practical difficulties of legal ordering in contemporary full-spectrum operations where force can be used both within and without the conduct of hostilities, but one which has, nevertheless, arisen due to the existence of individual complaints procedures under IHRL. Furthermore, the decisions of the ICJ referred to earlier are stated at a high level of abstraction and do not provide clear guidance on the applicability or the interplay of IHRL and IHL in the contemporary full-spectrum operational environment, for example, during armed confrontations in situations of occupation. In this regard, the decisions lack utility in that they do not clearly spell out where the use of force is (a) a matter for IHL, (b) a matter for IHRL or (c) a matter for both branches of law, with IHL as the *lex specialis*.[134] It is suggested that this decision does not provide definitive guidance on how to resolve what Hampson describes as 'the ongoing debate as to how to make the law of armed conflict and human rights law interoperable'.[135] Indeed, other experts in the field of IHL have described the ICJ's articulation of the *lex specialis* principle as being at best 'unclear' and at worst 'utterly unhelpful' as a methodological tool for resolving conflict laws issues in relation to the parallel application of IHRL and IHL in conflict situations, particularly, it is submitted, with regard to targeting and weaponry issues under IHL that are closely connected with the substantive and procedural aspects of the right to life.[136] Hampson notes that although the approach taken by the ICJ 'has been clear and consistent in what it has said', unfortunately '[t]he same cannot be said for what it might *mean* by what it has said'.[137] In particular, Hampson notes various legal and logical problems with the ICJ's dictum in its Advisory Opinion. First, the ICJ does not resolve the apparent contradiction in relation to how any situation can be purely a matter for humanitarian law given that the ICJ states that human rights law applies in all circumstances. Second, the ICJ gave no pragmatic elucidation of *lex specialis* and how this can be used to address questions of priority or 'horizontal collisions' between the human rights law framework and the humanitarian law framework in any of the three situations identified by the ICJ. Additionally, when handling this issue in the contentious case of *Congo v Uganda*, Hampson notes that the ICJ did not provide sufficient reasoning with regard to how the same acts could violate both API and the International Covenant on Civil and Political Rights.[138] Ultimately, for the purposes of this study, the general approach of the ICJ does not provide sufficiently clear guidance on interoperability in this regard, for example, how to operationalise or sequence the transition from a threat-based targeting paradigm (HRL) with a status-based targeting paradigm (IHL) with regard to members of an organised

---

134 *Construction of a Wall in OPT* (Advisory Opinion), above n 127, 106.

135 Françoise Hampson, above n 2, 187.

136 The University Centre for International Humanitarian Law, 'Expert Meeting on the Right to Life in Armed Conflict and Situations of Occupation' (September 2005) <www.geneva-academy.ch/docs/expert-meetings/2005/3rapport_droit_vie.pdf> accessed 1 October 2013.

137 Françoise Hampson, above n 2, 192.

138 Ibid., 193.

armed group. Chapter 3 elucidates this issue with reference to targeting in order to provide further guidance on how to operationalise these two paradigms in this regard, but does not specifically deal with the issue of detention.[139]

According to the International Law Commission, the *lex specialis* principle generally means that 'special law' serves to derogate from 'general law' and may be employed as a 'pragmatic' tool for 'legal interpretation', reasoning and argumentation or even 'the resolution of conflict of norms'[140] by establishing 'definite relationships of priority' between two opposing sets of equally valid and applicable norms.[141] Its particular form follows its function, which is entirely context dependent or, in other words, influenced by the particular 'normative environment'.[142] This is important, as it permits the suggestion that IHL can be a 'cutting-edge' area of law that is not limited by the restricted modes of conventional reasoning in other areas of public international law. However, beyond that, it cannot be conceived of as a rigidly defined and clear-cut general principle, but as a general principle whose 'operation [is] always conditioned by its legal systematic environment' given that what is to be considered as a 'special' rule is entirely relative to a particular overarching normative context[143] or, indeed, the requirements of context.[144] Thus, in the absence of a formal normative hierarchy within international law, the application of the *lex specialis* principle will be entirely relative to a particular context and its own idiosyncratic or 'informal hierarchy' that emanates from the fabric or the structure of the norms and the 'natural' and 'forensic' reasoning that flows from the embedded norms, which can indicate in specific or general terms the will of the parties bound by the provisions and their consent to evolutive approaches to the law.[145]

The closest thing we have to an 'informal hierarchy' of norms is Article 38 of the Statute of the ICJ, but this does not itself represent an adequate tool for resolving tensions between treaty-based norms of IHRL and IHL in complex factual situations, but rather a general tool that prioritises treaty-based rules over customary norms. Rather than having a clear-cut and single definition, the International Law Commission, on the basis of a wide survey of case law, has suggested that international case law indicates that it has various permutations. For example, it can be used to determine priority between special and general provisions within the same treaty, between two provisions that are contained within separate treaties, between a treaty-based and a nontreaty–based standard

139 Françoise Hampson, above n 2, 187.
140 ILC (A/58/10), above n 120, 305.
141 ILC (A/58/10) Ibid., 304; ILC (A/CN.4/L.682), above n 207, 56, 57, 58.
142 ILC (A/58/10), Ibid., 311.
143 Ibid., 304.
144 UNGA (ILC) 'Report of the Study Group On Fragmentation of International Law: Difficulties Arising from the Diversification and Expansion of International Law' (28 July 2004) Fifty-sixth Session (Geneva, 3 May-4 June 2004 and 5 July-6 August 2004) UN Doc A/CN.4/L.663/Rev.1, 12.
145 ILC (A/58/10), above n 120, 307.

and between two nontreaty–based standards.[146] According to the International Law Commission, these permutations can be further refined into two basic premises: first, a special rule can be viewed as 'an application, elaboration or updating of a general standard'; or second, a special rule can be viewed 'as a modification, overruling or setting aside of the general standard' which remains in the background and can still inform the interpretation of the special rule.[147] Accordingly, it can serve two broad functions: namely, it can serve as a way of derogating from general standards or, alternatively, as a way of developing general standards.[148]

The general *lex specialis* principle is thus said to ensure that there is an adequate fit between particular norms and particular contexts and that this also respects the will of parties bound by specific norms in specific contexts.[149] However, this notion of ensuring an 'adequate fit' is predicated on accurate and consistent situational and contextual status determination, and the *lex specialis* principle alone does not provide a sufficiently clear normative or factual conceptual classification scheme in order to undergird and guide the proposition that 'when a situation reaches the level of armed conflict, the question of what constitutes an arbitrary deprivation of life is interpreted according to the standards of international humanitarian law'.[150] The possible form that a clearer scheme could take will be discussed in Chapter 3 of this study.

The *lex specialis* principle can thus serve only as a general and insufficient basis for clearer legal ordering. What is needed are criteria that can offer more protection by promoting clarity with regard to those standards which govern the use of force in contemporary full-spectrum operations, that is, targeting law, weaponry law, the finding of procedural violations relating to failure to carry out effective investigations and supervision of the lawfulness of derogations. This aspect of the discussion suggests that arguments which use the *lex specialis* principle to suggest that the applicability of IHL displaces the HRL *in toto* are flawed.[151] Moreover, this type of argument is also flawed in the sense that it is predicated on overly simplistic binary categorisations that are not sensitive to complex normative and factual environments. This is problematic as it assumes the applicability of IHL as the *lex specialis* on the basis of very general and limited situational and contextual

146 ILC (A/58/10), Ibid., 306; ILC (A/CN4/L682), above n 207, 68–72.

147 ILC (A/58/10), Ibid., 308 and 311.

148 Ibid., 311.

149 Ibid., 307.

150 *Prosecutor v Boškoski and Tarculovski* (Trial Judgment) ICTY-04–82-T (10 July 2008), 178.

151 Naz Modirzadeh, above n 8, 379: This is to take issue with Modirzadeh's suggestion that 'even if there was parallel application, then according to this [*lex specialis*] principle the effect of IHRL would be limited or non-existent because IHL contains relevant norms specific to the situation at hand' which 'functions to render relatively meaningless the legal principle of convergence', as it is simply not the case that in 'any given factual situation the relevant human rights norm [such as the right to life] would be trumped by the more specific or clearly applicable IHL rule'. This rhetorical assertion is based on the premise that it has a clear and general meaning and plays an instrumental displacement function.

status determination schemes and does not permit hybrid status determination which may prove to be more protective to civilians and civilian populations. In other words it can serve to assume that which has to be fully established – that is, that the use of all force takes place within the conduct of hostilities *in toto* and that IHL is sufficiently clear, precise and unambiguous as to guide adequately the means and methods of force, as well as to take into account both military and humanitarian considerations, which, it is suggested, it is not (for example, on the issue of what it means to participate directly in hostilities).

According to Modirzadeh's conception, this approach assumes that where there is conflict, then IHL is *lex specialis* and so this approach does not accommodate a complex and hybrid *de facto* and *de jure* context where IHRL norms can provide substantive or at least procedural safeguards.[152] This is all the more remarkable given that embedded within the fabric of IHL itself are *renvois* to other sources and branches of law, which may, in the words of McCarthy, 'speak to aspects of a particular factual scenario in a more sophisticated and relevant manner than the specially tailored law'.[153] Furthermore, it is a premise that gives undue weight to the historic and 'original' intent and interests of parties as embodied in one particular legal framework, which, it is suggested, may have to be modulated and attenuated in view of subsequent normative, doctrinal and material developments, rather than being treated in a hermetically sealed fashion. Thus, as McCarthy notes, '*lex specialis* is not simply a question of law' vis-à-vis the specificity and sophistication of a set of rules relative to another, but also a question of fact, or, in other words, the specificity and sophistication of the 'rules relative to the factual context in which they are being applied'.[154]

Essentially, a limited conception of the principle as a heuristic device can serve to preclude any further nuanced process of contextual analysis and legal reasoning and thus enhanced protection through progressive and dynamic legal interpretation in 'hybrid' contexts. Thus, rather than a conclusory heuristic tool, it should be taken as a multifaceted concept that aids the process of credible legal interpretation within a normatively and factually diverse landscape.[155] In such a diverse environment, it is submitted that 'voluntarist' concerns surrounding the intention of states to receive certain benefits and endure certain obligations can be dealt with through clearer classification schemes.

In terms of being able effectively to evaluate and respond to complex and hybrid *de facto* and *de jure* contexts, it is suggested that hybrid status determination may serve the twin aims of promoting the effective use of force and ensuring that appropriate protections are in place for civilians and civilian populations. As

152 Conor McCarthy, 'Legal Conclusion or Interpretative Process? Lex Specialis and the Applicability of International Human Rights Standards' in R Arnold and N Quenivet (eds), *International Humanitarian Law and Human Rights Law: Towards a New Merger in International Law* (Brill, Leiden/Boston, 2008) 108.

153 Ibid., 109.

154 Ibid., 117.

155 Ibid., 110.

discussed in Chapter 1, whereas contemporary military doctrine foresees 'full spectrum' operations within one operational theatre, namely, operations that combine elements of law enforcement and combat, the geographical scope of IHL is called into question given that *Tadić* provides that

> whenever there is a resort to armed force between States or protracted armed violence between governmental authorities and organized armed groups or between such groups within a State, international humanitarian law applies from the initiation of such armed conflicts and extends beyond the cessation of hostilities until a general conclusion of peace is reached; or, in the case of internal conflicts, a peaceful settlement is achieved. Until that moment, international humanitarian law continues to apply in the whole territory of the warring States or, in the case of internal conflicts, the whole territory under the control of a party, whether or not actual combat takes place there.[156]

However, as will now be discussed, as we read further into the decision, this dictum may not be as restrictive as it first appears.

On first glance, this approach in *Tadić* implies that if there is violence reaching the threshold of a particular type of armed conflict in one part of a country, then the rules applicable to that conflict may apply throughout the territory of that country, even in relatively calm parts. Such broad geographical scope being given to IHL is of concern in those situations where violence reaching the threshold of an armed conflict is occurring only in a certain part of a territory, whereas other parts of the territory are relatively calm or have violence that can be characterised merely as internal tensions or disturbances. The AC noted that the Geneva Conventions were silent on the geographical scope of armed conflicts.[157] Moreover, treaty-based IHL is unclear as to whether hybrid status determinations are permitted in such circumstances or, in other words, whether IHL foresees that different forms and levels of violence may be prevalent in different parts of one country, and thus whether different legal frameworks relative to law enforcement and hostilities may be applicable. After surveying various contributions on this issue, Wilmshurst notes that such questions 'remain unresolved'.[158] Nevertheless, Hampson notes that the issue of national contingents that are part of UN forces having to respond to differing levels and types of violence in different parts of a country raises the question of whether the different frameworks relating to law enforcement as well as non-international armed conflict can apply at the same time according to the level of violence in any given place, or whether there

156 *Prosecutor v Tadić*, above n 53, 70.
157 Ibid., 68.
158 Elizabeth Wilmshurst, above n 119, 490.

ought to be a general classification that reflects the highest level of violence.[159] In response, Hampson argues that in the context of international armed conflicts, 'it may be preferable to assume that LOAC applies throughout the relevant territories and to use the definition of a military objective to limit the geographical scope of the fighting'.[160] Moreover, Hampson suggests that a reading of the ICTY case law actually indicates that in situations of non-international armed conflict,

> it is equally important that a LOAC paradigm should only be used when it is necessary . . . [e]mergency measures that are genuinely required are usually accepted . . . [a] population is, however, likely to be alienated by reliance on emergency measures not perceived to be necessary . . . [o]n that basis, NIAC rules should apply to those parts of the territory in which fighting is occurring and to conflict-related activities in other parts of the territory.

In other words, it is possible that NIAC rules may be restricted to conflict-affected areas.[161] Hampson proposes that 'it is indeed possible to have different classifications of armed conflict in different parts of the territory'.[162] Such an interpretation is indeed borne out by the decision in *Tadić*.

In relation to the GCs, the AC found that some of the provisions had a geographical and temporal frame of reference that was broader than the vicinity and duration of the actual hostilities. Indeed, the AC noted that 'some of the provisions are clearly bound up with the hostilities and the geographical scope of those provisions should be so limited'. In contrast, the AC found that provisions relating to the protection of prisoners of war under GCIII and provisions relating to the protection of civilians under GCIV, for example, are not geographically or temporally limited. With regard to prisoners of war, according to Article 5 GCIII, the protections under this convention apply as soon as combatants fall into the hands of the enemy, regardless of whether they are in the vicinity of hostilities, and they apply until their final release or repatriation. With regard to civilians, the AC interpreted GCIV to protect civilians anywhere in the territory, and although GCIV ceases to apply on the general close of military operations, according to Article 6 certain provisions continue to apply during occupation, or otherwise, protected persons continue to be protected by GCIV until their release, repatriation or reestablishment. This could be interpreted to mean that there may be a more restricted geographical scope of applicability for provisions that are 'clearly bound up with the hostilities', for example, the Hague rules on

---

159 Françoise Hampson, 'Afghanistan 2001–2010' in Elizabeth Wilmshurst (ed.), *International Law and the Classification of Conflicts* (OUP, 2012) 257; Elizabeth Wilmshurst, above n 206, 490.

160 Françoise Hampson, above n 2, 190–192.

161 Ibid; Françoise Hampson, above n 159, 257.

162 Ibid., 257 and 262.

the conduct of hostilities, whereas some Geneva rules have a broader geographical scope of applicability.[163] The AC in *Tadić* interpreted the geographical and temporal scope of the rules relative to non-international armed conflicts in a similarly broad fashion. In particular, the AC interpreted the protections under CA3 available to those taking no active part in hostilities 'also apply outside the narrow geographical context of the actual theatre of combat operations'. With regard to APII, the AC found that certain provisions relating to deprivation of liberty for reasons related to the conflict may reach beyond the actual hostilities and apply until the end of such deprivation or restriction of liberty.[164]

It is suggested that this interpretation is consistent with military doctrine applicable to different types of 'full spectrum' military operations, as discussed in Chapter 1, which foresees that there can be varying levels and types of violence occurring in different places and at different times within one operational theatre and which call for differing tactical, operational and strategic responses ranging from law enforcement to conventional combat operations. In this vein, Hampson notes that a study of state practice and the approach taken by human rights bodies dealing with derogation during states of emergency indicates a similarly restrictive approach, in that where a crisis is occurring only in part of a territory, states will often only declare a state of emergency in relation to that particular part, which could accordingly serve to confine the geographical scope of emergency powers, or even the applicability of the laws of armed conflict.[165] Moreover, as discussed in Chapter 1, military doctrine prioritises situational awareness and training so that forces can adapt and respond to a range of conditions within any given operational theatre, which may itself be in a state of flux in terms of escalating or deescalating. Hampson notes that because the applicability of LOAC in NIACs can vary at different times according to the level or intensity of violence, then this 'may be relevant when determining whether a geographical limitation to the applicability of NIAC rules is, in principle, acceptable'. Accordingly, Hampson asserts that NIAC rules 'only apply to the areas of the territory in which the conflict is occurring, and to conflict-related issues elsewhere'; otherwise, '[i]n other parts of the territory, domestic law, including relevant human rights obligations of the State will be applicable'.[166] However, the question then becomes how we classify a situation in order to determine and modulate the applicable normative frameworks together with their concomitant approaches to the use of force.

In terms of coordinating such a geographic division, it is suggested that the *Boškoski* indicative guidelines can assist with modulated or regionalised status determination in order to avoid general territorial classifications and concomitant broad and general application of IHL that reflects the highest level of violence in any given region. This allows for the possibility of domestic law and human rights

163 *Prosecutor v Tadić*, above n 53, 68.
164 Ibid., 69.
165 Françoise Hampson, above n 2, 190–192.
166 *Ibid.*, 191.

law to apply as far as is practicable. However, that still leaves open and unresolved the issue of the nature and extent of the applicable NIAC rules. As will be discussed in Chapter 3, this discussion suggests that rather than limiting the legal regulation to the treaty-based rules and their customary equivalents regarding the conduct of hostilities set out in APII, the whole range of customary Hague law should apply where a conflict has reached the level at which CA3 applies according to the *Boškoski* indicative guidelines. The reason for this is that these indicative guidelines which authoritatively elucidate the treaty-based applicability criteria also suggest that the law enforcement paradigm is not practicable once hostilities have reached this threshold of an 'armed conflict'. As stated, regionalised or modulated status determination can ensure that human rights standards and threat-based rather than status-based targeting apply as far as possible, and in this regard *Boškoski* sets the threshold at an appropriately high level.

Conclusions: exploring the cutting-edge of public international law

On the issue of customary law formation and identification in the context of armed conflict, Jean-Marie Henckaerts argues that 'violations of existing rules can be derived only from the way they are received by the international community through verbal acts, such as military manuals, national legislation, national and international case-law, resolutions of international organizations and official statements'.[167] Accordingly, Henkaerts notes that '[t]hese verbal acts provide the lens through which to look at operational practice'.[168] Indeed, as stated previously, it may not be feasible to obtain evidence of 'operational state practice in connection with actual military operations', because, in the words of the Trial Chamber in *Tadić*,

> it is difficult, if not impossible, to pinpoint the actual behaviour of the troops in the field' because 'not only is access to the theatre of military operations normally refused to independent observers [. . .] but information on the actual conduct of hostilities is withheld by the parties to the conflict.[169]

Thus, rather than viewing the approach to CIHL in *Tadić* and *Nicaragua* as 'trashing customary law',[170] Meron, a distinguished scholar and jurist, notes that they may be observable manifestations of an evolutionary processes and that rather than being a sudden 'mutation', these cases have 'important antecedents in

167 Jean-Marie Henckaerts, '*Customary International Humanitarian Law*: a response to US comments' (2007) 89 (866) *International Review of the Red Cross* 473–488, 473–488.

168 Ibid.

169 *Tadić* (Jurisdiction), above n 53, 99; Michael Byers, above n 92, 119.

170 A D'Amato, 'Trashing Customary International Law' (1987) 81 *American Journal of International Law* 101–102.

its earlier jurisprudence, especially that implicating important human and humanitarian rights'.[171] According to Meron and the late Cassese, arguably two of the foremost distinguished legal scholars of our time, there is the cautious acceptance and accommodation of changing principles, concepts and processes that undergird international public law.[172] Arguably, these two eminent jurists have been integral to identifying a trend in this particular field of public international law towards liberalising the normative process, and, in part, this has involved a necessary and legitimate shift in the premises, values and perspectives that serve to define and sustain the normative process of customary international humanitarian law formation and interpretation, given the values that it seeks to protect, as well as the exceptional and challenging circumstances in which it has to operate.[173]

Weil strongly critiqued such an approach, arguing that it gives rise to the spectre of 'relative normativity'. Namely, that its deviation from 'classic' doctrine serves to 'graduate' and 'dilute' legal norms. This served to 'destabilize the whole international normative system and turn it into an instrument that can no longer serve its purpose'.[174] Regarding the 'graduation' of norms, he argued that 'relative normativity' unjustifiably created a hierarchy of norms dependent upon their relative importance to the international community with the effect that some norms received differential treatment due to the values they embody. Connected to this, Weil argued that 'relative normativity' leads to the meaning and scope ascribed to norms becoming unjustifiably broad and indeterminate, which served to 'dilute' integrity and coherence of norms. Thus, according to Weil, his own statist conception of normativity is 'inspired by unimpeachable moral concerns' and so he argued that what he described as a 'relativist' trend must be halted and reversed 'before the dislocation of the normative structure of international law and the perversion of its functions become irreversible facts'.[175] According to Weil, the essential feature for legal validation within the 'normative structure of international law' is voluntarism, a normative conception described in *Lotus* whereby '[t]he rules of law binding upon States . . . emanate from their own free will'. In other words, the authority and integrity of norms are premised purely on the basis of state consent,[176] moral and ideological neutrality and positivist

171 Theodor Meron, *Human Rights and Humanitarian Norms as Customary Law* (Clarendon, 1989) 113.

172 Theodor Meron, 'The Continuing Role of Custom in the Formation of International Humanitarian Law' (1996) 90 (238) *The American Journal of International Law* 239–240: as noted by Meron, the explicit rationale of the ICTY's approach of attaching significant weight to *opinio juris* was to 'compensate for the scarcity of supporting practice' which Meron argues 'requires stretching the traditional meaning of customary law'.

173 John Perkins, 'The Changing Foundations Of International Law: From State Consent to State Responsibility' (1997) 15 *Boston University International Law Journal* 433.

174 P Weil, 'Towards Relative Normativity in International Law?' (1983) 77 *American Journal of International Law* 431.

175 Ibid., 442.

176 *The Lotus Case*, above n 86; Antony Anghie, 'Finding the Peripheries: Sovereignty and Colonialism in Nineteenth-Century International Law'(1999) 40(1) *Harvard International*

methodology.[177] The functional goals of this statist approach are coexistence and cooperation between states, which Weil respectively defined as 'reducing anarchy through the elaboration of norms of conduct enabling orderly relations to be established among sovereign and equal states' and 'serv[ing] the common aims of members of the international community'.[178]

Falk criticised Weil's absolutist account of international law as 'the work of a highly intelligent person' who 'dislikes the problems of tension and diversity that exist in the world' and as such 'is translating into jurisprudence a kind of ideological nostalgia for an earlier period of certainty and consensus'.[179] According to Tasioulas, Weil's doctrinal approach is contradictory in the sense that it is not sufficiently value free or value neutral, and therefore lacks validity and plausibility as a theoretical account of international law.[180] Indeed, voluntarism may not truly be described as an amoral political morality, but rather an immoral one that has a state sovereignty–oriented approach rather than a human being–oriented-approach at its core. In particular, consent as a basis for determining normative legitimacy is problematic in situations of succession and where there are gross and systematic violations of human rights by oppressive and undemocratic regimes.[181]

Interpretive approaches to international law may thus suffer from 'definitional closures' and pragmatic deficiencies that arise from what Harding and Lim have described as 'the confines of a monolithic doctrinalism that has previously inhibited experiment and thus in some respects intellectual progress'.[182] Indeed, when faced with altered or novel factual contexts, positivist methodology rigidly adheres to codified rules of IHL created by states in past circumstances that are arguably very different from our own. For example, the Geneva Conventions and their Additional Protocols were created before the jurisprudence of HRL and ICL really began to flourish. A traditional positivist account does not assist

---

Law Journal 2; Aaron Fichtelberg, 'Legal Rules and International Society' (2001) 15 *Emory International Law Review* 157, 161; Duncan Hollis, 'Why State Consent Still Matters – Non-State Actors, Treaties, and the Changing Sources of International Law' (2005) 23(1) *Berkeley Journal of International Law* 137, 141.

177 P Weil, above n 174, 442, 415–421; John Tasioulas, 'In Defence of Relative Normativity: Communitarian Values and the Nicaragua Case' (1996) 16(1) *Oxford Journal of Legal Studies* 88.

178 P Weil, Ibid., 418–419.

179 R A Falk, 'To What Extent Are International Law and International Lawyers Ideologically Neutral?' in A Cassese and J Weiler (eds.), *Change and Stability in International Law-Making* (Walter de Gruyter & Co, 1989) 137.

180 John Tasioulas, above n 177, 93.

181 John Tasioulas, 'Customary International Law and Quest for Global Justice' in Amanda Perreau-Saussine and James Bernard Murphy (eds.), *The Nature of Customary Law: Legal, Historical and Philosophical Perspectives* (Cambridge University Press, 2009) 313; Brian Lepard, *Customary International Law, a New Theory with Practical Applications* (Cambridge University Press, 2010) 77.

182 Christopher Harding and C L Lim (eds.), *Renegotiating Westphalia: Essays and Commentary on the European and Conceptual Foundations of Modern International Law* (Martinus Nijhoff, 1999) 21.

in mediating, coordinating and ultimately unifying a more complex international framework of norms and institutions of public international law. On this point, it is submitted that since 1949, the landscape of international law has become richer in diversity, particularly with regard to the emergence and growth of international and regional human rights mechanisms, as well as international criminal tribunals during the second half of the twentieth century. Moreover, it is suggested that political imperatives have seen states increasingly accepting the gradual limitation of their sovereignty by consenting to the regulatory and/or supervisory capacity of the subsidiary and auxiliary organs of supranational and intergovernmental organisations that make up international civil society.[183]

In these regulatory and/or supervisory capacities, such nonstate entities can be seen as contributing to the process of normative evolution through the invocation, interpretation and application of treaty-based and customary norms approved and adopted by states.[184] This approach to normativity can thus give more meaning and clarity to the indeterminate substance and ordering of conventional IHL because it can derive innovative solutions regarding the substance and ordering of existing legal frameworks, for example, with regard to targeting and weaponry norms, as well as individual and contextual status determination. A more inclusive and progressive approach to legal interpretation captures the practical solutions to current problems that are to be found in military doctrine, as well as the 'authoritative pronouncements' of international civil society mechanisms,[185] such as UN treaty and charter-based mechanisms and regional human rights systems, which derive their competencies from states.[186]

Indeed, it is suggested that such a broader conception of normativity was envisaged by the International Law Association, which viewed the process of customary law formation as one which is

> created and sustained by the constant and uniform practice of States *and other subjects of international law* in or impinging upon their international legal relations, in circumstances which give rise to a legitimate expectation of similar conduct in the future [emphasis added].[187]

This reference to 'other subjects of international law' suggests that in addition to states, there are other politically and legally relevant actors that can embody a spectrum of practice or interpret existing standards and, in so doing, play a role in shaping and ordering norms, especially where their reports and findings receive

183 Ibid., 8.

184 Ibid.

185 K Knop, *Diversity and Self-Determination in International Law* (Cambridge University Press, 2002), 477–504, 499; Robert McCorquodale, 'An Inclusive International Legal System' (2004) 17 *Leiden Journal of International Law* 477–504, 499.

186 Siegfried Wiessner and Andrew R Willard, 'Policy-Oriented Jurisprudence and Human Rights Abuses in Internal Conflict: Toward a World Public Order of Human Dignity' (1999) 93 (2) *The American Journal of International Law* 316–334, 317.

187 ILA, above n 73, 8; Mendelson, above n 73, 172–176.

endorsement from their parent bodies.[188] This is in keeping with the ICJ's observation regarding the inclusive nature of the international community, namely that

> [t]hroughout its history, the development of international law has been influenced by the requirements of international life, and the progressive increase in the collective activities of states has already given rise to instances of action upon the international plane by certain entities that are not states.[189]

This approach to normativity is essential and justified in relation to ensuring an adequate level of procedural and substantive protection within a broad spectrum of unconventional hostilities. Indeed, the extended reach of a range of international civil society mechanisms can be seen as a pragmatic and evolutionary response to contemporary gaps, challenges, demands and expectations vis-à-vis the use of force and standards of protection.[190]

Developments within human rights law, humanitarian law and international criminal law indicate a 'coincidence of interests'[191] with military doctrine. Common policy preferences suggest that substantive and structural progression are plausible and justified and that IHL, together with its related branches of HRL and ICL, have not been and can never be insulated from the underlying doctrinal policy considerations that are integral to their substance and function. As indicated in Chapter 1, common policy preferences indicate a shift towards a population-centric approach to a range of unconventional hostilities. This discussion now proposes a number of solutions that in many cases are essentially already being applied by states in practice as an outcome of their learning experience in dealing with unconventional conflict situations, and so this learning process may therefore be regarded as a basis upon which existing standards may develop by way of progressive interpretation. Rather than diluting already nebulous general norms or fragmenting an already fragmented and decentralised international legal system, this discussion seeks to add clarity to the meaning and scope of humanitarian and human rights norms on the use of force as well as their interrelationship in a way which, because of its grounding in military doctrine, should therefore prove amenable to the civilian and military leaders of states who wish to be guided by the military expertise and experience relative to the effective use of force.

---

188 Wiessner and Willard, above n 186, 316–334; UNGA 'Report of the Special Rapporteur on extrajudicial, summary or arbitrary executions, Philip Alston, submitted in accordance with General Assembly resolution 61/173' (16 August 2007) UN Doc A/62/265, 22–54, 53.

189 *Reparation for Injuries in the Service of the United Nations* (Advisory Opinion) [1949] ICJ Rep 174, 178.

190 UN Doc A/62/265, above n 188, 53.

191 Jack L Goldsmith and Eric A Posner, 'A Theory of Customary International Law, the Law School' (2006) *The Chicago Working Paper Series, John Olin Law & Economics Working Paper No. 63*, 2 <www.law.uchicago.edu/Publications/Working/index.html> accessed 1 October 2013.

3 Reconceptualising the regulation of the use of force in situations of crisis and unconventional conflict

Enhanced contextual status determination

Introduction: the importance of classifying situations of violence

Chapter 1 identified some of the key trends across the milieu of unconventional operational theatres. The analysis indicated that conventional normative analysis and frameworks of protection are not fit for contemporary contexts, and so this warrants progressive normative reconceptualisation in terms of the substance and ordering of existing standards relative to the use of force – that is, the meaning to be given to general rules and how separate but related legal frameworks interact and work together. In the context of this study, it covers three main aspects: first, the sequencing of law enforcement and combat activities along a continuum of force and, as a corollary of this, the sequencing of the legal paradigm of law enforcement and of the legal paradigm of hostilities; second, the development of clearer objective criteria for individual and contextual status determination; and, third, the progressive realisation and sequencing of targeting and weaponry norms within the continuum of force required in a full-spectrum operational environment. In short, the term 'sequencing' is used as a shorthand expression for identifying the point at which there is a shift or transition from a law-and-order paradigm to an armed conflict paradigm in relation to targeting and weaponry law, and particularly in relation to targeting by status. The importance of this discussion is that the high threshold for a basic CA3 armed conflict indicated by the ICTY *Boškoski* guidelines suggests a preference for treating contemporary situations of violence as crises to which human rights–based law enforcement approaches to targeting and weaponry apply, rather than conflicts where more permissive Hague rules on the use of force apply. In this way, this discussion takes issue with the argument that the application of 'IAC rules or principles in a CA3 situation would mean reducing the current level of protection afforded by HRL'.[1]

1 Françoise Hampson, 'The Relationship between International Humanitarian Law and Human Rights Law', in Scott Sheeran and Sir Nigel Rodley (eds), *The Routledge Handbook of International Human Rights Law* (Routledge, 2013) 201.

As alluded to earlier, one of the main consequences of classifying a situation as an 'armed conflict' is that any civilian directly participating in hostilities can be targeted (which has an equivalence with the human rights law approach of using lethal force only where absolutely necessary), but this turns on the issue of what constitutes 'participation' in hostilities, and, as will be discussed later, further clarity is needed on this issue. However, what is most significant about the transition to the paradigm of hostilities is the permissibility of targeting individuals on the basis of status alone, rather than a targeting decision being based on an individual posing a direct and immediate lethal threat. In other words, individuals can be targeted if and for as long as they are members of an organised armed group exercising a continuous combat function. It is suggested that a lot more clarity and analysis are required in relation to this issue because it results in a general loss of immunity at the same time as there is a significant amount of legal and practical uncertainty surrounding its meaning.[2] In this regard, targeted killings of members of organised armed groups exercising a continuous combat function may be planned and based on 'kill lists' rather than being based on an individual taking a direct part in hostilities at the time of the attack. Targeted killings on this basis thus depend on accurate intelligence, as they are not based on a direct and immediate lethal or harmful threat to a party to the hostilities and, furthermore, will usually be executed in the form of missile strikes from drones or fixed-wing aircraft.[3] As will be discussed further later, attacking individuals on the basis of their membership in an organised armed group exercising a continuous combat function may only plausibly occur in the context of targeted operations. It is suggested that this is because a certain degree of intelligence and evidence gathering, together with the requisite analysis and planning, has to have occurred in order to ensure that an individual has gone beyond spontaneous, sporadic or unorganised direct participation in hostilities and has become a member of an organised armed group belonging to a party to the conflict who is exercising a continuous combat function. In other words, it is suggested that where an individual does not represent an immediate threat through their direct participation in hostilities, then the presumption of membership of an organised armed group has to have a reasonable evidential basis in order to overcome any doubt as to their civilian status.

Classification is important as it has a bearing on the lawfulness of such targeted killings because they may only be deemed lawful where the given situation has reached the threshold of an armed conflict. In situations which have not reached the threshold of an armed conflict, then such targeted killings on the basis of status may be regarded as unlawful.[4]

---

2 Françoise Hampson, 'Direct Participation in Hostilities and the Interoperability of the Law of Armed Conflict and Human Rights Law', in Raul Pedrozo and Daria Wollschlaeger (eds), *International Law Studies* (Vol. 87, US Naval War College, 2011) 187.

3 Françoise Hampson, 'Afghanistan 2001–2010' in Elizabeth Wilmshurst (ed), *International Law and the Classification of Conflicts* (OUP, 2012) 262.

4 Elizabeth Wilmshurst, 'Conclusions', in Elizabeth Wilmshurst (ed), *International Law and the Classification of Conflicts* (OUP, 2012) 495.

In view of the unconventional challenges posed by the contemporary contexts of crisis and conflict, unconventional normative and institutional responses may serve to elucidate progressively and to order norms contained within relevant and interrelated legal frameworks of IHL, HRL and ICL.

Enhanced contextual status determination

The status mixus *of contemporary conflicts*

According to Garraway, the distinction between 'war' and 'peace' 'was never more than theoretical and in the last 50 years has broken down completely', arguably in the face of unconventional operational theatres.[5] Furthermore, Garraway notes two major trends in the post–Second World War normative landscape, namely 'international humanitarian law has spread from international armed conflict into non-international armed conflict and in turn, human rights law has spread from peacetime and internal disturbances and tensions into full-scale armed conflict including war.'[6] There has been a substantive and institutional expansion of HRL into the grey area of low-intensity conflict situations, which has also been described as the 'threshold between less-than-NIAC law enforcement and NIAC'.[7]

Given its propensity for being *status mixus*, determining and responding to the range of violence in this type of milieu is one of the most important yet challenging and contentious tasks in ensuring legal protection of civilians.[8] As discussed in Chapter 1, the propensity for *status mixus* arguably stems from the dynamics of asymmetric warfare which renders conflict patterns relatively amorphous, fluid, chronic and insidious.[9] In this context, accurate and appropriate determinations are of vital humanitarian and strategic importance as they condition the type of force that is used. Accurate classification can therefore act as a safeguard against inappropriate types and degrees of force which military doctrine recognises as having the potential to be counterproductive, for example, by serving to escalate crises or conflicts which render the return to peace and public order unnecessarily difficult. Thus, in any given operational theatre, non-international conflicts

---

5 Charles Garraway, '"To Kill or Not to Kill?" – Dilemmas on the Use of Force' (2010) 14 (3) *Journal of Conflict & Security Law* 500–501.

6 Ibid.

7 Rob McLaughlin, 'Legal-Policy Considerations and Conflict Characterisation at the Threshold between Law Enforcement and Non-International Armed Conflict' (2012) 13(1) *Melbourne Journal of International Law* 28.

8 G Schwarzenberger, 'Jus Pacis ac Belli?' (1943) 37 *American Journal of International Law* 460, 470; P C Jessup, 'Should International Law Recognize an Intermediate Status between Peace and War?'(1954) 48 *American Journal of International Law* 98, 100.

9 Kenneth Watkin, 'Stability Operations: A Guiding Framework for "Small Wars" and Other Conflicts of the Twenty-First Century?' in Michael N Schmitt (ed), *The War in Afghanistan: A Legal Analysis* (US Naval War College Press, 2009) 411, 417; G Schwarzenberger, Ibid.; P C Jessup, Ibid.

may become internationalised or transnational through the involvement of third parties. Non-international armed conflicts may even comprise forms of violence that are not connected to the surrounding hostilities or which do not reach the threshold of armed conflict.

The challenge of contextual qualification

In view of the suggestion that the protection gaps resulting from substantive differences in the conventional rules of international and non-international armed conflicts have been mitigated through the development of customary international law, Milanovic suggests that 'the question of classification of armed conflict is at best redundant and at worst dangerous'.[10] This section takes issue with this proposition for the reason that in the contemporary milieu there is still the need to distinguish NIAC from 'less-than-NIAC' situations and to determine when rules relating to the conduct of hostilities apply in uncertain operational environments, for example, in postconflict environments such as where a state of occupation has been established following an international armed conflict. As will be discussed later, clear guidelines on conflict classification are vitally important in grey area situations of low-intensity violence as, it is suggested, they can serve to promote a human rights–oriented approach to the use of force where the *Boškoski* guidelines have not been satisfied. Furthermore, their application may serve to bolster the subject matter jurisdiction of human rights mechanisms over situations of low-intensity violence. Indeed, in these types of situation it will be a challenge to apply the appropriate legal framework given the absence of more detailed threshold criteria and given that there may be no clear or apparent boundary between different forms of violence.[11] Thus, although it may be suggested that the factual determination of the existence of IACs is relatively straightforward due to their 'overwhelmingly overt and highly visible' manifestation of 'uniformed militaries of two of more states engaged in hostilities', the same cannot be said for NIACs, especially at the lower end of their spectrum of intensity.[12]

As will be discussed later, legal ordering in this milieu is complicated by the indeterminate threshold criteria for the existence of an armed conflict under IHL, as well the human rights frameworks for the use of emergency powers, which Simpson asserts were 'handled in an amateurish fashion' by states when establishing international and regional mechanisms of HRL protection.[13] It is suggested that the threshold criteria for an armed conflict under IHL constitute a weak schematic framework with which to assess unconventional full-spectrum

10 Marko Milanovic and Vidan Hadzi-Vidanovic, 'A Taxonomy of Armed Conflict' in Nigel While and Christian Henderson (eds), *Research Handbook on International Conflict and Security Law* (Edward Elgar, 2012), Ch. 7.

11 Ibid.

12 Rob McLaughlin, above n 7, 2.

13 A W Brian Simpson, *Human Rights and the End of Empire: Britain and the Genesis of the European Convention* 875 (2nd rev edn Oxford University Press, 2004) 875.

operational environments. This is especially so given that international and regional HRL frameworks were not in existence at the time that the Geneva Conventions were drafted and, furthermore, given that the Geneva Conventions and their Additional Protocols left unresolved the issue of how to regulate hybrid conflicts that contain a full spectrum of violence. Conventional IHL principles constitute a weak tool for addressing and elucidating the *lex specialis* in any given situation. Accordingly, this section will attempt to elucidate practical tests for the sequencing and the priority to be given to treaty-based and customary IHL or HRL in order to regulate responses to the continuum of violence prevalent in the full-spectrum operational environment. In other words, this section will attempt to elucidate the sequenced framework proposed by Veuthey, whereby rather than having a war/not-war dichotomy, a continuum of legal protections can track a continuum of conflict categories by means of 'a series of flexible provisions, an absence of rigidity in [the conditions of] their application, [and] a range of protective rules',[14] or what McDougal posited as a 'multiple-factor approach'.[15]

It is suggested that this is most important in a context where HRL mechanisms are playing an expanded role in assessing alleged violations of IHL and HRL arising out of conflict situations. Although this is a vital palliative in the absence of a compulsory and centralised international mechanism for quick and accurate status determinations, a clearer schema for the legal ordering of the paradigms of law enforcement and hostilities can serve to ameliorate the risk of normative downgrading. For example, this may occur where a mechanism interprets HRL expressly or by implication through the prism of IHL and thus mixes them without any express and systematic correlation with the violence continuum or any reasoned attempt at ensuring systemic coherence. When dealing with alleged HRL or even IHL violations arising out of conflict situations, investigative and judicial fact finding, as well as adjudication mechanisms, need to ensure that there is detailed factual analysis and legal reasoning that includes a systematic and coherent application of relevant legal frameworks so that their determinations can be regarded as credible and authoritative.

Furthermore, a clearer schema could assist primary duty bearers with what has been described as self-classification or autoqualification.[16] This is important as it constitutes a way of reducing contestation and uncertainty in classification, and thus applicable rules for primary duty bearers that, as indicated in Chapter 1, may have to shift between 'destruction' and 'preservation' or 'war performance'

---

14 Michel Veuthey, *Guérilla Et Droit Humanitaire* (Institut Henry-Dunant, 1983) 355–356; Nathaniel Berman, 'Privileging Combat? Contemporary Conflict and the Legal Construction of War' (2004) 43(1) *Columbia Journal of Transnational Law* 23–24.

15 Myres McDougal and Florentino Feliciano, *Law And Minimum World Public Order* (Yale University Press, 1961) 97–120.

16 René Provost, *International Human Rights and Humanitarian Law* (Cambridge University Press, 2002) 338.

and 'police performance'.[17] Clearer doctrine, combined with clearer classification guidelines, can make the role of primary duty bearers less of a 'dangerous guessing game'.[18] Indeed, although IHL is said to apply automatically to a factual state of armed conflict without the need for a formal declaration of war, the application of open-textured norms by human agents is an integral part of the construction of armed conflict or a state of emergency,[19] yet IHL does not expressly spell out who can and who cannot make authoritative status determinations.[20] This allows for a broad spectrum of status determinations that vary in terms of their degree of objectivity, or what Provost describes as 'often numerous, usually contradictory and sometimes legally unfounded' characterisations.[21]

Proposed solution to the challenge of qualification

It is suggested that a clearer systematic approach to classification can lead to greater legal protection as it compels a population-centric and presumptively human rights–based approach to the use of force.[22] Rather than inventing such a classification framework *de novo*, this chapter carries out an examination of the classification models developed in the jurisprudence of the ICTY and suggests that these form the basis of a pragmatic and clear approach to legal ordering of the paradigms of law enforcement and combat vis-à-vis the use of force. In particular, it is suggested that contemporary military doctrine combined with the jurisprudence of the ICTY assists with addressing what may be described as the fundamental question, which is as follows: When does a situation become such that it exceeds the capacity of law enforcement mechanisms and thus may become subject to the paradigm of hostilities? In other words, how can we identify situations that exceed the capacity of the law enforcement model to make individualised threat assessments and use law enforcement techniques? This section proposes a model based on international criminal law (ICL) jurisprudence that can serve to guide the escalation and sequencing of force in a clear and pragmatic fashion so as to be of use to primary duty bearers as well as protection actors.

---

17 *'The Einsatzgruppen Case': United States v Ohlendorf et al.* (15 September 1947–10 April 1948), in IV Trials of War Criminals Before the Nuremburg Military Tribunals Under Control Council Law No 10 Volume IV (US Government Printing Office, 1951) 492.

18 Major Timothy P Bulman, 'A Dangerous Guessing Game Disguised as Enlightened Policy: United States Law of War Obligations during Military Operations Other than War' (1999) *Military Law Review* 152, 159.

19 Provost, above n 16, 260.

20 Provost, Ibid., 264; Jean S Pictet (ed), *Geneva Convention Relative to the Protection of Civilian Persons in Time of War* (International Committee of the Red Cross, Geneva, 1958) ('Commentary IV') 35–36.

21 Provost, Ibid., 338.

22 Ariel Zemach, 'The Unpleasant Responsibilities of International Human Rights Law' (2010) 38 *Denver Journal of International Law and Policy* 111–112: Zemach argues that 'hostilities that do not meet the threshold of armed conflict-such as the conflict between the United States and al-Qaeda-are governed by human rights law . . .'

The scope *ratione materiae* of treaty-based IHL

The practical challenge of classifying armed hostilities

The discretion of military and political decision makers to classify an armed conflict as either international or non-international is limited by the ability of courts of law to make *ex post facto* determinations to this effect.[23] It is suggested that international and regional HRL mechanisms have a major role to play in making status determinations as part of derogation review and in order to assist primary duty bearers through a process of dialogue. Nonetheless, in the absence of any capable and recognised determining body, such preliminary self-classification and self-regulation by parties to a conflict are unavoidable. The application of this binary classification system poses an acute practical challenge for decision makers on the ground, in that they may face complex factual situations that are oscillating, changing or mixed in character.[24] Indeed, the recent ICC TC decision in *Lubanga* endorsed the view that 'conflicts taking place on a single territory at the same time may be of a different nature' and that 'international and non-international conflicts may coexist'.[25] In this respect, and despite all the goodwill in the world, a major difficulty that will often arise for warring parties during the constraints of hostilities, especially in the initial phase and during the process of

23 *Prosecutor v Akayesu* (Trial Judgment) ICTR-96-4-T (2 September 1998) 603.

24 *Prosecutor v Tadić* (Decision on the Defence Motion for Interlocutory Appeal on Jurisdiction) ICTY-94-1-AR72 (2 October 1995) 72.

25 *Prosecutor v Lubanga* (Judgment pursuant to Article 74 of the Statute) ICC-01/04-01/06 (14 March 2012), 540 & footnote n 1644: 'The International Court of Justice ("ICJ") also acknowledged the principle of coexistence in the Case Concerning the Military and Paramilitary Activities in and against Nicaragua (*Nicaragua v United States of America*) (Merits), Judgment of 27 June 1986, para 219: "The conflict between the contras' forces and those of the Government of Nicaragua is an armed conflict which is 'not of an international character'. The acts of the contras towards the Nicaraguan Government are therefore governed by the law applicable to conflicts of that character; whereas the actions of the United States in and against Nicaragua fall under the legal rules relating to international conflicts. Because the minimum rules applicable to international and to non-international conflicts are identical, there is no need to address the question whether those actions must be looked at in the context of the rules which operate for the one or for the other category of conflict"'; Chris de Cock, 'Counter-Insurgency Operations in Afghanistan. What about the '*Jus ad Bellum*' and the '*Jus in Bello*': Is the Law Still Accurate? in M Schmitt et al. (eds), *Yearbook of International Humanitarian Law* (Volume 13, T M C ASSER Instituut, 2010) 127: 'in Afghanistan, [u]p until the take-over by the new Government of the Islamic Republic of Afghanistan there existed: An international armed conflict between the US (and allies) and the Taliban; A non-international armed conflict between the US (and allies) and Al Qaeda (Al Qaeda not de facto organ of the Taliban); An internationalized non-international armed conflict between the Northern Alliance and the Taliban. Today, the situation can be résumed as follows: An enforcement action (Chapter VII) between the ISAF and the insurgents, in which ISAF Forces are engaged therein as combatants; A non-international armed conflict between the OEF Forces and Al Qaeda; A non-international armed conflict between the ANSF and the insurgents; A law enforcement operation between the GIRoA and the drug traffickers'.

deescalation, is in identifying where a given situation that may be in constant flux is to be placed on the sliding scale ranging from internal tensions and disturbances to internal and international armed conflicts.[26] The ICRC has noted that contemporary situations of violence can be highly volatile. For instance, a situation of civilian unrest inside or outside the context of an armed conflict can quickly escalate into an actual combat situation, which can make it a challenge to identify the appropriate legal framework.[27] The UK armed forces have for some time been unclear about what rules will apply to their operations and whether or not their actions will be scrutinised by coroners' courts, public inquiries or cases brought under human rights law. There is anxiety that this will undermine the willingness of armed forces personnel to accept responsibility and take necessary risks.[28]

The rationale of the following discussion on qualification is to stress the importance of applying customary IHL to armed conflicts *ab initio* (that is, in relation to NIACs, from the point when the CA3 threshold criteria outlined in the *Boškoski* guidelines have been satisfied) and sequencing this with a presumptively human rights–oriented law enforcement model which may be escalated where necessary.[29] In these cases, rather than trying to draw a distinction between conventional IAC and NIAC, the jurisprudence relating to the threshold criteria for an armed conflict under CA3 offers a radical and progressive way systematically to regulate mixed and full-spectrum situations of violence; namely, where the threshold criteria for an armed conflict are met, then this triggers the application of CIHL.

Classifying international armed conflicts

The Trial Chamber in *Tadić* set the threshold for the existence of an international armed conflict at a relatively low level, namely "whenever there is a resort to armed force between States".[30] The detailed humanitarian protections contained in the Fourth Geneva Convention[31] and Protocol I[32] will not apply where one or both parties to a conflict do not qualify, or indeed, are not recognised, as a

---

26 Andrew J Carswell, 'Classifying the Conflict: A Soldier's Dilemma' (2009) 91 (873) *International Review of the Red Cross* 4.

27 International Committee of the Red Cross, 'The Use of Force in Armed Conflicts: Interplay Between the Conduct of Hostilities and Law Enforcement Paradigms (Report of Expert Meeting) (ICRC, November 2013) Foreword.

28 UK House of Commons Defence Committee, 'UK Armed Forces Personnel and the Legal Framework for Future Operations' (Twelfth Report of Session 2013–14) (House of Commons, 2 April 2013) 11.

29 Lindsay Moir, *The Law of Internal Armed Conflict* (Cambridge University Press, 2002) 51.

30 *Tadić* (Jurisdiction) above n 24, 70.

31 Geneva Convention (IV) relative to the Protection of Civilian Persons in Time of War, Geneva, 12 August 1949, Article 2(1).

32 Protocol Additional to the Geneva Conventions of 12 August 1949, and relating to the Protection of Victims of International Armed Conflicts (Protocol I), 8 June 1977 ('API').

contracting state within the meaning of Article 2 common to the Geneva Conventions and Article 1(1) of Protocol I or as a national liberation movement within the meaning of the latter's Article 1(4).[33] These limitations are problematic given that states such as India, Israel and the United States have not ratified Protocol 1,[34] and that movements such as Hezbollah and Hamas have not generally been recognised as state entities despite their status as *de facto* authorities which perform quasi-state functions.[35] The main exception to the said limitations is where the conduct of a nonstate entity can be attributed to a foreign state, effectively 'internationalising' the conflict. Therefore, making the distinction between international and non-international conflicts is complicated in situations where there is foreign intervention in a non-international armed conflict or situations of proxy war.[36] In part this is because there is controversy regarding the test for when the rules of international armed conflict apply to such situations or, in other words, regarding the test for the internationalisation of non-international armed conflicts where a foreign state supports a nonstate group. Assessing whether internationalisation has occurred in this regard involves an assessment of the level of involvement of a foreign state in the combat activities of a nonstate actor[37] or, put another way, the degree to which the combat activities of a nonstate actor can be attributed to a foreign state. Indeed, according to *Tadić*, the issue is whether a nonstate actor can be regarded *de facto* as an organ of a foreign state.

There is some controversy surrounding the test to be used for the application of the rules relative to international armed conflicts to an internationalised non-international armed conflict,[38] and one of the uncertainties has been whether this test is based on the rules of attribution in the law of state responsibility.[39] The Appeals Chamber in *Tadić* interpreted the ICJ's test for attribution under the law of state responsibility set out in *Nicaragua v United States of America* as one of 'effective control of a military or paramilitary group', which entailed that 'the control be exercised with respect to the specific operation in the course of which breaches may have been committed'.[40] However, the ICJ judgment in the *Bosnia Genocide Convention Case* indicated that the ICTY's interpretation was overly simplistic, as its primary test for attribution is that of 'complete dependence' or, more specifically, where 'persons, groups or entities act in 'complete dependence' on the state of which 'they are ultimately merely the instrument', they may be

33 Nils Melzer, *Targeted Killing in International Law* (Oxford University Press, 2009) 248.
34 See ICRC Treaty Ratification Table <https://ihl-databases.icrc.org/ihl>
35 Ekaterina Stepanova, *Terrorism in Asymmetrical Conflict: Ideological and Structural Aspects* (Stockholm International Peace Research Report No 23, Oxford University Press, 2010) 114–115.
36 Dapo Akande, 'Classification of Armed Conflicts: Relevant Legal Concepts', in Elizabeth Wilmshurst (ed), *International Law and the Classification of Conflicts* (OUP, 2012) 56.
37 Ibid., 58.
38 Ibid.
39 Ibid., 60.
40 *Prosecutor v Tadić* (Appeals Chamber Judgment) ICTY-94-1-A (15 July 1999) 84–141.

'equated with State organs'.[41] However, the ICJ went on to set out a secondary test for situations where there is no relationship of 'complete dependence' per se, but rather, where persons have 'acted in accordance with [a] State's instructions' or, in other words, are under the 'effective control' of a state. For this test to be satisfied, it must be proved that 'the State's instructions were given, in respect of each operation in which the alleged violations occurred, not generally in respect of the overall actions taken by the persons or groups of persons having committed the violations'.[42]

Therefore, the AC in *Tadić* noted that the ICJ essentially set out two tests for determining state responsibility, in that where there is no relationship of 'complete dependence' that indicates that a nonstate group is a *de facto* state organ,[43] then the acts of a nonstate group can nevertheless be attributed to a state where it has 'effective control' in the form of specifically directing 'each operation' thought its 'instructions'.[44] An analysis of the relevant ICTY and ICJ case law suggests different tests for attribution that apply in the following distinct situations: first, in assessing the degree and nature of a state's involvement in an armed conflict on another state's territory for the purposes of assessing whether or not the conflict is to be characterised as international; second, in assessing the degree and nature of involvement of a state with a nonstate actor outside its territory for the purposes of assessing the responsibility of that state for a specific act of the nonstate actor.[45]

The ICJ itself noted that the Appeals Chamber in *Tadić* used the 'overall control' test to determine whether or not an armed conflict was international.[46] The court found that although this test was suitable for the sole question which the Appeals Chamber in *Tadić* was called upon to decide – that is, whether the conflict was international in character so that the grave breaches regime applied – the argument that this 'overall control' test was equally applicable for the purpose of determining state responsibility was unpersuasive.[47] In particular, the ICJ emphasised that 'logic does not require the same test to be adopted in resolving the two issues which are very different in nature', and that the test for assessing whether a state's involvement in a non-international armed conflict on another state's territory internationalises it, can 'without logical inconsistency differ' from the test

41 *Application of Convention on Prevention and Punishment of Crime of Genocide* (Bosnia and Herzegovina v Serbia and Montenegro) (Judgment) [2007] ICJ Rep 43, 392.

42 Ibid., 400.

43 *Tadić* (Appeals Chamber Judgment), above n 40, 100–114, that is: 'responsibility arising out of unlawful acts of State officials'.

44 Ibid., 114, that is: 'responsibility generated by acts performed by private individuals acting as de facto State organs . . . [where] private individuals [are] not only [. . .] paid or financed by a State, and their action [. . .] coordinated or supervised by this State, but also that the State [. . .] issue[s] specific instructions concerning the commission of the unlawful acts in question'.

45 *Bosnia Genocide Convention Case*, above n 41, 405.

46 Ibid., 404.

47 Ibid.

used to determine state responsibility for wrongful acts committed in the course of a conflict situation.[48]

Accordingly, this discussion suggests that in contrast with the law on state responsibility, IHL has developed a different test for assessing whether or not a non-international armed conflict has become internationalised.[49] The Appeals Chamber in *Tadić* noted that the rules in this regard do not require the same degree of control in that the degree of control required varies vis-à-vis private individuals and individuals not having the status of state officials, but are nevertheless regarded as constituting a *de facto* organ of the state.[50] In relation to the first category, namely 'a single private individual or a group that is not militarily organised', then the Appeals Chamber stated that the test for attribution is whether 'specific instructions concerning the commission' of particular acts had been issued by the state to the individual or group, or whether unlawful acts had been subsequently endorsed or approved.[51] In relation to the second category, the Appeals Chamber stated that 'control by a State over subordinate armed forces or militias or paramilitary units may be of an overall character'. In contrast with the former test regarding private individuals or groups that are not militarily organised, this 'overall control' standard does not require 'the issuing of specific orders by the State, or its direction of each individual operation'. In this way, it is not necessary for the state authorities to 'plan all the operations of the units dependent on them, choose their targets, or give specific instructions concerning the conduct of military operations . . .' Rather, 'overall control' will be established where a state party to an armed conflict 'has a role in organising, coordinating or planning the military actions of the military group, in addition to financing, training and equipping or providing operational support to that group'.[52] Accordingly, there do not need to be specific instructions vis-à-vis the acts performed by subordinate groups that are organised militarily.

Indeed, the ICC Trial Chamber, in its judgment in *Lubanga*, confirmed that the 'overall control' test applied by the ICTY is the 'correct approach' for assessing

48 Ibid., 405; See also, *Tadić* (Appeals Chamber Judgment) above n 40, paras 100 and 104: although the Appeals Chamber in *Tadić* did note that the issue before the ICJ in *Nicaragua v United States of America* (above n 25) 'revolved around state responsibility', whereas the issue before the ICTY was 'criminal culpability . . . for serious violations of international humanitarian law', or, in other words, whether the grave breaches regime relative to international armed conflicts was applicable, it somewhat erred in its assertion that 'what is at issue is not the distinction between State responsibility and individual criminal responsibility', but rather 'the question is that of establishing the criteria for the legal imputability to a State of acts performed by individuals not having the status of State officials . . . [i]n the one case these acts, if they prove to be attributable to a State, will give rise to the international responsibility of that State; in the other case, they will ensure that the armed conflict must be classified as international'.

49 Dapo Akande, above n 36, 60.

50 *Tadić* (Appeals Chamber Judgment) above n 40, 137.

51 Ibid.

52 Ibid.

attribution in the context of determining whether or not a non-international armed conflict has become internationalised. According to the Trial Chamber, this standard will be satisfied where a state 'has a role in organising, co-ordinating or planning the military actions of the military group, in addition to financing, training and equipping or providing operational support to that group'.[53] In this way, it is suggested that the general approach under IHL for assessing whether the acts of a nonstate group can be attributed to a foreign state for the purpose of the internationalisation of non-international armed conflicts is not dependent on or derived from the general law of state responsibility, but rather those standards developed under IHL in the case law of International Criminal Law.[54]

Even though this approach may extend the humanitarian protections of the Fourth Geneva Convention and Protocol I to civilians caught up in proxy wars – that is, international armed conflicts between states fought indirectly through third parties (states or nonstate entities) as substitutes – this evidential burden creates the risk of underclassification, that is as a non-international armed conflict rather than an international armed conflict, especially during the initial stages of armed hostilities when adequate intelligence is likely to be at a premium. Thus, according to *Tadić*, an internal armed conflict 'may become international (or, depending on the circumstances, be international in character alongside an internal armed conflict)' in two main circumstances: first, where 'another State intervenes in that conflict through its troops' or second, where 'some of the participants in the internal armed conflict act on behalf of that other State'.[55] This allows for mixed rather than global status determinations.[56]

Situations of occupation may follow on from international armed conflicts, and this raises the issue of which legal frameworks apply to targeting and weaponry decisions where armed violence breaks out in such situations. Article 3 (b) of Protocol I ensures the applicability of the international humanitarian law rules of

53 *Prosecutor v Lubanga*, above n 25, 541.

54 Dapo Akande, above n 36, 60–61.

55 Ibid., 84.

56 *Lubanga*, above n 25, 564: 'there is evidence that during the relevant timeframe the UPDF [Ugandan armed forces] occupied certain areas of Bunia, such as the airport. However, it is unnecessary to analyse whether territory came under the authority of the Ugandan forces, thereby amounting to a military occupation, because the relevant conflict or conflicts concern the UPC and other armed groups', 565: 'Focussing solely on the parties and the conflict relevant to the charges in this case, the Ugandan military occupation of Bunia airport does not change the legal nature of the conflict between the UPC/FPLC, RCD-ML/APC and FRPI rebel groups since this conflict, as analysed above, did not result in two states opposing each other, whether directly or indirectly, during the time period relevant to the charges. In any event, the existence of a possible conflict that was "international in character" between the DRC and Uganda does not affect the legal characterisation of the UPC/FPLC's concurrent non-international armed conflict with the APC and FRPI militias, which formed part of the internal armed conflict between the rebel groups'; James Stewart, 'Towards a Single Definition of Armed Conflict in International Humanitarian Law: A Critique of Internationalized Armed Conflict' (2003) 85 (850) *International Review of the Red Cross* 333.

international armed conflict not only until 'the general close of military operations', but also 'until the termination of occupation'. However, 'for those persons whose final release, repatriation or re-establishment takes place thereafter . . . [t]hese persons shall continue to benefit from the relevant provisions of the Conventions and of this Protocol until their final release, repatriation or re-establishment'. Accordingly, Geneva law protections may continue to apply long after Hague-type rules on the conduct of hostilities have ceased to be applicable.

According to Cassese, where there are hostilities between 'an occupying Power and rebel or insurgent groups . . . in an occupied territory', this should trigger the resurgence of treaty-based and customary Hague law permissions vis-à-vis targeting and weaponry law relative to international armed conflicts.[57] In a similar fashion to Cassese, Melzer's account of the Expert Meeting on the Right to Life in Armed Conflict was that the

> prevailing view among the experts participating . . . was that the use of force by an occupying power to maintain public order and safety and to provide for its own security should be governed by the law enforcement model unless there was either a resumption of international hostilities or, alternatively, an outbreak of hostilities distinct from the original international armed conflict, possibly even of non-international nature.[58]

Thus, unless an individual represents a direct and immediate threat, they should not be subject to lethal force 'on sight', on the basis of status as a member of an organised armed group exercising a continuous combat function or as a method of first resort unless there has been a resumption or outbreak of hostilities.[59]

However, treaty-based human rights law and humanitarian law provide no clear guidelines for identifying when any escalation, 'resumption' or 'outbreak' of armed hostilities within a situation of occupation may give rise to Hague law permissions vis-à-vis targeting and weaponry law. Participants at the University Centre for International Humanitarian Law (UCIHL) expert meeting suggested that the standards to be applied are dependent upon the facts on the ground, which can vary significantly, in that certain parts of a territory may be relatively calm, whereas in other parts there may be active hostilities. Accordingly, it was generally agreed at the expert meeting that in 'calm' areas the human rights–based 'law enforcement model' should apply relative to the use of force.[60]

As will be suggested later, the CA3 threshold criteria elucidated in *Tadić* and *Boškoski* may be used to identify when any escalation, 'resumption' or 'outbreak'

---

57 Antonio Cassese, *International Law* (2nd edn Oxford University Press, 2005) 420.

58 The University Centre for International Humanitarian Law, 'Expert Meeting on the Right to Life in Armed Conflict and Situations of Occupation' (September 2005) <www.geneva-academy.ch/docs/expert-meetings/2005/3rapport_droit_vie.pdf> accessed 1 October 2013, 22.

59 Ibid., 5.

60 Ibid., 5, 22; Louise Doswald-Beck, 'The Right to Life in Armed Conflict: Does International Humanitarian Law Provide All the Answers?' (2006) 88 (864) *International Review of the Red Cross* 892–894.

of armed hostilities within a situation of occupation may give rise to Hague law permissions vis-à-vis targeting and weaponry law. In other words, these criteria may be used to make a distinction between 'calm' situations that are governed by the human rights–based law enforcement paradigm and those areas where there are active hostilities that are governed by the humanitarian law–based paradigm of hostilities. It is suggested that this approach provides a workable standard for guiding the application of the most appropriate legal framework governing the use of force, particularly in situations of belligerent occupation, which are likely to contain different forms and levels of violence.

As will be discussed later, a clearer classification scheme can be used to prioritise human rights–based approaches to the use of force vis-à-vis forms of sporadic and low-intensity armed activities, rather than automatically treating such armed activities as grounds for applying the legal framework relative to hostilities. As stated, these threshold standards are important, as they may be used to identify those situations that exceed the capacity of law enforcement approaches to restore and maintain public order and security.[61]

Classifying non-international armed conflicts

This section discusses the threshold criteria for the qualification of a situation as a non-international armed conflict, which is complicated by the fact that the analytical framework provided by IHL is vague and the reality of non-international armed conflict is multifarious.

Kretzmer provides an illustrative typography of forms of non-international armed conflict which is suggestive of the potential factual complexity classifying dynamic and fluid situations on the ground.[62] For example, types of violence that may not be regarded as armed conflicts, but rather as internal tensions and disturbances include '[p]rotracted low threshold conflicts between organized armed groups and governmental forces in a State' and 'protracted low or high threshold conflicts between organized armed groups in a State'.[63] In contrast with situations of internal tensions or disturbances, types of violence that more closely resemble non-international armed conflicts include 'high-threshold conflicts between organized armed groups and governmental authorities in a State' which meet the threshold of APII, 'conflicts between dissident armed forces and the armed forces of the State' and 'civil war between armies representing different regions or different ethnic/national/religious groups in a State'.[64] Finally, an example of a non-international armed conflict that has become internationalised includes 'high-threshold conflicts between dissident groups, or organized armed

61 Ibid.
62 David Kretzmer, 'Rethinking Application of IHL In Non-International Armed Conflicts' (2009) 42 *Israel Law Review* 34.
63 Ibid.
64 Ibid., 34–35.

groups, and the authorities of the State, which has agreed to the involvement on its side of the forces of another State, or other States'.[65]

Elucidating treaty-based classification criteria for non-international armed conflicts

The ICRC position has been to ensure that the definition of 'armed conflict' extended down to as low a level of violence as possible so as to extend the protections given by Geneva law to people who are not or are no longer taking part in hostilities: these include the sick and wounded of armed forces on the field; wounded, sick and shipwrecked members of armed forces at sea; prisoners of war; and civilians. The Appeals Chamber in *Tadić* ruled that the minimum threshold for the application of Common Article 3 to the Geneva Conventions is 'protracted armed violence between governmental authorities and organized armed groups or between such groups within a State'[66] as opposed to lesser forms of armed violence such as 'banditry, unorganized and short-lived insurrections, or terrorist activities', which are covered by municipal criminal law and applicable international human rights norms.[67] According to the ICRC and the Appeals Chamber in *Tadić*, such a basic distinction is to be made on a case-by-case basis and involves an evaluation, first, of whether the nongovernmental groups have a sufficient level of organisation to be regarded as parties to a conflict, and, second, whether the hostilities are of a sufficient intensity to amount in fact to a non-international armed conflict.[68]

In both these regards, on the basis of a broad and systemic survey of ICTY jurisprudence, as well as decisions from international, regional and domestic courts and organisations, the Trial Chamber in *Boškoski* set out a number of 'indicative factors' that serve as 'useful practical guidance to an evaluation'[69] of whether or not a factual situation of armed hostilities can be classified as a non-international armed conflict.

There is no agreed threshold at which customary Hague law becomes applicable in the context of non-international armed conflicts, that is, CA3 or APII, as well as the content of these rules and the extent to which they vary between CA3 and APII non-international armed conflicts.[70] The ICRC does not see any difference in the threshold under customary IHL. In practical terms, it is suggested that the *Boškoski* indicative criteria discussed later may be used as a gateway for the application of customary Hague law rules which have emerged over the course of the past two decades. Furthermore, these indicative criteria represent a crucial way of guiding the transition from a law enforcement

65 Ibid., 35.
66 *Tadić* (Jurisdiction) above n 24, 70.
67 *Prosecutor v Tadić* (Opinion and Judgment) ICTY-94–1-T (7 May 1997) 562.
68 Ibid.
69 *Prosecutor v Boškoski and Tarculovski* (Trial Judgment) ICTY-04–82-T (10 July 2008) 193.
70 Elizabeth Wilmshurst, above n 4, 482; Françoise Hampson, above n 3, 261, 262.

approach to the paradigm of armed conflict. The indicative criteria set out in *Boškoski* are pitched at the CA3 level and arguably represent the type of minimum conditions at which the law enforcement model may no longer be feasible, as there is a *de facto* 'armed conflict', and thus justify the transition into the paradigm of hostilities wherein, notwithstanding the nonapplicability of APs I and II, customary IHL standards on the conduct of hostilities apply. This is justified because as discussed in Chapter 2 in relation to the arguments presented by Abresch, customary IHL is a freestanding body of law that applies in situations of *de facto* armed conflict, notwithstanding its omission from the preamble of APII.

In this regard there is no need to peg customary Hague law rules onto the high-threshold criteria of APII on the basis that they are its customary equivalents.[71] Furthermore, setting the gateway for the applicability of customary Hague law to the threshold for APII non-international armed conflict is perhaps too elevated a requirement in this context, given that CA3 is itself pitched at a high threshold, but without the complicating features of APII, such as the criteria of control over territory within a state and sustained and concerted military operations which are set out in Article 1(1) APII. Indeed, these threshold requirements represent the preconditions for the applicability of the particular provisions of APII rather than the threshold criteria for the existence of a non-international armed conflict under customary international humanitarian law, which is arguably set at the CA3 NIAC threshold. As will be discussed further later, although this threshold is not as stringent as APII, it is nevertheless set at a sufficiently high level to warrant the applicability of prohibitive and permissive customary Hague rules on the conduct of hostilities.[72] To assert that prohibitive and permissive customary Hague rules can only apply where the threshold of an APII NIAC has been reached on the basis that the only reference to NIAC Hague-type rules is found in APII as opposed to CA3 is to overstate the Hague law content of APII and to overgeneralise the scope of its threshold criteria to include customary Hague law in an unwarranted fashion. Arguably this is because customary Hague law rules are better suited to the dangerous and chaotic type of situation envisaged by the *Boškoski* criteria than those under the framework of law enforcement. Therefore, in addition to the point that both CA3 and APII apply to conflicts of a non-international character, it is also worth mentioning that the jurisprudence of the ICTY suggests that the CA3 threshold may be used as a gateway not only for the application of the same rudimentary treaty-based provisions, but also for detailed customary Hague norms applicable to 'armed conflicts'. Hampson notes that '[t]his is surprising given that there are no Hague-law-type treaty rules in Common Article 3 NIACs . . . [t]hey only appear in treaty law when a NIAC crosses the very high threshold for the applicability of [APII]'.[73] As will

71 Ibid., Hampson, 256.
72 Dapo Akande, above n 36, 54.
73 Françoise Hampson, above n 2, 195.

be discussed later in the section on the parameters of immunity from attack, this study begs to differ.

However, for present purposes, it is to be noted that, as indicated by *Tadić*, customary rules 'have developed to govern internal strife' as a way of unifying the law applicable to IAC and NIAC and thus overcoming the traditional gaps in subject matter jurisdiction associated with the bifurcation of the treaty-based rules relative to IAC and NIAC. It does this by providing for the customary

> protection of civilians from hostilities, in particular from indiscriminate attacks, protection of civilian objects [. . .] protection of all those who do not (or no longer) take active part in hostilities, as well as prohibition of means of warfare proscribed in international armed conflicts and ban of certain methods of conducting hostilities.[74]

Indeed, the compelling dictum of *Tadić* is that '[w]hat is inhumane, and consequently proscribed, in international wars, cannot but be inhumane and inadmissible in civil strife'.[75]

This indicates acceptance, 'borne out by national military manuals', that the 'basic core' Hague law principles on the conduct of hostilities are, according to *Tadić*, essentially reflected in CA3 and are, therefore, 'a part of generally accepted customary law'.[76] The argument presented here is that gaps in the regulation of hostilities created by API and APII are remedied by the application of a parallel system of customary Hague law relevant to armed conflicts once the *Boškoski* CA3 threshold criteria have been surpassed. Those customary Hague rules identified by the ICRC in its CIL study that are relevant to this discussion will be discussed later, as they indicate that state practice has developed to broaden the customary Hague law applicable to NIAC.

Because APII makes reference to 'organized armed groups' and contains some Hague-type rules, it does mean that customary Hague law cannot apply as a matter of course in situations where the threshold criteria of APII have not been reached. Having the threshold set at the CA3 level can thus ensure that a broader range of customary IHL standards can apply to the conditions of contemporary non-international armed conflicts where parties are unlikely to seek to control territory but rather to deny their adversary's ability to do so. Once this situation has reached the threshold envisaged by *Boškoski*, then it is unclear how systems of criminal justice and human rights can practically apply given the organisation of the parties, including organised armed groups, the intensity of the hostilities and any operational and strategic-level policy decisions on the part of states. In this sense, it is not problematic to shift to the paradigm of hostilities to the threshold of CA3 as opposed to APII. The core question is whether types of violence

74 *Tadić* (Jurisdiction) above n 24, 127; Dapo Akande, above n 36, 35.
75 *Tadić* (Jurisdiction) above n 24, 119.
76 Ibid., 117.

illustrated as being in the grey area in Figure 3.1 meet the high threshold of a CA3 armed conflict.

It is suggested that these guidelines are of great practical utility for situational and contextual status determination, both to primary duty bearers in their decision making at different levels of intervention, and also to supervisory mechanisms when it comes to *ex post facto* review of the use of force. This is particularly important when it comes to decision making and *ex post facto* review of grey area situations that are otherwise on what can be described as the non-international armed conflict/less-than non-international armed conflict border and which, for example, may involve counterinsurgency or counterterrorism operations.

As will be discussed further later, application of a clearer classification framework for the purposes of applying HRL or IHL can serve to clarify the rules applicable in such unconventional 'grey area' situations of violence. One of the main reasons for this is that application of the indicative guidelines discussed later should also make it harder for states to be able to justify shoot-to-kill policies, that is, to use lethal force as a first resort, even where not absolutely necessary to pursue a legitimate aim, as these indicative guidelines give a clearer idea as to the level of intensity and organisation required for there to be an armed conflict in which such permissive rules of engagement may be lawfully employed.

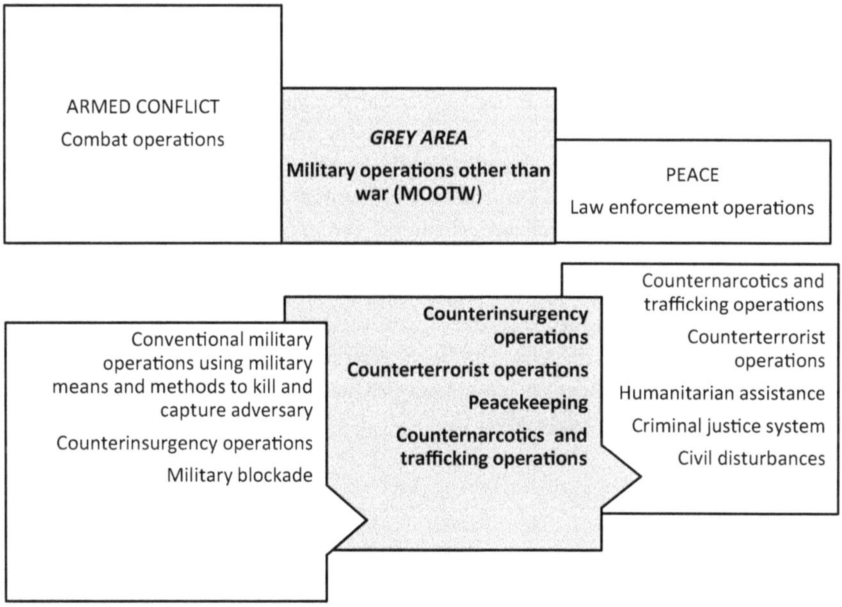

Figure 3.1 The 'grey zone' of military operations.

Source: Adapted from Figure 2–1 Stability in Full Spectrum Operations FM 3–07 2–15, 6 October 2008.

Accurate reference to the law is predicated on adequate determination of the status of a particular situation or a general context, as this affects the relevant and applicable legal framework. This is a major challenge in the context of full spectrum operations, which may include operational theatres involving many levels of conflict and also postconflict situations, such as belligerent occupation, when there are frequent outbreaks of armed activity. In this context, adequate legal analysis is predicated upon adequate status determination, and this can include the challenging legal issue of where and when a factual state of armed conflict begins and ends. As will be discussed further later, it is submitted that there may often be confusion surrounding the characterisation of types of violence outlined in this grey area. Although 'low intensity' forms of organised violence may be generally likened to NIACs, this may not be sufficient for them to satisfy the minimum threshold criteria for a CA3 NIAC and thus technically be described as an 'armed conflict' to which prohibitive and permissive Hague rules may apply. Where they do not reach the minimum threshold criteria for a CA3 NIAC as outlined in *Boškoski*, then they may be appropriately regarded as situations of crisis, emergency or even 'military operations other than war' to which the law-and-order paradigm can and should apply. As will be discussed later, it is crucial to look at the intensity of the violence and the organisation on the part of non-state actors' hostilities, but also the way that organs of the state use force against armed groups and how rights are interpreted so as to determine at a systematic level whether the situation has reached the threshold of an armed conflict.[77] As will be argued later, in situations falling short of the armed threshold as indicated by the *Boškoski* CA3 guidelines, the state has the right to use force to maintain law and order in accordance with human rights restrictions, and so implicitly within human rights standards, states may generally use lethal force in situations where it is absolutely necessary and where it is strictly proportionate to the achievement of specific legitimate objectives (for example, under Article 2 of the European Convention on Human Rights, such objectives are (a) self-defence [including defence of others], (b) in order to make a lawful arrest or to prevent the escape of a person lawfully detained or (c) action lawfully taken for the purpose of quelling a riot or insurrection). In contrast with permissive Hague rules, human rights standards of necessity and proportionality do not permit the use of lethal force on the basis of status-based targeting. Outside the restrictions on the use of force, human rights standards generally permit people to be free from arbitrary detention.[78]

The intensity criterion

Pertinent to the issue of where the framework of law enforcement cannot be expected to operate are the *Boškoski* guidelines for evaluating whether the

---

77 *Boškoski* (Trial Judgment) above n 69, 178.
78 Ibid.

hostilities are of a sufficient intensity to qualify as an armed conflict.[79] Another way of putting this is whether the hostilities can be considered sufficiently serious and whether there has been an increase in and a spread of armed clashes over territory and over time.[80] In this regard, account ought to be taken of the casualty levels[81] and the extent of the destruction[82] caused by the fighting, as well as the effect of hostilities on civilians, for example, by forcing them to flee from combat zones, and whether civilians and/or civilian objects have been subject to direct or indiscriminate attacks.[83]

An assessment should also be made as to whether there has been any increase in the size of government armed forces as well as evidence of mobilisation and distribution of weapons among both parties to the conflict.[84] Indicators in this regard include troop and unit deployment numbers, the formation and change of front lines between belligerent parties[85] and whether high-intensity 'weapons of war' such as 'heavy weapons and other military equipment, such as tanks and other heavy vehicles' have been used.[86] Also relevant to the issue of mobilisation of forces and materiel is whether military tactics and formations have been employed, such as the mass deployment of forces to a crisis area, the closure of roads and the blocking and encirclement of conurbations and the use of mortar or artillery fire against them.[87] Another key factor that is relevant to the intensity criterion is whether international organisations such as the UN Security Council have become involved over concerns about the situation presenting a threat to domestic, regional and international stability, and whether any resolutions have been passed in this regard.[88] As will be discussed later, this affirms the importance of UN charter and treaty mechanisms in the classification and thus the regulatory process.

Boškoski suggests that an account of the intensity or seriousness of hostilities can take place at a 'more systematic level'.[89] This may involve an analysis of the policy decisions that lie behind 'the way that organs of the State, such as the police and military, use force against armed groups' at the various levels of conflict. The rationale of this systemic approach is that such considerations may indicate a tactical and operational shift away from the framework of law enforcement to that of armed conflict because the former has become unfeasible or too dangerous in the circumstances.[90] In this regard, account may be taken of the

79 *Lubanga*, above n 25, 537.
80 *Boškoski* (Trial Judgment) above n 69, 177.
81 Ibid.
82 Ibid.
83 Ibid.
84 Ibid.
85 Ibid.
86 Ibid.
87 Ibid.
88 Ibid.
89 Ibid., 178.
90 Ibid.

nature of the orders and instructions given to forces engaging in clashes with organised armed groups and whether forces are limited to using force that is 'no more than absolutely necessary and which is strictly proportionate to certain objectives' or whether forces have been permitted to use lethal force under broader and more permissive rules of engagement.[91] In other words, according to *Boškoski*, an analysis of how the right to life is interpreted in practice can be used to evaluate whether a situation is one of armed conflict,[92] and this, it is suggested, is particularly important in grey areas where there has been no formal declaration of war or a state of emergency. In such instances, an analysis of orders and instructions running down a chain of command may be probative of strategic and operational assessments that the intensity and seriousness of the violence is such that the law enforcement model is too restrictive of the use of force and that the framework of armed combat has become necessary to restore control, public order and security. In this way, strategic and operational decisions are part of a number of factors that may go towards a broad assessment of how the underlying state of affairs should be qualified. The existence of these factors suggests that the law enforcement paradigm consisting of individualised threat assessments and law enforcement techniques may no longer be practicable, and so we must introduce the framework of hostilities out of military necessity.

The challenge for making assessments in this area is that states will respond to exceptional circumstances, such as terrorism cases, in a range of ways. Some states may respond through their ordinary criminal procedures, whereas others have established exceptional procedures and rules on the use of force, detention, evidence and trial procedure that are enforced through specialised or even military courts.[93] In order to assess whether or not this law enforcement paradigm is practicable, we need to assess whether the police, prosecutorial and judicial institutions and their general or specialised law enforcement tools can operate effectively in the face of the exceptional circumstances within the overall security environment. To this effect, the United Nations Counter-Terrorism Committee has provided technical guidance to states which would suggest that exceptional criminal procedures and special investigative tools can be employed across a broad spectrum of serious criminality, including serious organised crime and terrorism.

The first issue to consider is whether there is a system of prosecution that can respond effectively to the exceptional challenges posed, for example, by terrorism-related cases. At an institutional level we should assess whether the prosecution has a central agency; whether it has internal and external coordination mechanisms with police, judicial and government bodies; whether it has human resources and technical resources to carry out its investigatory and

91 Ibid.

92 Ibid.

93 United Nations Counter Terrorism Committee, Technical Guide to the Implementation of Security Council Resolution 1373 of 2001 (2009) (Counterterrorism Committee Executive Directorate) 27.

prosecutorial functions; whether it has mechanisms for the domestic and international exchange of information; or whether it has specialised counterterrorism agencies.[94] Factors that we may take into account in assessing systemic capabilities in responding to exceptional challenges include whether the police, prosecution and judicial services have the capability to guide, instruct and supervise the work of the investigatory agencies and whether the police/military investigators themselves can operate within the security environment. For example, there may be 'no go' areas for the police/military, precluding them from gathering evidence, carrying out crime scene investigations and interviewing victims and witnesses; from controlling the use of special investigative techniques by investigative and prosecutorial agencies; from handling complex cases involving conspiracy, charity law, finance and human rights, as well as being able to map out complex networks and typologies of incitement and recruitment; from handling and securing forensic, technological and financial aspects of investigation and prosecution; from cooperating internationally both formally and informally; from executing correctly mutual legal assistance and extradition requests; from supervising the use of special investigative techniques by the investigative agencies; from handling intelligence collected by the different investigative agencies and converting it into admissible evidence when appropriate; from handling evidence collected by different states; from accessing special training or educational programmes concerning criminal networks and criminal financing; from accessing intelligence and intelligence techniques such as covert surveillance and infiltration; from handling antiterrorist-financing measures (for example freezing, confiscation); from responding to transnational crimes that can support or facilitate terrorist activity; from handling witness protection for victims, witnesses and collaborators before, during and after statements and testimony are given, bearing in mind that they will be subject to intimidation and death threats; from handling investigative and pretrial detention of suspects, potentially in large numbers, in accordance with procedures established in law, without having to resort to prolonged or indefinite periods of detention due to security risks or political exigencies and without causing the security situation to escalate further in intensity; and from running special courts and court procedures, without necessarily resorting to military courts, and ensuring that there are fair and, where possible, public trials by independent and impartial tribunals (that is, investigating and judicial authorities that are, and are seen to be, operationally independent of the military chain of command).[95]

The organisational criterion

The second factor to consider in assessing whether IHL can apply is whether an armed group has the requisite level of organisation. The more organised an armed group is, the greater the threat it represents and therefore the greater the

94 Ibid., 26.
95 Ibid.

challenge it will be for the 'normal' framework of law enforcement to respond. This organisational prerequisite is an important factor to consider in determining whether standard means and methods of law enforcement are inadequate and military means and methods are needed to reimpose public order or, in other words, whether an armed group is so well organised that it exceeds the capacity of law enforcement mechanisms to respond. Zemach frames this in a slightly more nuanced fashion by describing situations that exceed the capacity of the law enforcement model as those which generally preclude the possibility for individualised threat assessments and law enforcement techniques.[96]

In these ways, the organisational criterion is related to the intensity criterion, but it is also an important element in its own right in that IHL can only apply in a pragmatic and functional sense where a group has the requisite organisational structure and capabilities. Thus, in general terms, to constitute an organised armed group for the purposes of CA3, there needs to be 'some hierarchical structure' and furthermore the 'leadership requires the capacity to exert authority over its members'.[97] Thus, where the law enforcement model cannot functionally operate, for IHL to apply, basic organisational features need to be in place so that it can. As stated in *Boškoski*, '[s]ome degree of organisation by the parties will suffice to establish the existence of an armed conflict' and that '[t]he leadership of the group must, as a minimum, have the ability to exercise some control over its members so that the basic obligations of CA3 of the Geneva Conventions may be implemented'.[98] Without the functional prerequisite in place, it would suggest that 'those who regard its actions as mere acts of anarchy or brigandage are right',[99] which in turn suggests that a law enforcement model is the appropriate and necessary legal and policy framework with which to regulate the use of force in response to 'irregular, anarchic armed groups with no responsible command'.[100]

In general terms, it may be suggested that 'irregular, anarchic armed groups with no responsible command' may not exceed or undermine the capacity of an intelligence-led and evidence-based law enforcement model to respond, as they are not sufficiently organised to confront police and military forces with military means. However, for the purposes of the CA3 threshold criteria, they do not need to be 'as organised as the armed forces of a State' in order to satisfy

96 Zemach, above n 22, 421.

97 *Boškoski* (Trial Judgment) above n 69, 196; *Prosecutor v Slobodan Milošević* (Rule 98 *bis* Decision) IT-02-54-T (16 June 2004), 23; *Prosecutor v Limaj et al.* (Trial Judgment) ICTY-03-66-T (30 November 2005), 89.

98 *Boškoski*, Ibid.

99 Jean S Pictet (ed), *Geneva Convention for the Amelioration of the Condition of Wounded, Sick and Shipwrecked Members of Armed Forces at Sea, Commentary* (International Committee of the Red Cross, Geneva, 1960) (Commentary II) 34.

100 *Ministère public et Centre pour l'égalité des chances et la lutte contre le racisme v C et B* (17 December 1997) Belgian Military Court, Journal des Tribunaux, 4 April 1998, 286–289 (unofficial French translation from the Dutch original ruling) (Violations of IHL in Somalia and Rwanda) 286–289.

the criterion of organization, and they do not need to control territory.[101] The threshold criteria for CA3 are set at a lower level than APII, and so the CA3 criteria represent a minimum standard to determine situations which may be viewed as exceeding the capacity of law enforcement mechanisms to respond.

Boškoski sets out five indicative and interrelated criteria of what constitutes a sufficient degree of organisation for there to be an armed conflict for the purposes of IHL.[102] First, there must be some form of command structure in place. This may be evidenced by the existence of what can be regarded as a 'general staff' or a 'high command' which can issue political statements and communiqués as well as organise personnel, logistics and weapons, such as by appointing personnel to specific roles or tasks, giving orders and authorising military operations.[103] Furthermore, IHL can only apply where there is a command structure which allows the 'high command' to receive reports from all operational units within the chain of command and to establish and disseminate internal regulations that set out the hierarchical organisation and structure of the armed group in terms of roles and duties at each level of the chain of command.[104]

Second, for a group to qualify as being 'organised', it must have the ability to carry out military operations in an organised fashion and control territory. Factors to consider in this regard are whether the group has the ability to establish a 'unified military strategy' so as to be able 'to conduct large scale military operations', whether it has 'the capacity to control territory' (rather than actually controlling it) and whether 'there is territorial division into zones of responsibility'. Furthermore, there must be some evidence that commanders and operational units can 'co-ordinate their actions' and effectively disseminate 'written and oral orders and decisions'.[105]

Third, an organised armed group is one which has a sufficient level of logistical and organisational capabilities. For example, an assessment is to be made of a group's ability to recruit new members and to provide them with military training and to control and organise the supply of weapons and uniforms, as well as its ability to link and coordinate all levels of the chain of command through a communications system.[106]

Fourth, an armed group must also be sufficiently organised so as to ensure a level of discipline and to demonstrate the ability to implement CA3. Factors relevant in this respect include whether a system of internal regulations and disciplinary rules is in place, as well as mechanisms such as proper training and supervision to ensure that they are disseminated to members of the organised armed group.[107]

---

101 *Boškoski* (Trial Judgment) above n 69, 197.
102 *Lubanga*, above n 25, 537.
103 *Boškoski* (Trial Judgment) above n 69, 199.
104 Ibid.
105 Ibid., 200.
106 Ibid., 201.
107 Ibid., 202.

Fifth, *Boškoski* suggests that an 'organised' armed group is one with the ability to 'speak with one voice' in the course of political negotiations.[108] In this regard, account may be taken of the group's capacity 'to act on behalf of its members in political negotiations with representatives of international organisations and foreign countries', as well as its ability to negotiate and conclude agreements such as cease fire or peace accords'.[109] The existence of these organisational features may indicate that standard law enforcement means and techniques may not be able to remove or reduce the threat from an organised armed group, and so Hague rules on the conduct of hostilities are needed to respond effectively.

'Protracted armed violence'

For situations of violence to fall within the paradigm of hostilities, they need to be sufficiently connected to a 'protracted campaign' that has reached the threshold of 'hostilities'. Thus, a material issue to be determined for IHL to apply is 'whether the acts are perpetrated in isolation or as part of a protracted campaign that entails the engagement of both parties in hostilities'.[110] Unfortunately, the meaning of the term 'protracted armed violence' has not 'received much explicit attention in the jurisprudence' of the ICTY.[111]

Although *Boškoski* does not offer a clear definition of this temporal element per se, it nevertheless contributes to our understanding by providing some examples of how acts of violence can be connected so as to fulfil the 'protracted armed violence' requirement.[112] In this regard, the decision in *Boškoski* noted the 'significant pattern' within the jurisprudence of the ICTY of considering and examining evidence of 'incidents of violence outside the temporal limits of an indictment to determine whether armed violence in question is "protracted"'.[113] The approach of identifying whether particular violent acts are part of 'protracted' hostilities is thus relative to the surrounding context. In other words, in order to determine the law applicable to violent acts occurring within a circumscribed period, particularly short periods of a year or less, this approach seeks to establish whether or not they were factually connected with surrounding acts of violence, thus constituting 'protracted' hostilities subject to the legal paradigm of hostilities. For example, in *Furundžija* it was found that the indicted acts which occurred on or around 15 May 1993 were connected to hostilities occurring between January and July 1993;[114] in *Čelebići*, it was found that the indicted acts which took place between May and December 1992 were connected to an armed conflict

108 Ibid., 203.
109 Ibid.
110 Ibid., 185.
111 Ibid., 186.
112 Ibid.
113 Ibid.
114 *Prosecutor v Furundžija* (Trial Judgment) ICTY-95-17/1-T (10 December 1998), 51–57, 59.

in Bosnia-Herzegovina that occurred between 6 March 1992 and November 1995[115]; in *Milošević Rule 98 bis Decision*, it was found that the indicted acts occurring between 1 January and 24 March 1999 were connected to KLA operations against the police in 1996, as well as a 'large scale offensive' of Serbian forces in 1998.[116]

The threshold criteria for the applicability of APII

Although CA3 is *prima facie* limited to armed conflicts 'not of an international character" that occur "in the territory of one of the High Contracting Parties', contemporary jurisprudence and academic discourse indicate that it applies to armed conflicts with a 'transnational' dimension, in other words, to conflicts that involve cross-border hostilities, either between state and nonstate entities or between nonstate entities.[117] Furthermore, the *Commentary* by the International Committee of the Red Cross (ICRC) points out that the threshold of applicability of APII is set at a higher level than that of CA3.[118] It explicitly does not apply to internal disturbances, a term the ICRC interprets as serious acts of violence carried out by 'more or less organised groups' and which 'call upon extensive police forces, or even armed forces, to restore internal order.'[119] The Trial Chamber in *Akayesu* has interpreted the requirement of Protocol II that nonstate entities must have the ability 'to carry out sustained and concerted military operations' to mean that 'operations must be continuous and planned',[120] as opposed to CA3's criterion of 'protracted' armed conflict, a standard which may include sporadic violence. In addition, Protocol II requires nonstate groups to be able to exercise 'control over a part of [the] territory' of the state in question. The Trial Chamber further elucidated this criterion as 'usually that which has eluded the control of the government forces' in that a nonstate entity is able to 'dominate a sufficient part of the territory' and 'impose discipline in the name of a *de facto* authority'.[121]

---

115 *Prosecutor v Delalić et al.*, the 'Čelebići Case' (Trial Judgment) ICTY-96–21-T (16 November 1998) 186.

116 *Milošević* (Rule 98 *bis* Decision), above n 97, 28.

117 *Nicaragua v United States of America*, above n 25, 218; *Hamdan v Rumsfeld, Secretary of Defense, et al.*, Supreme Court of the United States, Judgment of 29 June 2006, 126 SCt 2749 (2006), 67; *Tadić* (Jurisdiction) above n 24, 102; Melzer, above n 33, 258; Andreas Paulus and Mindia Vashakmadze, 'Asymmetrical War and the Notion of Armed Conflict – A Tentative Conceptualization' (2009) 91 (873) *International Review of the Red Cross* 199.

118 Protocol Additional to the Geneva Conventions of 12 August 1949, and relating to the Protection of Victims of Non-International Armed Conflicts (Protocol II), 8 June 1977 ('AP II'), Article 1 (1); Y Sandoz, C Swinarski and B Zimmermann (eds), *Commentary on the Additional Protocols of 8 June 1977 to the Geneva Conventions of 12 August 1949* (ICRC/Martinus Nijhoff, Geneva, 1987), (*'Commentary'*) 4447.

119 *Commentary*, APII, Ibid., 4475–4477.

120 *Akayesu*, above n 23, 626.

121 Ibid.

The Trial Chamber in *Boškoski* set out a number of 'indicative factors' of territorial control, such as the establishment of alternative structures of authority in liberated territories, zones, cities and even villages.[122]

Protocol II is limited in that it is not applicable where a state is engaged in hostilities against nonstate parties in the territory of a foreign state, where a conflict is taking place on the territory of a state that has not ratified it or where the only parties are nonstate actors. Moreover, in the context of unconventional asymmetric conflicts, the elements of organisation and control of territory are likely to be highly contentious and difficult to determine in practice. One of the main reasons for this is that if a weaker party does adopt conventional forms of territorial control, organisation and military engagement, this is likely to result in its swift isolation, suppression and destruction.

The dynamics of asymmetric conflict force weaker adversaries into a counterstrategy of 'organic organisational adaptation' whereby they adopt horizontal, clandestine and hybrid systems and networks of command and control as well as 'defenceless defence' in order to promote their survivability.[123] Thus a symptomatic outcome of asymmetric conflicts may be spatial and geographical uncertainties such as 'fronts' that are in a constant state of flux across urban areas, if indeed there are fronts at all. In situations of what Veuthey describes as wars 'without a front', there is likely to be 'interpenetration and reciprocal encirclement', and according to Veuthey, this 'territorial uncertainty relativizes, if not effaces, the fundamental notions of the classical law'.[124]

In this regard, the dynamics of asymmetric warfare make it extremely difficult to identify the material conditions where the meagre protections under APII apply,[125] but, nevertheless, from a conventional point of view, where intelligence is at a premium, there is the risk of underclassification, that is, where there is weak evidence of territorial control, then the basic protections under CA3 apply. Accordingly, to mitigate these issues surrounding the application of APII, the approach advocated here is that the indicative guidelines set out in *Boškoski*, which elucidate the threshold criteria for an armed conflict, may not only be used as a gateway for the application of the basic protections under CA3, but also customary Hague law.

It is suggested that setting the threshold for the applicability of customary Hague law at the APII level is arguably too high given the contemporary conditions of non-international armed conflicts and, furthermore, there is no plausible basis for setting it at the APII level rather than the CA3 level.[126] Indeed, it is suggested

---

122 *Boškoski* (Trial Judgment) above n 69, 242–249.

123 Stepanova, above n 35, 105; Rupert Smith, *The Utility of Force: The Art of War in the Modern World* (Allen Lane, London 2006), 329; Brian Steed, *Piercing the Fog of War* (Zenith Press, 2009), Chapter 9.

124 Veuthey, above n 14; Berman, above n 14.

125 Stepanova, above n 35, 104–134; Ivan Arreguín-Toft, *How the Weak Win Wars: A Theory of Asymmetric Conflict* (Cambridge University Press, 2008) 33.

126 For a contrary view see Françoise Hampson, above n 3, 256.

that a CA3 non-international armed conflict set at the threshold indicated by the *Boškoski* indicative guidelines marks the point where the law enforcement framework comprising domestic law and human rights law may no longer be practicable given the intensity of the hostilities, the organisation of the parties to the conflict and the overall strategic policy decisions on the part of a state. In other words, the *Boškoski* indicative guidelines are useful benchmarks for assessing which framework is most suited for the situation on the ground and for which they have been designed. As noted by Hampson, 'in normal circumstances, a decision on opening fire is based on a law and order paradigm' or in other words, 'it should be taken as a last resort and based on the behaviour of the person targeted' and that this is 'dependent on the immediacy and severity of the threat that person poses at the time'.[127] However, Hampson also notes that this law-and-order paradigm may be appropriate 'most of the time and in most of the territory, even during an emergency, but that '[i]n most situations of armed conflict, that is inappropriate as a bottom line', and furthermore, 'in many situations of armed conflict it is in everyone's interest, including that of the civilian population, for such decisions to be based on a LOAC paradigm'.[128] It is suggested that the CA3 threshold criteria as elucidated in *Boškoski* are not only an appropriate 'bottom line' for marking the threshold of an armed conflict, and thus marking the ceiling at which the law-and-order paradigm is no longer practicable, but are also critical in operationalising the relationship between international human rights law and the law of armed conflict, particularly when it comes to targeting issues. In other words, to assert that human rights law applies in situations that have surpassed the threshold indicated by these guidelines is arguably not only 'to assert an unrealistic protection of civilians in situations of armed conflict', but also 'unrealisable expectations on the part of civilians and increased violation of the rules on the part of the armed forces'.[129] In short, the IHL classification criteria are thus useful in elucidating the distinction between 'armed conflict on the one hand and armed violence not amounting to armed conflict' as this is 'of major relevance to the rules on the application of force'.[130]

In any case, despite the advantages of customary IHL in this regard, such an approach is still required in order to distinguish non-international armed conflict situations from less-than-non-international armed conflict situations. Given the high threshold indicated by these indicative guidelines, this fosters the presumptive application of the law enforcement framework and its sequencing with the framework of hostilities. This is vitally important in order to maintain high levels of protection in view of 'grey area' situations of violence which may contain military counterterrorism and counterinsurgency operations. In this regard, it is suggested that the indicative guidelines outlined in *Boškoski* being used as a

127 Françoise Hampson, above n 2, 192.
128 Ibid.
129 Ibid.
130 Elizabeth Wilmshurst, above n 4, 495.

threshold for the shift from a law-and-order paradigm to an armed conflict, and thus also as a gateway for the application of customary IHL, is in no way to set the threshold at 'an inappropriately low level of disruption',[131] given that the intensity of violence required, as well as the level of organisation needed on the part of an organised armed group, strongly suggests that normal law enforcement measures and restrictions on the use of force may not be practicable under such exceptional conditions where there is such a high level of violence and, furthermore, may be considered 'unrealisable expectations', namely human rights–oriented, threat-based targeting, as well as human rights standards of necessity, precautions, proportionality and effective investigations. For example, in a situation of violence that has reached the threshold of CA3, it is unlikely that it would be possible to gather evidence of a quantity, type or character so as to enable a criminal prosecution of someone suspected of actively participating in hostilities on a frequent basis or of being a member of an organised armed group exercising a continuous combat function. The CA3 threshold represents a high intensity of violence beyond what can be regarded as mere states of crisis or emergency to which human rights law can apply. Therefore, it is argued that it is not problematic for prohibitive or permissive customary Hague law principles to apply once a situation has reached the CA3 NIAC threshold, in particular vis-à-vis targeted operations against members of organised armed groups. As will be suggested in more detail, the CA3 threshold outlined in the indicative guidelines in *Boškoski* marks the base level at which there is a paradigm shift from the law enforcement framework to that of the law of armed conflict framework. In a complex operational environment, this threshold can be used to identify what is permitted and prohibited in different situations with greater clarity. As will be discussed later, given that the *Boškoski* indicative criteria are set at a very high level in terms of the requisite intensity of violence and level of organisation needed on the part of an armed group, it is suggested that there are no real difficulties with having the paradigm shift at this threshold, as opposed to the APII threshold, to enable the applicability of customary Hague prohibitions and permissions. In view of the high threshold established by the *Boškoski* indicative criteria, it is unclear what grounds there are for the proposition that the armed conflict paradigm is more clearly applicable in situations in which APII is applicable.[132] This is all the more so given the obstacles to the applicability of APII, such as a requirement that the non-international armed conflict occurs in the territory of the state party to the conflict (that is, it would not apply where a state is fighting a nonstate actor on the territory of another state that is not party to the conflict), as well as the criteria that an organised armed group exercises control over territory within a state and demonstrates the ability to carry out sustained and concerted military operations. All these obstacles could serve to create a gap in LOAC regulation if customary norms were not applicable at the CA3 threshold. Arguably, the human

131 Françoise Hampson, above n 2, 197.
132 Ibid., 199.

rights paradigm is not suited to the type and level of armed violence foreseen at this threshold between state and nonstate actors, or solely between nonstate actors, and so it is argued that the armed conflict paradigm is appropriately and clearly applicable at this threshold rather than the APII threshold.

Terrorism

As outlined earlier, the Geneva Conventions and their two Additional Protocols do not provide clear guidelines on when IHL becomes applicable to conflicts with terrorist organisations per se. This constitutes a major protection issue in that there is the heightened risk that Hague law permissions on both targeting and means and methods of warfare apply at too low a level of violence, or in other words, that it effectively overreaches or 'goes down' into an excessively broad range of organised forms of violence and essentially 'comes down' from what should be its high threshold of applicability into states of emergency or crisis. It is suggested that the overreaching of Hague law prohibitions to what may be objectively construed as less-than-NIAC situations should be circumscribed through the rigorous application of objective classification criteria, because otherwise there is the risk that means and methods of force that are far too permissive and arbitrary are applied in situations where there is a low level of violence and would constitute an escalatory factor. As suggested earlier, the application of the clearer classification scheme envisaged in *Boškoski* can ensure that, as far as possible, terrorist acts are treated as criminal in nature and thus subject to the paradigm of law enforcement with its due process requirements as well as appellate and 'constitutional' oversight. This can serve to prevent any unnecessary militarisation of public order and also can serve to ensure the supervision and regulation of the exercise of executive power through military means. Nevertheless, it is submitted that terrorist acts may rise to the level of an armed conflict and that this is entirely consistent with the logic of IHL.[133] Furthermore, it is suggested that the *Boškoski* objective criteria set the threshold for Hague law permissions at an appropriately high threshold; that is, these threshold criteria appropriately mark the point at which it may be deemed fitting to shift from a law-and-order paradigm to an armed conflict paradigm in the case of targeting. This is because it is suggested that *Boškoski* provides reasoned and authoritative objective criteria for identifying those situations that exceed the capacity of the law enforcement paradigm or, in other words, those situations where individualised threat assessments and standard law enforcement techniques are not generally practicable.

According to *Tadić*, a non-international armed conflict exists where there is 'protracted violence between governmental authorities and organised groups or between such groups within a State'.[134] Accordingly, *Boškoski* noted that the

---

133 *Boškoski* (Trial Judgment) above n 69, 187.

134 *Tadić* (Jurisdiction) above n 24, 70; *Limaj et al.* (Trial Judgment), above n 97, 84; *Prosecutor v Haradinaj* (Trial Judgment) IT-04-84-T (3 April 2008) 37.

core threshold criteria of intensity and organisation 'may be used solely for the purpose, as a minimum, to distinguish an armed conflict from lesser forms of violence such as "terrorist" activities',[135] and, furthermore, that the drafters of the Geneva Conventions 'did not intend the term "armed conflict" to apply to any and every isolated event involving the use of force and obliging officers of the peace to have resort to their weapons'.[136] It is argued that customary IHL, together with CA3, applies to 'conflicts which are in many respects similar to an international war, but take place within the confines of a single country', that is, where 'armed forces' on either side are engaged in 'hostilities'.[137] Accordingly, it does not apply to 'isolated acts of violence, such as terrorist activities . . .',[138] or as stated in *Kordić* '[t]he requirement of protracted fighting is significant in excluding mere cases of civil unrest or single acts of terrorism'.[139] Similarly, Article 8(2)(d) of the ICC Statute provides that CA3 applies in the context of 'armed conflicts not of an international character and thus does not apply to situations of internal disturbances and tensions, such as riots, isolated and sporadic acts of violence or other acts of a similar nature'.[140]

Therefore, the crucial dictum set out in *Boškoski* is that '[i]t is immaterial whether the acts of violence perpetrated may or may not be characterised as terrorist in nature'.[141] It undergirded this stance by noting that both 'national courts and UN bodies have not discounted acts of a terrorist nature in their consideration of acts amounting to armed conflict'.[142] In this regard the labelling and condemnation of 'terrorist acts' by domestic authorities or international

135 *Boškoski* (Trial Judgment) above n 69, 185; *Tadić* (Opinion and Judgment), above n 67, 562.

136 *Boškoski*, ibid; *Commentary* GC II, above n 99, 33.

137 Ibid.

138 Ibid; *Tadić* (Jurisdiction) above n 24, 70; *Limaj et al.* (Trial Judgment), above n 97, 84; *Haradinaj* (Trial Judgment), above n 134, 37.

139 *Prosecutor v Kordić and Čerkez* (Appeals Chamber Judgment) ICTY-95–14/2-A (17 December 2004) 341.

140 UN General Assembly, Rome Statute of the International Criminal Court (last amended 2010), 17 July 1998, Article 8(2)(d) ('ICCS').

141 *Boškoski* (Trial Judgment) above n 69, 185.

142 *Boškoski*, Ibid., 190. Municipal authorities cited in *Boškoski* include: *Case of Abimael Guzmán Reinoso and others*, Peru, Expediente acumulado No 560–03, Decision of 13 October 2006 (National Criminal Chamber), paras 470–476; *Pius Nwaoga v The State*, Nigeria, Supreme Court, 3 March 1972, All Nigeria Law Reports, Part 1, Vol. 1, p. 149; ILR Vol. 52, 1979, p. 494, at p. 497: 'To our mind, deliberate and intentional killing of an unarmed person living peacefully inside Federal Territory as in this case is a crime against humanity, and even if committed during a civil war is in violation of the domestic law of the country, and must be punished'; *Hamdan v Rumsfeld*, above n 117, 66–68; *Ajuri v IDF Commander*, HCJ 7015/02; HCJ 7019/02, Israel, Supreme Court, Judgement of 3 September 2002, para 1; *Public Committee Against Torture v The Government of Israel*, Israel, Supreme Court, Judgment of 14 December 2006, HCJ 769/02, 16; *El Saka v The State of Israel* (unpublished), HCJ 9255/00; *Kn'aan v The Commander of IDF Forces in the Judea and Samaria Area* (unpublished), HCJ 2461/01; *Barake v The Minister of Defence*, 56(2) PD, HCJ 9293/01; *Almandi v The Minister of Defence*, 56(3) PD 30, HCJ 3451/02;

organisations does not prevent the classification of a situation as one which amounts in fact to an armed conflict.[143] Put another way, it was held in *Boškoski* that

> while isolated acts of terrorism may not reach the threshold of armed conflict, when there is protracted violence of this type, especially where they require the engagement of the armed forces in hostilities, such acts are relevant to assessing the level of intensity with regard to the existence of an armed conflict.[144]

This is both a useful and pragmatic stance in that although the perpetration of 'terrorist acts' may indicate that an organised armed group or 'terrorist' group has 'poor discipline' or lacks the requisite hierarchical structure, they are not conclusive in this regard. Indeed, to the contrary, it may not be appropriate 'to infer a lack of organisation of the armed group by reason of the fact that international humanitarian law was frequently violated by its members'.[145] Instead, a pattern of 'violations of rules of IHL such as terrorist attacks' may satisfy the threshold criteria of CA3 where there is evidence to suggest that they were 'part of a military strategy' and 'involve a high level of planning and a coordinated command structure for their implementation' rather than 'members deciding to commit attacks of their own accord'.[146]

In this regard, the indicative guidelines outlined earlier can help us distinguish situations where terrorist acts become subject to the legal framework of hostilities from situations where they remain subject to the legal framework of law enforcement. In other words, where the intensity and organisation of group violence becomes such that the framework of law enforcement can no longer function due to the breakdown in the security environment, for example, where it poses 'totally unreasonable risks to law-enforcement officials' and where 'the State does not have sufficient control to carry out an arrest', then recourse may be had to the legal framework of hostilities.[147] In this way, the previously mentioned indicative guidelines may be put forward in order to answer in the affirmative the question of whether it is possible in general terms to set out the type of situations that can and the type of situations that cannot be contained under a human rights–oriented law enforcement framework.[148]

The application of these indicative guidelines which set a clear and high threshold for the existence of an armed conflict would suggest that primary duty bearers

---

Ibrahim v The Commander of IDF Forces in the West Bank (unpublished), HCJ 8172/02; *Mara'abe v The Prime Minister of Israel*, HJC 7957/04.

143 *Boškoski* (Trial Judgment) above n 69, 192.

144 Ibid., 190.

145 Ibid., 204–205.

146 Ibid.

147 Kretzmer, above n 62, 35.

148 Ibid.

as well as international and regional oversight mechanisms should give primacy to a human rights–oriented law enforcement approach in the context of unconventional conflicts. In other words, this scheme of indicative guidelines serves to assist primary duty bearers and oversight mechanisms in identifying those situations where the use of lethal force as a method of first resort should only be used where 'absolutely necessary', or, in other words, where there is an obligation to use less-than-lethal measures primarily and to escalate the degree of force where necessary. Arguably, this can serve to prevent, as far as possible, any premature recourse to Hague law permissions that may result in unwarranted 'extrajudicial' killing of suspected 'terrorists' and any consequent 'collateral' deprivation of life in grey area situations characterised by low levels of violence. The CA3 threshold represents a high intensity of violence beyond what can be regarded as mere states of crisis or emergency to which the law enforcement regime of human rights law can apply.

Kretzmer suggests that the law enforcement regime is one that protects individuals and secures public order by containing threats from other individuals and groups through the mechanism of the criminal justice system. This model focuses on prosecuting and convicting criminal acts, or at least preventing and deterring them, on the basis of actual criminal actions and complicity in them.[149] Furthermore, it has been suggested that departing from criminal law concepts and mechanisms may serve to retard or undermine a state's capacity to identify and respond to a continuum of violence in an appropriate and effective manner.[150] Moving away from this paradigm, for example, in the form of effectively applying Hague law permissions at too low a level of violence, risks using force that may cause an escalation in hostilities and is thus counterproductive. Contemporary jurisprudence thus assists with policing this border between states of emergency, where the right to life under the human rights–based law enforcement model applies, and states of armed conflict, where customary and treaty-based IHL on targeting and weaponry applies. The following discussion in relation to the Bloody Sunday incident illustrates this point.

The British military was involved in security operations in Northern Ireland from August 1969 to July 2007 effectively to give 'military aid to the civil power'.[151] As noted by Haines, this raises the question of whether the violence that occurred, for example, during the course of Bloody Sunday crossed the threshold for the existence of an armed conflict and, if it did, into which category of conflict did it fall?[152] Haines notes that the 'troubles' in Northern Ireland can be divided into discrete stages, namely civil disturbances between 1968 and 1971,

149 Pierre Hauck and Sven Peterke, 'Organized Crime and Gang Violence in National and International Law' (2010) 92 (878) *International Review of the Red Cross* 407, 410.

150 Rob McLaughlin, above n 7, 26–27.

151 Steven Haines, 'The Nature of War and the Character of Contemporary Armed Conflict', in Elizabeth Wilmshurst (ed), *International Law and the Classification of Conflicts* (OUP, 2012) 118.

152 Ibid.

an insurgency between 1972 and 1974, a campaign of terrorism between 1975 and 1994 and a period of conflict resolution between 1994 and 1998.[153] Haines notes that towards the end of the phase of civil disturbances, there were episodes of intense sectarian rioting, and so large numbers of British Army troops were deployed to help restore public order through the imposition of measures such as curfews. As civil disturbances were growing in intensity, the Irish Republican Army (IRA) and the Provisional Irish Republican Army (PIRA) took advantage of this unstable security situation, became more organised and intensified their operations against British forces in Northern Ireland. Haines notes that by early 1971 PIRA was sufficiently organised and resourced to carry out direct attacks on the British Army and the Security Forces of Northern Ireland. This stage also saw the introduction of the policy of internment, which in turn saw increased IRA and PIRA recruitment.[154]

On 30 January 1972 fourteen people were shot dead and many others injured by members of the British Army during a civil rights march in the Bogside area of Derry. This led to a dramatic worsening of the security situation with attacks on the British Army resulting in over 100 servicemen fatalities and a dramatic escalation in the PIRA bombing campaign with high numbers of civilian casualties as well as increased Unionist paramilitary violence and assassinations of suspected Nationalists. As a result of this deteriorating security situation, the UK Parliament dissolved the Northern Ireland administration at Stormont.[155]

Despite this dire security situation, combined with the fact that the IRA and PIRA were able to mount direct attacks upon the British Army as well as the Security Forces of Northern Ireland, together with an insurgent bombing campaign, Haines suggests that 'the security situation was not uniformly serious' and, furthermore, even though the PIRA claimed control over certain areas, it was nevertheless not sufficiently organised or resourced to withstand any intervention by the British Army, which it either did or was able to do throughout the insurgency period. Furthermore, Haines notes that the British Army did not have to resort to any 'high-intensity urban warfare' to gain access to and control over 'high risk areas'. Rather, it merely reinforced the Security Forces of Northern Ireland with a mass mobilisation of troops which occurred without any fatalities on the part of the security forces and only two 'terrorist' fatalities.[156] The question is thus: If Bloody Sunday, as well as the events surrounding it, occurred today, could opening fire against suspected members of the IRA be considered lawful?

On the basis of his analysis of the situation, Haines writes that the events that occurred during 1972 provide grounds for suggesting that the intensity of the violence rose beyond that of mere internal disturbances or tensions and reached

153 Ibid., 119.
154 Ibid., 124.
155 Ibid., 125.
156 Ibid.

the threshold of a CA3 non-international armed conflict,[157] but that this CA3-type NIAC did not extend into the post-1974 phase despite lack of clarity about the exact point at which the level of violence dropped from being an armed conflict to that of civil disturbances and tensions.[158] It is suggested that the main weakness of Haines's account is that it did not give a full account of the *Boškoski* criteria. In particular, as discussed earlier, *Boškoski* suggests that an account of the intensity or seriousness of hostilities can take place at a 'systematic level' and this may involve an analysis of the policy decisions that lie behind 'the way that organs of the State, such as the police and military, use force against armed groups'.[159] Indeed, the rationale of this approach is that such considerations may indicate a shift away from the framework of law enforcement to that of armed conflict and in this regard, account may be taken of the nature of the orders and instructions given to forces engaging in clashes with organised armed groups and whether forces are limited to using force that is 'no more than absolutely necessary and which is strictly proportionate to certain objectives' or whether forces have been permitted to use lethal force under broader and more permissive rules of engagement. In this regard the British authorities denied the existence of a NIAC in Northern Ireland[160] and furthermore, as noted by Haines, the evidence suggests that British rules of engagement were based on the law enforcement paradigm in that the 'yellow card' instructions given to armed forces concerning opening fire set out 'general rules' such as 'never use more force than the minimum necessary to enable you to carry out your duties' and '[a]lways first try to handle the situation by other means than opening fire'.[161] In this regard, the instructions set out restrictions on the use of automatic fire 'where persons not using firearms are in, or may be close to, the line of fire'. In addition, the instructions stated in bold that 'whenever possible a warning should be given before you open fire' unless the situation fell within one of the defined circumstances where such a warning was considered 'impractical' such as self-defence in response to a direct armed attack. Further to this, forces were only permitted to open fire '[a]gainst a person carrying what you can positively identify as a firearm . . . and . . . he refuses to halt when called upon to do so, and there is no other way of stopping him' or where a person was doing specified acts that were 'likely to endanger life'. In these circumstances, forces were only permitted to fire 'aimed shots'.[162]

These instructions thus indicated a revised policy on the part of the UK Ministry of Defence to apply law enforcement standards vis-à-vis the use of force. Even though the level of PIRA and IRA organisation combined with the intensity of armed violence from 1972–1974 indicates the threshold of a CA3 armed conflict

157 Ibid., 134.
158 Ibid., 135.
159 *Boškoski* (Trial Judgment) above n 69, 178.
160 Steven Haines, above n 151, 134.
161 Ibid., 137.
162 UK Ministry of Defence, Instructions by the Director of Operations for Opening Fire in Northern Ireland, Army Code 70771.

may have been reached, the UK government did not overtly regard or treat the situation as an armed conflict.[163]

The Bloody Sunday incident was an example that law enforcement standards on the use of lethal force, as outlined in the 'yellow card', were breached. This was confirmed in the report of the Saville Inquiry of June 2010 which concluded that '[t]he firing by soldiers of 1 PARA on Bloody Sunday caused the deaths of 13 people and injury to a similar number, none of whom was posing a threat of causing death or serious injury'.[164] Furthermore, the report concluded that British paratroopers 'lost control' in that, without warning, they fired live rounds which killed unarmed civilians trying to flee the situation as well as unarmed civilians who tried to help the wounded.[165] The Saville Inquiry found that the civilians who were fired upon posed no lethal threat to British paratroopers before they opened fire upon them[166] and, furthermore, the inquiry found that the paratroopers involved had tried to cover up the situation by providing false accounts in order to justify opening fire and, in addition, there was insufficient evidence to suggest that members of the IRA who were present did anything to justify British paratroopers opening fire in the first instance.[167]

If the Bloody Sunday incident happened today, then, in addition to the criteria of organisation and intensity, an analysis must also take place at the 'systematic level' in order to determine fully the character of the situation. The UK government at the time did not overtly shift away from a law enforcement approach in policy or significantly in practice, despite the numerous breaches of its policy on the use of force. There is nothing to suggest that if such civil disturbances rose to such extreme levels as they did in 1972, then the current UK government would shift from the framework of law enforcement to that of an armed conflict. Rather, it is suggested that this was and would be regarded as an extreme law enforcement situation to which criminal law and human rights standards would apply rather than the permissive standards of IHL.

Accordingly, it is suggested that by applying the *Boškoski* criteria, then the overt policy and practice of the United Kingdom, would suggest that, all things considered, this was a situation just falling below the threshold of a CA3 non-international armed conflict to which human rights standards would apply, as they did then in key cases relating to the use of force such as *McCann v UK* as well as detention cases such as *Lawless v Ireland*, *Ireland v UK* and *Brannigan and McBride v UK*. Indeed, what is interesting about incidents such as Bloody Sunday is that although law enforcement rules of engagement rather than IHL standards were officially deemed sufficient to respond to the security situation, those situations where law enforcement rules of engagement were breached only

---

163 Steven Haines, above n 151, 138.

164 Report of the Bloody Sunday Inquiry, 15 June 2010, 'The overall assessment'.

165 Ibid.

166 Ibid., Volume I, Ch. 3.

167 Ibid.

served to complicate further and worsen the security situation. The *Boškoski* criteria are thus useful in restricting customary Hague rules to a high threshold of applicability set at the CA3 level. Indeed, it is suggested that an analysis involving the *Boškoski* criteria is sufficiently nuanced to ensure that the law enforcement paradigm may be deemed to be the appropriate and practicable framework even in those situations where an armed group claims control over certain areas but is not able to withstand normal modes of state intervention; that is, where only exceptional law enforcement means and methods of force, as opposed to high-intensity military means and methods, are needed to gain access to and control areas purportedly controlled by organised armed groups.

Even if, all things considered, this could be catagorised a CA3 non-international armed conflict, then as indicated by the report of the Saville Inquiry, there was nothing to indicate that the activities of those civilians killed on Bloody Sunday amounted to direct participation in hostilities, nor was there any evidence upon which it could be presumed that those killed were members of the IRA. Accordingly, it is doubtful whether these killings could even be justified from an IHL perspective.

War and peace in the information environment

Increasingly, contemporary operational environments may also be conceived of as 'virtual theatres' which arise from globalised communications systems and which allow nonstate actors to organise attacks.[168] This part of the discussion aims to contribute to the discourse on conflict classification by suggesting that legal guidelines should take into account military doctrine relating to our 'information environment', which is defined as 'the aggregate of individuals, organisations, and systems that collect, process, disseminate, or act on information'.[169] Importantly, when attempting to categorise a state of affairs for legal purposes, account ought to be taken of an armed group's information-related capabilities (IRCs), which are defined as 'tools, techniques, or activities using data, information, or knowledge to create effects and operationally desirable conditions within the informational, physical and cognitive dimensions of the information environment'. More specifically, IRCs are part of cyberspace which comprises interdependent networks of information technology infrastructures and resident data, including the Internet, telecommunications networks, computer systems and embedded processors and controllers.[170] Counterinsurgency doctrine defines the 'information dimension' as the place where the physical and

168 David Kilcullen, 'Future Land Operational Concept – Complex Warfighting' (Report) (The Australian Army, 7 April 2004), 1.

169 US Joint Chiefs of Staff, Information Operations, Joint Publication 3–13 (27 November 2012 Incorporating Change 1 20 November 2014), Chapter I, 1(b).

170 US Department of the Army (Training and Doctrine Command) Counterinsurgency (COIN) Field Manual (FM) 3–24 and Fleet Marine Force Manual (FMFM) 3–24 (Final Draft) (Headquarters, Department of the Army, Washington, DC & Marine Corps Combat

cognitive dimensions interact, or, in other words, the place where information is collected, processed, stored, disseminated, displayed and protected; the physical dimension comprises targetable command-and-control systems in the real, tangible world such as information systems, human beings (including decision makers, leaders and military forces) and organisations, as well as the supporting infrastructure and physical networks (microwave towers, computers, smart phones) that connect them and which enable individuals and organisations to create effects conduct operations across air, land, maritime, space and cyberspace domains and across national, economic, and geographical boundaries.[171] The cognitive dimension is defined as existing in the minds of individuals such as those who plan, instigate or order, or those who follow them. It is the dimension where people think, perceive, visualise, influence and decide, and includes their values, ideologies, ideas, beliefs, intentions, motivations, influences, decisions and perceptions.[172] Accordingly, the cognitive dimension is viewed as the most important component of the information environment because it is where effects can be created.[173]

In order to provide appropriate regulation, legal and military doctrine must keep up with the means and ends with which IRCs are increasingly being used to produce effects within the physical domain in particular. For example, advanced wired and wireless information technology is used to foster global networked connectivity in order to gain strategic, operational and tactical advantages and effects, namely, influencing international, national, regional and local audiences in near real time, anonymously and/or securely. Global networked connectivity brings countries, groups and people around the world closer together. It has a stimulating effect on crises and conflicts in that it provides for the freer flow of weaponry, information and finances for groups and individuals and it allows them to have wider strategic and operational effects than in the past.[174] John Arquilla et al. suggested that 'network based conflict and crime will become major phenomena in the decades ahead' – in other words, information-related capabilities will increasingly enable small and dispersed groups to communicate, coordinate and conduct armed violence without a precise central command or hierarchy, and that control over networks confers distinct advantages.[175] Global communications are increasingly used to increase the military capabilities of organised armed groups. Technological advances in communications allow insurgent groups to communicate with other groups and individuals outside

---

Development Command, Department of the Navy, Headquarters, United States Marine Corps, Washington, DC, 16 June 2006), 8–6.

171 FM 3–13, above n 169, Chapter I, 1(b), Chapter I, 2(a).

172 FM 3–24, above n 170, 2–34 and 2–35.

173 FM 3–13, above n 169, Ch. I, 2(c).

174 FM 3–24, above n 170, 2–5.

175 David Ronfeldt, John Arquilla, Graham E Fuller, and Melissa Fuller, *The Zapatista "Social Netwar" in Mexico* (Rand, 1998) 9.

areas that they physically control.[176] The ability to create and control the flow of information brings with it organisational, doctrinal, strategic and tactical advantages.

According to Burke, networked connectivity allows for three main types of networks to operate and constantly adapt. First, there are major groups or networks that are able to organise a centralised command structure in order to resource and coordinate large-scale military operations, control territory and incorporate subnetworks. For example, Islamic State has been able to integrate a number of Sunni militant networks into its preexisting overarching networks. Second, there are smaller networked militant groups that have some degree of organised structure: affiliates may have allegiance to and follow orders from major groups, whereas independents or factions may act autonomously of the central leadership of a major network or merely offer loose support. There is an increasing trend of affiliates and independents establishing links and loose coalitions with each other in order to coordinate their operations without directly involving the senior leadership of a major network. Third, there are self-radicalised individuals or small groups that are not directly connected to major groups or smaller militant groups, but who plan and carry out acts of violent extremism, sometimes in the name or ideology of major groups, or engage in nonviolent extremism online.[177]

According to Kilcullen, major groups such as Al-Qaeda and Islamic State are exploiting developments in information-related capabilities, such as social media, smart phones, YouTube and Google Earth, to disseminate propaganda instigating isolated acts of violent extremism as well as to develop new and dynamic forms of command and control that are overdiffuse transnational networks. These are enabling the widespread but seemingly isolated use of guerrilla or unconventional warfare techniques – not just the 'expeditionary approach' of organising in one country, training in another and then infiltrating the target country, but forming cells within countries, evading law enforcement agencies and international travel security measures and carrying out small-scale but mass-casualty attacks.[178] Similarly, Atwan notes that modern IRCs have enabled Islamic State to develop and expand a 'digital caliphate' in cyberspace, which has enabled it to network with individuals and groups around the world so as to finance and direct simultaneous and protracted acts of violence that range from small-scale attacks to large-scale military operations. Atwan suggests that part of the reason for this is that Islamic State's online social media and publications have enabled it to influence, recruit, train and operationalise a vast target audience around the world by inculcating a shared ideology and militant praxis. According to Atwan, off-the-shelf

176 FM 3–24, above n 170, 2–35.

177 Jason Burke, *The New Threat From Islamic Militancy* (Vintage, 2016) 16–22.

178 David Kilcullen, *Blood Year: Islamic State and the Failures of the War on Terror* (Hurst & Company, London 2016), 120–122.

anonymity products have facilitated the development and survivability of this 'digital caliphate'.[179]

In this complex environment, it is vital to engage in social network analysis of the information environment in order to determine how it affects the capabilities of actors to engage in armed hostilities as opposed to criminal acts of terrorism. In our complex information environment, it will be a constant challenge to identify what we can conceive of as hierarchical or centralised and coordinated forms of military organisation. We must be constantly on the lookout for new, dynamic and adaptive forms of organisation and ways of linking actors and groups within belligerent networks, as these are increasingly not based on formal hierarchical and networked structures of command and control involving two-way communication systems or face-to-face interaction for disseminating plans and orders. Furthermore, the cluttered information environment, mass use of social media and sophisticated 'off-the-shelf' encryption tools and techniques, especially for jihadist propaganda, make it harder to detect those actors who are recruiting, training and planning potentially numerous attacks with long lead times, as well as to detect concerted efforts to this effect.[180] In this regard, understanding the precise nature, scope, characteristics and effects of individuals, organisations and systems that collect, process, disseminate or act on information is essential in order to assess whether or not there is a state of internal or transnational non-international armed conflict in existence and, if not, to respond by using and developing law enforcement methods at the domestic and international levels.

It is suggested that as the constant evolution of terrorist methods – for example, of financing using Internet-based systems, new payment methods and development in wire transfers and electronic payments – quickly renders counter-terrorist measures obsolete, we need to remain vigilant about understanding the social dynamic and nuances that underlie both criminal activity and warfighting, in order that we do not overextend the permissiveness of the framework that governs the latter out of political and military expediency. Kilcullen suggests that the advances made in cloud computing, complex systems theory, big data analysis, remote observation and crowd-sourced analytics are enabling us to map and gain insights into virtual/human support networks as well as complex patterns of violence far more easily than in the past.[181]

In other words, we must gain a clear understanding of the transnational information environment at any given time so as to identify the adaptive and unconventional methods of command and control and to assess whether a group's organisational, fighting and logistical abilities mean that it has the ability to carry out sustained and concerted military operations in such a way that exceeds the

179 Abdel-Bari Atwan, *Islamic State: The Digital Caliphate* (Saqi Books, 2015) 1, 2, 9, 10.
180 Kilcullen, above n 178, 122.
181 David Kilcullen, *Out of the Mountains: The Coming Age of the Urban Guerrilla* (Hurst & Company, London, 2015), vii.

capacity of law enforcement agencies to respond.[182] According to Kilcullen, with regard to the consequences of our ability to map and gain insights into virtual/human networks in cyberspace, theories of conflict that are framed around a single threat or simple binary distinctions do not fit the complex information environment that we inhabit where there are many actors within a global network competing for influence and control and where nonstate actors are using organised violence with greater ease, frequency and reach.[183]

However, as the *Boškoski* guidelines do not specifically take into account the peculiarities of our global information environment and networked connectivity, the purpose of this discussion is to discuss the guidelines with reference to military doctrine on these issues so as to elucidate the conditions that are sufficient for a group to be regarded as 'organised' for the purposes of applying the law of armed conflict. Modern IRCs mean that the use of military force and approaches alone will, arguably, not be sufficient to combat the constantly evolving ways in which acts of terrorism are being instigated, planned and financed. It is suggested that domestic and international developments in criminalising the financing, planning and instigation of terrorist acts and developing expertise and techniques for the investigation and prosecuting of such offences, the freezing of assets and increased border security will be vital in ensuring that the use of targeted killings are kept in check and that fragile security environments are prevented from escalating. Indeed, the Terrorist Financing Convention of 1999 represents a valuable strategic approach of criminalising the planning and preparation of terrorist acts before they are committed and before they escalate in nature and scope, as well as only pursuing those networked individuals who provide support for unlawful terrorist acts either intentionally or knowingly.

Command and control

Increasingly, we see that IRCs, such as cell phones and social media, are used to plan and order attacks. In view of *Boškoski*, we need to examine whether the physical, information or cognitive dimensions present elements of a basic command structure with a recognised leader, structure and hierarchy, and internal regulations that establish a chain of command and disciplinary measures. A network analysis of the information environment may help us understand the organisational dynamics and thus the nature of the threat that we face. Furthermore, it may help us understand where the leadership resides and how it is distributed among members within the network.[184] For example, Kilcullen notes that from mid-2015, Islamic State *wilayat* networks had been established in Libya, Algeria, Tunisia, Yemen and Egypt. Rather than being viewed as mere guerrilla or terrorist groups, these were seen as formal territorial, legal and political entities with

182 FM 3-24, above n 170, 2-33 and 2-34.
183 Kilcullen, above n 181, 16.
184 FM 3-24, above n 170, 7.53.

direct connections to a centralised caliphate organisation and a central figure by the name of Abu Bakr al-Baghdadi who was able to set out the overall aims and objectives of the group together with his two deputies, Abu Muslim al-Turkmani and Abu Ali al-Anbari, and a variety of advisory councils and departments such as the military council and the security and intelligence council. Through this effective chain of command over large fighting and auxiliary forces, Islamic State conducted operations within a set of defined strategic guidelines and collaborated with networks in neighbouring regions which were able to carry out larger, widespread and coordinated attacks in Syria, Libya and Iraq. Some of these were coordinated large-scale attacks, whereas others were smaller self-radicalised attacks. Islamic State executive leadership began to establish territorial control comprising a network of cities linked by narrow strips of territory in Syria and Iraq and to carry out state-like functions, such as running courts, taxation and public services as well as intelligence and security services. Islamic State has also been able to recruit and receive vast numbers of foreign fighters travelling to Iraq, Syria, Libya, Yemen and Somalia. In areas such as these, Islamic State represents more of a conventional military threat to other nonstate actors as well as other states rather than a terrorist group per se. This is especially so that it can finance its operations from a diverse range of revenue streams such as control over oil fields; trafficking in weapons, drugs and artefacts; kidnapping; and robberies. However, although major groups such as Islamic State and Al-Qaeda may be able to launch conventional attacks in the Middle East, we must closely examine their links with peripheral actors and networks in other regions in the Middle East, Europe, Asia and the United States, as well as the roles and capabilities these peripheral actors are performing, in order to assess whether the overarching network has the organisational resources and capabilities to launch widespread and coordinated attacks in these regions.[185]

Accordingly, at the strategic and operational levels, where a group's IRCs allow for an identifiable leadership to plan, order and coordinate large-scale attacks, even if this is done remotely and by dispersed groups outside their physical control, then there is the potential for this to reach the level of transnational non-international armed conflict. However, it is important for there to be some control and effect over an insurgent network that exists in the physical and cognitive domains. It is suggested that there does not have to be complete control over these domains at all times, as this is not realistic in an information environment with a high degree of surveillance that compels groups to avoid detection by adopting diffuse structures.[186] Accordingly, there may be no clear organisational structure that mirrors a conventional chain of command involving a core leadership, guerrillas, cadres, auxiliaries and underground cells. Thus, rather than a hierarchical leadership structure, the organisational structure may be diffusely networked within a complex and cluttered information environment involving a

185 Kilcullen, above n 178, 127, 128, 133, 214. Atwan, above n 179, 140–144.
186 FM 3-24, above n 170, 10-36.

range of actors or entities that provide basic support functions, and this network will be constantly learning and adapting.[187]

In a networked organisation it is important to understand the roles that actors play in a network and the links that exist between them for financing, as well as providing tactical and operational support, to produce effects that are adverse to the military operations or military capacity of a party to an armed conflict or, alternatively, that inflict death, injury or destruction on persons or objects protected against direct attack. What we are looking for primarily are 'critical actors' or central points of communication or influence that have an influence or measurable impact on a network that is capable of carrying out military operations in the physical domain.[188] Critical actors have a great influence over what flows through the network and are able, directly or indirectly, to influence other actors within that network.[189]

In particular, they will have a measurable impact upon what we may describe as underground 'guerrilla units' or 'cells' which are able to carry out small-unit tactical operations or which can mass or coordinate for larger operations, for example, directly recruiting and providing some tactical support or indirectly providing general guidance and support, thus enabling a pattern of individuals to self-recruit and operationalise in the name of the cause or strategy, for example, what may be described as a digital *levée en masse* or mass uprising.[190] The information environment may indicate a highly centralised network that is dominated by one or more centralised actors. However, if these actors are removed or damaged, then the network may fragment into unconnected subnetworks.[191] Where such fragmentation or disaggregation occurs, then a decentralised network may result. A characteristic of this is that there is now no single point of failure, as operational and tactical decisions may be made by different actors within the network rather than by a central or critical actor. A major network may fragment into numerous subnetworks that have numerous connections to the operational environment, but not necessarily with each other. Here, subnetworks may have direct multiple connections with each other; they may have only very loose and indirect links with a few central actors and other subnetworks; they may now be completely isolated and freestanding.[192]

Under such circumstances, it is important for us to gauge network density, which is a general indicator of how connected individuals are in a network – the more links that actors have to other actors within a network, the greater the density.[193] Decentralised networks may have low network density and be complex to map. In other words, unlike a hierarchical network, low network density means

187 Ibid., 4–79, 4–88.
188 Ibid., 4–77.
189 Ibid., 4–96.
190 Ibid., 4–80.
191 Ibid., 4–95.
192 Ibid., 4–89 and 4–95.
193 Ibid., 4–99.

that such networks are not acting as a unified force, but rather as a disaggregated and atomised force.[194] Under such circumstances, it is unlikely that a central actor will be able to enforce discipline, ensure that orders are carried out and that there is compliance with humanitarian law. However, a central actor may still be able to issue general, albeit one-directional, ideological, operational and tactical guidelines to their target audience. They may still control what flows through the network and have great influence over peripheral actors without having direct links to them or direct influence over them.[195] Kilcullen notes the contemporary phenomenon of self-recruited individuals or groups acting upon general directions, propaganda, tactics and techniques, usually disseminated openly on the Internet by 'symbolic' or charismatic figures without their having to give any direct communication, support or coordination. Kilcullen terms this form of remote radicalisation and operationalisation as 'leaderless resistance'. More specifically, the individuals and groups who carry out violence ranging from small acts of violent extremism to large-scale military operations may be extremely peripheral in that they have no direct ties to central figures or networks and are operating in a clandestine fashion in foreign countries. Central figures do not have to establish a formal hierarchical structure or chain of command based upon two-way communication systems in order to disseminate secret plans and orders, but merely make public statements and general commands on YouTube or social media. These then become linked via social media platforms to other actors who issue detailed operational and tactical guidance enabling individuals or small groups to act autonomously and on their own initiative. For instance, Anwar Al-Aulaqi was designated as a 'Specially Designated Global Terrorist' because he was said to have provided financial, material or technological support for actors of terrorism that included recruiting, influencing and training persons to fight, such as Nidal Hassan who fatally shot thirteen people and injured more than thirty others in the Fort Hood mass shooting on 5 November 2009, and Umar Farouk Abdulmutallab who is popularly referred to as the 'Underwear Bomber'. Al-Aulaqi is also said to have inspired the London 7/7 attacks as well as plots in Toronto in 2006 and Fort Dix in 2007 through his sermons available on the Internet and on DVD.[196]

This state of affairs necessitates rigorous social network analysis of the information environment in order to understand the organisational dynamics of a network and its leadership. We need to identify the nature and scope of leadership and how it is distributed throughout a network. It may be that members have a high degree of autonomy which enables the network to avoid detection and increase its operational capabilities.[197] It is suggested that even though central actors may be unable directly to enforce discipline, to ensure that orders are

194 Ibid., 4–89.
195 Ibid., 4–96.
196 Kilcullen, above n 178, 123.
197 FM 3–24, above n 170, 7–53.

carried out and that there is compliance with humanitarian law, this is not necessarily detrimental to a networked group being sufficiently organised for the purposes of applying the paradigm of hostilities. Under such conditions, we should be careful to ensure that there is reliable intelligence that indicates a pattern of individuals or cells indirectly responding to and operating in a manner that is consistent with the general guidance issued by central actors (for example, by following instructional videos or audio files or training manuals and by publicly professing a commitment to the cause). Furthermore, in the absence of a hierarchical structure made up of a direct chain of command, we would need sufficient intelligence to demonstrate a pattern indicative of a unified fighting force. Namely, that remote leadership is inculcating similar ideological, tactical and operational decisions and effects across a decentralised network. Where this is not the case, then this would indicate that the network does not constitute a sufficiently unified or organised fighting force capable of mounting adverse military operations.[198]

Ability to mount protracted operations

In response to *Boškoski*, we need to examine the information environment in order to assess whether a group's information-related capabilities and network dynamics enable it to conduct sustained and concerted military operations, such as manoeuvring fighters and carrying out coordinated hit-and-run operations. We also need to examine whether IRCs are being used to coordinate military-grade logistics, such as supplying weaponry and equipment, financing, providing military training and recruiting new members. There should be evidence in the information environment that a network has some unity and the ability to speak with one voice. In our modern information environment, IRCs, such as cell phones, text messaging, Voice over Internet Protocol, GPS devices, Google Earth and the Internet, are being used to organise and coordinate actors within networks. Urban populations within developing countries are now highly connected and networked, expanding their reach, influence and support.[199] According to Kilcullen, the same connectivity that enables licit trade also enables people to self-organise in 'dark networks' where illicit trade, trafficking, piracy and terrorism flow.[200] Furthermore, 'dark networks' may be used to enable violence across a spectrum ranging from criminal activity through to transnational terrorism and transnational non-international armed conflict.[201] Accordingly, we need to be careful in examining IRCs in order to assess whether they are being used to conduct coordinated and large-scale military attacks, even by what may appear to be a decentralised and fragmented organisation in the physical domain.[202] For exam-

198 FM 3–24, above n 170, 4–89.
199 Kilcullen, above n 181, 32.
200 Ibid., 34.
201 Ibid., 51.
202 FM 3–24, above n 170, 2–36.

ple, Kilcullen notes that in the 2011 Libyan uprising, groups used social media platforms and networks through improvised satellite phones and Internet uplinks for remote and decentralised command and control. The command system was distributed through multiple networks and remote platforms and was used to play a practical coordination and logistics function for self-organising corps of volunteers and nonstate armed groups, for example, by developing a narrative or common cause and distributing military intelligence and tactical and operational guidance, as well as sending out requests for assistance. According to Kilcullen, this allowed 'a diverse movement of small groups, spread across several coastal cities to act in a unified manner against the regime, making this a true case of networked-enabled insurgency [with] supporters of the uprising from all over the world'. Effectively, Libya in 2011 was a novel example of a mass networked mobilisation emerging in cyberspace that had direct physical effects rising to the basic intensity threshold of an armed conflict.[203] Thus, where a group's IRCs allow for the detailed planning, organisation and coordination of attacks as part of large-scale military operations, then a group's network may be regarded as sufficiently organised for the purposes of applying the paradigm of hostilities.

Returning to the idea of network density, where the information environment reveals a high network density among a range of actors and entities, this would indicate that a group has the networked capabilities to conduct widespread, coordinated and protracted military operations. This means that they may be sufficiently organised to constitute a dangerous military threat and thus subject to the framework of hostilities.[204] Accordingly, this involves an assessment of a network's ability to share information in near real time, anonymously and securely, and then to act on it in a coordinated fashion.[205] To this end, we would need intelligence regarding direct and/or indirect links between auxiliary cells and guerrilla cells, as well as the ways in which a group is using IRCs to recruit, train and motivate followers and organise the logistics of weaponry and people as well as the financing of military operations.[206] For example, we would need evidence that there are auxiliary cells that perform logistics operations such as maintaining safe houses, moving weapons, intelligence gathering, propaganda, recruitment and communications support.[207] Auxiliaries may also include economic support systems that directly fund military and political operations, such as fundraising, unlawful appropriation, illicit trade and trafficking, banking and finance operations and laundering through businesses.[208] We would need intelligence demonstrating that leadership and/or auxiliaries have direct and/or indirect ties to guerrilla units or cells that can conduct coordinated and protracted small-unit tactical military operations or which can mass for larger protracted military

203 Kilcullen, above n 181, 203–204.
204 FM 3-24, above n 170, 4-100 and 4-102.
205 FM 3-13, above n 169, Ch. 1(a).
206 FM 3-24, above n 170, 8-6.
207 Ibid., 4-85.
208 Ibid., 4-84.

operations.[209] For instance, the Mumbai terror attacks of 2008 saw a leadership cell operate from a safe house in Pakistan by giving intelligence, directions, instructions and warnings to small attack units on the ground in India by using Skype, SMS text messages and mobile phone calls. Although this caught Indian security forces by surprise and enabled attack forces to take diversionary countermeasures for a short period, ultimately it did not exceed the capacity of India's counterterrorism force to contain the attackers eventually; this small-unit tactical operation was directed at civilians rather than a large military operation or a coordinated series of assaults against police or military forces.[210] This can be contrasted with the unrest in Kingston in 2010 when Jamaican authorities attempted to enforce a US extradition request of Christopher Coke – the head of an international crime syndicate named 'the Shower Posse' which controlled the Tivoli Gardens area of Kingston and had previously attacked police stations. It exceeded the capacity of civilian law enforcement to respond as it required a full-scale military effort lasting around a week and involving over 1,000 police and soldiers engaged in house-to-house fighting with large numbers of casualties to gain control over Tivoli Gardens.[211] Nevertheless, the situation was declared a state of emergency and, overall, it was treated as a law enforcement operation to arrest and extradite, rather than kill, Christopher Coke. He eventually pled guilty to racketeering and drug-related charges in a New York federal court.

Returning to the idea of network density, a decrease in network density indicates that a group is becoming fragmented and isolated and that its organisational ability is reduced. As a network's capability to act as a unified fighting force is diminished, it becomes less of a military threat and more amenable to law enforcement methods. Furthermore, disaggregated and atomised groups are more difficult to detect and disrupt, and so may require a more intelligence-led and individualised social network assessment in order to understand their capabilities and the threat that they pose over time.[212] Another complicating feature of social network analysis is that a network may be diffusely made up of a range of criminal, guerrilla and auxiliary entities as well as individuals acting alone without any direct connections to any other individuals or groups within the network.[213] Some of these entities may not be aware that they are playing indirect support roles within a network that contains belligerent elements. Changes to network density and belligerent functions across a network should be continuously monitored and mapped out over time, allowing states to develop and change their tactics so that they are more in line with law enforcement operations as a group's IRCs become reduced, its network becomes more fragmented and its military capabilities diminished.[214] For example, Kilcullen notes that at the time of 9/11, Al-Qaeda had an organised

209 Ibid., 4–80.
210 Kilcullen, above n 181, 52, 62, 64.
211 Ibid., 90.
212 FM 3-24, above n 170, 4–89.
213 Ibid., 4–77.
214 FM 3-24, above n 170, 4–101, 4–78 and 4–77.

and hierarchical network of commanders, committees, camps, groups and support networks. This high network density exposed it to attack, and so it quickly fragmented and developed forms of 'leaderless resistance' using IRCs to influence target audiences to support its efforts and to mount attacks. This process of disaggregation led to a proliferation of smaller attacks from isolated groups, factions and affiliates. However, as seen with Islamic State, its major networks have been able to disaggregate under aerial bombardment and move into safe zones, only to reform and expand military capabilities in and across new areas.[215]

However, even where network density is low and its elements are atomised, in our modern information environment the network may still be able to carry out what amounts to tacitly coordinated military operations where central or critical actors issue general and one-way operational and tactical guidelines that are operationalised and acted upon by isolated but free-standing and autonomous individuals, auxiliaries, guerrilla units or underground cells. Under such circumstances isolated subnetworks may have their own leadership, fighters and auxiliary forces enabling them to mount widespread attacks.[216] Kilcullen notes that groups such as Al-Qaeda and Islamic State are increasingly disseminating their tactics and techniques via online magazines, such as *Inspire* and *Dabiq* which enable individuals and groups to operationalise and mount attacks without any direct contact or formal membership of a terrorist organisation.[217]

Under such circumstances, it may be sufficient for individuals or cells to act in a manner that is consistent with general guidance without the need for further centralised operational and tactical support and coordination as long as there is intelligence revealing a pattern to this effect. It may be the case that there is a small networked group with actors on the periphery with very few, if any, links to this central core. This may be the case where there is a group within one country and a number of 'lone wolf' actors on the periphery in other countries. This would tend to indicate that the organisation has a low network density and has a weak connection to its centre. In order to understand the nature of the threat they present, it is important to examine the nature and scope of their connection to a central network, as well as networks outside the theatre of operations, and in order to assess whether they contribute to the efficiency, cohesion and operational capability of a network.[218] In this regard it is important to make a cautionary note with reference to Kilcullen, who suggests that global connectivity has increased the threat of 'home-grown terrorists', whereby individuals and groups become remotely radicalised and organised online through propaganda on social networks and social media, very often with little or no face-to-face contact with foreign terrorist groups, and gain basic training on tactics and weaponry to carry out small-scale attacks. Kilcullen argues that many, if not

215 Kilcullen, above n 178, 124.
216 FM 3-24, above n 170, 4–87.
217 Kilcullen, above n 178, 122.
218 FM 3-24, above n 170, 4–97 and 4–98.

most, of these remotely organised plots and attacks do not represent a strategic or military threat to their countries as they are disaggregated and atomised individuals or cells which are amenable to counterterrorism operations by law enforcement agencies, that is unless they begin to become more widespread, coordinated and protracted, which is generally not the case at present due to Western and European domestic counterterrorism efforts. For example, Kilcullen suggests that in some instances, attacks may not be viewed as a single terrorist incident, but rather as one part of a sustained campaign of guerrilla warfare. This might be said of the Paris attacks of January and November 2015. However, Kilcullen argues that although they represent an escalation in terms of the guerrilla means and methods of warfare, and although there is evidence linking the Paris attacks to a transnational support network as well as attacks in other countries, it is suggested that these are not sufficiently widespread, networked or intense enough to rise to the level of a transnational armed conflict. Furthermore, even though individuals or groups acting in the name of Islamic State increasingly claim responsibility for attacks, there is often little or no evidence to suggest that they actually planned, resourced and coordinated attacks. Accordingly, it is suggested that many instances of what Kilcullen describes as 'leaderless resistance', 'guerrilla terrorism' and 'remote radicalisation' are to be situated within the framework of law enforcement. Just because actors or small networks can remotely radicalise and launch attacks in the belief that they are part of a bigger network does not mean that they are actually part of a network that can launch widespread and coordinated operations in the face of a system of law enforcement that can effectively respond to this complex threat, whilst at the same time upholding human rights and civil liberties. This is an important issue given that we will be dealing with these types of threats over a long period and so we must resist attempts to aggregate atomised attacks and plots into a persistent and long-term armed conflict.[219] Similarly Atwan and Burke suggest that although Islamic State has developed a global jihadist network in cyberspace, this may not translate into a network that has military capabilities or the ability to create effects in the physical dimension. Instead, it may be regarded as a set of subnetworks that create effects, most of which do not rise above the level of what we could describe as nonviolent or even violent extremism, which expresses similar, if not shared, ideas and statements. Individuals may republish propaganda on social media, condone militant activities in comments on or profess allegiance or sympathy on YouTube.[220]

As the notion of a 'conflict zone' is not defined within IHL treaties, and thus the geographical scope of application is unclear, it is suggested that social network analysis is important to try and confine 'war zones' to physically confined areas where enemy forces are engaged directly, conducting or supporting

219 Kilcullen, above n 178, 202–28.

220 Atwan, above n 179, 4; and Burke above n 177, 206–207.

combat operations, and to resist spillover into 'peace zones', where the intensity of violence does not reach that indicated in the *Boškoski* guidelines, but that may contain concealed and supportive elements of a unified virtual network. However, even though global connectivity renders it increasingly difficult to create legal, strategic and operational boundaries between such zones, we should constantly attempt to ensure that the physical domain of the paradigm of hostilities does not track and extend out into the peripheries of the virtual domain, especially because, as noted by Kilcullen, this can draw in populations and forces anywhere on the planet that have no geographical connection to the conflict, in the sense of being directly involved in conduct or support. This creates the risk that the conduct of hostilities paradigm can spill over and prevail outside of combat zones. In this sense 'virtual theatres' can serve to undermine the spatial conception of a war zone.[221] This renders the requirement that a group controls territory or has the ability to do so even more critical in setting out spatial boundaries of the paradigm of hostilities, and we must closely scrutinise the ability of central actors to maintain direct and continuous connectivity with coordinated fighting units over vast virtual networks which create effects in the physical domain of hostilities. Where actors are 'virtually' in a remote 'war zone' but physically present in a 'peace zone' that is geographically disconnected from actual hostilities, then we should consider whether law enforcement methods are sufficient to respond to the 'virtual threat' that they present in their peace zone and, if not, then ensure that any targeted killing is as attenuated as possible so as to be in accordance with what is justifiable on the basis of Hague targeting principles and self-defence. However, outside the context of an international armed conflict, the city, region or country where they are residing should not be treated as a war zone subject to the paradigm of hostilities.

Where individuals and underground cells are self-recruited and freestanding, it will be extremely difficult to demonstrate that a 'critical actor' has caused their actions and that they are actually part of a networked organisation that can adversely affect the military operations or military capacity of a party to an armed conflict or, alternatively, to inflict death, injury, or destruction on persons or objects protected against direct attack. Central networks may claim responsibility for attacks, but this may often be mere pretence. It will also be a challenge to identify the ability of a network to 'speak with one voice' and for central actors to ensure uniform disengagement from a digital *levée en masse*. Although certain parts of a network may be disrupted or neutralised, other parts may continue fighting or lie dormant and opportunistically launch an attack where the opportunity arises. This suggests that such an organisation will be more amendable to law enforcement methods.[222]

---

221 Kilcullen, above n 181, 171–172.
222 FM 3–24, above n 170, 4–89.

Assessing belligerent nexus in the information environment

Finally, in an unconventional environment it is a major challenge to establish a nexus between an individual and any surrounding hostilities, either on the basis of their direct participation in hostilities or their membership of an organised armed group, in order to categorise them as a lethal threat. Where an individual does not constitute a direct and immediate lethal threat, recourse will have to be made to the information and cognitive dimensions in order to ascertain their intentions and motivations, as, more often than not, this will be the decisive issue when it comes to targeting on the basis of status and ensuring that it is done legitimately and lawfully. This requires us to understand the information environment in order to build up a picture not only of an armed group but also of the population in which it resides. We must engage in social network analysis to build up an intelligence picture of the 'social dynamic that sustains ongoing fighting', how individual actors interact with one another and how networks are being used for warfighting. In most civilianised operational environments, this will require an individual-level analysis, and the IRCs that states have at their disposal render this practical and feasible in many situations. Not only that, the use of IRCs can also help us distinguish between those who foresee or intend adversely to affect the military operations or military capacity of a party to an armed conflict or, alternatively, to inflict death, injury or destruction on persons or objects protected against direct attack and take some practical contribution to this end from those who merely provide indirect support without foresight or awareness or those who merely sympathise with the cause. From the information environment, we may be able to glean intelligence of an individual's subjective state of mind through statements, pictures, photographs, media files and private communications in cyberspace or to make an objective assessment on the basis of their behaviour or tacit knowledge.[223] Although it is beyond the scope of this discussion, one of the implications of violence within our information environment is that although there may be many purportedly justifiable invasions into our privacy within the information domain and public physical domain, the very existence of the global information environment should help states understand the nature, scope and capabilities of networks and the roles that individuals play within them and take greater mitigation and precautionary approaches – in particular through real-time data coming from virtual/human networks, big data analysis, remote observation and crowd-sourced analytics. This should enable states to regulate themselves predominantly within the paradigm of law enforcement without having to resort to the permissive Hague rules on the use of force – but this will require ongoing dialogue between governments and their intelligence and police services.

---

223 FM 3-24, above n 170, 4–90.

Limits on autoqualification

The general notion is that primary duty bearers are best suited to making self-classifications/autoqualifications of situations of armed conflict or states of emergency as they are closest to 'facts on the ground', and so in the best position to classify the prevailing state of affairs. Indeed, as stated in the *Commentary* to the Geneva Conventions, '[a]ll international conventions . . . are primarily the affair of Governments . . . and it is upon Governments that the duty of applying them devolves'.[224] However, it is suggested that this is a slightly outdated notion in that following the Geneva Conventions, we have seen the development of jurisprudence from international criminal tribunals regarding classification, as well as HRL mechanisms vis-à-vis the supervision of derogation regimes.

International criminal tribunals

As discussed earlier, the ability of primary duty bearers, that is, states, to self-classify or autoqualify a situation is limited by the ability of courts of law to make *ex post facto* determinations to this effect.[225] The jurisprudence of the ICTY which elucidates the scope *ratio materiae* of customary IHL, CA3 and APII may be viewed as setting limits on states' discretion when it comes to classification. *Boškoski* suggests that the labels that parties to a conflict attach to a situation are 'immaterial' in the sense that they are not binding in the context of international criminal law proceedings. The rationale for this is that status determinations 'by States or their officials, are made on a political, not legal basis, and cannot be directly interpreted as evidence of, or a legal interpretation of, a factual state of affairs . . .'[226] Therefore, self-classification by primary duty bearers can be regarded as declaratory rather than constitutive or, in other words, 'provisional and not definitive'.[227]

It is suggested that it is not only international criminal tribunals that have set limits on autoqualification, but international and regional human rights mechanisms also. In this regard, although the Trial Chamber in *Boškoski* ruled that although the factual and legal classification of a state of affairs by national courts and UN bodies is not binding within the context of international criminal proceedings, they 'may have legal consequences'.[228] Accordingly, the Trial Chamber

---

224 Jean S Pictet (ed), *Geneva Convention for the Amelioration of the Condition of the Wounded and Sick in Armies in the Field* (International Committee of the Red Cross, Geneva, 1952) (Commentary I) 39.

225 *Akayesu*, above n 23, 603.

226 *Boškoski* (Trial Judgment) above n 69, 192.

227 *Asylum Case (Columbia v Peru)* (Judgment) [1950] ICJ Rep 266, 274–275.

228 *Boškoski* (Trial Judgment) above n 69, 192; See also, Dapo Akande and Hannah Tonkin, 'International Commissions of Inquiry: A New Form of Adjudication?' (2012) *EJIL: Talk!* <www.ejiltalk.org/international-commissions-of-inquiry-a-new-form-of-adjudication/> accessed 1 October 2013.

in *Boškoski* accorded, *inter alia*, UN resolutions with persuasive value in the course of its own reasoning on subject matter jurisdiction and in this way they can be considered 'authoritative determinations' on the status of a situation.

Human rights mechanisms

As suggested earlier, human rights mechanisms have a vital role to play in carrying out derogation review which can ensure that the right to life continues to apply in extreme situations of violence, which, as discussed earlier, can take place in what can be regarded as a 'grey area' of legal regulation, for example, situations of occupation, security operations with the consent of a host nation or multinational force and counterterror operations. In this regard, derogation regimes need close supervision as they may justify emergency powers in response to actual or imminent threats, whereas the use of military force under IHL requires an actual armed conflict. Care thus needs to be taken to ensure that military force under the permissive framework of IHL is not used in response to imminent threats – for example, the anticipated threat of an armed conflict – but rather the framework of IHRL vis-à-vis the right to life.[229]

It is submitted that the threshold criteria discussed earlier should be used by human rights mechanisms in conjunction with their own threshold criteria for the existence of states of emergency in order to have a clearer objective framework with which to ascertain the credibility of claims that there is an actual or imminent state of emergency or, more pertinently to this discussion, in order to distinguish situations that have reached the threshold of an armed conflict from those that have not. Such a development is necessary given that human rights frameworks establishing emergency powers were 'handled in an amateurish fashion'[230] by not clearly spelling out what constitutes the ceiling vis-à-vis the substantive and procedural aspects of the right to life or, in other words, sequencing the frameworks of HRL and IHL in relation to the use of force.[231] Furthermore, reference to the indicative guidelines on status determination described earlier can serve to bolster their own qualification of a state of affairs for the purposes of applying and contextualising human rights law standards relative to the use of force in exceptional situations of violence.

---

229 Provost, above n 16, 271.

230 Simpson, above n 13.

231 Siracusa Principles on the Limitation and Derogation Provisions in the ICCPR, adopted by an expert meeting convened by the International Commission of Jurists in Siracusa, Italy from 30 April to 4 May 1984, submitted for circulation to the UN Commission on Human Rights by the Government of the Netherlands; ECOSOC (UNCHR) 'Siracusa Principles on the Limitation and Derogation Provisions in the International Covenant on Civil and Political Rights' (24 September 1984) UN Doc ECOSOC E/CN.4/1985/4, Article 40 underlines this general omission by stating that '[i]nternal conflict and unrest that do not constitute a grave and imminent threat to the life of the nation cannot justify derogations under Article 4'.

As will now be discussed, under the ECHR derogation regime, the ECHR has proved willing to intervene in order to challenge a state's self-classification or autoqualification of a state of emergency. Thus, it is possible to suggest that derogation regimes and armed conflict threshold criteria are not merely autointerpretative, but also justiciable in the sense that there is increasing scope for international review that can serve to promote the right to life in situations of extreme violence by qualifying them as not objectively amounting to an armed conflict.[232] Human rights mechanisms may use such criteria to filter out cases reaching the threshold of an armed conflict at the admissibility or merits stages and refer on to more appropriate mechanisms. This may serve to placate states who feel that cases brought under human rights law impede the operational effectiveness through the 'judicialisation of war'. If a human rights body can classify a situation as an armed conflict, then this may ensure that if a state becomes involved in a situation or operation amounting to such, then there is no prospect of a detailed investigation into the lawfulness of each and every death and the ability to claim compensation in the case of unlawfulness, and vice-versa. Alternatively, courts could entertain the merits of a case and apply Geneva Convention rights, but interpret them in a way that takes account of international humanitarian law, that is, by reading down Article 2, for instance, so that if an individual is killed in the context of an armed conflict, it will be deemed to be lawful as long as the use of force is consistent with IHL even if it is not absolutely necessary as required by Article 2. However, it may be preferable for human rights courts to recognise their lack of legal capacity and competence to adjudicate situations that amount to an armed conflict and give states a wide margin of appreciation, but be clearer about where this will apply.

Reviewing states of crisis and conflict

The European Court of Human Rights

In *Lawless v Ireland*, the former European Commission defined a 'public emergency' as 'a situation of exceptional and imminent danger or crisis affecting the general public, as distinct from particular groups, and constituting a threat to the organised life of the community which composes the State in question'.[233] Similarly, in the Greek case, the commission developed these objective standards by stating that to constitute a 'public emergency', a crisis 'must be actual or imminent', 'its effects must involve the whole nation', 'the continuance of the organised life of the community must be threatened' and 'the crisis or danger must be exceptional, in that the normal measures or restrictions, permitted by the convention for the maintenance of public safety, health, and order, are plainly inadequate'.[234]

232 Provost, above n 16, 339.
233 *Lawless v Ireland* European Commission Decision, Series B (1960–61) 90.
234 *The Greek Case (Denmark, Norway, Sweden and the Netherlands v Greece)* (Application No 3321/67) (1969) 12 Yearbook 170 (EComHR) 113.

However, in *Lawless v Ireland* it was stated that 'it is for the Court to determine whether the conditions laid down in Article 15 for the exercise of the exceptional right of derogation have been fulfilled'[235] and this indicates that a state's discretion to 'autoqualify' is limited in that the court may objectively review whether or not there existed a 'public emergency threatening the life of the nation'.[236] This principle grants states 'a certain measure of discretion in assessing the extent strictly required by the exigencies of the situation',[237] or in other words states have a margin of appreciation vis-à-vis the enforcement of human rights and the measures taken in response to crisis situations.[238] According to this doctrine, the state is presumptively in a better position than a supranational body to make a status determination.[239] Indeed, as stated in *Brannigan and McBride*, the rationale for this presumption is that

> [b]y reason of their direct and continuous contact with the pressing needs of the moment, the national authorities are in principle in a better position than the international judge to decide both on the presence of such an emergency and on the nature and scope of derogations necessary to avert it. Accordingly, in this matter, a wide margin of appreciation should be left to the national authorities.[240]

Furthermore, in *Lawless* the commission stated that

> having regard to the high responsibility which a government has to its people to protect them against any threat to the life of the nation, it is evident that a certain discretion – a certain margin of appreciation – must be kept by the Government in determining whether there exists a public emergency which threatens the life of the nation and which must be dealt with by exceptional measures derogating from its normal obligations under the Convention.[241]

Thus, although the general proposition is that states are in a better position than supranational bodies to qualify a state of affairs, this proposition does not

---

235 *Lawless* (Commission), above n 233, 22.
236 Ibid., 90.
237 *Lawless* (Commission), above n 233, 28.
238 O Gross and F Ni Aolain, *Law in Times of Crisis, Emergency Powers in Theory and Practice* (Cambridge University Press, 2006) 262.
239 *Brannigan and McBride v UK* (Application Nos14553/89 and 14554/89) (1993) Series A No 258-B [43]; *Ireland v UK* (Application No 5310/71) (1978) Series A No 25 [79]; *Aksoy v Turkey* (Application No 21987/93) ECHR 1996-VI [68].
240 Given modern communications systems, it is suggested that the proposition that national authorities will always be better informed and appraised of the facts on the ground than supranational bodies is no longer necessarily valid or plausible. Indeed, with the support of modern telecommunications systems, it may be the case that IGOs and NGOs may be better appraised of the facts on the ground than national authorities.
241 *Lawless* (Commission), above n 233, 90.

preclude judicial supervision and review of autoqualifications under certain circumstances. Indeed, in the Cyprus case, the European Commission stated that it had the 'competence and the duty' to review the validity of Article 15 derogations by assessing whether the objective conditions of a state of emergency are in place'.[242] This was subsequently affirmed by the ECtHR in a series of cases where it set out the objective conditions for the existence of a state of emergency and held that it had the power to intervene in order to assess claims regarding the existence of a state of emergency.[243] Thus, with regard to the power to intervene, in the *Greek* case the commission found that the government's claim that there was a state of emergency to be unfounded,[244] and in *Brannigan and McBride* both the commission and the court made their own determinations of the existence of a state of emergency. However, this power is qualified in that the power to intervene and override a state's characterisation of a situation as constituting a state of emergency may only occur where it is unreasonable and falls outside its 'margin of appreciation', or where the facts do not satisfy the objective threshold criteria for a state of emergency.[245] Thus although 'national authorities' such as domestic courts have a wide margin of appreciation under Article 15, the ECtHR may intervene to review a state's determination of a state of emergency and whether the measures taken in response were strictly required by the exigencies of the situation 'only if satisfied that the national court had misinterpreted or misapplied Article 15 or the Court's jurisprudence under that Article or reached a conclusion which was manifestly unreasonable'.[246]

Although in *Lawless*, the commission demonstrated a high degree of deference by stating that the 'existence at the time of a "public emergency threatening the life of the nation" was reasonably deduced by the Irish government from a combination of several factors',[247] the commission showed itself willing and capable to take a much more interventionist and nondeferential approach in the Greek case where the government under the 'The National Revolution' invoked Article 15 in order to suspend human rights and introduce martial law. In particular, the commission carried out an objective review of the facts that were submitted to it by the parties and also which were gathered as part of an independent fact-finding exercise. On the basis of the evidence it was able to collect, it rejected the government's factual and substantive claim that there was an imminent threat

---

242 *Cyprus v Turkey* (Application no 25781/94) (1996) DR 86-A, 13.

243 Provost, above n 16, 317; *Ireland v UK*, above n 239 [78] – [82]; *Brannigan and McBride*, above n 239, [569]–[570]; *Aksoy v Turkey*, above n 239, [586]–[587]; *Lawless v Ireland* (Application No 332/57) (Judgment of 14 Nov 1960) (Merits) Series A No 3 [56]; See also, UNHRC 'Report of the Human Rights Committee on the Work of its 48th Session' (1996) UN Doc A/51/40, 349.

244 *The Greek Case*, above n 234, 125.

245 Lawless (Merits) above n 243 [56]; *Ireland v UK*, above n 239 [78]–[82]; *Brannigan and McBride*, above n 239 [43] & [569]; *Aksoy v Turkey*, above n 239, [68].

246 *A and Others v UK* (Application No 3455/05) ECHR (Grand Chamber) 19 February 2009, 174.

247 *Lawless* (Commission), above n 233, 90.

as the evidence suggested that a *coup d'etat* was 'neither planned at the time, or seriously anticipated by either the military or police authorities'.[248] The court in *Lawless* left open the question of whether a breach of the notification of derogation requirement under Article 15 paragraph (3) of the ECHR would prevent reliance on Article 15 paragraph (1), that is, the ability to derogate in that Sir Humphrey Waldock, speaking on behalf of the commission, stated that 'the Commission, as at present advised, hesitates to say that the right of the State to justify its actions . . . may never be affected by its failure to keep the Secretary-General informed'.[249]

The United Nations Human Rights Committee

The UN Human Rights Committee has stated that derogations are justified only where they are 'exceptional and temporary in nature',[250] and in this respect it has the mandate to 'conduct a careful analysis under each article of the Covenant based on an objective assessment of the actual situation'.[251] However, its ability to carry out derogation review is precluded in situations where a state has not ratified the Optional Protocol to the ICCPR allowing individuals to bring complaints under the covenant before the committee. However, failing this, derogation review may still occur to a limited extent through the mechanism of country reports pursuant to Article 40(4) ICCPR.

The Inter-American Court and Commission of Human Rights

This notion that states of emergency are exceptional and temporary phenomena is also reflected in the decisions of the Inter-American Court and Commission of Human Rights. Under Article 27 of the American Convention on Human Rights, derogations are justified only in 'extremely serious circumstances' or 'exceptional situations' and do not affect that applicability of nonderogable rights.[252] Thus, the Inter-American Court and the Commission of Human Rights also play a role in derogation review to ensure that emergency powers are not abused by unbridled executive power. They do this by closely monitoring whether derogating

248 *The Greek Case*, above n 234, 159; Gross & Aolain, above n 238, 274.

249 *Lawless* case, Publications of the European Court of Human Rights, Series B, Pleadings, Oral Arguments, Doc 1960–61, p. 388; Rosalyn Higgins, 'Derogations under Human Rights Treaties' (1976–1977) 48 (1) *British Yearbook of International Law* 290.

250 *Sergio Euben Lopez Burgos v Uruguay* (1981) UNHRC Communication No R.12/52, UN Doc Supp No 40 (A/36/40), 110 and 176.

251 UNHRC 'CCPR General Comment No 29: Article 4: Derogations during a State of Emergency' (24 July 2001) UN Doc CCPR/C/21/Rev1/Add11, 6.

252 *Report on the Situation of Human Rights in Argentina*, Inter-American Commission on Human Rights, OEA/Ser L/V/II 49 Doc 19 corr 1 (11 April 1980), 25–27; *Habeas Corpus in Emergency Situations*, Advisory Opinion OC-8/87, Inter-American Court of Human Rights Series A No 8 (30 January 1987) 23.

measures are actually justified by the circumstances,[253] and this depends on the 'character, intensity, pervasiveness, and the particular context of the emergency and upon the corresponding proportionality and reasonableness of the measures'.[254] To promote this, the commission has a fact-finding capacity to carry out missions and on-site visits at the consent of a state party under Article 18 of the ACHR.

Actual and imminent threats

As discussed earlier, derogation review can play a role in reviewing emergency powers by assessing whether there is a credible basis for stating that they are being invoked in response to an actual or imminent threat, or that IHL applies because there is an actual armed conflict. With regard to the imminence of a threat, commentators such as Zeidy have argued that states of emergency of a purely preventative nature are not justified,[255] and Oraá similarly argues that it is not possible for states 'to derogate from situations that have not yet arisen . . . [t]he emergency, therefore, must be present or at least imminent'.[256] In the Greek case, the European Commission stated that

> with regard to the actual or imminent character of the emergency, it imposes a limitation in time, that is to say, the legitimacy of a derogation undertaken at a certain date depends upon there being a public emergency, actual or imminent at that date.[257]

However, it is suggested that the Greek case offers no clear standards on this, and Zeidy and Oraá provide no definitive authorities for their arguments.

Instead, it is suggested that states have a relatively wide margin of appreciation in this regard. Indeed, *Brannigan and McBride* implies that states are responsible for the safety of their citizens and that the mere threat of an armed attack is sufficient to justify recourse to emergency powers, and furthermore, the government is in the best place to appreciate and respond to any perceived threat. Despite this wide margin of appreciation, the ECtHR still has the power to assess whether the measures taken were strictly required by the exigencies of

253 *Judicial Guarantees in States of Emergency*, Advisory Opinion OC-9/87, Inter-American Court of Human Rights Series A No 9 (6 October 1987), 24; Gross and Aolain, above n 238, 290; *Castillo Petruzzi et al. Case* (Judgment) Inter-American Court of Human Rights Series C No 52 (30 May 1999) 204.

254 *Habeas Corpus in Emergency Situations*, above n 252, 24.

255 Mohamed El Zeidy, 'The ECHR and States of Emergency: Article 15 – A Domestic Power of Derogation from Human Rights' (2002) *MSU-DCL Journal of International Law* 261, 268.

256 Jaime Oraá, *Human Rights in States of Emergency in International Law* (New York: Oxford University Press, 1992) 221.

257 *The Greek Case*, above n 234.

the situation and proportionate to that threat. In this way the ECtHR can play a major role in the regulation of the use of force in states of emergency. Nevertheless, it is suggested that the notion that states have a margin of appreciation in invoking emergency powers under the permissive rules of IHL in response to imminent threats of armed conflict is not plausible. In order to justify derogation measures pursuant to the laws of war on the basis of an armed conflict, there has to be a factual state of armed conflict per se, and in this regard the HRL mechanisms should employ the clearer indicative guidelines in *Boškoski* as a basis for closely supervising any recourse to martial law. In other words, the threat of armed conflict is insufficient to justify recourse to martial law, but it does allow recourse to emergency powers under a law enforcement model according to which the use of force is subject to review on human rights standards where violence is actual or imminent.[258]

It is suggested that the HRL framework is itself sufficient for responding to threats that are not immediate per se as long as they are subject to escalation of force within but not exceeding the law enforcement paradigm, and as long as the force used is no more than absolutely necessary and proportionate in pursuit of a legitimate aim.[259] Kretzmer argues that HRL does not permit 'pre-emptive targeting of a suspected terrorist' on the grounds that it is not absolutely necessary.[260] Zemach takes issue with this argument, suggesting that 'neither the language of the main human rights conventions nor the jurisprudence of international human rights tribunals provides ample support for such conclusion'.[261] Although Zemach's point that the 'imminent' standard is ambiguous is reasoned, it is suggested that the net outcome of his argument is largely speculative. HRL is structured in such a way that lethal force may only be used where absolutely necessary, and this means that the circumstances where it may be used where the threat is not direct and imminent will be extremely rare and unlikely. In other words, if nonlethal means are available, then the use of lethal force will not have been absolutely necessary, and furthermore, this standard has been interpreted as obliging state security forces to take preventative and precautionary measures so as to avoid the resort to lethal force as well as to protect civilian bystanders from being injured or killed.[262]

Nevertheless, Zemach's argument that the 'imminent' standard is ambiguous and can accommodate extreme law enforcement measures has a reasoned basis.

258 Hernan Montealegre, 'The Compatibility of a State Party's Derogation under Human Rights Conventions with Its Obligations under Protocol II and Common Article 3' (1983–1984) 33 *American University Law Review* 34 and 41.

259 Zemach, above n 22.

260 David Kretzmer, 'Targeted Killings of Suspected Terrorists: Extra-Judicial Executions or Legitimate Means of Self-Defence?' (2005) 16 *European Journal of International Law* 171, 189.

261 Zemach, above n 22.

262 Françoise Hampson, above n 2, 201; *McCann and Others v UK* (Application No 18984/91) (1995) Series A no 324, [149].

For example, rather than condemning Israel's policy of targeted killing in absolute terms, the UN Human Rights Committee merely stated that it was 'concerned' that the practice of attacking 'those in the process of committing acts of terror' – in other words, attacking individuals where the threat they posed is not, strictly speaking, imminent, but merely preparatory or supportive – 'would appear to be used at least in part as a deterrent or punishment, ***thus raising issues under article 6***' [emphasis added].[263] Furthermore, the Human Rights Committee noted that the principle of proportionality should be adhered to, that state policy should be set out in written guidelines and that, before using lethal force, 'all measures to arrest a person suspected of being in the process of committing acts of terror must be exhausted'.[264]

The Inter-American Commission on Human Rights, in its Report on Terrorism and Human Rights, stated that

> in situations where a state's population is threatened by violence, the state has the right and obligation to protect the population against such threats and in so doing may use lethal force in certain situations. This includes, for example, the use of lethal force by law enforcement officials where strictly unavoidable, to protect themselves or other persons from imminent threat of death or serious injury, or to otherwise maintain law and order where strictly necessary and proportionate.[265]

This second condition, namely that the use of potentially lethal force 'to otherwise maintain law and order', is not expressly constrained by the need for an 'imminent threat of death or serious injury', but instead may be used for the more broader goals of 'maintaining law and order'.[266] In this regard, the commission's stance on the use of force equivocally left the matter open by stating that 'the state may resort to the use of force only against individuals that threaten the security of all'. The commission thus left a wide lacuna for preemptive strikes where strictly necessary in that it qualified this proposition accordingly:

> in their law enforcement initiatives, states must not use force against individuals who no longer present a threat . . . such as individuals who have been apprehended by authorities, have surrendered, or who are wounded and abstain from hostile acts [as] the use of lethal force in such a manner would constitute extra-judicial killings.[267]

---

263 UNHRC 'Concluding Observations: Israel' (21 August 2003) UN Doc CCPR/CO/78/ISR, 13; Zemach, Ibid.

264 UNHRC 'Concluding Observations: Israel', Ibid., 15.

265 *Report on Terrorism and Human Rights*, Inter-American Commission on Human Rights, OEA/Ser.L/V/II.116 Doc 5 rev 1 corr (22 October 2002) 87.

266 Zemach, above n 22.

267 *Report on Terrorism and Human Rights*, above n 265, 90–91; Zemach, Ibid., 125–126.

In order to further elucidate the question of whether a threat of harm needs to be strictly imminent, Zemach carried out a brief survey of domestic laws given the indeterminacy prevalent in decisions at the international and regional levels. Zemach argues that 'the construction of the right to life under human rights law should be informed by the domestic laws of the various states' and accordingly proposes that 'the domestic law of self-defense is indicative of the social attitudes in the various states toward the use of lethal force'.[268] In this regard, conduct in self-defence may be used to justify the use of lethal force and so such conduct may not amount to a human rights violation. Although Zemach's remarks are illuminating, it is submitted that they may not be wholly pertinent to standards on state or governmental use of force, but rather that they relate primarily to the justified use of what may amount to lethal force by private actors in stations where 'the police are no longer in a position to intervene and exercise the state's function of securing public safety'.[269] Nevertheless, Zemach notes that although some US states and jurisdictions such as Scotland only allow self-defence to be raised in situations where the defendant 'believed that he was in imminent danger and that he held that belief on reasonable grounds',[270] many other jurisdictions do not attach such a condition to the operation of the defence. For example, English and Canadian law are similar in that

> [t]here is . . . no formal requirement that the danger be imminent. Imminence is only one of the factors which the jury should weigh in determining whether the accused had a reasonable apprehension of danger and a reasonable belief that she could not extricate herself otherwise than by killing the attacker.[271]

This, combined with the wealth of authority provided by Zemach, suggests that imminence is not generally to be equated with 'immediately necessary'.[272]

Concluding statements on status determination

As stated earlier, the indicative guidance in *Boškoski* represents a concrete schema against which state justification of emergency or military force may be assessed.

268 Zemach, Ibid., 126–127.

269 George Fletcher, 'Domination in the Theory of Justification and Excuse' (1996) 57 *University of Pittsburgh Law Review* 553, 570.

270 *Owens v HM Advocate* 1946, JC 119, 125; *Whipple v Indiana* 523 NE2d 1363, 1367 (1988); The Code of Alabama (1975), 13(A)-3–23(a); The Code of Arkansas (1975), 5–2–606(a)(1); Colorado Revised Statutes (1975), 18–1–704(1); Georgia Code (2001), 16–3–21(a); Maine Revised Statutes (2006), 14(A)–108(1); Montana Code (2009), 45–3–102 cited in Zemach, above n 22, 126–127.

271 *R v Pétel* [1994] 1 SCR 3; *R v Shaw* [2001] UKPC 26 (Jamaica), 19; *R v Palmer* [1970] AC 814, 831.

272 *Tennessee v Garner*, 471 US 1, 3 (1985); United States Model Penal Code (2001), 3.04(1); Penal Law of Israel (626/1996), 34(J) cited in Zemach, above n 22, 128.

Furthermore, they provide clearer objective criteria for sequencing HRL and IHL in order to ensure that, as far as possible, a presumptively HRL approach to the use of force is applied in problematic grey area conflicts where IHL and IHRL seemingly overlap. HRL mechanisms may play a major role in regulating the use of force by supervising emergency or crisis situations and ensuring that, as far as possible, the right to life is applied so as to ensure that crisis powers are not used to justify extrajudicial killing. Indeed, given that the right to life is non-derogable, but to be assessed according to IHL standards within a situation of armed conflict, the process of derogation review represents an important mechanism for restraining and minimising the use of force, as it gives HR mechanisms the opportunity to state that the right to life cannot be suspended or interpreted in view of IHL because the objective conditions for an armed conflict are not in place, or in other words, the exceptional circumstances are not in existence so as to justify the deprivation of life according to the laws of war.[273] This is particularly so in the context of complex and protracted *de facto* emergency situations where, over time, executive powers may be used to make extrajudicial killing the norm rather than the exception.

In such contexts, HRL mechanisms can play an important role in confining the applicable legal framework to HRL by stating that the application of IHL is not justified due to the absence of the objective conditions for a state of armed conflict. This can assist with the prevention of extrajudicial killings resulting from the 'unregulated or unproclaimed use of martial law', that is, the application of Hague rules on targeting and weaponry to situations that do not factually amount to an armed conflict.[274] In overseeing the resort to emergency powers, HRL mechanisms thus have an important role to play in policing the 'fuzzy' intersection between crisis and conflict. Indeed as Gross and Ni Aolain suggest, derogation review can instigate procedures and elicit contextual information that 'can act as a brake on the worst of state excesses . . .'[275] It is suggested that derogation review necessarily requires an express understanding and application of threshold criteria for an armed conflict under IHL, as well as the jurisprudence that elucidates this, in a clear and pragmatic fashion.

International and regional HRL mechanisms have resorted to carrying out status determinations, and they have the capacity and the competence to perform this function in pursuing their mandates. However, it is suggested that a key lesson to be learned is that their analyses need to take into account in an express

273 Council of Europe, European Convention for the Protection of Human Rights and Fundamental Freedoms, as amended by Protocols Nos. 11 and 14, 4 November 1950 ('ECHR'), Article 15: 'time of war or other public emergency'; Organization of American States (OAS), American Convention on Human Rights, "Pact of San Jose", Costa Rica, 22 November 1969, entry into force 18 July 1978 ('ACHR'), Article 27: 'time of war, public danger, or other emergency that threatens the independence or security of a State Party'.

274 Colm Campbell and Ita Connolly, 'A Model for the "War Against Terrorism"? Military Intervention and the 1970 Falls Curfew' (2003) 30 *Journal of Law and Society* 341.

275 Gross & Aolain, above n 177, 268.

fashion the indicative guidance discussed earlier in order to make their decisions substantively and contextually clear, coherent and credible. This discussion of the elucidation of the threshold criteria for an armed conflict, as well as the progressive role that derogation review can play in unconventional conflict situations, can serve to narrow what McLaughlin describes as the 'wide margin for legal-policy influence' that can distort the process of self-classification.[276] Indeed, clearer criteria and judicial and quasi-judicial oversight can serve to limit the 'fierce controversy of a political nature'[277] and 'strategic instrumentalisation'[278] that surrounds the classification process and which may serve to undermine legal protections under humanitarian or human rights law.

A stricter interpretative framework for assessing the 'facts on the ground' combined with and more robust and interventionist system of review of autoqualifications can play a role in promoting the primacy of the substantive and procedural aspects of the right to life in situations of extreme violence by ensuring that it is only justifiably departed from in situations where the high threshold of organised and intense armed violence, as discussed in this section, means that it cannot reasonably be contained without resort to the armed conflict model.[279] In this respect, it is suggested that the clearer interpretative framework and system of review discussed in this section accords with states' own interests in employing force that is strategically effective as discussed in Chapter 1. Furthermore, improvements in these regards can serve to guide autoqualifications and thus operational and tactical responses in a principled and coherent fashion. The employment of clearer objective criteria that serve to analyse war in terms of a 'continuum of armed conflict' would, it is suggested, actually assist with the 'demarcation between war and peace' rather than lead to its erosion as Hew Strachan and Sibylle Scheipers suggest.[280] Indeed, this would prevent the dangerous approach of subjecting what can be viewed objectively as less-than-non-international armed conflict situations to the law of war, rather than to the law enforcement model, on a perpetual and indefinite basis.

The outcomes of this discussion serve to clarify and further contextualise the boundaries between situations where the 'ordinary' or 'normal' law enforcement model applies, situations where exception to the 'ordinary' law enforcement model may be taken and human rights standards interpreted in a broad and flexible manner, and then situations of armed conflict where IHL applies. It is suggested that this could assist with preventing the mixing of IHL and IHRL rules relative to the use of force and their subsequent spillover into situations characterised by general civil peace and security.

276 Rob McLaughlin, above n 7, 28.
277 Stewart, above n 54, 342.
278 Berman, above n 14.
279 Kretzmer, above n 62, 36.
280 Hew Strachan and Sibylle Scheipers (eds), *The Changing Character of War* (Oxford University Press, Oxford, 2011) 10–11.

As discussed earlier, the threshold for the applicability of treaty-based and customary rules to international armed conflicts is set at a low level. However, in relation to non-international armed conflicts, the situation is a lot more contentious and complex. For example, as noted in Chapter 2, Abresch regards the customary humanitarian law of internal armed conflict and the human rights law of internal armed conflicts as competing projects for the legal regulation of contemporary non-international armed conflicts. In particular, he argues that the sparse treaty provisions of APII and the inapplicability of customary protections even at the APII threshold creates a normative lacuna which, in his opinion, can and should be filled by human rights law.[281] In contrast, Hampson suggests that the armed conflict paradigm of treaty-based and customary Hague law prohibitions and permissions is more clearly applicable and should be confined to situations where the level of violence has reached the threshold foreseen by APII, but not CA3.[282] Similarly, Sivakumaran proposes that low-intensity internal armed conflicts should be governed by human rights law, but high-intensity internal armed conflicts should be governed by international humanitarian law with the threshold being set at the APII level.[283] As argued earlier, human rights standards are not practicable or appropriate once armed hostilities between state and nonstate groups have reached the threshold of a CA3 armed conflict, according to the guidelines set out in *Boškoski*. Furthermore, as discussed elsewhere, given that one or both of the parties to a non-international armed conflict must be a nonstate actor, it makes little sense to promote the application of rules to a conflict situation that only bind a state party to a non-international armed conflict. Importantly, this contribution suggests that *Boškoski* may have the effect of ensuring that the varied typology of non-international armed conflicts fall more clearly within the scope of CA3 non-international 'armed conflicts', providing that the demanding threshold criteria are satisfied, but also that, given these demanding criteria, applicable human rights frameworks relating to the use of force and detention apply as far as practicable to what may be described as states of crisis or emergency. Thus, rather than confuse the discussion by trying to draw a distinction between 'low intensity' and 'high intensity' internal conflicts, this discussion attempts to maintain and clarify a more traditional distinction between states of crisis, to which human rights frameworks apply, and factual states of armed conflict, to which the law of armed conflict framework applies. With regard to non-international armed conflicts, it is suggested that this proposal can serve to maintain the truly exceptional status of the law of armed conflict framework by ensuring that it is not applied to situations that do not factually meet the minimum yardstick of an armed conflict.

281 William Abresch, 'A Human Rights Law of Internal Armed Conflict: The European Court of Human Rights in Chechnya' (2005) 16 (4) *The European Journal of International Law* 749–765.

282 Françoise Hampson, above n 2, 200.

283 Sandesh Sivakumaran, 'Re-envisaging the International Law of Internal Armed Conflict' (2011) 22 *European Journal of International Law* 235–236.

Furthermore, Wilmshurst has surveyed a broad spectrum of primary and secondary legal sources, including the writings of leading academics on this topic, and has posited that 'there is no agreement on what the threshold is for non-international armed conflict in respect of the application of all the rules of customary law' and, furthermore, that it 'is difficult to show that there are two thresholds of non-international armed conflict as a matter of customary law and to establish the law that is applicable to them'.[284] Pejic notes that the ICRC Study on Customary International Humanitarian Law did not assess this issue and did not set out differing thresholds in this regard 'because it was found that in general states did not make this distinction in practice'.[285] In terms of the ICC system, although Article 8(2)(e) of the ICC Statute does not make a distinction in this regard, it does use two different formulations for the trigger of NIAC rules: Article 8(2)(c) uses the vocabulary of CA3, and Article 8(2)(f) uses a modified form of the *Tadić* formula,[286] that is, it applies to armed conflicts that take place in the territory of a state when there is protracted armed conflict between governmental authorities and organised armed groups or between such groups but contains no reference to territorial control. Despite the difference in wording between subparagraphs (d) and (f) of Articles 8(2) (in that the latter refers to the element of 'protracted conflict'), Akande suggests that this is 'better interpreted as simply stating the intensity test with the protracted nature of the conflict being a factor to be assessed in determining intensity',[287] and Pejic suggests that Article 8(2)(f) should be regarded as having the same threshold of applicability as CA3.[288]

As will be discussed further later, this study argues that customary Hague law prohibitions and permissions on the use of force are applicable at the CA3 threshold as illustrated by the indicative guidelines in *Boškoski*, because, as noted by Akande, they provide more elaborate rules for non-international armed conflicts than those to be found in treaty-based CA3 or APII. Thus, customary norms have a much more significant role to play in non-international armed conflicts than international armed conflicts. Furthermore, it is suggested that customary Hague rules are more appropriate for situations of armed conflict than human rights norms on the use of force, in that they are applicable to both state and nonstate parties to a non-international armed conflict. In terms of the blurring of the distinction between the regulation of international and non-international conflicts, this is partly reflected within the ICC system in that Articles 8(2)(c) and (e) of the ICC Statute contain a broader set of Hague- and Geneva-type rules

---

284 Elizabeth Wilmshurst, above n 4, 482.

285 Jelena Pejic, 'Status of armed conflicts', in Elizabeth Wilmshurst and Susan Breau (eds), *Perspectives on the ICRC Study on Customary International Humanitarian Law* (Cambridge University Press, Cambridge, 2007) 88; Elizabeth Wilmshurst, above n 4, 482.

286 *Tadić* (Jurisdiction) above n 24, 70.

287 Dapo Akande, above n 36, 56.

288 Jelena Pejic, The Protective Scope of Common Article 3: More than Meets the Eye, *International Review of the Red Cross*, Volume 93, Number 881, March 2011, 192.

that are applicable to situations of non-international armed conflict.[289] However, Akande also notes that in comparison with the rules applicable to situations of international armed conflict, the customary rules applicable in non-international armed conflict as outlined in the provisions of Article 8 of the ICC Statute are not as broad as the approach taken by the ICTY and the ICRC in its Customary International Humanitarian Law Study, and so this 'indicates a reluctance on the part of states to go as far as the ICTY and the ICRC' in terms of criminalising violations of IHL in situations of non-international armed conflict.[290] Furthermore, Akande notes that the law relating to the status of fighters and the detention of combatants and civilians still differs depending on the status of the armed conflict.[291]

The final part of this concluding section aims to develop the discussion on the difference between Geneva law (that is, rules on the protection of victims, who are, by definition, in the power of the party concerned) and Hague law (that is, rules on the conduct of hostilities). In particular, after discussing the preliminary issue of the threshold of applicability of LOAC to international armed conflicts, it addresses the question whether the threshold for the applicability of Geneva law in NIACs is lower than that for Hague law, namely as a way of restricting Hague rules, particularly permissive Hague rules, on the conduct of hostilities. Accordingly, it will be suggested that an assessment of the latter issue depends on the parties to the hostilities and the context in which they occur. In particular, there are two types of scenarios where the latter issue is particularly significant: first, traditional or classic NIACs between a state and its own nationals in the form of an organised armed group within its territory; and, second, conflicts that arise between an invading or occupying power and enemy or foreign nationals who organise themselves into armed groups that are not linked to state entities per se. It will be suggested that the threshold for permissive Hague rules is higher in the latter type of scenario, that is, where an occupation meets with armed resistance on the part of nonstate actors, or where there is a subsequent outbreak or reemergence of armed resistance from organised armed groups of enemy nationals in a situation of occupation (that is, hostilities within an occupation). This is problematic, as IHL and HRL are not clear as to the law applicable to prolonged occupations. In the former situation, that is, traditional or classic NIAC, applicable treaty-based and customary Geneva and Hague rules will apply once the threshold of a CA3 or APII NIAC has been surpassed, and up to that point, domestic criminal law will apply and applicable human rights standards will apply. The legal regulation of the latter situation is a more complex and contentious issue, which is why there is a discussion on the extraterritorial effect of human rights obligations in Chapter 8, as the interplay between IHL and HRL becomes problematic in such situations.

289 Dapo Akande, above n 36, 36.
290 Ibid.
291 Ibid.

As noted in Chapter 2, CA2 and CA3 of the Geneva Conventions and their Additional Protocols do not set out a clear definition of what constitutes the threshold of an international armed conflict and what constitutes the threshold of a non-international armed conflict. The AC in *Tadić* elaborated on this issue by stating that 'an armed conflict exists whenever there is a resort to armed force between States or protracted armed violence between governmental authorities and organised armed groups or between such groups within a State'.[292] In contrast with the threshold for a NIAC, writers such as Akande[293] and Vité, as well as the ICRC *Commentary*, suggest that the threshold for an IAC, and, in particular Geneva rules, is set at a comparatively low level. This issue will be discussed further before contrasting it with the applicability of Hague and Geneva rules in NIAC situations.

According to the ICRC *Commentary* '[a]ny difference arising between two States and leading to the intervention of armed forces is an armed conflict within the meaning of Article 2, even if one of the Parties denies the existence of a state of war'. Moreover, in further contrast with the threshold criteria for a CA3 NIAC set out in *Boškoski*, in relation to CA2, this *Commentary* states that

> it makes no difference how long the conflict lasts, or how much slaughter takes place . . . [t]he respect due to human personality is not measured by the number of victims. . . . [i]f there is only a single wounded person as a result of the conflict, [Article 12 of GCIII] will have been applied as soon as he has been collected and tended. . .[294]

Akande notes that predicating the subject matter jurisdiction of the rules in the four Geneva Conventions and API on any intensity requirement would mean that military operations between two states below that threshold would not be covered by the law of international armed conflict, and that this would raise problems vis-à-vis the applicability of Hague and Geneva law during the opening phase of hostilities.[295] In this way, IHL ensures that Geneva Law prohibitions are available in the context of hostilities between two states during any opening phase of hostilities, and this is not linked to the type of threshold criteria elucidated in relation to CA3 in *Boškoski*, in that the Geneva protections will apply regardless of the intensity of violence between state parties. As will be discussed further later, this can be contrasted with NIAC in that the thresholds for the applicability of Geneva and Hague rules to NIACs are set at a high level, and so the opening phases of many confrontations between the armed forces of states and organized

292 *Tadić* (Jurisdiction) above n 24, 70.
293 Dapo Akande, above n 36, 41; Sylvain Vité, 'Typology of Armed Conflicts in International Humanitarian Law: Legal Concepts and Actual Situations' (2009) 91 (873) *International Review of the Red Cross* 39–56.
294 Jean S Pictet, above n 224, 28 and 32.
295 Dapo Akande, above n 36, 41.

armed groups will generally not reach the CA3 or APII thresholds, and are thus regulated by domestic criminal law and applicable human rights standards.

In particular, in the framework of international armed conflict between states, it may be argued that Geneva rules may have the broadest temporal and geographical scope, that is, they have a lower threshold of applicability compared with Geneva and Hague rules in NIAC as well as Hague rules on the conduct of hostilities in IAC. According to *Naletilić* and *Martinović*, 'the law of occupation as it affects "individuals" as civilians protected under Geneva Convention IV does not require that the occupying power has actual authority', because otherwise 'civilians would be left, during an intermediate period, with less protection than that attached to them once occupation is established', and accordingly this protection 'becomes applicable to individuals, ie to the protected persons, as they fall into the hands of the Occupying Power'.[296] For this reason, in *Naletilić* and *Martinović*, on its reading of the *Commentary* to Geneva Convention IV, the Trial Chamber made clear that the application of the law of occupation under GCIV to the civilian population is broader than Article 42 of the Hague Regulations in that GCIV 'becomes applicable to individuals, ie to the protected persons, as they fall into the hands of the Occupying Power' and so '[t]here is no intermediate period between what might be termed the invasion phase and the inauguration of a stable regime of occupation'. In particular, according to Article 42 of the Hague Regulations, '[t]erritory is considered occupied when it is actually placed under the authority of the hostile army' and '[t]he occupation extends only to the territory where such authority has been established and can be exercised'.

Thus Article 6 has been interpreted to the effect that the Geneva protections under GCIV have broader applicability than Article 42, in that territory need not be occupied in terms of a belligerent party exercising effective control, substituting the territorial state's authority with its own by exercising functions of government or exercising territorial control through a subordinate administration that it controls.[297] As Akande notes, this creates two different thresholds for the law of occupation, as under Article 6 GC, the protections outlined therein will apply where individuals find themselves in the hands of a party to the conflict or an occupying power of which they are not nationals, whereas Article 42 of the Hague Regulations covers those situations where there is a form of effective territorial control.[298] This is important as Part II and Part III of GCIV set out obli-

296 *Prosecutor v Naletilić and Martinović* (Trial Judgment) ICTY-98–34-T (31 March 2003), 219 and 221.

297 Dapo Akande, above n 36, 44; As noted in the ICRC Commentary IV (above n 20), belligerent occupation as defined in Article 42 of the Hague Regulations does not need to be established for GCIV to apply, as Article 6 has 'a wider meaning than it has in Article 42 . . . [s]o far as individuals are concerned, the application of the Fourth Geneva Convention does not depend upon the existence of a state of occupation within the meaning of the Article 42'.

298 Dapo Akande, above n 36, 46.

gations on occupying powers vis-à-vis the protection and treatment of persons who have protected status. Furthermore, Article 6 GCIV suggests that within the framework of IAC, of which the law of occupation is a subset, Geneva protections may have broader temporal and geographical applicability than Hague rules on the conduct of hostilities, in that they provide for the beginning and end of application of Geneva Law, and that they may apply beyond the military operations to which Hague rules on the conduct of hostilities apply.

According to Article 6 of GCIV, Geneva law will apply until general close of military operations, unless there is a situation of belligerent occupation, in which case certain specified Geneva rules apply beyond the cessation of hostilities and for the duration of occupation where the occupying power exercises functions of government.[299] Indeed, the *Commentary* to GCIV notes that the convention applies 'from the outset' of 'any armed conflict' within the meaning of Article 2. As noted earlier, the applicability of Geneva rules under this convention are not predicated on any intensity requirement in that they are applicable as soon as the first acts of violence, such as mere frontier incidents, are committed, as they may be the beginning of a more widespread conflict. In contrast, Geneva and Hague rules applicable to NIAC are not necessarily applicable 'from the outset' of confrontations between a state and its nationals, as they may begin as mere internal tensions or disturbances to which domestic criminal law and applicable human rights standards will apply.

Furthermore, according to the *Commentary*, GCIV will apply 'from the outset', whether occupation meets with armed resistance or not, and so will apply 'even if the armed struggle did not continue'. This indicates that in situations that fall within the scope of CA2, in comparison with Hague rules, Geneva protections apply beyond the conduct of hostilities to which Hague rules are applicable. This is because 'the relations between the civilian population of a territory and troops advancing into that territory, whether fighting or not, are governed by the present Convention' and as such 'there is no intermediate period between what might be termed the invasion phase and the inauguration of a stable regime of occupation'. Indeed, the *Commentary* notes that 'the Convention should be applied as soon as troops are in foreign territory and in contact with the civilian population there' even where no military resistance is encountered. Thus GCIV will apply where there is 'occupation during war' as well as, more importantly, where there is 'occupation without war'. Accordingly, the *Commentary* to Article 6 GCIV further states that '[t]he Convention is quite definite on this point: all persons who find themselves in the hands of a Party to the conflict or an Occupying Power of which they are not nationals are protected persons. No loophole is left'.

---

299 *Tadić* (Jurisdiction) above n 24, 70, 'until a general conclusion of peace is achieved, or in the case of internal conflicts, a peaceful settlement is achieved . . . IHL continues to apply in the whole territory of the warring states or, in the case of internal conflicts, the whole territory under the control of a party, whether or not actual combat takes place there'.

Although the convention has been interpreted to be 'quite definite' on the applicability of Geneva protections in situations that fall within the scope of Article 2, that is, above and beyond Hague-type rules on the conduct of hostilities, this point is being raised as confrontations between occupying states and enemy/foreign nonstate actors may arise in situations of occupation, and, as such, it must be considered whether this has any possible bearing on the threshold of Geneva and Hague rules in pure NIAC situations between the armed forces of a state and its own nationals who have formed organised armed groups.

Although Geneva protections may apply in situations of occupation above and beyond the legal framework relative to the conduct of hostilities, where hostilities break out in situations of occupation between an occupying power and a nonstate organised armed group, the question arises as to what legal framework applies, as the hostilities here are not between two states and thus do not have an international character per se. Akande notes that in such situations, it must be ascertained whether the violence reaches the threshold of an armed conflict governed by the paradigm of hostilities or whether it constitutes internal disturbances or tensions to which the paradigm of law enforcement applies, which, broadly speaking, may be made up of domestic criminal law and applicable human rights law.[300] Furthermore, if the hostilities are such that they reach an intensity over and above that of mere internal disturbances, the question then becomes whether they are to be regulated by the conduct of hostility framework relative to international armed conflict, given that there is a situation of occupation, or the framework relative to non-international armed conflict, given that the hostilities are between a state acting as an occupying power and nonstate–organised armed group.[301] Akande notes that the answer will depend on whether the nonstate–organised armed group is fighting on behalf of the state that is occupied, as foreseen by Article 4 paragraph (2) GCIII or Article 43 API, or whether they are functionally separate and independent of the occupied state. If it is the former, then the treaty-based rules relative to IAC will apply. This then raises the question of what legal framework relative to the conduct of hostilities applies if it is the latter type of situation, that is, hostilities between a state actor and an organised armed group that is functionally separate and independent of the occupied state.[302]

As discussed earlier, according to the Israeli High Court of Justice[303] and Cassese,[304] in both types of situations, such hostilities are to be regulated by the legal framework relative to international armed conflicts, namely the Hague rules on the conduct of hostilities.[305] Akande and this author agree with this legal stance.[306] Furthermore, it is suggested that this interpretation is borne out

300 Dapo Akande, above n 36, 46.
301 Ibid.
302 Dapo Akande, above n 36, 46.
303 *Public Committee Against Torture v The Government of Israel*, above n 142, 16–23.
304 Antonio Cassese, above n 55, 420–423.
305 Dapo Akande, above n 36, 46–47.
306 Ibid.

from a reading of Articles 1, 72 and 75 of API, together with Article 2 of GCIV. Namely, this interpretation is premised on the notion that part of the purpose of GCIV as well as API is to ensure that 'the relations between the civilian population' (GCIV Commentary) and an invading or occupying power are governed not only by GCIV, but also by the additional rules contained in API that relate to the humanitarian protection of civilians and civilian objects in the power of a party to an armed conflict.[307] As noted by Akande, in such situations the material issue is 'not what type of conflict exists between the state and the nonstate group, but what law applies to the acts of an occupying power within occupied territory', that is, between an occupying power and foreign or enemy nationals.[308] Accordingly, Article 1 of API states that it applies in situations covered by Article 2 of GCIV, namely to 'all cases of declared war or of any other armed conflict which may arise between two or more of the High Contracting Parties' and also 'to all cases of partial or total occupation of the territory of a High Contracting Party, even if the said occupation meets with no armed resistance'. Furthermore, in addition to certain provisions of GCIV and API themselves, the decisions of the International Court of Justice and the International Criminal Court also confirm that the law of occupation regulates how an occupying power may respond to civilians suspected of or engaged in activities hostile to the security of the state, and it is suggested, therefore, that where such hostile activities reach the threshold of an armed conflict, then treaty-based targeting and weaponry law relative to international armed conflict apply, that is, permissive and prohibitive Hague rules.[309] In other words, according to this reasoning, where a conflict is of an

307 API, above n 32, Article 72: Geneva Convention (IV), above n 29, Parts I and III; Commentary IV, above n 20; Akande, Ibid., 47.

308 Dapo Akande, above n 36, 47.

309 Dapo Akande, Ibid., 47–48; See also DRC v Uganda; *Prosecutor v Lubanga* (Pre-Trial Chamber I Decision on Confirmation of Charges) ICC-01/04–01/06 (29 January 2007), para 220: 'on the evidence admitted for the purpose of the confirmation hearing, the Chamber considers that there is sufficient evidence to establish substantial grounds to believe that, as a result of the presence of the Republic of Uganda as an occupying Power, the armed conflict which occurred in Ituri can be characterised as an armed conflict of an international character from July 2002 to 2 June 2003, the date of the effective withdrawal of the Ugandan army': *Prosecutor v Katanga* (Decision on Confirmation of Charges) para 240: 'There is also sufficient evidence to establish substantial grounds to believe that Uganda directly intervened in this armed conflict through the Ugandan People Armed Forces ("the UPDF"). The evidence presented establishes direct participation of significant numbers of UPDF troops in several military operations on behalf of different armed groups including the UPC takeover in Bunia in early August 2002, the FNI/FRPI takeover in Bogoro in February 2003, para 319 and of Bunia in early March 2003 . . . Uganda was one of the main suppliers of weapons and ammunitions to these armed groups . . . and that the respective recipients' ability to successfully attack other groups was aided by this Ugandan military assistance . . . As a result, the Chamber finds that there is sufficient evidence to establish substantial grounds to believe that the conflict that took place in Ituri District between, at least, August 2002 and May 2003, was of an international character'; Armed Activities on the Territory of the Congo (*Democratic Republic of the Congo v. Uganda*), ICJ Reports (2005), para 216: where both violations of IHL and IHRL were found in

international character, then constraints on waging war relative to targeting law in IAC are also applicable in situations of belligerent occupation, as it is a subset of conflicts of an international character.

As alluded to earlier, it may also be suggested that GCIV and API foresee and provide for situations where there is no armed resistance, but also, *a contrario*, situations where there is armed resistance from within the civilian population in the context of an occupation. Furthermore, in calm situations of occupation, arguably GCIV and API not only provide a range of Geneva law protections (which may be supplemented by human rights standards), but may also be construed as providing requirements to use measures short of lethal force in some situations. For example, Article 68 of GCIV provides that

> protected persons who commit an offence which is solely intended to harm the Occupying Power, but which does not constitute an attempt on the life or limb of members of the occupying forces or administration, nor a grave collective danger, nor seriously damage the property of the occupying forces or administration or the installations used by them, shall be liable to internment or simple imprisonment . . .

Furthermore, according to Articles 64, 65 and 68, an invading or occupying power cannot execute a civilian without trial. Additionally, according to Article 68, penal provisions promulgated by the occupying power may only impose the death penalty on a protected person in cases where they are found guilty of espionage, serious acts of sabotage against the military installations of the occupying power or of intentional offences which have caused the death of one or more persons, provided that such offences were punishable by death under the law of the occupied territory in force before the occupation began. Article 45 paragraph (3) of API provides that '[a]ny person who has taken part in hostilities, who is not entitled to prisoner-of-war status and who does not benefit from more favourable treatment in accordance with the Fourth Convention shall have the right at all times to the protection of Article 75 of this Protocol'. Additionally, Article 45 paragraph (3) makes reference to Article 5 GCIV, which provides that where 'an individual protected person is definitely suspected of or engaged in activities

---

the context of an armed conflict thus giving *res judicata* effect to this interpretation of the *lex specialis* principle which views IHL and IHRL as complementary. In this case, the ICJ found that Uganda had violated Article 6 of the ICCPR as well as Articles 48, 51, 52, 57, 58 and 75 of API; Ibid., para 345: 'Uganda [. . .] violated the following provisions of the international humanitarian law and international human rights law instruments, to which both Uganda and the DRC are parties: [. . .] International Covenant on Civil and Political Rights, Articles 6, paragraph 1, and 7; First Protocol Additional to the Geneva Conventions of 12 August 1949, Articles 48, 51, 52, 57, 58 and 75, paragraphs 1 and 2 [. . .]' (para 219); 'Uganda is internationally responsible for violations of international human rights law and international humanitarian law committed by the UPDF and by its members in the territory of the DRC and for failing to comply with its obligations as an occupying Power in Ituri' (para 220).

hostile to the security of the State, such individual person shall not be entitled to claim such rights and privileges under the present Convention'. In other words, civilians may be subject to internment and have rights as internees (for example, the right of communication) unless they are held as a spy or saboteur.

Therefore, the provisions of GCIV and API combined with the commentary lend credence to Akande's suggestion that the law of occupation is not only concerned with regulating the belligerency between two states, but also about governing what he describes as the often 'tense relationship' between the civilian population within the occupied territory and the occupying power. Akande notes that this tension may give rise to hostilities between the civilian population and the occupying power, and that under such circumstances this 'does not free the occupier from the restraints it otherwise has' but rather 'it ought to strengthen those restraints'.[310] In other words, although Geneva protections will apply at a very low threshold, above and beyond the Hague rules on the conduct of hostilities, it is suggested that restraints on the conduct of hostilities relative to IACs apply to those situations where hostilities between an occupying state and a non-state–organised group made up of enemy nationals break out in the context of an occupation, which is connected to a preexisting international armed conflict, and so is regulated within the framework of the rules relative to international armed conflict. Importantly, this raises the issue of where the threshold of an armed conflict is to be set in such situations where there is an outbreak or resurgence of violence between an occupying power and elements of the civilian population.

In view of the restrictive effect that provisions such as Articles 5, 64, 65 and 68 of GCIV and Articles 45, 72 and 75 API have on the use of lethal force against civilians who have engaged in harmful activities, it is suggested that the threshold of prohibitive and permissive Hague rules on the conduct of hostilities should be set at a much higher threshold than those Geneva protections that apply to enemy or foreign nationals which apply as soon as they fall into the hands of the enemy. Given that hostilities between a state and nonstate actor may occur within the context of belligerent occupation, it is suggested that the CA3 threshold criteria for an 'armed conflict' should be used, as this is the core basic test that has emerged to distinguish between situations of internal strife, tensions and disturbances to which domestic law and human rights law apply, and non-international armed conflicts to which treaty-based and customary Hague rules on the conduct of hostilities apply. Although CA3 does not provide express threshold criteria itself, its scope of applicability has been subsequently elucidated in ICTY cases such as *Tadić*, *Haradinaj* and *Boškoski*, that set out the requirements of a certain level of organization on the part of a nonstate actor and hostilities having reached a certain level of intensity. Furthermore, it is suggested that CA3 constitutes the basic gateway for customary Hague and Geneva standards. In this way, it is suggested that in comparison with the threshold for the applicability of Hague law to international armed conflicts, the threshold for the applicability of Hague law

310 Dapo Akande, above n 36, 47.

to non-international armed conflicts, such as NIACs between the armed forces of a state and its nationals, as well as outbreaks of violence between an occupying power and foreign or enemy nationals, is set at a higher threshold. This implies that the threshold for the applicability of Geneva law in instances of IAC and belligerent occupation is lower than Hague law, in that Geneva protections will apply as soon as protected persons fall into the hands of an occupying power, even where there is no armed resistance on the part of the enemy state or its nationals.

In situations of IAC, Hague law relating to the general conduct of hostilities may not apply if the occupation meets with no armed resistance, or will cease to apply upon the general cessation of hostilities (where Geneva protections as supplemented by domestic law and applicable human rights law will continue to apply), unless there is an outbreak of hostilities between the occupying power and elements of the civilian population and those hostilities reach the threshold of a CA3 armed conflict, which as it occurs within an international armed conflict framework (that is, belligerency between two states followed by occupation) will trigger prohibitive and permissive treaty-based and customary Hague rules on the conduct of hostilities. In other words, given that this is a situation of occupation, the law of occupation relative to the status and treatment of civilians outlined in Parts II and III of GCIV and supplemented by Articles 75 of API constitute the core Geneva law that applies, and, as indicated earlier vis-à-vis Article 6 GCIV, this has a lower threshold than that required for the introduction of Hague law in view of any hostilities in such situations between the occupying power and elements of the civilian population. This situation of occupation (relations between an invading/occupying force and enemy nationals) can be considered distinct from a purely non-international armed conflict where the territorial state is engaged in an armed conflict with an organised armed group (between a state and its own nationals). Here, as will be discussed in further detail later, it is suggested that once the threshold for a CA3 NIAC is met, this triggers the application of customary Hague and Geneva law. Below this threshold, domestic law and human rights law apply. As will be discussed later, the CA3 threshold represents a high intensity of violence beyond that which can be regarded as mere states of crisis or emergency to which human rights law can apply. Therefore in situations that are covered by the international framework relative to belligerent occupation, where there is an outbreak of violence between the occupying power and elements of the civilian population that reach the threshold of CA3, it can be argued that Hague permissive rules have a higher threshold of applicability than much of the Geneva rules (and any domestic law and applicable supplementary human rights standards) that would be applicable to an ongoing situation of occupation. In situations that do not fall within the framework of belligerent occupation, that is, situations of internal violence between the armed forces of a state and nonstate actors who are nationals of that state, then it is suggested that human rights standards on issues such as detention, use of force and effective investigations apply up to the ceiling of CA3, as it is questionable as to whether human rights standards relative to these issues are practicable or realisable once this intensity of violence has been reached.

It is suggested that it is more problematic for human rights mechanisms not just to apply standard peacetime human rights norms to situations that have reached the CA3 threshold, but also to modify them through the express or implicit extrapolation of the language and logic of humanitarian law principles. This risks downgrading human rights standards and creating expectations that are both unrealisable and unrealistic. In terms of CA3 constituting the ceiling for the applicability of the law-and-order paradigm in situations of NIAC between the armed forces of a state and its own nationals or between an occupying power and foreign or enemy nationals, Hampson has proposed that the derogation threshold in human rights law should be linked to the threshold of CA3 of the Geneva Conventions in that 'at least [CA3] is applicable if the State asserts the right to derogate.'[311] Although it is accepted that the threshold of the transition from the paradigm of human rights law to that of the law of armed conflict should be set at CA3 in situations of NIAC, it is suggested that IHRL derogation threshold criteria are not necessarily linked to IHL threshold criteria, nor should they be linked.

IHL is linked to factual states of armed conflict and does not require any official recognition, formal derogation or declaration of war by any of the parties to a conflict.[312] In other words, a formal derogation from human rights treaties is not a prerequisite for the application of IHL. In this way, it is erroneous to suggest that where no martial law or state of emergency is declared, then the situation is to be judged against the 'normal background' of IHRL.[313] Indeed, IHL may apply even where one of the state parties to an international armed conflict does not recognise a state of war (CA2), or where a state fails to issue a formal declaration derogating from its human rights obligations. In the alternative, the proposal of linking human rights derogation thresholds that apply to states vis-à-vis their obligations that are capable of derogation with the application of IHL may be considered to lack efficacy in non-international armed conflicts fought exclusively between nonstate–organised armed groups.[314] Moreover, arguably, notwithstanding the continued applicability of nonderogable rights, whereas emergency powers may be resorted to in the face of 'actual or imminent' danger or crisis,[315] the paradigm of hostilities may only be entered into where there is an actual state of armed conflict as opposed to an 'imminent' threat of armed conflict.

The satisfaction of HRL derogation criteria is neither a necessary nor sufficient cause to apply a law of armed conflict framework. In other words, just because there may in fact be a 'public emergency which threatens the life of the nation',[316] this does not mean that it amounts to a factual state of armed conflict or that

311 Françoise Hampson, 'International Humanitarian Law in Situations of Acute Crisis' in Mukesh Kapila and Nigel Rodley (eds), Conference on the Promotion and Protection of Human Rights in Acute Crisis (Report) (11–13 February 1998), Chapter 3, 13.
312 API, above n 32, Article 1, (1)–(4); APII, Article 1; *Boškoski* (Trial Judgment) above n 69.
313 *Isayeva v Russia* (Application No 57950/00) ECHR 24 February 2005, [191].
314 Dapo Akande, above n 36, 54.
315 *The Greek Case*, above n 234; *Lawless* (Commission), above n 233.
316 UNHRC ICCPR General Comment No. 29, above n 251, Article 4.

the threshold for a CA3 or APII non-international armed conflict has been met. Furthermore, there is nothing in the provisions of the ICCPR, ECHR or the ACHR to suggest that there is such a linkage in practice.[317] Thus, just because a state declares a state of emergency it does not mean that the law of armed conflict will apply; nor should it. Additionally, Akande questions how derogation thresholds could trigger the application of IHL in situations where a state is not party to a particular human rights treaty and thus does not formally apply, or where the applicable human rights treaty does not provide for derogation, such as is the case with the African Charter on Human and People's Rights.[318]

As will be suggested later, having the paradigm shift for the transition from the law enforcement paradigm to that of armed conflict set at the CA3 threshold is a satisfactory state of affairs given that its threshold criteria, and thus the threshold for prohibitive and permissive customary Hague rules on the conduct of hostilities, are set at a high threshold. Indeed, it is suggested that the *Boškoski* threshold criteria, discussed later, mark the point at which normal measures or restrictions on the use of force associated with the right to life become inadequate in the face of an extremely dangerous and chaotic situation on the ground. This means that human rights law has a very broad spectrum of applicability in situations of internal and acute crisis that do not amount to an armed conflict, and human rights mechanisms have a very valuable role to play in this regard in terms of overseeing the resort to emergency powers so as to prevent the unregulated or unproclaimed resort to the framework of armed conflict and that the right to life applies as far as possible.[319] In other words, in situations where members of the civilian population, state agents or institutions are threatened by extreme violence in the form of internal tensions, disturbances or terrorist acts, then human rights standards are sufficiently permissive to allow for responses that are strictly unavoidable to guard against imminent threat of death or serious injury, or to otherwise maintain law and order where strictly necessary, without needing to resort to permissive Hague rules that allow for status-based targeting. Indeed, in situations not meeting the CA3 threshold criteria, normal measures and restrictions on the use of force are to be applied, not exceptional and permissive Hague rules on targeting. This means that human rights mechanisms can play a valuable role in assisting with the condemnation of targeted killings of individuals on the basis of status, rather than their representing a direct and immediate lethal threat which can only be prevented through the application of lethal force. In this regard, the *Boškoski* threshold criteria discussed later mark the point at which normal measures and restrictions on the use of force are no longer feasible or practicable, and more permissive standards on targeting are needed and become permissible.

To conclude this part of the discussion, it is suggested that even though human rights derogation criteria and humanitarian law threshold criteria are independent

---

317 Dapo Akande, above n 36, 52.
318 Dapo Akande, Ibid., 54.
319 UNHRC ICCPR General Comment No. 29: above n 251, Article 4 para (2).

of each other, it is nevertheless submitted that they are mutually reinforcing, in that when read together, they can ensure that human rights law applies as far as is practicable. This is to suggest that although IHL does not necessarily require linkage with human rights threshold criteria or, indeed, additional criteria imported from human rights law, to clarify its threshold of applicability, human rights law reasoning could benefit from reference to the IHL threshold criteria as elucidated by international criminal law jurisprudence so as to clarify the upper limits of its subject matter jurisdiction, or whether the use of force in question falls within the scope of the regulatory framework associated with the right to life. This could assist with evaluating whether a state of affairs falls within the legal framework of law enforcement or that of hostilities, and thus whether or not there is a permissible resort to permissive Hague rules on the conduct of hostilities. In particular, one of the criticisms that may be made of the reasoning employed by the European Court of Human Rights in cases such as *Isayeva v Russia* is that in the face of violence that indicated a factual state of non-international armed conflict, it proceeded to state that the situation was nevertheless 'outside wartime' and applied a law enforcement framework, albeit in a modified form in that it incorporated terminology and concepts associated with the paradigm of hostilities.[320] It is suggested that the reasoning of human rights mechanisms when dealing with situations involving extreme violence between state and nonstate actors could be bolstered by providing reasoned analyses of whether or not the threshold criteria for an armed conflict have been met, and in this regard human rights mechanisms should refer to updated guidelines in the jurisprudence of the ICTY in order to assess whether or not a given situation is 'outside wartime' or, more specifically, whether or not there is a factual state of armed conflict. To date, this does not appear to have occurred. If on such an assessment a situation is assessed to be 'outside of wartime' and so the 'normal legal background' of HRL applies, then it is suggested that human rights mechanisms should avoid the express or implicit extrapolation of the language and logic of IHL when interpreting the right to life, as this risks downgrading human rights protections that are per se sufficient to respond to crisis situations (but not conflict situations), such as the strict or absolute necessity threshold for the use of lethal force under human rights law, and potentially widening the scope of permissive IHL principles (from conflict into crisis situations or even lesser 'peacetime' law enforcement operations) such as status-based rather than threat-based targeting decisions.[321]

---

320 *Isayeva v Russia*, above n 313, 180 and 191.

321 *Özkan and Others v Turkey* (Application no 21689/93) ECHR (Second Section) 6 April 2004, [178]–[179]; *Ergi v Turkey* (Application No 23818/94) ECHR 1998-IV [70] [72] [79] [80] [81]; *Isayeva*, Ibid., [175] [177] [176] [182] [185] [189] [198] [199]; *Isayeva, Yusupova and Bazayeva v Russia* (Application Nos 57947/00, 57948/00 and 57949/00) ECHR 6 July 2005, [184] [190] [191] [205].

4 Reconceptualising the regulation of the use of force in situations of crisis and unconventional conflict

Individual status determination

Introduction: direct participation in hostilities and the loss of noncombatant immunity: an 'admixture of military sternness with basic humanitarianism'[1]

Chapter 1 suggested that the dynamics of asymmetric power relations of contemporary conflicts have led to them becoming increasingly unconventional in that they are irregular in nature and urban in context. In other words, the dynamics of asymmetric warfare compel weaker adversaries to adopt concealment methods of warfare whereby they operate within high-density civilian-populated areas. In this way, civilians not only 'saturate the modern battlefield', but this 'battlefield' is characterised by a high degree of irregularity in terms of civilians 'often engaging in activities that have traditionally been performed by members of the armed forces'.[2] As discussed in Chapter 1, in a civilianised operational environment, there are increased pressures for civilians to play a variety of direct and indirect roles within the internal support structure of a party to an armed conflict. Furthermore indirect and direct forms of support can in fact be considered forms of participation in an internal support structure. In turn, these forms of support may be regarded, respectively, as 'nonlethal' or 'lethal' threats, which, to a greater or lesser extent may not be considered functionally or causally distant harm occurring or likely to occur during conduct of hostilities.

In a civilianised milieu, this poses a twofold challenge, namely to distinguish members of an organised armed group from civilians who are directly participating in hostilities and, more fundamentally, to distinguish direct participation in hostilities from general support provided by the mass base of popular support of the general population towards the general war effort. The next section will discuss the challenge of distinguishing the activities and the violence occurring within the mass base of popular support and the general population from a range

1 Emily Camins, 'The past as prologue: The Development of the 'Direct Participation' Exception to Civilian immunity' (2008) 90 (872) *International Review of the Red Cross* 862.

2 Michael Schmitt, 'Deconstructing Direct Participation in Hostilities: The Constitutive Elements' (2009–2010) 42 *New York University Journal of International Law and Politics* 697, 699.

of 'lethal' and 'nonlethal threats' emanating from organised armed groups that are embedded within and concealed amongst the people.

However, for present purposes this section suggests that treaty-based and customary rules of humanitarian law that serve to guide the process of making such distinctions were developed for conventional armed conflicts, and so a degree of 'dynamic interpretation' is required so that they are fit for the 'new reality' of unconventional and full-spectrum operational environments.[3] Accordingly, the 'dynamic' objective of this section is to consider whether modes of participation and perpetration adopted in international criminal law can be extrapolated in order to redress the substantive lacunae and indeterminacies within humanitarian law vis-à-vis what constitutes 'direct' or 'active' participation in hostilities. This is discussed as a means of redressing the absence of clear and uniform standards which creates a 'wide margin for legal-policy influence'[4] or 'strategic instrumentalisation'[5] in the targeting process. Accordingly, it is generally unclear who can be lawfully attacked in the complex operational environment of contemporary hostilities where conflicts are often fought 'amongst the people' or concentrations of civilians in urban areas.

Although the 'dynamic' approach considered in this section may be considered counterintuitive, it is suggested that it can actually serve to reconcile humanitarian and military considerations in a plausible fashion, as well as to promote rather than undermine humanitarian protections by putting the issue of direct participation in hostilities on sounder analytical foundations. As will be discussed, this approach may only apply once the threshold of an armed conflict has been reached as described earlier, and rather than undermining civilian immunity, it is suggested that it actually serves to subject the escalation of lethal force to stringent conditions that may be considered plausible in unconventional operational environments. Moreover, as described in Chapter 1, contemporary military doctrine suggests that 'nonlethal' human targets should be subject to an escalation of nonlethal force. Therefore, even though military doctrine may describe participation in hostilities in broad and functional terms, it does not automatically prescribe a conventional lethal military response as a primary response. In unconventional contexts, the irregular form of violence may belie its collective nature in the sense that whereas only a few individuals may physically perpetrate

---

3 *Public Committee Against Torture v The Government of Israel et al.*, above n 142, 28 *per* Justice Barak: '[r]ules developed against the background of a reality which has changed must take on dynamic interpretation which adapts them, in the framework of accepted interpretational rules, to the new reality'; Hilly Moodrick Even-Khen, 'Case Note: Can We Now Tell What "Direct Participation In Hostilities" Is?' HCJ 769/02 The Public Committee Against Torture in Israel v the Government of Israel' (2007) 40 (1) *Israel Law Review* 213, 229.

4 Rob McLaughlin, 'Legal-Policy Considerations and Conflict Characterisation at the Threshold between Law Enforcement and Non-International Armed Conflict' (2012) 13(1) *Melbourne Journal of International Law* 28.

5 Nathaniel Berman, 'Privileging Combat? Contemporary Conflict and the Legal Construction of War' (2004) 43(1) *Columbia Journal of Transnational Law* 23–24.

harmful hostile acts, the activities of other individuals within multifarious support structures may actually facilitate their commission, or the likelihood of their commission, in a functional, material or otherwise causally proximate fashion through their underlying contributions.[6] This way of conceiving the fundamental issue of distinguishing forms of direct participation in hostilities from forms of general support towards a war effort raises the difficult, and essentially policy-based, question of whether forms of direct support or indirect participation that cause harm or are likely to cause harm can be equated with 'direct' or 'active' participation in hostilities so as to have a bearing on the modalities and parameters of civilian immunity from attack. As will be discussed later, although the ICRC elements of direct participation in hostilities spelled out in its interpretive guidance are useful in attempting to clarify the scope of civilian immunity from attack, it is suggested that its analysis was too narrow and conceptually weak to be capable of application in the realities of twenty-first-century conflicts. In particular, it fails to conceptualise adequately the grey area of direct and indirect participation in hostilities. Accordingly, following this section will be a discussion on the import of criminal law concepts of accessorial liability and coperpetration as a way of adding more analytical clarity to this issue as well as making it more amenable to states.

The principle of distinction in the unconventional operational environment and civilian status under international law

Distinction is a core principle of humanitarian law which is set out in Article 48 of API. It requires parties to a conflict to 'distinguish between the civilian population and combatants and between civilian objects and military objectives and accordingly shall direct their operations only against military objectives'. In *Martić*, the principle of distinction was described as 'the rule that the civilian population as such, as well as individual civilians, shall not be the object of attack' and that this 'is a fundamental rule of international humanitarian law applicable to all armed conflicts'.[7] The force of this 'fundamental rule' is thus premised on a clear definition of civilian status as well as clear and plausible parameters of civilian immunity from attack.

Civilian status

Article 50 of API defines a civilian as 'any person who does not belong to one of the categories of persons referred to in Article 4A(1), (2), (3) and (6) of the Third Geneva Convention and in Article 43 of this Protocol'. Accordingly, with regard to Article 4 of the Third Geneva Convention, civilians do not include '[m]embers of the armed forces of a Party to the conflict, as well as members of

6 *Prosecutor v Tadić* (Appeals Chamber Judgment) ICTY-94-1-A (15 July 1999) 191.
7 *Prosecutor v Martić* (Rule 61 Decision) ICTY-95-11-R61 (March 8 1996) 10.

militias or volunteer corps forming part of such armed forces'[8] and '[m]embers of other militias and members of other volunteer corps, including those of organised resistance movements, belonging to a Party to the conflict and operating in or outside their own territory . . .'[9] With regard to Article 43 of API, civilian status does not apply to those who belong to 'the armed forces of a Party to a conflict'. In *Dragomir Milošević*, the term civilian was interpreted to include 'any person who is not a member of the armed forces or an organised military group belonging to a party to the conflict'.[10] Therefore, the rules of international armed conflict only provide for the status of civilian and combatant. Combatants may not be prosecuted for carrying out lawful acts of war and can be targeted on the basis of their combatant status alone, unless they are *hors de combat*. As will be discussed, civilians may not be targeted unless they are directly participating in hostilities. APII relative to non-international armed conflicts does not provide a definition of what constitutes a civilian because proposals to include a definition were rejected during the drafting process.[11] Nevertheless, according to Rule 5 of the ICRC Customary Study, Article 50 of API is reflective of customary law and so applies in both international and non-international armed conflicts. However, combatant status pertains only to international armed conflicts. Therefore, members of organised armed groups may be prosecuted under domestic criminal law for violent acts committed against state armed forces as well as civilians. This raises the question of the status of those who directly participate in hostilities or who are members of organised armed groups within a non-international armed conflict.

The fuzzy legal parameters of noncombatant immunity from attack: 'direct' or 'active' participation in hostilities and where status-based targeting begins

Given its status as a 'fundamental rule of international humanitarian law',[12] it is of concern that the principle of distinction in terms of civilian immunity from attack rests on unclear and contentious foundations. Indeed, this 'fundamental rule' is qualified by Article 51 paragraph (3) of API and Article 13 paragraph (3)

8 Geneva Convention (III) relative to the Treatment of Prisoners of War. Geneva, 12 August 1949, Article 4(1).

9 Ibid., Article 4(2).

10 *Prosecutor v Dragomir Milošević* (Trial Judgement) ICTY-98–29/1-T (12 December 2007) 945–946.

11 Diplomatic Conference on the Reaffirmation and Development of International Humanitarian Law Applicable in Armed Conflicts (Conférence diplomatique sur la réaffirmation et le développement du droit international humanitaire applicable dans les conflits armés), 1974–1977, CDDH Official Records Volume I (3), 40: Article 25(1) and (2) of the draft Additional Protocol II submitted by the ICRC to the CDDH provided that 'any person who is not a member of armed forces is considered to be a civilian" and "the civilian population comprises all persons who are civilians'.

12 *Martić* (Rule 61 Decision), above n 7, 10.

of APII, which both provide that civilians are to enjoy protection against the dangers arising from military operations 'unless and for such time as they take a direct part in hostilities'.[13] As discussed earlier, one of the main consequences of classifying a situation as an 'armed conflict' is that any civilian directly participating in hostilities can be targeted, but this turns on the issue of what constitutes 'participation' in hostilities. This permissive rule on opening fire will be discussed in more detail later, but for present purposes it should be noted that it has an equivalence to the human rights permission to use lethal force where necessary. As discussed previously, this indicates that human rights standards may be interpreted in a highly permissive fashion so that they can be relevant and practicable to situations of crisis or emergency that involve extreme situations of violence but which do not reach the minimum threshold of an armed conflict as denoted by the indicative guidelines in *Boškoski*. Although the notion of direct participation in hostilities is important, arguably what is more significant about the transition to the paradigm of hostilities is the permissibility, according to the ICRC in its Interpretive Guidance, of targeting individuals on the basis of status (that is, on the basis of being a member of an organised armed group exercising a continuous combat function), rather than a targeting decision being based on an individual posing a direct and immediate lethal threat. In other words, according to the ICRC in its Interpretive Guidance, individuals can be targeted if and for as long as they are members of an organised armed group exercising a continuous combat function, because in such circumstances they will no longer be regarded as civilians per se, but neither will they be regarded as combatants in the sense of having combatants' privilege.[14] According to Schmitt, members of organised armed groups belonging to a party to a conflict who have a 'continuous combat function' are effectively disqualified as civilians.[15] In contrast, individuals who are directly participating in hostilities do not lose their civilian status, but, rather, may only be lawfully attacked 'for such time' as they are directly participating in hostilities. It is suggested that a lot more clarity and analysis are required in relation to this issue because although being a member of an organised armed group exercising a continuous combat function results in a general loss of immunity for as long as such a function is assumed, at the same time there is a significant amount of legal and practical uncertainty surrounding its precise scope and meaning.[16] This is problematic in that, according to the ICRC in its Interpretive Guidance, this notion of a 'continuous combat function' is in part premised on

---

13 Protocol Additional to the Geneva Conventions of 12 August 1949, and relating to the Protection of Victims of International Armed Conflicts (Protocol I), 8 June 1977 ('API'), Article 51(3): Article 51 was adopted by 77 votes in favour, one against and 16 abstentions; see also CDDH, above n 11, Volume VI, 16.

14 Françoise Hampson, 'Direct Participation in Hostilities and the Interoperability of the Law of Armed Conflict and Human Rights Law', in Raul Pedrozo and Daria Wollschlaeger (eds), *International Law Studies* (Vol. 87, US Naval War College, 2011) 199.

15 Michael Schmitt, above n 2, 704.

16 Françoise Hampson, above n 14, 187.

direct participation in hostilities as it states that '[i]ndividuals whose continuous function involves the preparation, execution, or command of acts or operations amounting to direct participation in hostilities are assuming a continuous combat function'.[17] As such, the Interpretive Guidance has been criticised in that as it accords a functionally narrow scope to the concept of continuous combat function, members of organised armed groups who do not perform continuous combat functions may not be attacked on the basis of their status alone and thus enjoy civilian immunity from attack unless and for such time as they directly participate in hostilities.[18] Watkin argues that creating the 'continuous combat function' test for membership and then restricting its scope by tying it to a narrow definition of direct participation in hostilities not only disadvantages states engaged in hostilities with organised armed groups, but is unlikely to be found credible by the soldiers of states asked to apply such guidance[19]:

> Consequently, under IHL, the decisive criterion for individual membership in an organized armed group is whether a person assumes a continuous function for the group involving his or her direct participation in hostilities (hereafter: 'continuous combat function')[20]

As noted by Hampson, targeting by reference to status rather than behaviour is likely to worsen a situation, for example, by leading to an escalation in violence, and is likely to be 'even less well tolerated' in what she describes as 'low-intensity armed conflicts' than in 'high-intensity' NIACs.[21] Furthermore, given the greater flexibility that the notion of loss of immunity 'unless and for such time' as an individual 'directly participates in hostilities' offers armed forces, Hampson questions the import or necessity of addressing the status of a fighter in NIAC.[22] For the sake of argument and definitional clarity within the context of this discussion, it is suggested the notion of what Hampson refers to as 'low intensity' NIACs, to which permissive Hague rules do not apply, are to be regarded as situations which do not reach the minimum threshold criteria for a CA3 NIAC as outlined in *Boškoski*. In this sense, this loose notion of a 'low intensity armed conflict' may be regarded as one which does not surpass the ceiling of a CA3 NIAC, and so rules based on the law-and-order paradigm, as opposed to the armed conflict paradigm, will apply. The argument here is that the indicative guidelines outlined

17 Nils Melzer, 'Interpretive Guidance on the Notion of Direct Participation in Hostilities under International Humanitarian Law' (International Committee of the Red Cross, Geneva 2009) 25 ('ICRC Interpretive Guidance') 27, 34.

18 Michael Schmitt, above n 2, 704.

19 Kenneth Watkin, 'Opportunity Lost: Organized Armed Groups and the ICRC "Direct Participation in Hostilities" Interpretive Guidance' (2010) 42 *New York University Journal of International Law and Politics* 655, 693–694.

20 ICRC (Interpretive Guidance), above n 17, 33.

21 Françoise Hampson, above n 14, 187.

22 Ibid., 199.

in *Boškoski* are practical and useful criteria in assisting armed forces in identifying those situations of organised armed violence to which the law-and-order paradigm applies and those to which the armed conflict paradigm will apply. It is suggested that *Boškoski* is most useful in that in addition to referencing municipal law, it consolidates and summarises the wealth of post-*Tadić* case law into a clear set of indicative guidelines that mark the minimum threshold for the applicability of the paradigm of armed conflict, and in this way, it is not helpful to try to distinguish between 'low intensity' and 'high intensity' NIACs when it comes to identifying those situations to which permissive customary Hague standards apply.

CA3 provides legal protection against 'violence to life and person, in particular murder of all kinds' for '[p]ersons taking no active part in the hostilities'.[23] According to *Akayesu* the terms 'direct participation in hostilities' and 'active part in hostilities' are synonymous.[24] It is thus suggested that this issue of direct participation in hostilities is not confined to APII situations, but also to situations reaching the threshold of a CA3 non-international armed conflict.[25] Furthermore, in contrast to Hampson's assertions that APII is 'a development of Common Article 3 [and] is principally an example of Geneva law' and that 'unlike Common Article 3', 'it does contain some Hague type provisions', it is suggested that these synonymous participation clauses are both referable to the targeting law principle of distinction, and thus both contain a basic Hague-type provision in that they represent a qualification to what may be considered a prohibition on targeting and opening fire on protected persons. In other words, they are referable to the principle of distinction in that in order to provide substantive protections, there must be a distinction between civilians and those who act like the armed forces of a party to a conflict. Similarly, the ICRC notes that

> [a]lthough Article 3 GC I-IV generally is not considered to govern the conduct of hostilities, its wording allows certain conclusions to be drawn with regard to the generic distinction between the armed forces and the civilian population in non-international armed conflict

and so 'each party to the conflict', that is, both state and nonstate parties to a conflict, must afford protection to 'persons taking no active part in the hostilities', which not only includes members of armed forces *hors de combat*, but also

23 Convention (I) for the Amelioration of the Condition of the Wounded and Sick in Armed Forces in the Field, Geneva, 12 August 1949, Article 3; Convention (II) for the Amelioration of the Condition of the Wounded, Sick and Shipwrecked Members of Armed Forces at Sea, Geneva, 12 August 1949, Article 3; Convention (III) relative to the Treatment of Prisoners of War, Geneva, 12 August 1949, Article 3; Convention (IV) relative to the Protection of Civilian Persons in Time of War, Geneva, 12 August 1949.

24 *Prosecutor v Akayesu (Trial Judgment) ICTR-96–4-T (2 September 1998)* 629.

25 For contrasting views see Françoise Hampson, above n 14, and Françoise Hampson, 'Afghanistan 2001–2010' in Elizabeth Wilmshurst (ed), *International Law and the Classification of Conflicts* (OUP, 2012).

civilians who are not directly participating in hostilities or who do not bear arms on behalf of a party to the conflict.[26]

CA3 thus provides rudimentary guidance on who may be targeted and on what basis, that is, those taking active part in hostilities. As it indicates that its beneficiaries are those who take no active part in hostilities, this suggests that it applies both within and without the conduct of hostilities.

Although CA3 and APII are silent on the issue of members of organised armed groups, they both nevertheless admit an important distinction between those who play a direct/active part in hostilities and those who do not, without conferring any combatant status or privilege on the former category.

In this way, in *Avila v Columbia*, although the commission recognised that Columbia had 'the full right to defend itself from violent actions . . . and to take military actions against . . . irregular armed groups', the commission also found a freestanding substantive breach of CA3 on the basis that

> once the members were hors de combat . . . the Columbian state had no right to attack or kill them . . . [t]hese combatants who were wounded or defenceless, like any wounded civilian, had the absolute right to the guarantees of humane treatment provided for in the non-derogable guarantees of Common Article 3 of the Geneva Conventions and of the American Convention.[27]

This would indicate that the state had the right to open fire on those participating in hostilities (Hague law aspect), but this did not affect the obligation of state agents 'to treat humanely all the persons within their power due to injury, surrender or detention, whether or not they had previously participated in hostilities' (Geneva law aspect).[28] In this way, the extrajudicial execution of the eleven victims constituted a flagrant violation of CA3, as they were effectively rendered *hors de combat* in an internal armed conflict and were in the power of the state, but, *a contrario*, opening fire on those participating in hostilities whilst not within the state's power would not constitute a violation of CA3.

This leads to the significant question of where targeting on the basis of status as a member of an organised armed group begins. Unfortunately, the ICRC in its Interpretive Guidance simply made a bifurcated distinction between conflicts of an international and non-international character. Accordingly, its general guidance seemingly applies to all the different permutations of NIAC without distinguishing between CA3 NIACs and APII NIACs. This was a significant omission given that Hampson suggests that it may not be permissible to target on the basis of membership of an organised armed group (that is, an individual exercising

26 Hampson, above n 14, 203; ICRC (Interpretive Guidance), above n 17, 28.
27 *Arturo Ribón Avila v Colombia* (Report No 26/97) Inter-American Commission on Human Rights, Case 11/142, OEA/Ser L/V/II.95 Doc 7 rev at 444 (30 September 1997), 135.
28 Ibid., 202.

a continuous combat function) at the level of a CA3 non-international armed conflict.[29] However, it is suggested that as Hampson did not expressly discuss *Boškoski*, then there is an absence of specific discussion in relation to whether human rights standards of threat-based targeting alone are practicable at the threshold of organised violence foreseen by the ICTY as being indicative of a factual state of CA3 non-international armed conflict. It is suggested that there are no compelling grounds for arguing that the Interpretive Guidance offered by the ICRC vis-à-vis direct participation in hostilities and, most significantly, membership in an organised armed group should be restricted to situations above the threshold of applicability of APII. Given the previously mentioned and upcoming obstacles to the applicability of APII, it is suggested that there is an absence of compelling reasons for arguing that status-based targeting on the grounds of membership should be confined to situations where, for example, an organised armed group controls territory or has the ability to mount sustained and concerted operations. Arguably, such a proposition does not reflect the operational reality of many contemporary armed conflicts of a non-international character and risks leaving armed conflicts below this particular threshold without any appropriate legal regulation in the form of treaty-based and customary IHL as opposed to human rights standards.

Furthermore, it is argued that even though organised armed groups are expressly provided for in Article 1(1) of APII, but not CA3, it is nevertheless suggested that the applicability criteria for CA3 are elucidated by *Boškoski*, which conditions its applicability on the *de facto* existence of sufficiently organised armed groups that integrate individuals and connect them to hostilities through recruitment, training and, most significantly, *de facto* systems of command and control. It is suggested that the *Boškoski* elucidation of the CA3 threshold criteria essentially foresees the notion of membership of an organised armed group. Furthermore, this is not only a factor to be taken into account in considering organisational aspects of the threshold question, but is distinct from questions of direct participation in hostilities, as it indicates a situation where the organisation is such that standard law enforcement responses may no longer practicable, and so at a minimum, CA3 applies and is supplemented by customary Hague Law.

However as stated earlier, in addition to the issue that in its Customary International Humanitarian Law study, the ICRC stated that 'a clear and uniform definition of direct participation in hostilities has not been developed in State practice',[30] the ICRC's Customary Law Study and Interpretive Guidance did not consider or clarify in any sufficient analytic detail what it means to target on the basis of status as a member of an organised armed group or whether there was more than one permutation of NIAC.

---

29 Françoise Hampson, above n 25, section 4.

30 Jean-Marie Henckaerts and Louise Doswald-Beck, *Customary International Humanitarian Law* (Volume 1: Rules, ICRC-Cambridge University Press, 2005) ('CIHL Study'), Rule 6, 23; *Prosecutor v Strugar* (Appeals Chamber Judgment) IT-01–42-A (17 July 2008) 66.

This is further complicated in that in *Kupreskić*, it was noted that loss of immunity may occur 'when civilians abuse their rights'.[31] In this way, in contrast to membership of an organised armed group, direct participation does not affect civilian status per se but rather, to an uncertain extent, results in loss of immunity from attack due to an 'abuse'. In the ICRC Commentary to the Geneva Conventions and in *Galić*, 'abuse' was defined as 'acts of war which by their nature or purpose are likely to cause actual harm to the personnel or materiel of the enemy armed forces . . . '.[32] *A contrario*, this is a major cause for concern given that there are no 'clear and uniform' standards for distinguishing direct participation from forms of indirect participation or support and given that 'acts of war' may be construed as activities which in fact 'are likely to cause actual harm'. This plausibly leaves a wide margin of discretion for belligerents to define broadly what constitutes a threat likely to cause actual harm. Put another way, conventional humanitarian law allows for a margin of appreciation to view forms of direct support or indirect participation as causing harm or likely to cause harm and on this basis equating them with direct participation in hostilities.[33]

31 *Prosecutor v Kupreškić* (Trial Judgment) ICTY-95–16-T (14 January 2000) 522.

32 *Prosecutor v Galić* (Trial Judgment) ICTY-98–29-T (5 December 2003), 48; *Prosecutor v Kordić and Čerkez* (Appeals Chamber Judgment) ICTY-95–14/2-A (17 December 2004), 51; *Strugar* (Appeals Chamber Judgment), above n 30, 64.

33 United States, *Manual for Military Commissions*, in Military Commissions Act (2006) Chapter 47 A of Title 10 United States Code (17 October 2006), 948 (a)(1), (2) & (3), Part IV 6 (26), IV-19, IV-20: With regard to the United States, in its Manual for Military Commissions, the elements of the offence of 'wrongfully aiding the enemy' include the knowing and intentional aiding of an enemy of the United States within the context and associated with an armed conflict. Examples of 'aiding an enemy' include 'providing arms, ammunition, supplies, money, other items or services to the enemy; harboring or protecting the enemy; or giving intelligence or other information to the enemy'. The United States also introduces an additional category of 'unlawful enemy combatant' which according to its Manual on Military Commissions includes any 'person who has engaged in hostilities or who has purposefully and materially supported hostilities against the United States or its co-belligerents who is not a lawful enemy combatant (including a person who is part of the Taliban, al Qaeda, or associated forces); or a person who, before, on, or after the date of the enactment of the Military Commissions Act of 2006, has been determined to be an unlawful enemy combatant by a Combatant Status Review Tribunal or another competent tribunal established under the authority of the President or the Secretary of Defense'; *Re Guantanamo Detainee Cases*, United States, District Court for the District of Columbia, Judgement of 31 January 2005: the US District Court found that 'the definition currently applied by the government, an "enemy combatant" "shall mean an individual who was part of or supporting Taliban or al Qaeda forces, or associated forces that are engaged in hostilities against the United States or its coalition partners. This includes any person who has committed a belligerent act or has directly supported hostilities in aid of enemy armed forces'; *Hicks Case*, Office of Military Commissions, Record of Trial (26 and 30 March 2007): in *Hicks*, the military judge held that '[t]he term "unlawful enemy combatant" as it is used here means a person who has engaged in hostilities or who has purposefully and materially supported hostilities against the United States or its co-belligerents . . .'

In trying to resolve this quandary of distinguishing direct and indirect forms of participation, the ICRC noted that

> to restrict this concept to combat and active military operations would be too narrow, while extending it to the entire war effort would be too broad, as in modern warfare the whole population participates in the war effort to some extent, albeit indirectly.[34]

More recently the ICRC proposed a number of interpretive guidelines on direct participation in hostilities, which will be discussed. However, for the present purposes, it is suggested that a major reason for the uncertainty surrounding the interpretation of what constitutes direct participation in hostilities is indicative of an approach which circumvents the issue of formulating general analytic criteria which cover functional or material contributions to hostile activities or 'acts which are likely to cause harm' on policy grounds. It is suggested that this acts as a barrier to discussing and conceiving this issue in a more detailed and analytic fashion. For example, numerous sources suggest that this issue of distinguishing between forms of direct participation in hostilities and forms of support for the general war effort are to be assessed on a case-by-case basis.[35]

Indeed, the Trial Chamber in *Tadić* stated that 'it is unnecessary to define exactly the line dividing those taking an active part in hostilities and those who are not so involved' and added that 'it is sufficient to examine the relevant facts of each victim and to ascertain whether, in each individual's circumstances, that person was actively involved in hostilities at the relevant time'.[36] It is suggested that this is a way of circumventing fundamental issues concerning the nature of harmful acts and their causative power. Moreover, it is suggested that such an approach is problematic in that it assumes the existence of that which has to be established, namely a clear analytical conception of what it means to be 'actively involved in hostilities' against which 'each individual's circumstances' can be assessed. To suggest that 'it is unnecessary' to forge a clearer normative understanding of what it means to participate directly in hostilities concedes that targeting largely takes place in a normative vacuum which allows for the possibility of arbitrary and erroneous targeting decisions in terms of allowing for both broad and narrow

34 Y Sandoz, C Swinarski and B Zimmermann (eds), *Commentary on the Additional Protocols of 8 June 1977 to the Geneva Conventions of 12 August 1949* (ICRC/Martinus Nijhoff, Geneva 1987), (*'Commentary'*), 514; United States Navy, Marine Corps & Coast Guard, The Commander's Handbook on the Law of Naval Operations, NWP 1-14M/MCWP 5-2.1/ COMDTPUB P5800.7 (Department of Navy, Naval Doctrine Command, Norfolk, Virginia October 1995), 11.3: The US Naval Handbook of 1995 states that '[d]irect participation in hostilities must be judged on a case-by-case basis [and that] [c]ombatants in the field must make an honest determination as to whether a particular civilian is or is not subject to deliberate attack based on the person's behavior, location and attire, and other information available at the time'.

35 Ibid.

36 *Prosecutor v Tadić* (Opinion and Judgment) ICTY-94-1-T (7 May 1997) 616.

interpretations of 'active' or 'direct' participation.[37] Furthermore, a case-by-case approach, together with the examples provided in numerous cases of forms of support for the general war effort or indirect participation that are claimed not to amount to direct participation in hostilities, do not, it is suggested, provide a clear and analytical conception that can assist with evaluating activities that are in the grey area between, for example, 'a civilian bearing arms (openly or concealed) who is on his way to the place where he will use them against the army' and a civilian 'sympathizing with one side's cause . . . or providing support for the general war effort, such as by selling food or medicine'.[38]

Arguably, the most cogent aspect of the reasoning employed by the Israeli High Court of Justice in *Public Committee Against Torture v The Government of Israel* was that 'function determines the directness of the part taken in the hostilities'.[39] In this way, it is not merely 'the person committing the physical act of attack' who causes harm, but also those who are 'involved in the terrorist chain of command'.[40] In this way, their indirect support roles[41] may be regarded as 'direct' and 'active' forms of participation.[42] Another key uncertainty concerns the temporal scope of direct participation in hostilities, and on this issue, although the Israeli High Court of Justice stated that there exists no 'consensus in the international literature,' on this issue, it nevertheless proceeded to elucidate it further.[43] In particular, in marked contrast to the approach taken vis-à-vis members of organised armed groups discussed later, it stated that 'a civilian taking a direct part in hostilities one single time, or sporadically, who later detaches himself from that activity, is a civilian who, starting from the time he detached himself from that activity, is entitled to protection from attack' and thus may not be attacked for the commission of previous hostile acts.[44]

---

37 Nils Melzer, *Targeted Killing in International Law* (Oxford University Press, 2009), 333–334.

38 *PCAT v Israel*, above n 3, 34; *Third Report on the Human Rights Situation in Colombia*, Inter-American Commission on Human Rights, OEA/Ser L/V/II 102 Doc 9 rev 1 (26 February 1999): '[c]ivilians whose activities merely support the adverse party's war or military effort or otherwise only indirectly participate in hostilities cannot on these grounds alone be considered combatants. This is because indirect participation, such as selling goods to one or more of the armed parties, expressing sympathy for the cause of one of the parties or, even more clearly, failing to act to prevent an incursion by one of the armed parties, does not involve acts of violence which pose an immediate threat of actual harm to the adverse party'.

39 *PCAT v Israel*, Ibid., 35.

40 Ibid., 37.

41 Ibid., 35: for example, the collection of intelligence relating to the hostilities, the transportation of combatants and the transportation, operation or servicing of weapons.

42 Ibid., 35–37, 39.

43 Ibid., 39.

44 Ibid; Michael Schmitt, 'Direct Participation in Hostilities and 21st Century Armed Conflict' in H Fischer (ed), *Krisensicherung und Humanitärer Schutz – Crisis Management and Humanitarian Protection: Festshrift fur Dieter Fleck* (Berliner Wissenschaftsverlag, Berlin, 2004) 505–509.

The ICRC Interpretive Guidance: overview

In view of these uncertainties, the ICRC Interpretive Guidance attempts to contribute to our understanding of the modalities and parameters of immunity from attack by attempting to clarify the distinction between civilians directly participating in hostilities and civilians becoming members of organised armed groups. This is set out diagrammatically[45] in Figure 4.1 before proceeding to discuss these two issues in turn.

The diagram illustrates the permutations of loss of immunity from attack. As this diagram suggests, the ICRC Interpretive Guidance attempts to make a clear distinction between loss of immunity from attack on the basis of direct participation in hostilities and loss of immunity from attack on the basis of a 'continuous combat function' which equates with *de facto* membership of an organised armed group. Respectively, the ICRC thus attempts to create a clear and distinct separation between these two separate bases of targeting, namely on the basis of threat and on the basis of status. The rationale for making such a distinction is based on an interpretation of Article 51 paragraph (3) of API to the effect that an act or even acts of participation in hostilities, without becoming a member of an organised armed group, should not result in a continuous loss of protection from attack, but rather a temporary loss of protection 'for such time' as an individual directly participates.[46] This interpretation is premised on the notion that using past participation as an indicator of a future propensity to commit hostile acts in order to render a civilian targetable for the duration of the hostilities 'would blur the distinction between temporary activity-based loss of protection and continuous status-based loss of protection (due to continuous combat function)'.[47] The reasoning embodied within the ICRC's Interpretive Guidance in making such a distinction will now be examined. With regard to direct participation in hostilities, the Interpretive Guidance attempts to provide general rules on the type of conduct that constitutes direct participation in hostilities. Furthermore, it attempts to clarify the temporal scope of participation in hostilities and thus the concomitant temporal scope of loss of immunity from attack. It does this by setting out three constitutive and cumulative elements of 'direct' or 'active' participation in hostilities which will be summarized and analysed next.

The elements of direct participation in hostilities: an overview

First, the requisite 'threshold of harm' has to be met. In this regard, an act does not need to amount to a direct 'attack' per se, but rather an act reaches the requisite threshold when it is likely to affect adversely the military operations or military capacity of a party to an armed conflict or, alternatively, to inflict death,

---

45 ICRC (Interpretive Guidance), above n 17; see also Nils Melzer, 'Keeping the Balance Between Military Necessity and Humanity: A Response to Four Critiques of the ICRC's Interpretative Guidance on the Notion of Direct Participation in Hostilities' (2009–2010) 42 *New York Journal of International Law and Politics* 831, 854.

46 Nils Melzer, above n 45, 887.

47 ICRC (Interpretive Guidance), above n 17, 44–45.

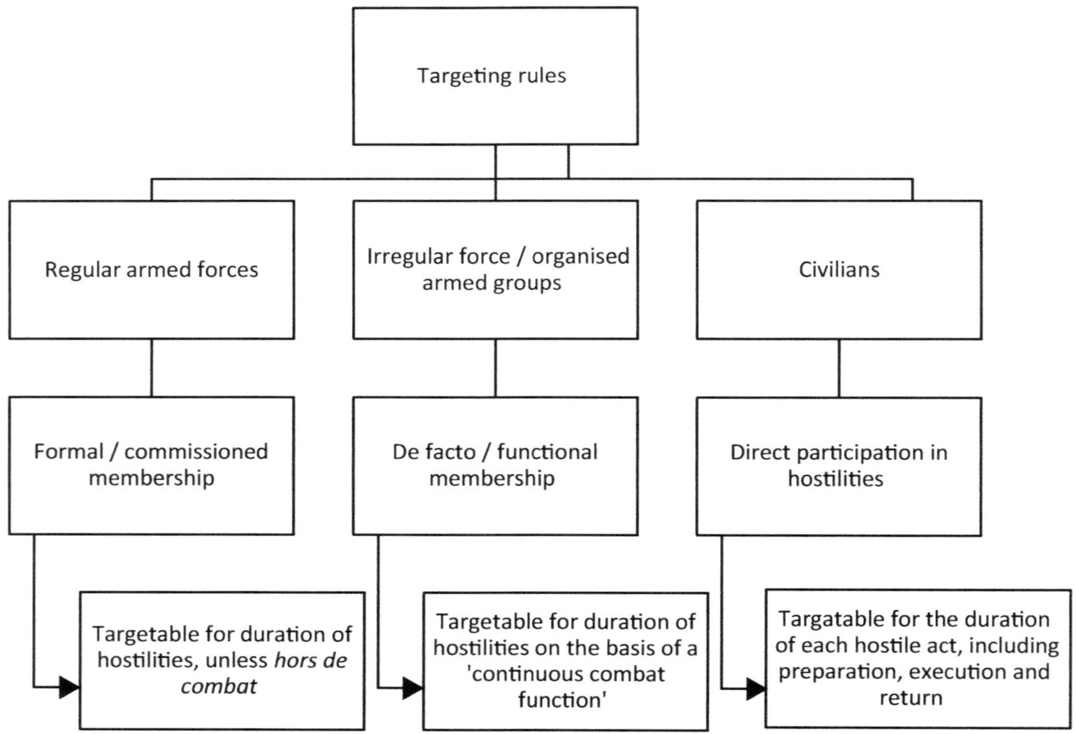

Figure 4.1 Distinguishing formal and functional membership from direct participation in hostilities.

injury or destruction. Second, there must be 'direct causation' between the act and the harm. In other words, there must be a direct causal link in the form of 'one causal step' between the act and the harm likely to result, either from that act or from a concrete and coordinated military operation that directly causes harm of which that act constitutes an integral part.[48] Third, in addition to satisfying the two previously mentioned criteria in terms of being 'objectively likely to inflict harm', there is the additional requirement of a 'belligerent nexus' between the act and the harm caused. This means that the act must be specifically designed to cause directly the required threshold of harm in support of a party to the conflict and to the detriment of another.[49] In this way, violent activities such as those involved in petty or organised crime may not be connected to the surrounding hostilities so as to amount to direct participation in them.

The threshold of harm

According to the Interpretive Guidance, the requisite 'threshold of harm' is met where an act is likely to affect adversely the military operations or military capacity of a party to an armed conflict or, alternatively, to inflict death, injury or destruction.[50] As will be discussed further in relation to causation, Schmitt has criticised this criterion in that it sets the threshold at too high a level and so does not adequately reflect military considerations. In particular, Schmitt suggests that this concept is underinclusive for the reason that civilian contributions that enhance military operations or capacity would not meet such a high threshold requirement, for example, with regard to the training and manufacturing processes involved in the use of improvised explosive devices.[51] In contrast to the position taken by the ICRC,[52] Schmitt notes that acts that are likely to enhance a party's military operations or military capacity should amount to direct participation in that a 'contribution to one side typically weakens its opponent', and, therefore, the ICRC's approach is too narrow in this regard.[53] Furthermore, Schmitt added that within any definition of harm, it was important to make a

---

48 ICRC (Interpretive Guidance), above n 17, 55.

49 Ibid., 53.

50 Ibid., 47.

51 Michael Schmitt, 'The Interpretive Guidance on the Notion of Direct Participation in Hostilities: A Critical Analysis' (2010) 1 *Harvard National Security Journal*, 27. See also US Department of Defense, *Law of War Manual* (12 June 2015), para 5.9.3: 'Taking a direct part in hostilities extends beyond merely engaging in combat and also includes certain acts that are an integral part of combat operations or that effectively and substantially contribute to an adversary's ability to conduct or sustain combat operations. However, taking a direct part in hostilities does not encompass the general support that members of the civilian population provide to their State's war effort, such as by buying war bonds. Whether an act by a civilian constitutes taking a direct part in hostilities is likely to depend highly on the context, such as the weapon systems or methods of warfare employed by the civilian's side in the conflict'.

52 ICRC (Interpretive Guidance), above n 17, 53.

53 Michael Schmitt, above n 2, 719.

distinction between acts that were directly related to the hostilities and acts that are criminal in nature.[54] This point is important in view of the fact that in hostilities, individuals and groups may take advantage of a breakdown in law and order to commit a range of petty and organised criminal offences.

One causal step

The ICRC suggested that 'direct causation' means that harm be 'brought about in one causal step', although as will be discussed later, this is subject to a significant exception.[55] The ICRC's discussion of 'direct causation' implies *a contrario* that there are indirect forms of causation, but that these do not amount to causation for the purposes of participation in hostilities. The 'one causal step' test is thus an approach to distinguishing 'direct' and 'indirect acts', and its plausibility will now be examined.

According to Schmitt, this criterion represents an underinclusive and contradictory approach to causation and suggests that states are only likely to be satisfied by a broader interpretation of causation that can work in practice.[56] He argues that it lacks plausibility by suggesting that harm may be brought about by acts that are more than one step removed from an attack and that indirectly contributing to capability may result in harm,[57] for example, through weapons production, logistical support and scientific as well as technological research and development.[58] In terms of weapons production and voluntary human shields, Schmitt notes that the ICRC's treatment of the manufacture of improvised explosive devices (IEDs) 'reflects a troubling ignorance of the realities of 21st century battlefield combat' and suggests that 'States that engage in conflict on a frequent or intense scale will certainly reject the Guidance's treatment of various examples'.[59]

This is because the ICRC asserts that the assembly and storage of IEDs as well as the purchase and smuggling of component parts may not amount to direct participation in hostilities as they do not specifically cause harm directly, such as with planting or detonating IEDs, but are rather 'connected with the resulting harm through an uninterrupted causal chain of events'.[60] Schmitt notes that legal experts were divided on this issue and comments that states would reject the notion that such indirect support activities would not be direct enough. Indeed, Schmitt argues that where there is 'actionable intelligence' going towards the performance of such indirect support activities, he notes that any attack would be justifiable, because assembly of IEDs amounts to an 'integral part of subsequent operations almost certain to occur in the near future and relatively nearby' and 'it would be absurd to expect [States] to delay attack, given the clandestine nature by

54 Ibid., 28.
55 ICRC (Interpretive Guidance), above n 17, 55.
56 Michael Schmitt, above n 2, 730.
57 Ibid., 726.
58 Schmitt, above n 51, 30.
59 Michael Schmitt, above n 2, 738.
60 ICRC (Interpretive Guidance), above n 17, 54; Michael Schmitt, Ibid., 731; Kenneth Watkin, above n 19, 658.

which such devices are emplaced, an immediate attack may be the only option for foiling a later operation employing the device'.[61] Schmitt also criticises the ICRC Interpretive Guidance for suggesting that where such devices are assembled by members of an organised armed group, this activity does not constitute a 'continuous combat function' as this is an insufficiently direct activity. Not only does this indicate that that the 'continuous combat function' standard as espoused by the ICRC is regarded by some legal experts and states as being too narrow to be applied in practice, but also that it should be broadened and only applied in the context of targeted operations where there is 'actionable intelligence'. Indeed, the Interpretive Guidance is problematic in that the examples given, such as IED production, narrow the notion of direct participation in hostilities to overtly hostile activities that occur at the tactical level. In other words, in unconventional operational environments, the employment of asymmetric tactics may mean that attacks rarely occur in 'one causal step leading to the hostile act' but rather are more likely to be 'achieved through a multiplicity of integrated steps' and that this ought to be taken into account in targeting decisions, which can only really occur from an analysis at an operational level of command.[62]

As will be discussed further, although it may be an evidential challenge to identify and to understand the ways in which indirect activities lead to harm, as the ICRC itself recognises, they cannot be ruled out in absolute terms given that they may be deemed to be 'an integral part' of a 'co-ordinated military operation'. Indeed, the ICRC significantly waters down the standard of 'direct causation' by stating that it 'must therefore be interpreted to include conduct that causes harm only in conjunction with other acts', or in other words:

> More precisely, where a specific act does not on its own directly cause the required threshold of harm, the requirement of direct causation would still be fulfilled where the act constitutes an integral part of a concrete and coordinated tactical operation that directly causes such harm.[63]

Schmitt notes that this '"integral part" qualifier . . . reveals the weakness of the "one causal step" criterion'[64] and is misplaced given its discussion of the assembly of IEDs. Indeed, asymmetric or irregular tactics may mean its integrated and coordinated operations are concealed and lie dormant and come into effect in an opportunistic fashion as and when a superior side exposes defensive weaknesses or blind spots and so is not able to prepare for and defend against such operations. For example, a civilian may give information of a military nature which is then passed along a 'chain of command' or through an irregular network, but this information

61 Michael Schmitt, Ibid., 731.

62 William Boothby, 'Direct Participation in Hostilities – A Discussion of the ICRC Interpretive Guidance' (2010) 1 *International Humanitarian Legal Studies* 159.

63 Michael Schmitt, 'The Interpretive Guidance on the Notion of Direct Participation in Hostilities: A Critical Analysis' (2010) 1 *Harvard National Security Journal* 30.

64 Schmitt, above n 2, 730–731.

is not used immediately to plan and execute an attack, but rather may be acted upon at an indeterminate time in the future as and when the opportunity arises.[65] In this way, it has been suggested that the notion of causation links in with the notion of temporal scope of participation, in that a civilian may cause harm 'for such time' as their act forms an integral part of and is closely linked to a specific and coordinated military operation.[66] Indeed, in critically assessing whether it is necessary or practicable to incorporate the 'continuous combat function' element into the ICRC's category of membership in an organised armed group, Schmitt provocatively asserts that 'it is necessary to . . . extend participation as far up and downstream as there is a causal link, and close the revolving door of participation'.[67] It is suggested that this assertion provokes the need for the issue of causation and the temporal scope of participation to be put on a more principled and structured foundation so as to be capable of application by states in the context of targeted operations. In particular, this is because, according to the ICRC, this element ultimately forms part of the 'continuous combat function' and thus may be used to decide questions of membership. In which case, Schmitt notes that in 'collective operations, the criterion of directly causing (in one step) the harm might not be met by all the individuals taking part in the operation, even though it is self-evident that they are deeply involved in the operation'. As will be discussed further, Schmitt notes that this is problematic in that 'individuals ordering or planning a mission, though plainly direct participants, might not be characterised as directly participating absent the integral component [. . .] element'.[68] This is to suggest that it is not only direct physical acts that can be construed as amounting to direct participation in hostilities, but also indirect support acts, or, more significantly, ordering or planning operations. Whereas direct combat activities are perpetrated and thus recognisable at a tactical level by soldiers on the ground, indirect command activities such as ordering and planning acts and operations amounting to direct participation in hostilities are not, and so they need to be analysed and responded to at an operational level by commanders with the benefit of legal, political and military analysis. Thus, given the abstract and indeterminate nature of the category of *de facto* membership in an organised armed group, there will be a discussion of criminal law concepts of participation and perpetration in order to further translate or operationalise the Interpretive Guidance into a framework that can be applied by military planners and commanders. Furthermore, it is suggested that this may serve to align further the parameters of civilian immunity with contemporary doctrinal considerations discussed in Chapter 1.

The ICRC attempts to work out the temporal aspect of 'direct causation' by suggesting that civilians lose protection from attack during the commission of acts

> preparatory to the execution of a specific act of direct participation in hostilities, as well as the deployment to and the return from the location of its

65 Schmitt, above n 63, 29.
66 Ibid., 36 and 38.
67 Melzer, above n 17, 868.
68 Michael Schmitt, above n 2, 731.

> execution, where they constitute an integral part of the act of such a specific act or operation.[69]

As noted by Watkin, this indicates that the Interpretive Guidance embodies a tactical focus in its assessment of direct participation, indicating that the 'preparation of a general campaign of unspecified operations would not qualify as direct participation in hostilities', and this could unduly serve to exclude planning for future attacks.[70]

Moreover, according to the Commentary to the Additional Protocols, 'thereafter, as he no longer presents any danger for the adversary, he may not be attacked'.[71] It is suggested that this guidance does not coherently clarify the temporal parameters of the 'for such time' standard in terms of when an act begins and when it ends. On the point of preparatory measures warranting loss of immunity, the Interpretive Guidance merely refers back to the vague treaty provisions that cover 'military operation[s]' and 'deployment' that are 'preparatory to an attack'.[72] In attempting to elucidate these terms, the Interpretive Guidance states that an 'attack' 'begins only once the deploying individual undertakes a physical displacement with a view to carrying out a specific operation', and that an attack 'ends once the individual in question has physically separated from the operation'.[73] By way of example, the Interpretive Guidance states that 'civilians should be liable to direct attack exclusively during recognisable and proximate preparations, such as the loading of a gun, and during deployments in the framework of a specific military operation'.[74] Again, this reasoning is flawed in that it assumes the existence of that which has first to be established, namely the existence of acts that are 'recognisable' as direct participation in hostilities. As discussed earlier in relation to the issue of causation of harm, 'recognisable' physical acts such as firing a weapon in self-defence or as part of the commission of a criminal offence may not be considered hostile, whereas a range of activities that result in harm may not be immediately 'recognisable' as harmful and thus hostile, or are in any case subject to a broad margin of judgment, or indeed mere suspicions or hunches without having any firm analytic foundations.

Furthermore, the Interpretive Guidance is contradictory in that whereas on the one hand it narrowly associates 'recognisable acts' with acts that constitute immediate and direct military threats or 'attack', it proceeds to state that '[m]easures preparatory to the execution of a specific act of direct participation in hostilities, as well as the deployment to and the return from the location of its execution,

---

69 ICRC (Interpretive Guidance), above n 17, 65.

70 Kenneth Watkin, above n 19, 644, 656, 659, 660, 688, 690; International Committee of the Red Cross, 'Interpretive Guidance on the Notion of Direct Participation in Hostilities under International Humanitarian Law' (2008) 90 (991) *International Review of the Red Cross* 1043–1044, 66.

71 *Commentary on the Additional Protocols*, above n 34, 4789.

72 ICRC (Interpretive Guidance), above n 17, 65.

73 Ibid., 67.

74 Ibid.

constitute an integral part of that act'.[75] It is suggested that the parameters of loss of immunity are thus extended from individual deployment in an attack to preparatory measures that are an integral part of such an attack. Accordingly, this undermines the ICRC's attempt to forge a clear and coherent distinction between acts, amounting to direct participation in hostilities and indirect acts not incurring a loss of immunity. Indeed, the Interpretive Guidance states that

> where a specific act does not on its own directly cause [that is, in one causal step] the required threshold of harm, the requirement of direct causation would still be fulfilled where the act constitutes an integral part of a concrete and coordinated tactical operation that directly causes such harm.[76]

The notion that an indirect act can amount to direct participation in hostilities in such circumstances constitutes such a broad exception to the 'one causal step' principle that it effectively effaces it.

The issue then becomes one of attempting to distinguish between activities that indirectly contribute to general military capacity from activities that 'can be linked to specific operations, or types of operations, that are relatively imminent',[77] or as the Interpretive Guidance states, distinguishing between activities that 'are of a specifically military nature and so closely linked to the subsequent execution of a specific hostile act that they already constitute an integral part of that act' from those activities that indirectly contribute to 'the general capacity to carry out unspecified hostile acts'.[78] However, as the notion of what constitutes an 'integral part' of a belligerent support structure is not placed on a principled or analytical basis, the Interpretive Guidance is essentially circular in the sense that it is merely an extended reformulation of the starting point set out in the Commentary to API of it being necessary to distinguish between activities that are part of 'combat and active military operations' and indirect activities that are part of the 'war effort'.[79] In this way, the Interpretive Guidance does not provide a clearer framework that delineates its concept of 'recognisable acts' that are causative of harm so as to avoid the erroneous or arbitrary use of force. Accordingly, building on the ICRC's third criterion for direct participation in hostilities, this contribution will attempt to elucidate further general principles for the identification of indirect acts that constitute direct participation in hostilities due to their causative power and the subjective intent behind them by extrapolating models of coperpetration and accessorial liability. The rationale for this contribution stems from Schmitt's criticism of the ICRC's 'direct causation' criterion: that it fails to take into consideration the approaches taken to causation in the domestic criminal

75 ICRC (Interpretive Guidance), above n 17, 65.
76 Ibid., 55.
77 Schmitt, above n 2, 727.
78 ICRC (Interpretive Guidance), above n 17, 66.
79 *Commentary on the Additional Protocols*, above n 34, 34.

or civil law of states.[80] This implies that an approach to indirect participation that reflects notions of causation and intention set out in criminal law could be regarded as more plausible than that proposed by the ICRC.

A belligerent nexus

According to the Interpretive Guidance, for an act to amount to direct participation in hostilities, it must have a 'belligerent nexus' or a connection with the surrounding hostilities; otherwise, it should be dealt with using law enforcement measures.[81] Yet the Interpretive Guidance construes the notion of 'belligerent nexus' in a narrower fashion than that developed in international criminal law jurisprudence and is, therefore, not harmonious with this related and interconnected branch of public international law.[82] In particular, according to the Interpretive Guidance, to amount to direct participation in hostilities, an act must not only be 'objectively likely' to injure or adversely affect the enemy, but it must also be 'specifically designed to directly cause the required threshold of harm in support of a party to the conflict and to the detriment of another'.[83] However, despite the obvious connotations of the term 'specifically designed', the Interpretive Guidance stated that this should be regarded as an objective standard that does not depend on the 'subjective' state of mind or 'hostile intent' of 'every participating individual'.[84] Indeed, where there is a direct and immediate threat, then subjective considerations are, according to the Interpretive Guidance, not generally relevant.[85]

Thus, according to the Interpretive Guidance, the belligerent nexus should be deduced 'objectively' from the acts themselves. However, this is a rather crude behaviour test which, it is suggested, does not help to resolve difficulties facing armed forces concerning the scope of the rule in the face of uncertain facts, or, in other words, how to establish that a person to be targeted is a member of an organised armed group that belongs to a party to the conflict and that the person fulfils a continuous combat function within the group. Indeed, the proposition that the belligerent nexus should be deduced 'objectively' from the facts themselves is to assume that which has to be first established: namely, what are the 'recognisable acts' from which one can reliably infer a belligerent nexus without making erroneous or arbitrary targeting decisions? Despite this proposition of an objective standard, the ICRC necessarily qualifies this by suggesting that subjective intent may be relevant in calling into question 'the belligerent nexus

---

80 Schmitt, above n 2, 726.

81 ICRC (Interpretive Guidance), above n 17, 59.

82 ICRC (Interpretive Guidance), Ibid., 58–59; *Prosecutor v Kunarac et al.* (Appeals Chamber Judgment) ICTY-96-23&IT-96-23/1-A (12 June 2002), 58; *Prosecutor v Rutaganda* (Appeals Chamber Judgment) ICTR -96-3 (26 May 2003), 570.

83 ICRC (Interpretive Guidance), above n 17, 58.

84 Ibid., 59.

85 Ibid., 58.

of their conduct', but only in 'exceptional cases'.[86] For example, this may be so 'when civilians are totally unaware of the role they are playing in the conduct of hostilities',[87] situations of self-defence and situations of law enforcement.[88] However, as implied by the Interpretive Guidance's discussion of the practical relevance of the 'belligerent nexus' criterion, in the context of unconventional, irregular and full-spectrum operational environments, subjective considerations may not be regarded as 'exceptional', but as a key way and, in many cases, arguably the only way, to distinguish a continuum of violence, which, as set out in Chapter 1, may range from petty and organised crime to isolated terrorist acts and then to combat activities. Indeed, the Interpretive Guidance actually states that '[m]any activities during an armed conflict lack a belligerent nexus even though they cause a considerable level of harm',[89] and furthermore that 'loss of protection against direct attack within the meaning of IHL, however, is not a sanction for criminal behaviour but a consequence of military necessity in the conduct of hostilities'.[90]

In this way, the Interpretive Guidance not only understates the vital practical importance of subjective considerations in unconventional operational environments, but does not indicate the modalities for distinguishing between those situations where subjective considerations should, as far as possible, be deduced in addition to doubtful activities, and those situations where the objective purpose of a 'recognisable act' can reliably and justifiably undergird the deprivation of immunity. In addition to this, despite the admission that subjective conditions are actually relevant to the question of belligerent nexus, the Interpretive Guidance does not make any attempt to describe the mental states that are relevant to establishing different forms of belligerent nexus. This is relevant to the following discussion in relation to elucidating the precautionary requirement to do everything feasible in the circumstances to verify that the objectives to be attacked

86 Ibid., 60. According to the US Department of Defence, above n 372, para 5.9.3, the following considerations may be relevant in determining whether a civilian is directly participating in hostilities: 'the degree to which the act causes harm to the opposing party's persons or objects, such as whether the act is the proximate or "but for" cause of death, injury, or damage to persons or objects belonging to the opposing party; or the degree to which the act is likely to affect adversely the military operations or military capacity of the opposing party; the degree to which the act is connected to the hostilities, such as the degree to which the act is temporally or geographically near the fighting; or the degree to which the act is connected to military operations; the specific purpose underlying the act, such as whether the activity is intended to advance the war aims of one party to the conflict to the detriment of the opposing party; the military significance of the activity to the party's war effort, such as the degree to which the act contributes to a party's military action against the opposing party; whether the act is of comparable or greater value to a party's war effort than acts that are commonly regarded as taking a direct part in hostilities; whether the act poses a significant threat to the opposing party'.

86 ICRC (Interpretive Guidance), above n 17, 65.

87 Ibid.

88 Ibid., 61.

89 Ibid., 60.

90 Ibid., 61.

are neither civilians nor civilian objects, which, as discussed in Chapter 1, may be described as the emerging requirement of 'positive identification' which can be described as an approach that 'requires reasonable certainty that the object of attack is verified and confirmed as a legitimate military target'.[91] Thus, at the very least, this may be viewed as requiring, as far as possible, that soldiers 'double-check' a target rather than being

> too hasty and careless in firing at anyone who [is thought to be] a combatant . . . [as] [t]here are times when it is too late to know that the supposed combatant is just carrying an airgun or a farm tool [or is a] [friend] . . .[92]

Accordingly, this discussion will explore models of indirect participation and perpetration of the commission of harmful acts in order to elucidate further this notion of a belligerent nexus. However, for present purposes, it is suggested that the approach taken in this discussion applies to the extent of the threshold for the existence of an armed conflict as discussed earlier and acts of self-defence in response to direct and immediate lethal threats.

Accordingly, it is suggested that the requirement that subjective considerations underlying a range of acts which are in some way directed to furthering an underlying common agreement, purpose or design to commit a harmful act should not pose too much of a challenge to armed forces. As discussed in Chapter 1, military doctrine has responded to the challenges associated with uncertainty concerning the facts by advocating social network analysis that seeks to 'understand the social dynamic that sustains on-going fighting'. As discussed in Chapter 1, in practice, social network analysis does not pose too much of a challenge for armed forces. Rather, it is viewed as an operationally and strategically important process which seeks to describe and analyse how an armed group operates in terms of the roles and functions performed in an organisation and how these can overlap and change over time. It also seeks to describe and analyse how armed groups operate within and exploit existing social, criminal and political structures and networks. Furthermore, it seeks to describe and analyse how social, criminal and political structures and networks support and contribute to hostilities, for example, in terms of financial, material, logistical or intelligence support. Indeed, it may be the case that criminal networks and insurgent groups are so highly interconnected that they can be construed as being functionally fused into a single organisation. Social network analysis thus advocates an intelligence-led and evidence-based approach to analysing threat levels and functional participation in hostilities that is predicated on accurate and reliable human and documentary intelligence in

91 Philippines, AFP Standing Rules of Engagement, Armed Forces of the Philippines, General Headquarters, Office of the Chief of Staff, 1 December 2005, 8(f); Netherlands, Humanitair Oorlogsrecht: Handleiding, Voorschift No 27–412, Koninklijke Landmacht, Militair Juridische Dienst, 2005, 0548.

92 Philippines, Philippine Army Soldier's Handbook on Human Rights and International Humanitarian Law, A Practical Guide for Internal Security Operations, 2006, 60, para (6).

order to develop a 'clear appreciation of the essential nature and nuances of the conflict' as a basis for effective tactical, operational and strategic responses. Furthermore, as discussed in Chapters 1 and 3, restricting status-based targeting to targeted operations can prevent an escalation in violence. Thus, a critical analytical approach to intelligence should be adopted when involved in confrontations and conflicts amongst the people, particularly with regard to human intelligence from informants and detained criminal suspects as well as fighters. In particular, there is a need to verify, cross-reference and corroborate intelligence in order to ensure that mistakes are not made on the basis of information that is purposefully inaccurate or given with the hostile intention, for example, of leading forces into compromising situations such as ambushes, overreacting and causing collateral damage and settling private disputes or vendettas. Social network analysis can construe the ambit of civilian status narrowly by focusing targeting analysis and target acquisition on the 'internal support structure' of an organised armed group engaging in hostilities. Thus in a purely functional sense the 'internal support structure' of an insurgency may be construed broadly so as to comprise 'military and political leaders', 'combatants', 'auxiliaries' and the 'political or ideological cadre'. The following discussion in relation to the importance of forms of participation in and coperpetration of hostile acts aims to add further clarity not only to the substance of direct perpetration and, more importantly, membership, but also factors that are relevant to social network analysis and positive identification that are absolutely critical in the context of status-based targeting within targeted operations.

Combatant status

As discussed previously, civilian status is defined *a contrario* to combatant status. Article 1 of the Hague Regulations[93] and Article 4 of the third Geneva Convention provide that certain 'irregulars' such as militias, volunteer corps and organised resistance movements 'belonging to a Party to the conflict' may be considered lawful 'combatants' entitled to prisoner of war status, providing that they meet four criteria set out in Article 4 paragraph (2) of the third Geneva Convention. These are that they are (a) commanded by a person responsible for his subordinates, (b) they wear a fixed distinctive sign recognisable at a distance, (c) they carry their arms openly and (d) they conduct their operations in accordance with the laws and customs of war. In unconventional hostilities, fighters or combatants may frequently fail to distinguish themselves by complying with these requirements for combatant status. In this

93 Convention (IV) respecting the Laws and Customs of War on Land and its annex: Regulations concerning the Laws and Customs of War on Land. The Hague, 18 October 1907 (Hague Regulations), Article 1: the law of armed conflict applies 'not only to armies, but also militia and volunteer corps that are 'commanded by a person responsible for his subordinates . . . have a fixed distinctive emblem recognizable at a distance . . . carry arms openly . . . and conduct their operations in accordance with the laws and customs of war'.

way, applying conventional notions to unconventional conflicts raises important questions regarding civilian status and immunity from attack.[94] Due to a recognition that because of 'the nature of hostilities', certain irregulars 'cannot so distinguish' themselves, and in order further to 'promote the protection of the civilian population from the effects of hostilities', Article 44 of API provides that combatant status shall be retained by those who carry arms openly 'during each military engagement' and 'during such time as he is visible to the adversary while he is engaged in a military deployment preceding the launching of an attack in which he is to participate'.

However, complicating this in the *Blaškić* case, the Appeals Chamber stated that the specific situation of a victim at the time they are attacked 'may not be determinative of his civilian or noncivilian status' as, for example, despite the fact that a member of an armed organisation is not armed or participating directly in hostilities at the time of attack, this does not affect their status as combatants or legitimate military objectives.[95] Thus, if a civilian is not directly participating in hostilities at the time they are attacked, this raises the question of what it means to attack an individual on the basis of their status as a 'member of an armed organisation'. This question is of major importance given that attacking on the basis of status as opposed to threat can seriously undermine the principle of distinction in that 'members of armed forces' may be attacked 'whether or not they are in combat, or for the time being armed'.[96]

Membership of and belonging to irregular forces or organised armed groups versus direct participation in hostilities

As discussed earlier, API recognises the status of irregular fighters, subject to the conditions outlined previously. APII merely refers to 'dissident armed forces or other organised armed groups' but provides no further guidance on how civilians become incorporated into such groups, how to distinguish between members of such organised armed groups and civilians directly participating in hostilities, and how to distinguish between civilians directly participating in hostilities and civilians who are not so involved. As discussed in Chapter 1, given the dynamics of asymmetric warfare, 'irregulars' are key players in contemporary

94 *PCAT v Israel*, above n 3, 24: The Israeli High Court of Justice, in dealing with the issue of whether members of the 'terrorist organizations' under its scrutiny had combatant status applied the relevant provisions the Hague Regulations, the Third and Fourth Geneva Conventions and Additional Protocol I, as discussed earlier, and found that they did not fulfil these conditions for combatant status because, inter alia, they had 'no fixed emblem recognizable at a distance, and they [did] not conduct their operations in accordance with the laws and customs of war'.

95 *Prosecutor v Blaskić* (Appeals Chamber Judgment) ICTY-95–14-A (29 July 2004), 113–114.

96 *Kordić and Čerkez* (Appeals Chamber Judgment), above n 32, 51.

'unconventional' conflicts. However, the status of 'irregulars' is unclear, and greater clarity is needed in order to clarify the parameters of civilian immunity. Indeed, it is problematic that civilian status is defined in opposition to what is essentially an equivocal general category that may be labelled in various ways, such as 'terrorists', 'guerrillas', 'unlawful combatants', 'unprivileged combatants' or 'criminals'. Thus the principle of distinction becomes blurred in the context of conflicts of a non-international character where individuals become members of an organised armed group belonging to a party to an armed conflict. It is vitally important to bring greater clarity and elucidation to this area because, as noted by the Appeals Chamber in *Blaškić*, in marked contrast to civilians directly participating in hostilities, as far as members of organised armed groups exercising a continuous combat function are concerned, their specific situation at the time of an attack may not be determinative of their status or, in other words, the fact that they are not armed or in combat at the time of an attack does not accord them civilian status, and therefore they are not immune from attack.[97]

Indeed, according to the ICRC Commentary,

> [a] civilian who is incorporated in an armed organization [. . .] becomes a member of the military and a combatant throughout the duration of the hostilities (or in any case, until he is permanently demobilized by the responsible command [. . .]), whether or not he is in combat, or for the time being armed.[98]

Again, this indicates that the notion of direct participation in hostilities may be equated with an individual, threat-based determination, whereas the notion of membership of an organised armed group may be equated with a status-based determination akin to that of a combatant. The ICRC Interpretive Guidance reasons that it was necessary to go beyond the notion of direct participation in hostilities by devising the category of members of an organised armed group exercising a continuous combat function in order to prevent an imbalance between organised armed groups and state armed forces that would result if organised armed groups could 'operate as farmers by day and fighters by night'.[99] However, in contrast to membership of state armed forces or other officially constituted irregular groups, membership of an organised armed group is difficult to define in clear and unequivocal terms. As discussed, in their own ways, both of these approaches of direct participation, but especially of membership, may have a negative impact upon civilian immunity, and so it is necessary to forge a clearer elucidation of this area. This general notion of membership of, or incorporation within, an organised armed group is problematic vis-à-vis irregularly constituted groups. This is because 'membership' can be based on a wide range

97 *Blaskić* (Appeals Chamber Judgment), above n 95, 114.
98 *Commentary on the Additional Protocols*, above n 34, 1676.
99 ICRC (Interpretive Guidance), above n 17, 72.

of overlapping and interconnected idiosyncratic, contextual and, in some cases, involuntary features, such as clan or tribal-based associations, political or religious affiliations, or ethnic or family ties.[100] However, given the indeterminacy of these ties, the ICRC Interpretive Guidance proposes that 'membership in such groups cannot depend on abstract affiliation, family ties, or other criteria prone to error, arbitrariness or abuse'.[101] Accordingly, the Interpretive Guidance attempts to make a categorical distinction between civilians participating in hostilities and membership of an organised armed group by adopting a narrow approach that equates membership with what it describes as a 'continuous combat function' or, to put it another way, functional combatancy. Hampson suggests that it is difficult to presume such functional combatancy on the basis of anything other than behaviour, and so this concept is just another type of behaviour test.[102] Although this is not disputed, it is suggested that the range of conduct from which we may infer functional combatancy is by no means an uncontroversial issue and, in part, this is because the significance that is to be attached to any given behaviour may be inextricably bound up with the intention or motive underlying any given activity as well as its surrounding context of diffuse organisational structures geared towards collective hostilities. For example, as will be discussed, when it comes to forms of indirect coperpetration, it will be necessary not only to establish an *actus reus*, but that the acts performed are in some way directed to furthering an underlying common agreement, purpose or design to commit a harmful act. Again, once a situation has reached the CA3 threshold of violence as indicated by *Boškoski*, then it is highly questionable as to whether the human rights paradigm is appropriate to govern the use of force in response to the hostile activities on the part of organised armed groups. Such a proposition may be regarded as being overly restrictive and thus tantamount to asserting an 'unrealistic protection of civilians in situations of armed conflict', as well as setting out 'unrealisable expectations on the part of civilians and increased violation of the rules on the part of the armed forces'.[103]

Although targeting on the basis of status in this case may be regarded as unduly permissive, it may be contended that premising targeting decisions not simply on overt behaviour, but also on underlying motives or common concerted plans or agreements to perform hostile operations, can serve to restrict such status-based targeting to planned targeted operations that have taken precautions into account in order to overcome doubt as to civilian status. According to the ICRC, an assessment of whether a civilian can be subject to lethal attack as a method of first resort at any time and in any place, regardless of whether or not they are directly participating in hostilities at the time, is premised on the notion that 'the continuous function assumed by an individual corresponds to that collectively exercised by

100 Melzer, above n 37, 321.
101 ICRC (Interpretive Guidance), above n 17, 33.
102 Françoise Hampson, above n 14, 199.
103 Ibid., 192.

the group as a whole, namely the conduct of hostilities on behalf of a non-State party to the conflict'.[104] Therefore, according to the ICRC Interpretive Guidance,

> where individuals go beyond spontaneous, sporadic, or unorganized direct participation in hostilities and become members of an organized armed group, IHL deprives them of protection against direct attack for as long as they remain members of that group . . . membership in an organized armed group begins in the moment when a civilian starts *de facto* to assume a continuous combat function for the group.[105]

According to the ICRC, this concept of membership based on the assumption of a continuous combat function was necessary to prevent any imbalance that could arise through what has been described as the 'revolving door' phenomenon where individuals could be part of organised armed groups which could attack state armed forces at any time, in any place and on a continuous basis, but those individuals could otherwise claim civilian immunity from attack when they were not directly engaged in such attacks.[106]

In contrast to a civilian participating in hostilities on a spontaneous, sporadic or temporary basis, the ICRC's notion of membership of an organised armed group is consonant with that described by the Israeli High Court of Justice. This states that where a civilian joins an organised armed group 'which has become his "home" and in the framework of his role in that organisation he commits a chain of hostilities, with short periods of rest between them', then, in such an instance they cease to be regarded as a civilian and they lose their immunity from attack 'for such time' as they are committing the chain of acts because 'the rest between hostilities' can be regarded as 'nothing other than preparation for the next hostility'.[107] Thus, in contrast to the threat-based approach to targeting denoted by the notion of direct participation in hostilities, the approach to targeting on the basis of *de facto* membership of an irregularly constituted group is equivalent to making a status-based targeting decision that infers an individual propensity to maintain a continuing hostile state of affairs from previous direct participation in active combat that is regular and consistent.[108]

However, in view of the ICRC's recognition that an individual may lose their status as a civilian and thus be deprived of their immunity from attack 'for such time' as their activities form an integral part of, and are closely linked to, a specific and coordinated military operation, it is suggested the notion of a 'continuous combat function' does not constitute a necessary or sufficient approach to distinguishing indirect acts that amount to direct participation in hostilities from *de facto* membership or affiliation with an organised armed group.[109] Rather, it

104 Ibid.
105 ICRC (Interpretive Guidance), above n 17, 72.
106 Ibid.
107 *PCAT v Israel*, above n 3.
108 Melzer, above n 17, 890.
109 Boothby, above n 62, 153.

maintains the existence of a 'grey area' that permits a broad margin of appreciation by reason of the previously mentioned 'integral part' qualification. This indicates that a 'continuous combat function' may not be the sole and definitive determinant of deprivation of immunity from attack on a continuous basis in view of the circumstances of specific operations.[110] Moreover, as indicated by Figures 4.2 and 4.3, due to the indeterminacy as to what amounts to 'continuous' and 'direct' hostile acts, the Interpretive Guidance does not satisfactorily make a clear and unequivocal distinction between 'temporary activity-based loss of protection and continuous status-based loss of protection' due to a continuous combat function.[111] This is particularly so where 'temporary acts' are performed on an intermittent or discontinuous basis. Schmitt notes that the concept of temporal scope of participation within the Interpretive Guidance is 'fatally flawed'.[112]

Furthermore, although the ICRC attempts to keep targeting on the basis of direct participation in hostilities and targeting on the basis of status categorically separate and distinct, a number of academics argue that the 'continuous combat function' is too indeterminate to be applied in practice, in that there is a grey area between a 'continuous combat function' and direct participation on a 'persistent recurring basis'. For example, according to Boothby, the seemingly high but indeterminate threshold for *de facto* membership may exclude 'members of such groups whose function is not continuous, and civilians who directly participate while not being members of such groups'.[113] Similarly, Watkin argues that in this regard the Interpretive Guidance is unlikely to be considered credible by the soldiers of states asked to apply such guidance, as they will face immense practical problems of putting it into practice, given that they operate at the tactical level, and as such will find it a challenge to distinguish between 'civilians who participate on a 'persistently recurring basis' and a member of an organised armed group who performs a 'continuous combat function'[114] and a member of an organised armed group who performs a 'continuous combat function''.[115] Arguably, therefore, the concept of direct participation in hostilities is only capable of application at the tactical level where soldiers are required to identify positively a hostile threat before using lethal force.[116] In contrast, to distinguish between a civilian who participates on a 'persistently recurring basis' or a civilian who has participated in hostilities merely on a spontaneous, sporadic or unorganised basis[117] and a member of an organised armed group who performs a 'continuous combat function' would require evidenced-based or intelligence-led analysis at the operational level in order to establish a pattern of conduct on

110 Kenneth Watkin, above n 19, 691.
111 Boothby, above n 62, 157.
112 Michael Schmitt, above n 2, 738.
113 Boothby, above n 62, 153.
114 ICRC (Interpretive Guidance), above n 17, 44. Kenneth Watkin, above n 19, 645.
115 Ibid.
116 Ibid., 659.
117 ICRC (Interpretive Guidance), above n 17, 35.

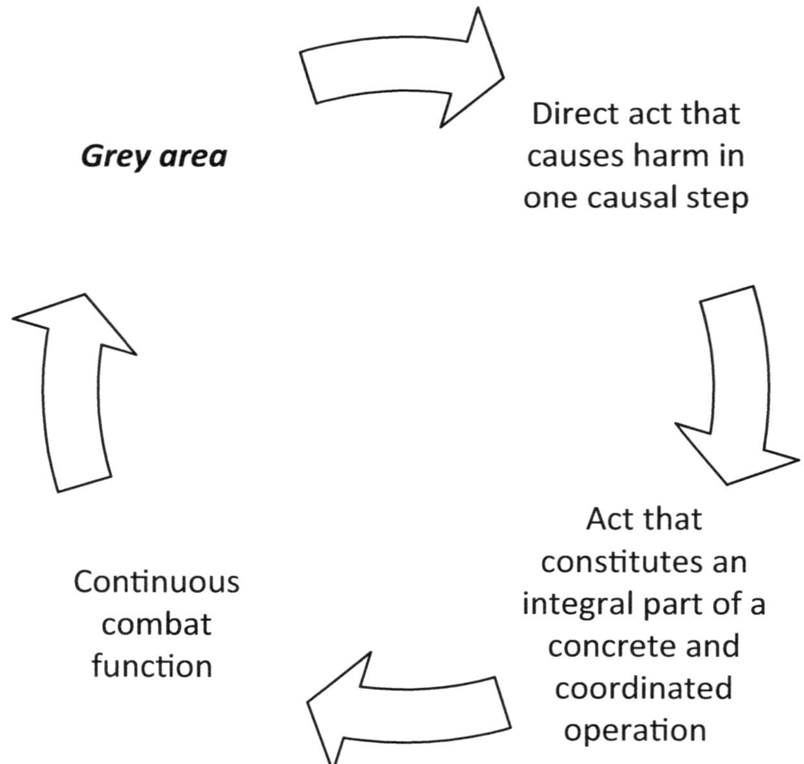

Figure 4.2 The grey area between continuous combat function and direct participation in hostilities.

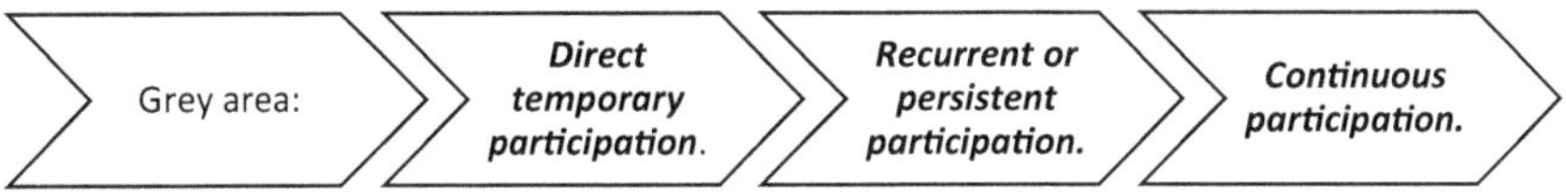

Figure 4.3 The temporal range of participation in hostilities.

which to base a presumption of future hostile propensity, and thus suggests that the 'continuous combat function' standard may only be applied in the context of targeted operations at this level of command. In this regard, Watkin argues that it is not difficult logically, operationally or factually to determine future activity from past conduct.[118]

Furthermore, to require that an individual 'assume a continuous combat function before he can become continuously targetable is to narrow the notion of membership to an unacceptable degree'.[119] Without clearly defining the scope of definition of terms, Boothby proposes that 'comparability of approach between organised armed groups, irregular armed forces and the armed forces of a State' would be achieved if it was instead recognised that, as a matter of fact, individuals lose immunity as members of organised armed groups where there is evidence of 'some combat function, which may be temporary or intermittent'.[120] Otherwise, the approach to functional combatancy, if narrowly construed to those who play a 'continuous combat function', would also serve to produce 'an unacceptable imbalance with members of the armed forces who can be targeted at any time during an armed conflict [and] this imbalance is likely to erode significantly the military acceptability of, and thus compliance with, the rule'.[121] However, Boothby's argument that 'any combat function, contingent, intermittent or continuous' will serve to deprive an individual of their immunity from attack represents a major threat to the fundamental rule of distinction.[122]

Nevertheless, a broad approach to *de facto* membership may be tempered and fundamental issues of reasonable doubt may be resolved when qualified with the proposition that status should be deduced from an intelligence-led and evidence-based process. In other words, this is to suggest that the continuous combat function requirement is only capable of application in the case of targeted operations that are based on adequate intelligence or evidence. Targeted killings on this basis thus depend on accurate intelligence, as they are not based on a direct and immediate lethal or harmful threat, and thus it is unclear how membership can otherwise be presumed. Where individuals are targeted on the basis of

118 Kenneth Watkin, above n 19, 688.
119 Boothby, above n 62,154.
120 Ibid.
121 Ibid., 153.
122 Ibid., 156.

membership of an organised armed group exercising a continuous combat function, then there is no need to establish any direct participation in hostilities per se. Nevertheless, as suggested earlier, a certain degree of intelligence and evidence gathering, together with the requisite analysis and planning, has to have occurred in order to ensure that an individual has gone beyond spontaneous, sporadic or unorganised direct participation in hostilities and has become a member of an organised armed group belonging to a party to the conflict who is exercising a continuous combat function. In other words, where an individual does not represent an immediate threat through direct participation in hostilities, then the presumption of membership of an organised armed group has to have a reasonable evidential basis in order to overcome any doubt as to their civilian status. It is suggested that appropriate responses to such situations ought to be premised on the escalation of lethal force, discussed in Chapter 1, which comprises precautionary measures such as effective warnings. In this way, a liberal approach to grey areas that has inbuilt safeguards can ensure that the law is plausible and effective from both military and humanitarian points of view, as will be suggested later, which also ties in with a more analytical and principled approach to the elements and causative power of 'recognisable acts' so as to restrict the use of force in situations where there are no manifestations of hostile force, as described in Chapter 1.

Both direct participation in hostilities and *de facto* membership raise the complex challenge of trying to define when an individual ceases to cause harm, or exercise a 'continuous combat function' so as to regain immunity, or in other words the modalities of the 'revolving door' phenomenon. It is suggested that rather than trying to define this in general terms, the better approach is, respectively, to escalate or graduate the application of nonlethal and lethal force so that in situations where there is doubt due to there being no perceivable threat that is direct and immediate, an individual who is suspected of being an integral part of specific military operations or a functional combatant has the opportunity to remove any such doubt or at least 'actively disengage' or 'overtly renunciate' from their directly or indirectly hostile activities, for example, by surrendering, demonstrating extended nonparticipation or giving up weapons.[123]

Public Committee Against Torture v *The Government of Israel: guiding case-by case determinations of direct participation in hostilities and membership of an organised armed group*

Given the doubt that will exist regarding direct participation in hostilities and membership in unconventional operational environment, the Israeli High Court of Justice ('HCJ') proposed four principles that serve to guide case-by-case determinations in a principled fashion. First, that 'most thoroughly verified' and reliable information 'regarding the identity and activity' of an individual 'who is

---

123 Schmitt, above n 51, 38; Boothby, above n 62, 162; ICRC (Interpretive Guidance), above n 17, 25; See also Melzer, above n 17.

allegedly taking part in the hostilities' is needed before making a status determination. The HCJ derived this norm from the ECHR case of *Ergi v Turkey* and stated that this places a 'heavy' burden of proof on forces to ensure combatant status before proceeding with an attack. Where there is any doubt as to civilian status, forces need to resolve this through a process of 'careful verification', the underlying policy being that basing attacks on a slight suspicion of hostile intent and action could serve to 'undermine' and 'erode' the foundational humanitarian law principle of distinction and lead to unwarranted extrajudicial or targeted killings of civilians.[124] Second, incorporating the human rights standard of proportionality in *McCann v United Kingdom*, the HCJ found that attacks against civilians directly participating in hostilities must be proportionate. They can only be carried out if absolutely necessary, or, in other words, only if less harmful means are not available. Accordingly, 'if a terrorist taking a direct part in hostilities can be arrested, interrogated, and tried, those are the means which should be employed'.[125] A key statement by the HCJ in this regard is that '[t]rial is preferable to the use of force' as '[a] rule-of-law state employs, to the extent possible, procedures of law and not procedures of force'.[126] Thus lethal force can only be used where '[a]rrest, investigation, and trial' are not possible or where they would involve 'a risk so great' of putting the lives of soldiers or other civilians lives in jeopardy.[127] The HCJ noted that 'arrest, investigation and trial' as opposed to a first resort to lethal force may 'be particularly practical' and 'realisable possibilities' in situations of occupation where forces have a degree of control over the area in which they are operating.[128]

Third, as expressly derived from *McKerr v United Kingdom*, the HCJ found that where lethal force has been used against 'a civilian suspected of taking an active part, at such time, in hostilities', effective investigations are to be carried out.[129] Finally, the HCJ held that the use of force against a civilian suspected of participating directly in hostilities must also meet the standard humanitarian law proportionality test, namely that the harm to innocent civilian bystanders must not be disproportionate to the advantage sought by such an attack.[130]

Thus, in recognition of the fact that current treaty-based and customary humanitarian law is unclear on the issue of direct participation in hostilities, this case is an important contribution in generally setting out when, in a situation of armed conflict, an individual can be deemed to take a direct part in hostilities or to be a member of an organised armed group and, pursuant to this, the stringent conditions that should be satisfied in order to overcome reasonable doubt as to whether or not an individual may be subject to lethal force.

124 *PCAT v Israel*, above n 3, 40.
125 Ibid.
126 Ibid.
127 Ibid.
128 Ibid.
129 Ibid.
130 *PCAT v Israel*, above n 3, 40.

Conclusions: doubt, direct participation in hostilities and membership of an organised armed group

In an unconventional context with irregular forms of organisation and asymmetric tactics, there will be much doubt as to the status of individuals, in particular, whether or not they can be presumed to be members of an organised armed group exercising a continuous combat function or playing an integral part in a concrete military operation. Treaty-based and customary law provide that where there is 'doubt [as to] whether a person is a civilian [then] that person shall be considered to be a civilian'.[131] The military doctrine surrounding social network analysis discussed in Chapter 1, the decision in *Public Committee Against Torture v The Government of Israel* discussed earlier and the decision in *Simić* suggest that where there is no immediate and direct threat, a 'heavy' burden of proof must be satisfied in order to remove reasonable doubt as to an individual's presumptive civilian status.[132] This reasoning opens the way for addressing the issue of how to make a distinction between notions such as direct participation in hostilities, what has loosely been referred to as 'participation in the war effort' and membership of an organised armed group exercising a continuous combat function, namely, it is to be done through an evidence-based and intelligence-led approach, which may, as far as possible, penetrate the underlying intention behind an act or otherwise that an individual is performing a continuous combat function. Accordingly, outside the framework of direct participation in hostilities, a heavy burden of proof is needed to remove reasonable doubt as to an individual's presumptive civilian status and in order to open the way for targeting on account of membership of an organised armed group on the basis of presumably exercising a continuous

---

131 Article 50 paragraph (1) of Additional Protocol I Protocol Additional to the Geneva Conventions of 12 August 1949, and relating to the Protection of Victims of International Armed Conflicts (Protocol I), Geneva, 8 June 1977, Article 50(1). Article 50 was adopted by consensus. CDDH, above n 11, Volume VI, 161; CIHL Study, above n 30, Rule 6.

132 *PCAT v Israel*, above n 3, 37; *José Alexis Fuentes Guerrero v Columbia* (Report No 61/99) Inter-American Commission on Human Rights, Case 11/519, OEA Ser.L/V/II.106, Doc 7 Rev (13 April 1999), 53; *Prosecutor v Simić* (Trial Judgment) ICTY-95–9-T (17 October 2003), 659: the ICTY Trial Chamber ruled that on the facts before it, it did 'not accept that allegations about possession of weapons, in itself, creates a reasonable doubt as to the civilian status of the persons arrested and detained for possession of weapons [as] [t]he fact that most of them were arrested from their homes, combined with a lack of evidence that they participated in the armed conflict, clearly shows that they were not combatants, but rather, civilians . . . '; UNHRC 'Summary record of the 2118th Meeting on 25 July 2003: Israel' (Aug 6, 2003) UN Doc CCPR/C/SR.2118: The Israeli government's statement to the United Nations Human Rights Committee stated that, '[e]ven persons known to be terrorists were legitimate targets only if there was reliable evidence linking them directly to a hostile act. . . . It would, of course, be preferable to arrest such persons, but in areas such as the Gaza Strip, over which Israel had no control, this Government did not have that option. Its security forces were instructed by the Attorney-General, however, to attack unlawful combatants only when there was an urgent military necessity and when no less harmful alternative was available to avert the danger posed by the terrorists'.

combat function. Furthermore, in addition to the previously mentioned discussion that argues that targeting members of organised armed groups arises at the CA3 threshold as illustrated by *Boškoski* and continues into APII NIACs, this notion of doubt under IHL suggests that the requirement of 'continuous combat function' for targeting members of organised armed groups is only capable of being applied in the context of targeted operations (as opposed to the general conduct of hostilities where the general basis of targeting will be direct participation in hostilities) where there is reliable intelligence or evidence going towards the element of membership. As targeting on this basis is not grounded on a direct lethal or harmful threat, it is unclear how membership can otherwise be presumed. Targeting on the basis of presumed membership where there is an absence of, or very limited, reliable intelligence or evidence hardly seems appropriate or sufficient to remove reasonable doubt as to an individual's presumptive civilian status and replace it with that of a 'continuous combat function'.

Although it is accepted that there is no obligation under IHL, circumstances permitting, to detain or use minimum force, rather than target by reference to status, it is nevertheless suggested that where there is reasonable doubt as to civilian status, then IHL foresees and provides for other measures short of lethal force, such as internment in relation to an occupying power or, precursory to the use of force, the obligation to provide effective warnings where feasible. Internment may be used where an individual is merely suspected of being a member of an organised armed group, without reasonable grounds for such a suspicion, and where they do not pose a direct lethal threat. Importantly, rather than representing what may be described as dangerous category confusion, this discussion elucidates how classic IHL can be interpreted so as to be fit for purpose and practicable in the complex and uncertain operational environment of unconventional or irregular urban warfare, for example, an NIAC within a situation of ongoing belligerent occupation.[133] Rather than regarding as 'incoherent' what may be seen as 'the combination of a right to use deadly force and a requirement to use the minimum force necessary',[134] it is suggested that the ICRC Interpretive Guidance, as well as this discussion, attempt to forge what is described later as a balanced interrelationship between two combatancy-related presumptions that should permeate the targeting law analysis, namely the humanitarian law presumption of 'mandatory civilian protection' or doubt on the one hand (that is, a person is to be considered to be a civilian for as long as there is doubt as to their real status, and they shall not be made the object of attack when it is not reasonable to believe in the circumstances that the potential target is a combatant, but still it may be necessary to take nonlethal action for imperative reasons of security) and, on the other, the closely related criminal law principles of *in dubio pro reo*

---

133 W Hays Parks, 'Part IX of the ICRC "Direct Participation in Hostilities" Study: No Mandate, No Expertise and Legally Incorrect' (2010) 42 *New York University Journal of International Law and Politics* 769, 801–802.

134 Françoise Hampson, above n 14, 201.

and *nullem crimen sine lege*, whereby any doubt is to be resolved in favour of the accused. Whereas the question of civilians directly participating in hostilities may, to a large extent, be determined at a tactical level by soldiers on the ground in response to direct and immediate lethal threats in a factual situation of non-international armed conflict commencing at the CA3 threshold, it is suggested that the questions of whether an individual is a member of an organised armed group exercising a continuous combat function or whether they are an integral part of a concrete and coordinated military operation are more convoluted and therefore involve a targeting analysis involving military, doctrinal and legal considerations on the part of those higher up in the chain of command, that is, at the operational level. Again, this is to suggest that targeting on the basis of status in situations that have at least reached the CA3 threshold as indicated in *Boškoski* can only plausibly be made at the operational level with reference to reliable intelligence and/or evidence and not at the tactical level, that is, by soldiers on the ground who are highly unlikely to have an awareness of the salient facts and legal issues necessary to arrive at a reasonable presumption of membership of an organised armed group.

Public Committee Against Torture v The Government of Israel referred to cases such as *McCann v UK* and *McKerr v UK* which concerned substantive breaches of Article 2 ECHR within the respective states' territory. Although the interpretations set out in the cases referred to only formally apply within the jurisdiction of contracting parties to the ECHR, they were nevertheless used as important subsidiary means for the determination of rules of law by the Israeli High Court of Justice, which attempted to set out the conditions that should be satisfied in order to overcome reasonable doubt as to whether or not an individual may be subject to lethal force. In this way, the decisions of regional human rights mechanisms can be seen as having wider import and impact on the issues such as the relationship between international human rights law and international humanitarian law. In this light, *Public Committee Against Torture v The Government of Israel* is as important as it is novel because it models an approach to resolving doubt inherent in civilianised conflict situations in favour of civilians and links this to broader strategic or policy goals, also evident in military doctrine discussed in Chapter 1, such as maintaining or transitioning towards the rule of law. In these regards, this case is significant as it attempted to establish rules governing 'targeted killings' which merge conduct of hostilities rules and law enforcement standards derived from human rights standards established by regional human rights treaty bodies.[135] In particular, it implies that threat-based assessments should be employed where feasible, and status-based targeting decisions should be restricted, in particular to targeted operations. *Public Committee Against Torture v The Government of Israel* is important as it indicates how complex targeting decisions can and should be made in the context of an unconventional and irregular operational environment,

135 Jelena Pejic, 'Conflict Classification and the Law Applicable to Detention and the Use of Force', in Elizabeth Wilmshurst (ed), *International Law and the Classification of Conflicts* (OUP, 2012) 112.

and thus this case, together with the authorities it used to reach its decision, constitute important subsidiary means for the interpretation of general standards of treaty-based and customary humanitarian law relating to precautions.

However, as alluded to earlier, the reasoning employed by the Israeli High Court of Justice in relation to what constitutes direct participation in hostilities has been described as 'nonanalytical in nature', in that although it provides some general principles and examples with which to make case-by-case assessments to this effect, it 'prevents the emergence of a general definition of direct participation in hostilities' as well as membership in an organised armed group and also 'undermines the . . . ability to . . . guide [the Courts] in making practical decisions in specific cases in which the policy of targeted killings is considered'.[136] This raises the question of whether it is possible to set out a 'general definition of direct part in hostilities' and, more significantly, membership of an organised armed group that can plausibly be applied to the complexities of irregular conflicts within a full-spectrum operational environment. The dictum of the Israeli High Court of Justice that 'function determines the directness of the part taken in the hostilities'[137] marks a useful but inadequate starting point in the analysis of how to distinguish between civilians on the one hand and members of organised armed groups, as well as civilians directly participating in hostilities on the other, and particularly in relation to members of organised armed groups, where and how it is appropriate to use lethal force on the basis of status-based determinations and where and how it is appropriate to use lethal force on the basis of threat-based determinations.

Accordingly, attention will now be turned to other meagre attempts to forge a general definition before contributing to the debate by proposing the extrapolation of criminal law models of indirect participation and perpetration in order to place operational and normative decision making vis-à-vis the escalation of nonlethal and lethal force in situations involving armed conflict on a clearer and more principled analytical foundation. Arguably, this represents an important contribution towards redressing what Hankaerts describes as the absence of a 'reference point for the general distinction' between those who 'participate directly in the hostilities and those to be protected as civilians',[138] as well as those who are to be regarded as members of organised armed groups exercising a continuous combat function and those who are to be protected as civilians which, as discussed previously, can lead to 'subjective or overly flexible' criteria emerging in practice which are 'prone to lead to erroneous and arbitrary targeting'.[139]

---

136 Moodrick Even-Khen, above n 3, 220.

137 *Public Committee Against Torture v Israel*, above n 3, 35–37. ('PCAT').

138 Jean-Marie Henckaerts, 'Study on CIHL: A Contribution to the Understanding and Respect for the Rule of Law in Armed Conflict' (2005) 857 *International Review of the Red Cross* 16; Dapo Akande, 'Clearing the Fog Of War? The ICRC's Interpretive Guidance on Direct Participation in Hostilities' (2002) 59 *International and Comparative Law Quarterly* 180–192.

139 Melzer, above n 37, 321.

5 Towards a clearer framework for distinguishing those who participate directly in hostilities from those who are to be protected as civilians

Extrapolating models of accessorial liability and coperpetration in the commission of harmful acts

Introduction

The previous discussion indicated that the law and Interpretive Guidance surrounding the issue of direct participation in hostilities and membership of organised armed groups is unclear and thus unsatisfactory. Indeed, as discussed earlier, the ICRC's criterion for 'direct causation' was criticised as lacking plausibility due to its failure to take into consideration established and pragmatic approaches taken to notions of participation and causation in international and domestic criminal law.[1] Seen in this light, individuals can foresee that general types of indirect contribution to the commission of proscribed acts or contributions to a common criminal plan or enterprise will lead to penal repression. In contrast, under the unclear rules and interpretations of humanitarian law relating to participation in hostilities and membership of organised armed groups, civilians are not able to foresee with sufficient clarity the forms of conduct that could lead to the deprivation of their immunity from attack as well as the duration of any deprivation, given that the rules as they stand grant states a broad margin of appreciation to construe broadly what constitutes harm and what is causative of harm in the context of hostilities. Moreover, it was suggested that this implied that established models concerning the harmful nature and causative power of forms of indirect participation and coperpetration in this regard could assist with clarifying the modalities and the parameters of depriving civilians of their immunity from attack.

Accordingly, this section will discuss how the rules on accessorial liability can elucidate the issue of what it means to participate directly in hostilities, subject to the proviso, as discussed in Chapter 1, that it is conditioned by the escalation

1 Michael Schmitt, 'Deconstructing Direct Participation in Hostilities: The Constitutive Elements' (2009–2010) 42 *New York University Journal of International Law and Politics* 697, 726.

of nonlethal force. The modes of liability here include indirect liability for aiding and abetting the commission of proscribed acts, followed by direct liability for planning, ordering and instigating the commission of proscribed acts. Following this, the discussion will then proceed to discuss how the framework of a joint criminal enterprise can elucidate the issue of *de facto* membership in an organised armed group, subject to the proviso, as discussed in Chapter 1, that it is conditioned by the escalation of lethal force. The rationale for this extrapolation, or 'cross-fertilisation', of models of accessorial liability and coperpetration from criminal law to issues of participation and membership in humanitarian law is that, as long as targeting is restricted according to the escalation of nonlethal and lethal force, then there appears no justifiable reason to exclude the clear, pragmatic and functional approaches of criminal law from humanitarian law analysis, especially given the former's clearer conceptual delineation of participation in the commission of an act, the coperpetration of an act and the distinction between them. In contrast to previous attempts at fostering clarity, it is suggested that the clarity offered by this approach can serve to restrict the conditions under which civilians may be deprived of their immunity from attack. Another way of describing this difference between the perpetration of an offence performed by the principal and 'participation' or 'complicity' in the perpetration of an offence performed by an accessory or accomplice is that 'perpetration of a crime [gives] rise to principal liability and participation in a crime committed by a third person [gives] rise to accessorial liability'.[2] By analogy with the Interpretive Guidance, this implies that perpetration may lead to deprivation of immunity for the duration of any given hostilities, whereas participation merely results in deprivation 'for such time' as there is indirect support or contributions to a hostile act or specific military operation. The distinction between the two modes of liability is thus of major practical relevance to humanitarian law. In other words, criminal law takes account of, and thus seeks to repress, acts that facilitate or support the direct or principle perpetration of proscribed and harmful acts and the logic inherent within this process is therefore relevant to the issue of participation in hostilities and thus targeting law.[3]

In *Tadić*, a justification for the repression of activities that support the commission of proscribed acts was that 'the moral gravity of such participation is often no less – or indeed – no different – from that of those actually carrying out the acts in question'.[4] In this way, *Tadić* noted that 'the participation and contribution of the other members of [a] group is often vital in facilitating the commission

2 Héctor Olásolo, *The International Criminal Responsibility of Senior Political and Military Leaders as Principles to International Crimes* (Hart, Oxford, 2010), 14.

3 *Prosecutor v Akayesu* (Trial Judgment) ICTR-96-4-T (2 September 1998), 530: '[a]s far as the Chamber is aware, all criminal systems provide that an accomplice may also be tried, even where the principal perpetrator of the crime has not been identified, or where, for any other reasons, guilt could not be proven'.

4 *Prosecutor v Tadić* (Appeals Chamber Judgment) ICTY-94-1-A (15 July 1999) 191.

Table 5.1 Comparing general elements of complicity and direct participation in hostilities

General elements of complicity or accessorial liability	*General elements of participation in hostilities*
Participation in the choate or inchoate perpetration of predicate act	Act likely to affect adversely the military operations or military capacity of a party to an armed conflict
Material contribution to perpetration of predicate act	There must be 'direct causation' between the act and the harm
Material contribution was intended, reckless or done with knowledge of the predicate act	Belligerent nexus: the act must be 'objectively likely' to inflict harm and 'specifically designed' to cause directly the required threshold of harm in support of a party to the conflict and to the detriment of another

of the offence in question'.[5] Furthermore, although the Appeals Chamber in *Strugar* noted that 'conduct amounting to direct or active participation in hostilities is not, however, limited to combat activities as such', it went on to state that 'to hold all activities in support of military operations as amounting to direct participation in hostilities would in practice render the principle of distinction meaningless'.[6] In this regard, it is suggested that the logic of criminal law modes of direct and indirect liability are not only relevant for the penal repression of activities that contribute to or support the direct perpetration of proscribed acts, but also have import concerning the modes and parameters of civilian immunity from attack under humanitarian law where civilians are deemed to be engaged in sufficiently harmful activity, so as to put the principle of distinction on a clearer analytic foundation. In this regard, it is also worth noting that if a member of an organised armed group shoots at government soldiers during a non-international armed conflict, then this will usually constitute a crime under domestic law, and forms of indirect participation or coperpetration may also attract criminal censure under domestic law.

In this way, the key concern that this discussion aims to dispel is that this approach to addressing fundamental lacunae in humanitarian law can serve to undermine the principle of distinction by leading to what has been described as the 'complicity cascade'.[7] In other words, broad or cascading approaches to complicity in hostile activities constitute a slippery slope towards imposing collective

5 Ibid.

6 *Prosecutor v Strugar* (Appeals Chamber Judgment) IT-01–42-A (17 July 2008).

7 William Schabas, 'Enforcing International Humanitarian Law: Catching the Accomplices' (2001) 83 (842) *International Review of the Red Cross* 451.

guilt upon civilians or creating a state of total war on the basis of the presumption that all hostile acts can ultimately be linked back to civilian activities, and therefore civilians and civilian populations are collectively liable and thus open to attack. Wright's *A Study of War* related such forms of 'total war' and increased attacks upon civilians during the Second World War to the emergence of a broad and pervasive doctrine of military necessity, which perceived an increase in the 'proportion of the population contributing directly or indirectly to the making of the policy and the military of the enemy'.[8] Indeed, with regard to workers in munitions and armament factories great distances behind enemy lines, and thus far away from battle, Rolland stated that they 'occupy a position intermediate between the combatants proper and the noncombatants who are still employed on their peacetime trades and professions'. On this basis Rolland asserted that '[t]he reasons for sparing them are losing force [as] [f]undamentally they are almost in exactly the same position as the men of the auxiliary services of the armies, and the latter are certainly legitimate objects of attack'.[9] According to Nurick's account of the aerial campaigns of the Second World War, to begin with,

> bombing was confined to military objectives in the actual theatre of operations [t]hen . . . extended to military objectives, such as factories, communications, and the like in the rear of the enemy's lines . . . [then finally to] the bombing of cities in order to affect the morale of the civilians.[10]

Arguably the *raison d'être* for the Geneva Conventions and their Additional Protocols was to prevent a recurrence of the systematic and widespread aerial bombing of civilian populated areas and infrastructure that occurred during the major wars of the twentieth century by attempting to forge a clear and narrow distinction between lawful and unlawful military objectives. As discussed previously, formulating a distinction between military objectives and objects of protection based on a narrow range of material considerations can be viewed as being based on such policy considerations, as well as the notion that the more causal steps we take back from the direct perpetration of a hostile act, the more difficult it becomes to be sure about whether there is a material, causal and intended link to the surrounding hostilities.[11] However, *a contrario*, this speculative consideration must vie with the equally cogent notion that the net of complicity can be as wide as there is reliable

8 Q Wright, *A Study of War* (2nd edn University of Chicago Press, 1983) 131; Emily Camins, 'The Past as Prologue: The Development of the 'Direct participation' Exception to Civilian Immunity' (2008) 90 (872) *International Review of the Red Cross* 868.

9 L Rolland, 'Les pratiques de la guerre aérienne dans le conflit de 1914 et le droit des gens' (Pedone, Paris, 1916) 559, cited in J M Spaight, 'Legitimate Objectives in Air Warfare' (1944) 21 *British Yearbook of International Law*, 162.

10 Lester Nurick, 'The Distinction between Combatant and Non-Combatant in the Law of War' (1945) 39 *American Journal of International Law* 681.

11 Schabas, above n 7.

intelligence and evidence to demonstrate such a link. Accordingly, although speculative and policy-based considerations are of major importance in ensuring the existence of humanitarian protections, they can nevertheless belie and circumvent the 'problematic' existence of such links in practice, particularly in the context of unconventional and irregular forms of collective violence amounting to hostilities. This approach recognises that armed conflicts are situations of collective violence that institutions of civil society are no longer able to contain and control.

As stated in *Tadić*, widespread killing in the context of an armed conflict does 'not result from the criminal propensity of single individuals but constitute manifestations of collective criminality . . . often carried out by groups of individuals acting in pursuance of a common criminal design'.[12] In this sense, the issue still remains that the Geneva Conventions, their Additional Protocols and subsequent attempts at elucidation in the form of their Commentaries, as well as the ICRC Interpretive Guidance on Direct Participation in hostilities, have left unresolved the questions of what generally constitutes direct participation in hostilities and membership of an organised armed group. As such, this has been dealt with on a case-by-case basis and, it is suggested, without any cogent analytical or theoretical reasoning. Thus, if it is logical to propose that criminal acts with a nexus to surrounding hostilities can involve a multiplicity of persons contributing in a range of direct and indirect ways, then it is logical to make a similar proposition regarding hostile or belligerent acts.

Accordingly, individual crimes can be an expression of collective criminality and thus subject to penal repression in the same way that individual hostile acts can be an expression of collective hostility and thus subject to loss of immunity from attack. For example in the ICTY's Final Report to the Prosecutor by the Committee Established to Review the NATO Bombing Campaign Against the FRY, it was suggested that if the media are used to incite concrete and specific crimes by identifying targets as well as encouraging and coordinating their engagement (as opposed to generating support for the war effort), or if they are used for military command, control and communications, then it becomes a legitimate military target.[13]

The difficulty in both respects lies in pinpointing the specific contribution that an individual makes to the collective act or policy, and in this regard, criminal law is more highly developed than humanitarian law and can therefore serve to elucidate further its provisions relating to the parameters of immunity. Indeed, it is suggested that criminal law, with its analytical focus on the objective and subjective elements of a range of indirect participation and perpetration possesses less of a propensity towards collective guilt than humanitarian law as it currently stands.[14]

---

12 *Tadić* (Appeals Chamber Judgment), above n 4, 191.

13 ICTY, Final Report to the Prosecutor by the Committee Established to Review the NATO Bombing Campaign Against the Federal Republic of Yugoslavia, (Jun 13, 2000), 47.

14 *'The IG Farben Case': United States of America v Carl Krauch et al.*, (Judgment of 30 July 1948) in IV Trials of War Criminals Before the Nuremburg Military Tribunals Under Control Council Law No 10 Volume VIII (US Government Printing Office, 1951): the manufacturers of poison gas were deemed to be not liable as accessories to war crimes on

However, it is suggested that focusing on the different outcomes and functions of these interrelated branches of law is not sufficient to preclude cross-fertilisation of models of complicity. The reason for this is that the issue of a civilian's complicity in hostilities is material to the determination of the lawfulness of the attack against them. Indeed, as the Appeals Chamber held in *Strugar*, 'in order to establish the existence of a violation [. . .] a Trial Chamber must be satisfied beyond a reasonable doubt that the victim of the alleged offence was not participating in acts of war . . .'[15] Therefore, where 'a reasonable doubt subsists' with regard to a civilian's 'non-participation in acts of war' and thus to their immunity, then 'a Trial Chamber cannot convict an accused' for an unlawful attack.[16]

This suggests that *ex post facto* criminal adjudication must objectively take into consideration the circumstances of the victim as well as the outlook of the attacker in order to assess whether or not they were 'participating in acts of war which by their nature or purpose are intended to cause actual harm to the personnel or equipment of the enemy's armed forces'.[17] In this way, this implies the need for a balanced interrelationship between what Hayashi describes as 'two combatancy-related presumptions', namely the humanitarian law presumption of 'mandatory civilian protection' or doubt, on the one hand, and, on the other, the criminal law principles of *in dubio pro reo* and *nullem crimen sine lege*, whereby any doubt is to be resolved in favour of the accused.[18] Therefore, the presumption of *in dubio pro reo*, as manifest in the previously mentioned dictum in *Strugar*, is to be balanced against the presumption of doubt in favour of civilians as described in *Galić*, whereby '[a] person shall be considered to be a civilian for as long as there is a doubt as to his or her real status', and furthermore,

> that a person shall not be made the object of attack when it is not reasonable to believe, in the circumstances of the person contemplating the attack, including the information available to the latter, that the potential target is a combatant.[19]

Accordingly, this suggests that there is an important substantive and reflexive relationship between the *ex ante* and contemporaneous targeting decisions by

---

the basis that they did not have requisite knowledge of its end use. Furthermore, according to the United States War Crimes Tribunal, this knowledge could not be inferred as 'neither the volume of production nor the fact that large shipments were destined to concentration camps would alone be sufficient to lead us to conclude that those who knew of such facts must also have had knowledge of the criminal purposes to which this substance was being put'; See also Schabas, above n 7, 844.

15 *Strugar* (Appeals Chamber Judgment), above n 6, 178.

16 Ibid.

17 Ibid.

18 N Hayashi, (2006) 2 'The Role of Judges in Identifying the Status of Combatants' (2006) *Acta Societatis Martensis* 76.

19 *Prosecutor v Galić* (Trial Judgment) ICTY-98–29-T (5 December 2003), 50.

primary duty bearers which are governed by humanitarian law and *ex post facto* adjudication and jurisprudence of international criminal tribunals.[20]

In this way, it is suggested that international criminal law can serve to condition and regulate the use of force, in that it functions to assess and thus guide the parameters of immunity. It thus has a strong normative and practical connection with IHL in terms of setting reasonable parameters vis-à-vis the lawful use of military force in situations of conflict. In turn, this implies that a consideration of modes of indirect participation in and coperpetration of hostile acts are relevant to the issue of whether or not an individual was 'participating in acts of war' so as to adequately balance the two previously mentioned 'combatancy-related presumptions'. Therefore, criminal law models of accessorial liability and coperpetration are relevant to the issue of the parameters of civilian immunity, and this discussion will now proceed to outline and discuss them in turn. At a more general level, it is suggested that international criminal and humanitarian law are functionally related in the sense that they are branches of international public law centred around the lawfulness of repressing, respectively, criminal activities that are harmful to the state or society, or hostile activities that are harmful to a party to an armed conflict or an occupying power.[21]

Furthermore, it is suggested that classification of a situation is important *ex ante* and *ex post facto*, as it has a bearing on what may be considered reasonable and thus lawful in circumstances where there is doubt or factual uncertainty. Thus, in situations of armed conflict, there will be lower standards of reasonableness because, due to the intense and dangerous circumstances and the lack of information available, it may be more reasonable for a person to believe that a potential target is not immune from attack, whereas the same may not be said in situations not reaching the threshold of a CA3 conflict. The important thing to bear in mind here is that general classification has an impact on notions of standards of reasonableness.

Accessorial liability and direct participation in hostilities

International and domestic systems of criminal law not only provide for principal liability for the person who directly or physically perpetrates a crime, but also for forms of accessorial liability for support roles. Accessorial liability is widely recognised in domestic and international criminal law and it derives from supporting the perpetrator's or principal's intentional commission of an offence. Article 7(1) of the Statute of the ICTY, Article 6 (1) of the Statute of the ICTR and Article 25 of the Statute of the International Criminal Court cover various stages and forms of third party participation and support roles in the commission of a

20 Antonio Cassese, 'On Some Merits of the Israeli Judgment on Targeted Killings' (2007) 5 *Journal of International Criminal Justice* 344.

21 Convention (IV) respecting the Laws and Customs of War on Land and its annex: Regulations concerning the Laws and Customs of War on Land. The Hague, 18 October 1907 (Hague Regulations), Article 43: 'The authority of the legitimate power having in fact passed into the hands of the occupant, the latter shall take all the measures in his power to restore, and ensure, as far as possible, public order and safety, while respecting, unless absolutely prevented, the laws in force in the country'.

crime by the direct physical perpetrator. For example Article 7(1) of the ICTY statute provides that '[a] person who planned, instigated, ordered, committed or otherwise aided and abetted in the planning, perpetration or execution of a crime [. . .] shall be individually responsible for the crime'. Furthermore, as can be seen from the ICC pre-trial chamber's decision in Lubanga, the ICC Statute also makes a distinction between forms of accessorial, as opposed to principal liability provided for in Article 25 (3)(a) to (d).[22] It is suggested that criminal law models of accessorial liability and co-perpetration are relevant to the issues of what constitutes direct participation in hostilities and membership in an organized armed group. Not only that, but as this approach is grounded in military doctrine it is suggested that it is practicable in the context of planned or targeted operations where intelligence is available as part of the process of target analysis. Frameworks of accessorial liability provide useful and functional concepts for elucidating the notion of direct participation in hostilities because forms of liability in this regard are derived from the practical support given to the commission of a criminal wrong by a principal or physical perpetrator. International criminal law modes of liability set out evolving conceptual frameworks for connecting individuals to crimes across a multiplicity of fact patterns in situations of armed conflict, and therefore also suggest plausible ways of linking individuals to hostilities as well as the membership of organised armed groups, albeit not to the requisite standard of proof involved in a criminal trial. Extrapolating the principles from evolving criminal law modes of liability to guide intelligence-based targeting analysis can assist target planners to understand the social dynamic or interaction that sustains on-going fighting, in particular, by helping them to distinguish the indirect support activities, defensive activities or criminal activities within the general civilian population or mass base of popular support that lack proximity or a nexus with the surrounding hostilities, from what can be broadly defined as the internal support structure of an organized armed group that is party to an armed conflict, as opposed to other types or situations of violence such as those just mentioned. It can develop IHL discourse in this regard by putting our notions of participation and membership on a more analytical footing. In a highly civilianized context, making distinctions between hostile and non-hostile threats, especially in the absence of a manifest lethal threat, will often involve subjective considerations relating to an individual's awareness and intentions. As will be discussed below, the advantage of this approach in a battlefield context is that subjectivity may be inferred from reliable intelligence that indicates a pattern of coordinated cooperation between individuals which can only be explained through the existence of a common purpose or strategic plan, or at least an awareness of it combined with some form of practical support. As

22 Article 7(1) of the Statute of the ICTY, Article 6 (1) of the Statute of the ICTR and Article 25 of the Statute of the International Criminal Court. *Prosecutor v Lubanga* (Pre-Trial Chamber I Decision on Confirmation of Charges) ICC-01/04-01/06 (29 January 2007), 326–330; *Prosecutor v Lubanga* (Judgment pursuant to Article 74 of the Statute) ICC-01/04-01/06 (14 March 2012), 919–922.

will now be discussed, it is crucial that IRCs and target analysis attempt to make such distinctions within a civilianized operational theatre.

Aiding and abetting

This section contributes to a general framework of target analysis which may be used to assess whether the indirect support activities provided by civilians comprising the general population, the mass base of popular support [23] and 'auxiliaries' amount to direct participation in hostilities by extrapolating the objective and subjective elements of aiding and abetting as developed in international criminal law.[24] It is suggested that where there is intelligence or evidence that establishes these elements, then a civilian may be targeted for such time as their conduct amounts to direct participation in hostilities or for such time as their indirect activities constitute 'an integral part' of a specific and coordinated military operation.

Beginning with the objective elements, according to ICTY jurisprudence, an individual will be liable as an accessory for aiding and abetting a crime where it is demonstrated that they offered practical assistance, encouragement or moral support to a principal offender or perpetrator and this has a substantial effect on the perpetration of their crime(s). Rather than implying a causal relationship, the accomplice must make a significant difference to the commission of the criminal act by the principal before during or after its perpetration. In other words, the criminal act would have occurred in a different way had it not been for their factual contribution.[25]

Generally, a 'substantial contribution' will be self-evident where there is proximity between acts of support and the direct perpetrators.[26] For example, in the

23 British Army, Countering Insurgency, Field Manual Volume 1 Part 10 (Army Code 71876, October 2009) 2-15: The base of popular support comprises those elements of the civilian population who do not remain neutral, but who play a general, clandestine and indirect role in supporting an insurgency or armed groups in their activities. Rather than functioning as active auxiliaries, the base of popular support engages in normal every-day civilian activities, whilst at the same time providing general and occasional supportive functions such as providing intelligence, concealment, funding and transport. Importantly, it is recognized that insurgencies involving clans or tribes, roles and functions are difficult to define and are fluid in that individuals have no formal status, but constantly move between combat, auxiliary and follower functions.

24 Ibid: Auxiliaries have been defined as those 'active sympathizers' who play an active role in supporting combat activities rather than engaging directly in combat activities. Forms of support provided by auxiliaries may include collecting and transmitting intelligence, running safe houses, sending signals and warnings, procuring, transporting and storing weapons, supplies and documents; See also, US FM 3-24, ibid, 1 – 62.

25 *Prosecutor v Blagojević et al.* (Trial Judgment) IT-02-60-T (17 January 2005), 726 and 777. *Prosecutor v Šainović et al.* (Appeals Judgment) IT-05-87-A (23 January 2014) 1626, 1647 and 1649. *Prosecutor v Strugar* (Trial Judgment) ICTY-01-42-T (31 January 2005) 91. *Prosecutor v Simić* (Trial Judgment) ICTY-95-9-T (17 October 2003) 161. *Prosecutor v Tadić* (Opinion and Judgment) ICTY-94-1-T (7 May 1997) 688.

26 *Prosecutor v Perešić* (Appeals Chamber Judgment) ICTY-04-81-A (28 February 2013) 38.

Zyklon B Case before British Military Court Hamburg, arguments that the provision of poison gas to concentration camps amounted to general assistance for lawful purposes were rejected in view of evidence demonstrating that the owner and manager of a company which manufactured poison gas had provided training to the principal perpetrators in how to use it to kill humans in confined spaces and that they knew that the gas was to be used for the purpose of killing human beings.[27]

The ICTY Appeals Chamber previously held that in cases of geographical or temporal remoteness it will be necessary to demonstrate that acts of support or assistance are 'specifically directed' towards the commission of a crime so as to ensure that there is a sufficient 'culpable link'. For example, a six-month delay between an individual being observed unloading weapons and a subsequent attack was considered to reduce the likelihood that these weapons were specifically directed towards assisting in this attack.[28] However the Appeals Chamber has subsequently conducted a survey of ICTY jurisprudence, customary law and municipal law and has found that specific direction does not constitute an additional and free-standing element of aiding and abetting liability.[29] Nevertheless, it noted that specific direction may at times be factually implicit in a finding that an individual's provision of practical assistance amounts to a substantial contribution.[30] Moving onto the subjective elements, for an individual to be liable for aiding and abetting it must be demonstrated that they know that their acts assist in the commission of the principal perpetrator's crime. [31] This means that they must have knowledge or awareness that the acts they performed assist in the commission of a specific crime by the principal and that they knew of the principal's intention to commit this crime.[32]

If function determines the directness of the part taken in hostilities, then the concept of aiding and abetting provides a useful tool for target planners by elucidating the objective and subjective elements of what it means to participate

---

27 *'The Zyklon B Case': The trial of Bruno Tesch et al. (The Zyklon B Case)*, British Military Court Hamburg 1946 (United Nations War Crimes Commission, 1 Law Reports of Trials of War Criminals) 93-102.

28 *Prosecutor v Perešić*, ibid., 40; *Prosecutor v Kupreškić* (Appeals Chamber Judgment) ICTY-95-16-A (23 October 2001, 275–277.

29 *Prosecutor v Šainović et al.* above n 25 1625.

30 Ibid.

31 *Prosecutor v Blaskić* (Appeals Chamber Judgment) ICTY-95-14-A (29 July 2004) 49. *Prosecutor v Šainović et al.* (Appeals Judgment), ibid., 1649.

32 *Prosecutor v Delalić et al. the 'Čelebići Case'* (Trial Judgment) ICTY-96-21-T (16 November 1998) 162–163: 'the act of participation [must] be performed with knowledge that it will assist the principal in the commission of the criminal act'; at para 329: there must be 'awareness of the act of participation coupled with a conscious decision to participate by planning, instigating, ordering, committing, or otherwise aiding and abetting in the commission of a crime'; With regard to aiding and abetting under the ICCS, Article 25 paragraph (3) (c) provides that a person shall be criminally responsible for a crime within the jurisdiction of the Court where they aid, abet or otherwise assist in the commission or attempted commission. In addition, it requires that the assistance must be '[f]or the purpose of facilitating the commission of such a crime.'

in hostilities. Compared to previous attempts at substantive elucidation, this approach narrows the scope of what it means to participate in hostilities. Firstly, it requires practical assistance, encouragement or moral support that is substantial and which has in a substantial effect on the commission of a hostile act. This means that supportive acts that are remote from the commission of harmful acts by principal perpetrators may merely amount to acts that are 'in some way' directed rather than being regarded as substantial contributions towards hostile acts. In other words, indirect support activities that are geographically or temporally remote from the direct perpetration of hostile acts may be more appropriately described as general assistance directed towards a war effort rather than direct participation in hostilities, and so by themselves, they may be regarded as being insufficient to result in activity-based loss of immunity from attack. Conceivably, this is because a broader range of inferences may be drawn as to the nature and purpose of such indirect activities and so the analysis given to what constitutes a sufficient culpable link to the surrounding hostilities may be used to elucidate the notion of a belligerent nexus. This serves to ensure that there is a clear culpable link in situations where seemingly supportive acts are geographically or temporally remote from direct perpetration of harmful acts. Secondly, the participant needs to know that their participation assists the hostile act(s).

Accordingly, in the context of this discussion, activities that seemingly amount to 'substantial contributions' but which are geographically and temporally remote from directly hostile acts should attract the presumption of civilian immunity from attack as this remoteness decreases the likelihood of a sufficient belligerent nexus. In this way, an individual may only be targeted for such time as their support or assistance constitutes a substantial contribution towards a hostile act and where the intelligence suggests that they know that their acts play a facilitative role. Where there is a delay between an observable act of assistance or support and a subsequent hostile act, then the likelihood of that act constituting a substantial contribution with a significant effect on the perpetration of a hostile act is reduced. In such situations, evidence regarding an individual's state of mind constitutes important circumstantial evidence that may temporarily rebut the presumption of civilian immunity from attack if it indicates that they know that their support or assistance is having a significant effect on hostilities. This means that in many doubtful cases, temporary activity-based loss of immunity ought to be based on evidence or reliable information which suggests that the activities suspected of having a substantial effect on the preparation or commission of hostile acts are the sole reasonable inference that can be made in the circumstances.

Although aiding and abetting has been seemingly granted wide reach by the ICTY, for instance in cases involving aiding and abetting by omission and cases where psychological support is given through words or even physical presence at the scene of crime, it is suggested that the elements 'substantial contribution' and 'substantial effect' represent appropriate constraints in order to allay the risk of an overly broad approach to the principle of distinction in this context. With regards to the former, it must be demonstrated firstly, that an individual has failed to discharge a legal duty and that this has had a substantial effect on the realisation of a crime, and secondly that they knew of the principal's crime and that their omission assisted its commission.[33] With regards to the latter, it is necessary to demonstrate that facilitation through physical presence and/or psychological support is combined with a position of *de facto* authority which lends tacit approval or moral support that has a significant legitimising or encouraging effect.[34]

Aiding and abetting will now be distinguished from another mode of liability relevant to this discussion, namely the liability of co-perpetrators who participate in a common plan in order to distinguish between temporary activity-based loss of immunity on the basis of direct participation in hostilities and status-based loss of immunity on the basis of individual membership of an organized armed group and exercising a continuous combat function.

Aiding and abetting versus participation in a joint criminal enterprise

According to the Trial Chamber in *Furundžija*, the legal ingredients of participation in a joint criminal enterprise and aiding and abetting are categorically different. As discussed earlier, the legal ingredients for aiding and abetting are

> the *actus reus* [which] consists of practical assistance, encouragement, or moral support which has a substantial effect on the perpetration of the crime [and] [t]he *mens rea* [which requires] the knowledge that these acts assist the commission of the offence.[35]

Thus, according to Appeals Chamber in *Tadić*, '[t]he aider and abettor is always an accessory to a crime perpetrated by another person, the principal'.[36] In contrast, for conduct to amount to participation in a joint criminal enterprise, the Appeals Chamber in *Tadić* held that it is necessary to establish that an accused acted in pursuit of an agreement, common purpose or common design to commit a crime, and so it needs to be demonstrated that the perpetrator or coperpetrator has performed the *actus reus* of performing acts that are 'in some way directed to furthering [. . .] the common plan or purpose' and that they have the requisite *mens rea* which is the 'intent to perpetrate the crime or intent to pursue the common criminal design plus foresight that those crimes outside the criminal common purpose were likely to be committed'.[37] Thus, it can be said that the *actus reus* for aiding and abetting is more demanding than that of acting in

33 *Prosecutor v Mrkšić* (Appeals Judgment) ICTY IT-95-13/1-A (5 May 2009), para 49.
34 *Prosecutor v Delalić et al. the 'Čelebići Case'* (Trial Judgment) above n 32 327 – 328. *Prosecutor v Simić* (Trial Judgment) above n 25 165.
35 *Prosecutor v Furundžija* (Trial Judgment) ICTY-95–17/1-T (10 December 1998), 216, 249, 257.
36 *Tadić* (Appeals Chamber Judgment) above n 4, 229.
37 Ibid.

pursuance of a common purpose or design, because it is not necessary to demonstrate the existence of a 'common concerted plan' or an 'agreement'.[38]

However, in contrast to aiding and abetting, the *mens rea* standard for common purpose or design within a joint criminal enterprise (JCE) is set at a higher threshold in that mere knowledge alone will not suffice. What needs to be established is specific or basic intent or, in other words, *dolus specialis* or *dolus eventualis.*[39] Thus a coperpetrator in a JCE may indirectly contribute to the commission of the crime, but shares the *mens rea* of those perpetrators who perform the direct physical act, or, in other words, an 'intent to achieve the criminal objective is required'.[40] Moreover, it was held in *Kvocka*, that

> [d]epending on the level and nature of participation, the accused is either an aider and abettor or a co-perpetrator of the criminal enterprise. Once the evidence indicates that a person who substantially assists the enterprise shares the goals of the enterprise, he becomes a co-perpetrator.[41]

Thus according to the decision in *Krajisnic*, '[a] person's conduct either meets the conditions of JCE membership [. . .] in which case he or she is characterised as a co-perpetrator, or the conduct fails the threshold, in which case there is no JCE responsibility'.[42] Ultimately, as can be seen from *Vasiljević*, participation in a JCE is deemed to be a form of commission incurring principal liability, whereas aiding and abetting the commission of a crime incurs accessorial liability.[43] In this way, as reasoned by the Appeals Chamber in *Krnojelac*,

> [t]he acts of a participant in a joint criminal enterprise are more serious than those of an aider and abettor since a participant in a joint criminal enterprise shares the intent of the principal offender whereas an aider and abettor need only be aware of that intent.[44]

The question of liability as an accessory or coperpetrator thus turns on the issue of *mens rea* and, therefore, on the issue of participation in hostilities; this serves to inform the meaning to be given to the belligerent nexus criterion in relation to direct acts of participation or being an integral part of particular military operations on the one hand, or, on the other, *de facto* membership of

38 Olásolo, above n 2, Chapter 3.
39 Ibid.
40 *Prosecutor v Krajišnic* (Trial Judgment) ICTY-00–39-T (27 September 2006) 885.
41 *Prosecutor v Kvocka et al.* (Trial Judgment) ICTY-98–30/1-T (2 November 2001) 285.
42 *Prosecutor v Krajišnic* (Trial Judgment), above n 40.
43 Nils Melzer, 'Interpretive Guidance on the Notion of Direct Participation in Hostilities under International Humanitarian Law' (International Committee of the Red Cross, Geneva 2009) 25 ('ICRC Interpretive Guidance') 44–45.
Prosecutor v Vasiljević (Appeals Chamber Judgment) IT-98–32-A (25 February 2004), 102.
44 *Prosecutor v Krnojelac* (Appeals Chamber Judgement) IT-97–25-A (17 September 2003) 75.

an organised armed group.[45] With regard to the latter aspect, this suggestion accords with and further develops Watkin's criticism of the ICRC Interpretive Guidance that although '[i]ndicia of membership of an organised armed group should include whether a person is carrying out a combat function', this 'is not a definitive determinant . . . but rather one of a number of factors that can be taken into consideration'.[46] However, it does so on the basis of the presumption of civilian protection or doubt, namely that where a situation has reached the threshold of an armed conflict and where a suspected individual does not constitute a direct and immediate lethal threat because there are no 'objective' manifestations of hostile force or activities as described in Chapter 1, then, as stated earlier, there ought to be reliable and credible intelligence going towards members of an organized armed group status before proceeding with an attack.

JCE and Article 25(3)(a) of the ICC Statute

This section aims to contribute to the framework of target analysis by examining the import of the ICTY's approach to JCE as well as the three modes of perpetration or commission under Article 25(3)(a) of the Statute of the International Criminal Court (ICCS), namely individual perpetration, jointly with another person or co-perpetration and through another person or indirect perpetration as well as the fourth hybrid mode of indirect co-perpetration. On this basis, it aims to distinguish these modes of perpetration or commission from participation, e.g. in the form of aiding and abetting, as discussed above, in order to suggest they offer practical ways of distinguishing between status-based loss of immunity on the basis of individual membership of an organized armed group, e.g. as a leader, fighter or auxiliary, and temporary activity-based loss of immunity on the basis of direct participation in hostilities, e.g. by individuals within the general population or mass base of popular support.

It is suggested that these frameworks are not necessarily focused on high-level accused but may be used flexibly to encompass those who participate in common plans as leaders and as subordinates, and furthermore, they may encompass small-scale to large-scale common purposes, for example killing on a village, town or regional, national or international level. They may be construed as widely as the strategic plan or common purpose to adversely affect military operations or military capacity itself, and this is an objective matter that should be properly defined and supported by intelligence.[47] Status-based targeting in this respect can only

45 *Prosecutor v Kvocka et al.* (Trial Judgment), above n 41, 92: '[a]iding and abetting generally involves a lesser degree of individual criminal responsibility than co-perpetration in a joint criminal enterprise'.

46 Kenneth Watkin, 'Opportunity Lost: Organized Armed Groups and the ICRC "Direct Participation in Hostilities" Interpretive Guidance' (2010) 42 *New York University Journal of International Law and Politics* 655, 693–694.

47 *Prosecutor v Brđanin* (Appeals Chamber Judgment) IT-99-36-A (1 September 2004) 421, 422, 423, 424, 425, 438.

occur in the context of targeted operations where there is reliable intelligence that suggests the objective and subjective elements outlined below are in existence.

According to the ICTY jurisprudence on JCE, a plurality of persons that share an agreement, common purpose or common design should be identified, as should the general goal(s), temporal and geographical scope and intended victims of the common plan. This may be inferred from intelligence which suggests the existence of a common pattern.[48] Furthermore, an individual should intentionally make a significant contribution to the commission or furtherance of this common purpose, or in some cases they must also have foresight that hostile acts outside the common purpose were likely to be committed'.[49] Similarly, under ICC jurisprudence, co-perpetration refers to a situation where there is a common plan or joint agreement between two or more persons. This can be inferred from circumstantial evidence.[50] Furthermore, such persons must make 'essential contributions' to this plan in a combined and coordinated fashion.[51] Co-perpetrators must have an awareness that the consequences of the common plan would occur in the ordinary course of events.[52]

Extrapolating the jurisprudence on JCE and co-perpetration suggests that those who physically perform hostile acts may not be considered as members of organised armed groups where these abovementioned conditions are not satisfied, but rather as direct participants in hostilities only in those circumstances where it can be established that they are aiding and abetting hostilities, or are 'tools' of the members of organised armed groups.[53] According to ICTY jurisprudence, members may execute their common objective(s) by ordering or instructing such non-members who, unlike members, do not share their intention to further or achieve the common objective(s) *per se*.[54] Rather, in the absence of an express understanding or agreement, their acts may be regarded as forming part of a manifest common purpose, strategic plan or pattern of conduct which can only be explained through coordinated cooperation.[55] ICC jurisprudence takes a similar approach whereby perpetration may occur through another person. In other words, the physical perpetrator of the crime is used as a tool by an indirect

48 *Prosecutor v Tadić* (Appeals Chamber Judgment) ICTY-94-1-A (15 July 1999) 299. Prosecutor v Krajišnic (Trial Judgment) ICTY-00-39-T (27 September 2006) 885.
49 *Prosecutor v Kvocka et al.* (Trial Judgment) above n 41 285.
50 *Prosecutor v Lubanga*, (Trial Chamber) ICC01/0401/062842 (14 March 2012) 988.
51 *Prosecutor v Lubanga*, (Pre-Trial Chamber Decision on the Confirmation of Charges), ICC-01/0401/06803, (29 January 2007) 343. *Prosecutor v Lubanga*, (Trial Chamber), ibid, 994 & 1000.
52 *Prosecutor v Lubanga*, (Trial Chamber), ibid, 1008. *Prosecutor v Katanga*, (Pre-Trial Chamber Decision on the Confirmation of Charges) ICC01/0401/07717 (30 September 2008) 473.
53 *Prosecutor v Brđanin* (Appeals Chamber Judgment) above n 47 410, 412, 413, 414, 415, 418, 441, 445.
54 Ibid.
55 Ibid.

perpetrator who is masterminding or controlling the physical perpetrator behind the scenes.[56] Another means of committing a crime through another is by means of control over an organization, by an individual, or jointly by several leaders who act in concert and provide the contributions necessary for the execution of a common plan.[57] An organisation must be based on hierarchical relations between superiors and a sufficient number of subordinates so that orders given by the recognised leadership will generally be complied with by the subordinates.[58] Finally, the concept of indirect co-perpetration has been developed within the jurisprudence of the ICC for situations where there are two or more individuals involved in a common plan executed by subordinates who belong to military organisations that are under separate, rather than joint control, e.g. where subordinates only accept orders from the leader(s) of their own ethnic group, rather than any leader within a joint command.[59] Despite the lack of direct control here, where an individual acts jointly with another individual who controls the person used as a tool, then their acts may be attributed to the former on the basis of mutual attribution.[60]

In summary, where there is intelligence indicating that an individual shares the hostile intention(s) of other individuals party to a common plan to engage in hostilities, and makes substantial or essential contributions to its furtherance or achievement, then they may be subject to status-based targeting for the duration of hostilities as a member of an organised armed group as this hostile intent evinces a genuine and continuous combat function. [61] For those individuals who are participating in hostilities, but who do not share the hostile intention(s) of other individuals that are party to a common plan, then as this may be the equivalent of aiding and abetting, they may accordingly be subject to threat-based targeting for such time as they are participating in, or making substantial contributions to hostile acts but no longer. This approach does not advocate the need to prove these extrapolated elements for establishing membership in an organized armed group beyond reasonable doubt in battle-field context. Rather, it is suggested that where there is doubt as to any of these elements, then it is reasonable to resolve it through a process of careful verification[62] otherwise continuous status-based loss of protection based merely on a slight suspicion, and without 'objective' manifestations of hostile force or actions, could serve to undermine

---

56 *Prosecutor v Katanga*, (Pre-Trial Chamber Decision on the Confirmation of Charges) above n 52 488. *Prosecutor v Lubanga* (Appeals Chamber Judgment on the Appeal of Mr Thomas Lubanga Dyilo Against his Conviction) ICC01/0401/063121Red (1 December 2014) 465.

57 *Prosecutor v Katanga*, ibid., 498 and 524–526.

58 *Prosecutor v Katanga*, ibid., 512. *Prosecutor v Bashir*, (Pre-Trial Chamber Public Redacted Version of the Prosecution's Application under Article 58), ICC02/05157AnxA (12 September 2008) 248.

59 *Prosecutor v Katanga*, ibid., 492.

60 Ibid., 493.

61 *Prosecutor v Krnojelac* (Appeals Chamber Judgement) IT-97-25-A (17 September 2003) 75.

62 *Public Committee Against Torture v The Government of Israell*, Israel, Supreme Court, Judgment of 14 December 2006, HCJ 769/02, 40.

and erode the fundamental principle of distinction in non-international armed conflicts involving diffuse organisational structures.[63]

Planning

To begin with, planning as a mode of perpetration is very similar to the notion of conspiracy, but what makes planning different is that a planner designs the commission of an act which is then perpetrated by others.[64] According to Article 7(1) of the ICTY statute, planning the commission of offences is a distinct form of accessorial liability.[65] According to the jurisprudence of the ICTY, planning constitutes a distinct form of criminal liability punishable per se, that is, even if the planned crime is not in fact committed.[66] In contrast, according to Article 25 paragraph (3)(b) of the ICC statute, criminal liability for the planning of criminal offences can arise on the basis of attempted acts. In relation to Article 6(1) of the ICTR Statute, according to *Akayesu*,[67] *Rutaganda*[68] and *Musema*,[69] planning is only punishable when followed by the actual commission of the planned offence, for example, according to the ICTR in *Musema*, individual criminal responsibility 'implies that the planning or the preparation of a crime must actually lead to its commission.'[70]

Regarding the objective elements of planning, in *Kordić*, the Appeals Chamber held that 'the *actus reus* of "planning" requires that one or more persons design the criminal conduct . . .'[71] Thus, those held liable for planning do not participate in the implementation of the criminal plan. Rather, planners are considered accessories because of their participation in the formulation of a criminal plan but not its subsequent implementation.[72] If they were to participate in its implementation, then they would become perpetrators or coperpetrators

---

63 ICRC (Interpretive Guidance) above n 43 44–45.

64 *Akayesu*, above n 3, 480.

65 *Prosecutor v Kordić and Čerkez* (Appeals Chamber Judgment) ICTY-95–14/2-A (17 December 2004) 26.

66 *Prosecutor v Kordić and Čerkez* (Trial Judgment) ICTY-95–14/2-T (26 February 2001), 386: 'an accused may be held criminally responsible for planning alone' because 'planning constitutes a discrete form of responsibility under Article 7(1) of the Statute'. It is important to qualify this by stating that only the planning of large-scale international crimes may be punishable per se, due to the gravity of these crimes and the demands of policy to prevent them. In contradistinction, for crimes of lesser gravity, there is the argument that the doubt should be resolved in favour of the accused, and so the planning of lesser crimes may not be punished per se.

67 *Akayesu*, above n 3, 475.

68 *Prosecutor v Rutaganda* (Appeals Chamber Judgment) ICTR -96–3 (26 May 2003), 34.

69 *Prosecutor v Musema* ICTR-96–13-A (27 January 2000), 115.

70 Ibid.

71 *Kordić and Čerkez* (Appeals Chamber Judgment), above n 65, 26.

72 *Prosecutor v Bagilishema* (Trial Judgment) ICTR-95–1A-T (7 June 2001), 30.

incurring principal liability. 'Planning' is therefore a mode of accessorial liability to be applied where the accused's role is limited to participation in the process of formulating a criminal plan. Hence, in *Stakic* the Trial Chamber held that '[a]n accused will only be convicted for planning a crime where his contribution during the planning stage is of greater weight than at the execution stage'.[73]

The element of causation is also required for this mode of liability to be established. According to *Kordić*, the act of planning must be 'a factor substantially contributing to such criminal conduct'.[74] As for the subjective elements of planning, for an accused to be held liable for planning, 'it needs to be established that the accused, directly or indirectly, intended the crime in question to be committed'.[75] Thus in *Kordić*, the Appeals Chamber ruled that

> a person who plans an act or omission with the awareness of the substantial likelihood that a crime will be committed in the execution of that plan, has the requisite *mens rea* for establishing responsibility [for] planning. Planning with such awareness has to be regarded as accepting that crime.[76]

Compared with the instigation and ordering of an offence, an accused who formulates a criminal plan does not have the *mens rea* required by the underlying crimes.[77]

Where planning can be considered 'an integral part' of a specific and coordinated military operation, then this may thus lead to a deprivation of immunity from attack. Given that the majority of approaches described earlier base liability for planning on a choate offence, that is, actual perpetration or attempted perpetration, then it is suggested that, by itself, planning may only result in temporary loss of protection unless and for such time as it can be considered 'an integral part' of a specific and coordinated military operation in motion. Accordingly, this approach can be considered relevant for targeting the core leadership[78] as well as the political or ideological cadre[79] and the auxiliaries of an organised armed group.

---

73 *Prosecutor v Slobodan Milošević* (Rule 98 *bis* Decision) IT-02-54-T (16 June 2004), 104.
74 *Kordić and Čerkez* (Appeals Chamber Judgment), above n 65, 26.
75 Ibid.
76 Ibid., 31.
77 Ibid.
78 British Army, *Countering Insurgency*, above n 23, 2-15: The role and attributes of military and political leaders are generally organising and planning at the strategic and operational levels. They provide the strategic direction and ideological impetus to the movement that underpins the activities of auxiliaries, the political cadre, combatants and the mass base of support; See also FM 3-24, above n 23, 1-61.
79 British Army, *Countering Insurgency*, Ibid., 2-15: The political or ideological cadre is not necessarily formally constituted, for example, into a political party or extremist group, but in substance, its function is to assist with the organisation, planning and direction necessary for the implementation of the overarching political or ideological goals that stem from the leadership; See also US FM 3-24, Ibid., 1-65.

Instigating the commission of an act

Article 7(1) of the ICTY statute and 6(1) of the ICTR statute categorise 'instigating' the commission of an unlawful act as an offence, whereas a breach of Article 25 paragraph 3(b) of the ICC Statute will occur where an individual 'solicits or induces the commission of such a crime which in fact occurs or is attempted'. In terms of the objective elements, instigation has been described as 'prompting another person to commit an offence'[80] and is punishable only where it leads to the actual commission of an offence desired by the instigator.[81] It can be considered a form of indirect participation in that an instigator does not carry out the objective elements of the underlying crime in question, and, if they do, then they can be considered a coperpetrator.[82] According the jurisprudence of the ICTY/R, the *actus reus* requires a causal link between the act of instigation and the physical perpetration of a crime.[83] However, this requirement of a causal link does not mean that the act of instigation need be the primary cause of the offence, or, in other words, it does need not be established *but for* the instigation, the perpetration of an offence would not have occurred. Rather, all that needs to be established is that the instigation was a 'clear contributing factor to the conduct of other person(s)',[84] or, as stated in *Kordić*,

> [w]hile it is not necessary to prove that the crime would not have been perpetrated without the involvement of the accused, it is sufficient to demonstrate that the instigation was a factor substantially contributing to the conduct of another person committing the crime.[85]

As for the subjective elements of instigation, the Trial Chamber in *Brđanin* held that it must be established that 'the accused intended to provoke or induce the commission of the crime, or was aware of the substantial likelihood that the commission of a crime would be a probable consequence of his acts'.[86] Furthermore, those responsible for acts of instigation do not have the *mens rea* required for the underlying offence.[87]

80 *Akayesu*, above n 3, 482.
81 Ibid., 481–482.
82 Héctor Olásolo, above n 2, 142–143; *Kordić and Čerkez* (Trial Judgment), above n 66, 387; *Prosecutor v Orić* (Trial Judgment) ICTY-03-68-T (30 June 2006), 273. Instigation can take place by omission, with threats and menaces, or even with bribery and financial promises. An act can be instigated face to face as well as through intermediaries. It can be exerted over both small and large audiences, provided that the instigator has the intent to prompt the audience to commit an act.
83 *Prosecutor v Strugar* (Trial Judgment), above n 25, 86.
84 *Galić* (Trial Judgment), above n 19, 168.
85 *Kordić and Čerkez* (Appeals Chamber Judgment), above n 65, 32.
86 *Prosecutor v Brđanin* (Trial Judgment) ICTY-99-36 (1 September 2004), 269.
87 *Prosecutor v Orić* (Trial Judgment), above n 82, 279, fn 772.

Instigation differs from indirect forms of participation such as ordering, in that its influence on the perpetrator of an act need not be connected with a superior–subordinate relationship or an authority to order.[88] Furthermore, instigation differs from ordering in that they have different tests for causation. Whereas ordering requires, in the case of the ICC Statute, that crimes be committed in furtherance of the order or that the order has a 'direct and substantial effect on the commission of the crimes',[89] instigation merely requires that it be a 'clear and contributing factor' of the commission of the underlying crime. As indicated in *Blaškić*, instigation need not cause in the physical perpetrator the intention to commit the crime. Instead, all that need be established is that the instigation strengthens the perpetrator's will or resolve to commit the offence by providing additional motives or reasons for its commission.[90] In this regard, by itself, instigation can be considered a form of indirect participation in hostile acts. Given that it is not punishable per se, it is suggested that loss of protection from attack may not occur unless it is having a 'direct and substantial effect' on the commission of hostile acts, in which case its duration is temporary to the extent that loss of immunity occurs only for such time as there are hostile acts being committed. Accordingly, this approach can be considered relevant for targeting the core leadership as well as the political or ideological cadre and the auxiliaries of an organised armed group.

Ordering

Ordering could be considered a form of indirect perpetration of a crime incurring principal liability rather than a form of indirect participation incurring accessorial liability. However, Article 25 para (3) (a) and (b) of the ICC Statute, Article 7 para (1) of the ICTY Statute and Article 6 para (1) of the ICTR statute regard ordering the commission of an act as a form of indirect participation. Accordingly, it is important to get a clear idea of the objective and subjective elements of this offence in order to distinguish it from the notion of indirect perpetration.[91] Order-

88 Antonio Cassese, *International Criminal Law* (3rd rev edn Oxford University Press, 2013), 189; *Prosecutor v Orić* (Trial Judgment), above n 82, 272. As stated in *Orić*: '. . . although the exertion of influence would hardly function without a certain capability to impress others, instigation [is different from] 'ordering' [because ordering] implies at least a factual superior-subordinate relationship [whereas instigation] does not presuppose any kind of superiority'.

89 *Prosecutor v Kamuhanda* (Appeals Chamber Judgment) ICTR-99–54A-A (19 September 2005) 75.

90 *Prosecutor v Blaskić* (Trial Judgment) ICTY-95–14-T (3 March 2000), 270, 277; Héctor Olásolo, above n 2, 142–147; *Prosecutor v Orić* (Trial Judgment), above n 82: instigation 'does not necessarily presuppose that the original idea or plan to commit the crime was generated by the instigator. Even if the principal perpetrator was already pondering on committing a crime, the final determination to do so can still be brought about by persuasion or strong encouragement of the instigator'.

91 Héctor Olásolo, above n 2, 135.

ing requires no formal superior–subordinate relationship. Rather, it is sufficient to demonstrate that the individual who issued the order had a form of *de facto* authority to instruct the perpetrators of the act or acts ordered,[92] which has been interpreted to mean that the individual issuing an order has a significant influence over the perpetrators such that they are compelled to obey.[93] *De facto* authority to 'instruct' the physical perpetrators may be implied from the circumstances and, as such, there is no particular form in which an order must be given.[94] An order can be given orally or in writing, and it can be made expressly or implicitly. Accordingly, the existence of an order can be proven by circumstantial evidence.[95] Furthermore, each intermediary who is at least in a position of *de facto* authority and who passes on the order is considered to be reissuing the order and can thus be held liable for ordering the commission of the crimes.[96] According to the Trial Chamber in *Strugar*, 'a causal link between the act of ordering and the physical perpetration of a crime [. . .] also needs to be demonstrated as part of the *actus reus* of ordering, but this does not require it to be established that the offence would not have been perpetrated in the absence of the order'.[97] Additionally, the physical perpetrators must commit the crimes in execution or furtherance of an order, although, according to Article 25 para (3) (b) of the ICC Statute, it is sufficient if the physical perpetrators attempt to commit the crimes in execution or furtherance of the order.

With regard to the subjective elements of ordering, it must be established that the accused intended the crime to be committed or was aware of the substantial likelihood that the commission of the crime would be a consequence of his acts, and so ordering with such awareness is to be regarded as accepting the crime.[98] The *mens rea* of the accused does not need to be explicit. Rather, it may be inferred from the circumstances, but in such circumstances it must be the

92 *Prosecutor v Kamuhanda* (Appeals Chamber Judgment), above n 89, 75; *Prosecutor v Semanza* (Appeals Chamber Judgment) ICTR-97–20-A (22 May 2005), 361; *Kordić and Čerkez* (Appeals Chamber Judgment), above n 65, para 28; *Prosecutor v Galić* (Appeals Chamber Judgment) ICTY-98–29-A (30 November 2006), 176; Olásolo, ibid; C del Ponte, 'Investigation and Prosecution of Large-Scale Crimes at the International Level. The Experience of the ICTY' (2006) 4 *Journal of International Criminal Justice* 549.

93 Olásolo, Ibid., 136; *Semanza* (Appeals Judgment) Ibid., 92.

94 *Blaskić* (Appeals Chamber Judgment), above n 46, 660.

95 *Galić* (Trial Judgment), above n 19, 168; *Prosecutor v Strugar* (Trial Judgment), above n 28, 388. In this regard, the approving presence of a superior at the scene of the crime while the crimes are being committed, or immediately afterwards, can be a relevant factor to infer that the superior ordered the commission of the crimes.

96 *Prosecutor v Kupreškić* (Trial Judgment) ICTY-95–16-T (14 January 2000), 827, 862.

97 *Prosecutor v Strugar* (Trial Judgment), above n 25, 332.

98 *Blaskić* (Appeals Chamber Judgment), above n 31, 41 & 42. In this way the *mens rea* standard for this offence is one of specific intent or recklessness. The threshold of recklessness was set at a relatively high threshold in *Blaskić*, in that '[t]he knowledge of any kind of risk, however low, does not suffice for the imposition of criminal responsibility . . . an awareness of a higher likelihood of risk and a volitional element must be incorporated into the legal standard . . . a person who orders an act or omission with the awareness of the substantial likelihood that a crime will be committed in the execution of that order, has the

only reasonable inference from the evidence.[99] Essentially, the Appeals Chamber in *Blaškić* and *Kordić* have ruled that ordering is subjectively different from principal modes of liability in that it need not be established that a superior giving an unlawful order has the particular *mens rea* required for the underlying criminal act executed in pursuit of that order. Rather, the superior merely needs to be aware of the substantial likelihood that the physical perpetrators will act with the *mens rea* required by the particular crimes that have been executed. As such, ordering does not constitute a form of indirect perpetration, as the authority giving the order does not possess the *mens rea* of the physical perpetrators. In this regard, by itself, ordering can be considered a form of indirect participation in hostile acts.

Given that it is not punishable per se, it is suggested that loss of protection from attack may not occur unless there is some indication of *de facto* authority over the physical perpetrators, as well as some indication of a causal connection between the order and the hostile acts. However, once hostile acts have been committed, then given the existence of a relationship of *de facto* authority over the perpetrators, it is reasonable to suggest that this hierarchical relationship will persist for the duration of the hostilities and the escalation of lethal force can be applied on this basis. Accordingly, this approach can be considered relevant for targeting the core leadership as well as the political or ideological cadre of an organised armed group.

Conclusions: a framework for understanding participation in 'wars amongst the people'

Chapter 1 discussed doctrinal adaptations that have been made in the context of unconventional conflicts where asymmetric or irregular tactics and forms of organisation are adopted. These doctrinal developments lend credence to Van Creveld's prediction that 'the armed forces of the world will have to adjust themselves to this situation by changing their doctrine, doing away with much of their heavy equipment and becoming more like the police'.[100] Moreover, as discussed in Chapter 1, contemporary military doctrine indicates the existence of self-imposed restrictions on the use of force in excess of conventional or traditional interpretations of conventional free-standing humanitarian law and which are expressed in imperative terms. In this way, doctrinal reconceptualisations provide the conditions for normative reconceptualisations in order to ensure that there is an adequate fit between legal frameworks concerning the use of force and prevalent aspects of the contemporary strategic environment. This discussion has contributed towards a framework that better suits these changes in the strategic environment and in

---

requisite mens rea for establishing liability under Article 7(1) pursuant to ordering. Ordering with such awareness has to be regarded as accepting that crime'.

99 *Prosecutor v Strugar* (Trial Judgment), above n 28, 333.

100 M van Creveld, 'Through a Glass, Darkly – Some Reflections on the Future of War' (2000) 53(4) *Naval War College Review* 26.

military doctrine by suggesting principles to guide intelligence-led and evidence-based processes that can better 'understand the social dynamic that sustains on-going fighting'[101] so as to ensure that combat lines of operations do not end up being operationally and strategically counterproductive, which, it is suggested, is a corollary of perceived illegitimacy or unlawfulness within the diverse and rich normative environment that has emerged in the latter stages of the twentieth century and the early stages of the twenty-first. This is to suggest that where an individual is targeted on the basis of their status as a member of an organised armed group, then there is no need to establish any direct participation in hostilities. However, this is qualified on the basis that the situation must at least have reached the threshold of a CA3 NIAC as indicated by the criteria in *Boškoski*, and, furthermore, that the requirement of a 'continuous combat function' is only capable of application in the framework of targeted operations. Furthermore, this framework can serve to undergird normatively the doctrine of positive identification as discussed in Chapter 1, by elucidating the conditions and criteria for establishing 'reasonable certainty' vis-à-vis civilian participation in hostilities or membership in 'complex and diffuse organisational structures and networks'[102] in situations where there are no clear manifestations of hostile force or action. In this way, this discussion has sought to contribute towards the fundamental issue of distinguishing the indirect support activities of the general civilian population and mass base of popular support that lack proximity or a nexus with the surrounding hostilities from what can be broadly defined as the internal support structure of an organised armed group by putting participation and membership on a more analytical footing (see Figure 5.1). Furthermore, in view of the concept of 'positive identification', it is suggested that targeting on the basis of membership of an organised armed group may only occur in the context of targeted operations where doubt as to civilian status can be overcome through reference to a reasonable degree of evidence.

It is suggested that the approach taken to clarify and elucidate our understanding of this fundamental issue is plausible in the sense that it has a normative basis. Furthermore, building on the discussion in Chapter 1, it can be seen as being logically and pragmatically connected to the military doctrine of positive identification, together with the presumption of 'mandatory civilian protection' or doubt under humanitarian law. This suggests that primacy be given to an intelligence-led and evidence-based approach to situations within unconventional operational theatres where there are no observable manifestations of hostile acts or intent. Accordingly, notwithstanding the presumption of doubt, which arguably becomes weightier in unconventional environments where there are 'complex

101 US Department of the Army (Training and Doctrine Command) Counterinsurgency (COIN) Field Manual (FM) 3–24 and Marine Corps War fighting Publication (MCWP) 3–33.5 (Headquarters, Department of the Army, Washington, DC & Marine Corps Combat Development Command, Department of the Navy, Headquarters, United States Marine Corps, Washington, DC, 15 December 2006) Introduction. Appendix B – 47.

102 Christopher Harding, 'The Offence of Belonging: Capturing Participation in Organized Crime' (2005) *Criminal Law Review* 690.

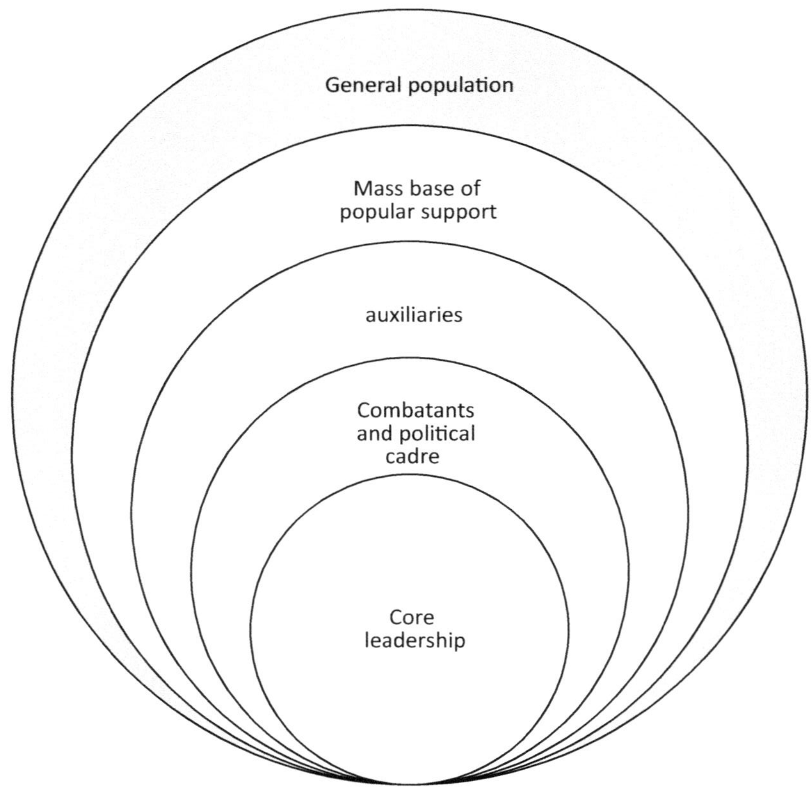

Figure 5.1 Core elements of an internal support structure.

and diffuse organisational structures'[103] embedded within a civilian population, this framework for understanding participation in hostilities does not obstruct the application of conventional military approaches and considerations where necessary. It merely serves to constrain targeting decisions by suggesting a clearer framework for resolving doubt in indeterminate situations vis-à-vis civilians that would otherwise fall into a 'grey area' within targeting law and connects this with what military doctrine describes as escalation of nonlethal and lethal force. Thus in situations of armed conflict, this approach seeks to constrain extrajudicial or 'targeted' killing of civilians who are suspected of being terrorists, criminals or participating in hostilities. Now that the parameters of immunity have been clarified, the next section will examine contemporary reconceptualisations of the law relating to the conduct of hostilities, that is, targeting and weaponry law in the context of unconventional or asymmetric urban armed conflicts.

103 Ibid.

6 Reconceptualising targeting and weaponry law for the unconventional theatre of operations

Introduction

International and regional human rights mechanisms have supplemented and filled lacunae within the substantive and institutional frameworks of protection under international humanitarian and criminal law. It is suggested that the oversight that these mechanisms of international civil society provide has, in many cases, necessarily comprised the consideration of existing norms under international humanitarian law, as well as a range of human rights law frameworks. Furthermore, it is suggested that the application of frameworks of humanitarian law and human rights law in response to alleged violations of these legal frameworks has in many cases involved the interpretation and ordering of those standards.

Procedural propriety contributes to the authoritativeness of the outcomes of a range of judicial or 'quasi-judicial' processes relating to alleged abuses occurring within conflict situations. In turn, this suggests that mechanisms of international civil society can, in addition to the role of derogation review, play an important and responsive role in the progressive elucidation of the meaning and ordering of existing norms relative to the use of force in full-spectrum operational environments. It is suggested that the reconceptualisations discussed so far in Chapters 3 through 5 and those discussed in this section in relation to targeting and weaponry law are consonant with the doctrinal developments outlined in Chapter 1. In addition to the argument that these doctrinal developments may be regarded as feeding into their own customary crystallisation process, it is suggested that this consonance goes towards the plausibility of the progressive elucidations of targeting law by mechanisms of international civil society that may, in their own ways, crystallise into norms. In this way, the evolutive and progressive approaches to legal interpretation highlighted in Chapter 2 may circumvent the 'definitional closures' arising from what Harding and Lim have described as 'the confines of a monolithic doctrinalism that has previously inhibited experiment and thus in some respects intellectual progress',[1] and so they pave the way for the progressive elucidation and systemic integration of human rights and humanitarian law.

---

1 Christopher Harding and C L Lim (eds), *Renegotiating Westphalia: Essays and Commentary on the European and Conceptual Foundations of Modern International Law* (Martinus Nijhoff, 1999) 2.

With regard to targeting law, on the basis of a liberal approach to normativity, this section proposes that higher standards of reasonableness may be imposed upon commanders of major military powers in order to ensure constant care for civilian populations, and furthermore, that civilian populations be spared more effectively from the effects of urban warfare by applying customary law *ab initio* where the *Boškoski* guidelines have been satisfied. This has the benefit of avoiding gaps in protection that may arise from the premature classification or underclassification of armed conflicts. In addition, this approach should be embedded within a framework that sequences the legal frameworks of law enforcement and combat. In practical terms, this takes the form of the escalation of nonlethal and lethal force in situations where there is no demonstrable hostile force or activities. This approach accepts and permits the *de minimis* core targeting and weaponry norms of treaty-based IHL, but suggests that their rigour may be modulated and essentially updated in view of the fact that they have to be applied in an increasingly complex and diverse normative and material environment which has seen major doctrinal shifts in the first decade of the twenty-first century.

As discussed earlier, the indicative guidelines that have emerged within the jurisprudence of the ICTY vis-à-vis situational and contextual status determination serve to add specificity to the notion of the continuum of violence as discussed in Chapter 1 and illustrated in Figures 1.1, 1.2, 1.3 and 1.5. In other words, where the CA3 threshold criteria have been met, as set out in *Boškoski*, this indicates that we have the type of socioeconomic, political or military violence which falls within the framework of hostilities rather than law enforcement. This serves to clarify when and where Hague rules, and status-based targeting in particular, become applicable to military operations that would otherwise fall within the 'grey area' of legal regulation as illustrated in Figure 1.2 in Chapter 1. Accordingly, this section proposes progressive reconceptualisations of treaty-based and customary IHL obligations.

Customary IHL obligations relating to the conduct of urban warfare: general targeting rules

According to the estimates made in the Geneva Declaration's report *Global Burden of Armed Violence*, in the period 2005–2007 civilian deaths in armed conflicts far exceeded combatant fatality rates,[2] and three-quarters of all direct conflict deaths that occurred during that period were concentrated in ten conflict-affected countries, including Iraq, Afghanistan, Sri Lanka, India, Somalia and Pakistan.[3] The report also found that the significant increase in the global number of direct

2 Geneva Declaration, *Global Burden of Armed Violence* (Report) (Geneva Declaration Secretariat, 2008) 11.

3 Ibid., 22.

conflict deaths witnessed during that period was primarily due to the armed conflicts in these countries,[4] and it is noteworthy that most of the major conflicts referred to in the report involved states, including the United States and Israel, that are not signatories to either Protocol I or II.[5]

In addition to the reports and studies cited earlier, this report further demonstrates the importance of customary IHL. In comparison with civilians caught up in armed conflicts classified as non-international, Protocol I provides civilians caught up in international armed conflicts with a broader and more detailed framework of humanitarian protection that is arguably better suited to regulating urban armed conflicts than Protocol II and CA3 because it includes rules on, *inter alia*, distinction, proportionality and precautionary measures.[6] Be that as it may, it is suggested that reliable evaluations of the precise dynamics of an armed conflict can only be made from the vantage point of hindsight.[7] In view of the enduring humanitarian quandary of classification lagging behind the actual situation, the inherent substantive limitations of Protocol II and CA3, the nonapplicability of treaty-based IHL to a range of contemporary asymmetric conflicts and the grave risks posed by insufficiently regulated urban conflict, application of the 'corpus of customary international law' relating to precautions in attack, proportionality and humanitarian assistance is warranted 'whenever there is a resort to armed force between States or protracted armed violence between governmental authorities and organised armed groups or between such groups within a State'.[8] This body of customary law is 'applicable to all armed conflicts irrespective of their characterisation as international or non-international'[9] and thus avoids any substantive gaps in humanitarian protection that may precede a reliable evaluation and concomitant application of treaty-based IHL, especially where there is likely to be disagreement, doubt or divergence as to the precise legal character of the hostilities in question *inter* and *intra* parties to a conflict.[10] As discussed earlier, this is especially so in relation to situations such as proxy wars and

---

4 Ibid., 9.

5 See ICRC Treaty Ratification Table <www.icrc.org/Web/eng/siteeng0.nsf/htmlall/israel-event-ihl-040509/$File/Treaty-Ratification-Table-IL-competition-2009.xls> accessed 1 October 2013.

6 Protocol Additional to the Geneva Conventions of 12 August 1949, and relating to the Protection of Victims of International Armed Conflicts (Protocol I), 8 June 1977 ('API'), Articles 48, 51(1)-(5), 52 and 57.

7 Andrew J Carswell, 'Classifying the Conflict: A Soldier's Dilemma' (2009) 91 (873) *International Review of the Red Cross* 151.

8 *Prosecutor v Tadić* (Decision on the Defence Motion for Interlocutory Appeal on Jurisdiction) ICTY-94–1-AR72 (2 October 1995), 70; *Prosecutor v Martić* (Rule 61 Decision) ICTY-95–11-R61 (March 8 1996), 11; Statute of the International Court of Justice, Article 38(b); James Stewart, 'Towards a Single Definition of Armed Conflict in International Humanitarian Law: A Critique of Internationalized Armed Conflict' (2003) 85 (850) *International Review of the Red Cross* 346.

9 *Martić* (Rule 61 Decision), Ibid.

10 *Prosecutor v Boškoski and Tarculovski* (Trial Judgment) ICTY-04–82-T (10 July 2008), 245.

"low-intensity conflicts" whose precise character can be hard to gauge as events unfold on the ground.[11] The advantage of applying the body of customary IHL when such uncertainty prevails is that it avoids parties to a conflict underclassifying a situation and subsequently being found to have violated a particular legal framework applied by a court of law on an *ex post facto* basis.[12] Furthermore, it is in the strategic interests of parties to an armed conflict, major military powers in particular, to incorporate customary obligations into their military doctrine and practice when using military force in urban areas, as this can enhance the utility of force in contemporary asymmetric armed conflicts.[13]

Precautions in attacking military objectives situated within urban areas

The concealment of military objectives within urban areas makes it difficult – if not impossible – to distinguish, as required by treaty-based and customary IHL, between the civilian population and combatants and between civilian objects and military objectives.[14] Within both legal frameworks, military objectives are defined as 'those objects which by their nature, location, purpose or use make an effective contribution to military action and whose total or partial destruction, capture or neutralisation, in the circumstances ruling at the time, offers a definite military advantage'.[15] In asymmetric armed conflict, the weaker side will often deem concealment within urban areas to be a necessity to survive any onslaught by its militarily superior adversary. Although the presence of military objectives among civilian populations in urban areas does not deprive the latter of their civilian character,[16] the presence of protected persons does not necessarily render the area in which such objectives are located immune from attack per se.[17] Whether or not the weaker side is merely benefiting from 'the presence or movements of the civilian population or individual civilians',[18] or is violating international law by using them or directing their movements so as to create shields from attack

11 Robin Geiß, 'Armed Violence in Fragile States: Low-Intensity Conflicts, Spill Over Conflicts, and Sporadic Law Enforcement Operations by Third Parties' (2009) 91 (873) *International Review of the Red Cross* 136.

12 Carswell, above n 7, 154–159.

13 Carswell, Ibid., 159; Arreguín-Toft, above n 120, 151–164; Smith, above n 123, 330–331.

14 API, above n 6, Article 48; Jean-Marie Henckaerts and Louise Doswald-Beck, *Customary International Humanitarian Law* (Volume 1: Rules, ICRC-Cambridge University Press, 2005) ('CIHL Study'), Rule 7.

15 API, Ibid., Article 52(2); CIHL Study, Ibid., Rule 8; Protocol on Prohibitions or Restrictions on the Use of Mines, Booby-Traps and Other Devices. Geneva, 10 October 1980 ('CCW Protocol II'), Article 2(6); Second Protocol to the Hague Convention of 1954 for the Protection of Cultural Property in the Event of Armed Conflict, 26 March 1999, Article 1(f).

16 API, above n 6, Article 50(3).

17 Ibid., Article 51(7); Geneva Convention (IV) relative to the Protection of Civilian Persons in Time of War, Geneva, 12 August 1949, Article 28.

18 API, Article 51(7).

or cover for military operations, Article 60(5) of the Vienna Convention on the Law of Treaties does not allow the militarily stronger adversary to suspend the operation of IHL.[19] On the contrary, it is still legally bound by those treaty-based obligations, of which some, according to the ICRC, "now bear the stamp of customary law",[20] and which may be identified, formulated or elucidated through a range of discrete processes under public general public international law.

Customary IHL thus stipulates that 'constant care shall be taken to spare the civilian population, civilians and civilian objects' and that 'all feasible precautions must be taken to avoid, and in any event to minimise, incidental loss of civilian life, injury to civilians and damage to civilian objects'.[21] Compliance with this customary obligation must be assessed according to the precautionary measures that were 'feasible' in the circumstances prevailing at the time.[22] Increasingly, nongovernmental organisations, international governmental organisations and international criminal tribunals have a major role in scrutinising the legality of attacks. This involves an examination of capabilities and capacities in terms of intelligence, surveillance and reconnaissance (ISR) and operational planning. Military superiority will often mean that as capabilities render more precautions feasible in practice, higher standards of reasonableness become attainable and are thus expected, especially in urban areas where the effects of hostilities are more acutely felt by the civilian population because such areas are usually the most densely populated.[23]

Customary IHL obligations to verify military objectives, take all feasible precautions in the choice of means and methods of attack and carry out ex ante *proportionality assessments*

Recent conflicts in Gaza, Chechnya, Iraq and Afghanistan have seen major military powers employing means and methods of high-intensity conventional warfare against weaker adversaries concealed among civilian populations in urban areas rather than on the open battlefield. The impact that these conflicts have had on civilian populations and civilian objects calls for a reappraisal of the customary rule that parties to a conflict must 'take all feasible precautions in the choice of

19 API, Article 51(8).

20 Y Sandoz, C Swinarski, and B Zimmermann (eds), *Commentary on the Additional Protocols of 8 June 1977 to the Geneva Conventions of 12 August 1949* (ICRC/Martinus Nijhoff, Geneva 1987), (*'Commentary'*), 1989.

21 CIHL Study, above n 14, Rule 15; API, Article 57(1) states that '[i]n the conduct of military operations, constant care shall be taken to spare the civilian population, civilians and civilian objects' and also in Article 13(1) of AP II which provides that '[t]he civilian population and individual civilians shall enjoy general protection against the dangers arising from military operations'. These obligations of constant care and general protection were passed, respectively, with a majority in favour and by consensus, and they are also recognised as having the status of customary law as can be seen from Rule 15 of the CIHL Study.

22 API, above n 6, Article 57(2).

23 *Commentary on the Additional Protocols*, above n 20, 2190.

means and methods of warfare with a view to avoiding, and in any event to minimising, incidental loss of civilian life, injury to civilians and damage to civilian objects',[24] as well as the rule that parties to an armed conflict are prohibited from '[l]aunching an attack which may be expected to cause incidental loss of civilian life, injury to civilians, damage to civilian objects, or a combination thereof, which would be excessive in relation to the concrete and direct military advantage anticipated'.[25] Assessing compliance with this obligation calls for an examination of the capabilities and circumstances prevailing at the material time.

A vital aspect of the principle of distinction is the obligation to do everything feasible to verify that prospective targets are indeed military objectives.[26] Military planners and decision makers must exercise great care, vigilance and precision at the planning stage to ensure that they are fully cognizant of all the facts and circumstances prevailing within their field of operations.[27] To do this, they must verify military objectives in good time[28] and carefully evaluate the accuracy and reliability of target information.[29] In particular, they must make careful and detailed assessments of the number and location of civilians as well as civilian objects surrounding prospective military objectives. The element of feasibility indicates that the ability to carry out an accurate and timely identification of military objectives is an obligation of means, which depends to a large extent upon the ISR capabilities available in the circumstances. In other words, the reasonableness of the precautionary measures taken is entirely context dependent. Essentially, parties can be expected to satisfy different standards of care according to their capabilities, their perception of the urgency of the situation and the military constraints upon them.[30] This does not amount to an obligation actively to acquire and employ state-of-the-art ISR technologies, but merely to employ the full range of feasible means in order to gather the most accurate intelligence possible and ensure that the object of attack is a military one. According to the ICRC *Commentary*, where there is even the slightest doubt, it is the responsibility of military planners and decision makers to issue orders for additional information or the gathering of further intelligence. The *Commentary* states that this is an issue where humanitarian and military interests coincide, as 'no responsible commander would wish to attack objectives which were of no military interest'. A failure to exercise due diligence and reasonableness in that regard, or a failure to carry out a serious evaluation of the accuracy of information, will amount to a violation of this precautionary rule. As discussed in Chapter 1, where there are advanced ISR combined with a basic targeting cycle that allows for targets to be found, fixed, tracked and targeted before being engaged, then heightened

24 CIHL Study, above n 14, Rule 17.
25 Ibid., Rule 14.
26 Ibid., Rule 16.
27 *Commentary on the Additional Protocols*, above n 20, 2194 and 2195.
28 Ibid., 2198.
29 Ibid., 2195.
30 Ibid., 2199.

standards of identification become increasingly feasible and important to reduce the risk of civilian harm, especially in areas outside active hostilities.[31]

The prohibition of indiscriminate attacks, defined in customary IHL, *inter alia*, as attacks '(. . .) which employ a method or means of combat which cannot be directed at a specific military objective; or (. . .) the effects of which cannot be limited as required by international humanitarian law',[32] is accentuated in situations of urban armed conflict, as military objectives will often be in close proximity to protected persons and objects. A core aspect of this prohibition is the obligation to avoid or minimise incidental loss by taking all feasible precautions in the choice of means and methods of attack.[33] This general requirement is to be applied on a case-by-case basis and does not amount to a prohibition of specific means or methods of warfare or an obligation to actively acquire the most discriminating means of warfare.

As with the obligation to verify military objectives to the best of one's means, the previous discussion indicates that this obligation is entirely context dependent and looks to what was feasible for the military decision makers in their particular circumstances. Again, the feasibility element serves to modulate the underlying principle that IHL applies equally to parties to a conflict by varying the

31 Ibid., 2195. See also US Department of Defense, *Law of War Manual* (12 June 2015), paras 5.5.3.1 and 17.5.1.3; The White House, Office of the Press Secretary, Fact Sheet: U.S. Policy Standards and Procedures for the Use of Force in Counterterrorism Operations Outside the United States and Areas of Active Hostilities, May 23, 2013 (In counterterrorism operations, 'lethal force will be used outside areas of active hostilities only when the following preconditions are met: . . . Third, the following criteria must be met before lethal action may be taken: 1) Near certainty that the terrorist target is present; 2) Near certainty that non-combatants will not be injured or killed'. Coalition Forces Land Component Command (CFLCC) Rules of Engagement (ROE) Card, Iraq (2003), reprinted in Center For Law And Military Operations, The Judge Advocate General's Legal Center & School, US Army, Legal Lessons Learned From Afghanistan And Iraq: Major Combat Operations (11 September 2001–1 May 2003) 314 (2004): '1. On order, enemy military and paramilitary forces are declared hostile and may be attacked subject to the following instructions: a. Positive Identification (PID) is required prior to engagement. PID is a reasonable certainty that the proposed target is a legitimate military target. If no PID, contact your next higher commander for decision'.; Final Report On The Persian Gulf War 177 ('Attack procedures specified that if the pilot could not positively identify his target or was not confident the weapon would guide properly (because of clouds, for example), he could not deliver that weapon. Several attack sorties were forced to return with their bombs for this reason.'); US Military Assistance Command Viet-Nam Directive 525–13, Military Operations: Rules of Engagement for the Employment of Firepower in the Republic of Vietnam, para 6a (May 1971), reprinted in 1975 Digest Of United States Practice In International Law 814, 815: 'All possible means will be employed to limit the risk to the lives and property of friendly forces and civilians. In this respect, a target must be clearly identified as hostile prior to making a decision to place fire on it'. 'All possible means will be employed to limit the risk to the lives and property of friendly forces and civilians. In this respect, a target must be clearly identified as hostile prior to making a decision to place fire on it'.

32 CIHL Study, above n 14, Rules 12(b) and (c).

33 API, above n 6, Article 57(2)(a)(ii); CIHL Study, Ibid., Rule 17.

precautionary standards according to means and circumstances. This customary rule will be deemed violated where it can be demonstrated that in the particular circumstances it was feasible for a party to choose certain means and methods of attack over others which could have avoided or minimised incidental loss, and there was an omission in this regard.[34] In such circumstances, it would be unlawful not only to choose weapons that are by their nature indiscriminate when used against military objectives concealed among civilian populations in urban areas, but also wilfully or recklessly to create the conditions in which their use becomes inevitable under the stress and pressure of combat or, in other words, to include certain conventional means of warfare within the operational arsenals of units deployed in urban areas to the exclusion of feasible alternatives that are more appropriate. The type of inappropriate weapons referred to here are those weapons that have wide fatal and destructive impact zones and includes missiles, mortars, flechettes, artillery shells, and shells containing hazardous materials which may remain in the urban environment after the cessation of hostilities, such as depleted uranium and white phosphorous. Although these weapons are not currently subject to specific treaty-based prohibitions, it must be assumed that a decision to choose such weapons over feasible and more discriminating or less destructive alternatives in such circumstances is a reckless violation of this obligation.[35] Those alternatives may include weapons of various lethality and destructiveness, including precision weaponry and nonlethal weaponry that is designed to incapacitate rather than destroy combatants and materiel. However, although there is no legal obligation to acquire and use such forms of weaponry per se, their use reduces the risk of violating the customary rule of proportionality.[36] This will be discussed in more detail later. The obligation to use more discriminating and less destructive means does not necessarily disadvantage poor states because, as stated, this is a question of feasibility. Furthermore, issues of force protection can be dealt with through the establishment of strategic cordons and front lines to isolate organised armed groups from the civilian population, sniper operations, clear-and-hold operations, area denial operations, etc. Giving priority to force protection in highly populated areas and proceeding to use explosive weaponry with a wide destructive area or proceeding to overuse explosive weaponry may serve to undermine force protection by alienating the civilian population and

34 For some examples *Commentary on the Additional Protocols*, above n 20, 2200; CIHL Study, above n 14, Rule 17.

35 UNGA (HRC) 'Human Rights in Palestine and Other Occupied Territories: Report of the United Nations Fact-Finding Mission on the Gaza Conflict' (25 September 2009) UN Doc A/HRC/12/48 ('Goldstone Report'), 698–699.

36 Michael Schmitt, 'War, Technology and International Humanitarian Law' (Summer 2005) Program on Humanitarian Policy and Conflict Research, Harvard University Occasional Paper Series, No 4, 23; Danielle L Infeld, 'Precision-Guided Munitions Demonstrated Their Pinpoint Accuracy in Desert Storm: But Is a Country Obligated to Use Precision Technology to Minimize Collateral Civilian Injury and Damage' (1992) 26 *George Washington Journal of International Law and Economics* 109.

cause the hostilities to escalate. Nor does it mandate or necessitate air strikes or drone strikes, as these do not represent an adequate solution to the problem of explosive violence in urban areas, but are rather part of the problem.

Ex ante proportionality assessments by those who plan or decide upon an attack are an integral feature of precautionary measures and must persist right up to the point at which an attack is launched.[37] Furthermore, an attack must be cancelled or suspended if it becomes apparent that the attack would be, *inter alia*, disproportionate.[38] One of the main issues with the principle of proportionality is that it requires military planners and decision makers to strike a balance between military and humanitarian considerations in good faith. This involves a subjective evaluation of whether the attack may be expected to cause incidental loss that is excessive in relation to the anticipated military advantage.[39] The ICRC *Commentary* notes that *ex ante* proportionality assessments should take into account factors such as the location of civilians and civilian objects in relation to the military objective; the accuracy of the weapons; the nature of the military objectives, including whether they can release dangerous forces; and the stability of the terrain, especially with regard to the risk of floods and landslides.[40] Wilfully launching an indiscriminate attack in the knowledge that it will cause disproportionate incidental loss constitutes a serious violation of treaty-based and customary IHL applicable to conflicts of an international and non-international character and may attract criminal sanction.[41] Where courts of law or political inquiries come to assess whether constant care has been taken to spare the civilian population from the effects of attacks, detailed examinations of the particular ISR, targeting and weapons capabilities and capacities will be made. In this sense, parties to a conflict will be judged according to the extent of their own means, and the greater the feasible means, the less scope there is for plausible deniability.[42]

A higher standard of due diligence is likely to apply in relation to attacks upon 'planned' targets where there is time for the application of rigorous precautionary measures. The joint targeting doctrine of the United States Joint Chiefs of Staff describes 'planned targets' as those which have been identified within an operational theatre and are then pursued in accordance with operational plans and schedules or attacked whenever the circumstances permit.[43] In contrast, the joint targeting doctrine categorises 'immediate' targets as those which are known in advance but not operationalised or those targets of which there is simply no prior

---

37 API, above n 6, Article 57(2)(a)(iii); CIHL Study, above n 14, Rule 18.
38 API, Ibid., Article 57(2)(b); CIHL Study, Ibid., Rule 19.
39 *Commentary on the Additional Protocols*, above n 20, 2208.
40 Ibid., 2212.
41 API, above n 6, Article 85(3)(b); CIHL Study, above n 14, Rule 155.
42 Jean-François Quéguiner, 'Precautions under the Law Governing the Conduct of Hostilities' (2006) 88 (864) *International Review of the Red Cross* 978.
43 Michael Schmitt, 'Precision Attack and international Humanitarian Law' (2005) 87 (859) *International Review of the Red Cross* 450.

knowledge.[44] This doctrine has major implications for regulating the conduct of urban warfare, as the respective categories of 'planned', 'on-call', 'unplanned' and 'unanticipated' targets may be designated as 'time sensitive' because they pose an immediate threat, or because they constitute high value but are 'fleeting' military objectives which may be lost if not immediately attacked.[45] The dynamics of asymmetric conflict may lead to a prevalence of 'unplanned' and 'unanticipated' military objectives, because in face of their opponent's overwhelming and insurmountable military capabilities the weaker side may have no option but to employ unconventional methods, such as 'defenceless defence' whereby rather than defending specific objectives they are organised into small and highly manoeuvrable units which can disperse to another location immediately upon launching an attack, and 'concealment warfare' which makes it difficult or impossible for the stronger side to distinguish between combatants and civilians until the former suddenly emerge to execute an attack.[46] In response, there is the increased risk that the militarily superior side will classify most military objectives as 'immediate targets' and subject them to truncated precautionary measures or take no precautionary measures whatsoever. Such an approach may be justified on the grounds that the application of diligent precautionary measures is not feasible in the circumstances. Although this does not necessarily violate rules on precaution, the results of such attacks may still be disproportionate and thus amount to indiscriminate forms of attack. That said, for parties to a conflict with advanced ISR capabilities, rapidly launching attacks upon purportedly 'time-sensitive', 'unplanned' and 'unanticipated' targets within urban areas may nevertheless be difficult to justify from tactical and legal viewpoints.

In asymmetric armed conflicts, unconventional tactics such as emerging, attacking and disappearing in a fleeting moment may mean that rapid responses directed at the *location* of an attack from within an urban area are ineffectual as a delayed response, and there is the further risk that responding to such provocative tactics increases the likelihood of violations of IHL. This argument has been made by Human Rights Watch and Open Society Foundations, which, respectively, claim that rapid responses directed at 'immediate' and 'emerging' targets, or in other words the use of unplanned airstrikes by US forces in Iraq and Afghanistan, were the primary driver of civilian harm in the form of misidentification of civilians as fighters and excessive incidental loss and collateral damage because such operations lacked the precautionary mitigation procedures and protocols used in planned strikes.[47] According an Open Society study, US and ISAF forces found that in cases not involving self-defence, greater use of 'tactical patience' and 'persistent ISR' could have been used to assess adequately whether

---

44 Ibid.

45 Ibid.

46 Brian Steed, *Piercing the Fog of War* (Zenith Press, 2009) Ch. 9.

47 Human Rights Watch, *Off Target: The Conduct of the War and Civilian Casualties in Iraq* (New York, 2003) 20, 23 and 38; Geiß above n 11, 798–799.

targets were hostile and to reduce collateral damage.[48] The general principle of proportionality will be discussed in greater detail later, but at this stage of the discussion it is suggested that incidental loss caused by attacks upon 'immediate' and 'emerging' targets among civilian populations within urban areas, and not requiring the use of force in self-defence, are likely to be indicative of a failure to take adequate precautionary measures and are likely to cause situations to escalate and result in strategic failures.[49] This, as noted earlier, constitutes a serious violation of customary IHL. As an alternative, and where feasible, advanced ISR capabilities should increasingly be used to identify, pursue, verify and destroy military objectives in real time, so as to ascertain the military objective and choose the most reasonable means, methods and locations of attack in order to avoid or minimise collateral damage.

Effective warnings

Article 57(2)(c) of API requires the following precautionary measure, namely that an '[e]ffective advance warning shall be given of attacks which may affect the civilian population, unless circumstances do not permit'. Customary IHL similarly requires that "[e]ach party to the conflict must give effective advance warning of attacks which may affect the civilian population".[50] This particular obligation applies insofar as the circumstances permit, and parties therefore have considerable latitude to derogate from it. Derogation may, for instance, be made where the element of surprise is deemed to be a necessary condition for the success of an attack.[51] In other words, if military planners or decision makers expect an attack which may affect the civilian population proportionately, they are, in principle, required to give a warning, unless to do so would undermine the success of the attack or otherwise render the attack useless. Adherence to the precautionary measures outlined earlier means that attacks on military objectives concealed among civilian populations in urban areas can be perfectly proportionate even though no warning, or no effective warning, has been given. Considering that precautionary measures, such as giving an effective warning, are of 'greatest importance in urban areas because such areas are most densely populated'[52] and there is thus an increased risk of incidental loss or damage, it is suggested that in circumstances where there is a significant inequality of arms between parties to an urban armed conflict, the stronger attacking side's discretion to derogate from this obligation should be limited by careful scrutiny of any justifications for noncompliance, as part of any *ex post facto* judicial or political inquiries.

48 Christopher Rogers, Rachel Reid, and Chris Kolenda, The Strategic Costs of Civilian Harm – Applying Lessons from Afghanistan to Current and Future Conflicts (Report) (Open Society Foundations – Washington, DC, June 2016), 18, 19, 22, 23.

49 Quéguiner, above n 42, 799.

50 CIHL Study, above n 14, Rule 20; API, above n 6, Article 57(2)(c).

51 *Commentary on the Additional Protocols*, above n 20, 2223.

52 Ibid., 2190.

Indeed, the ICRC *Commentary* suggests that the possibilities of giving warning are increased where an attacking side has complete air supremacy over an urban area concealing a weaker side which has either no air defences or only very basic capabilities, such as rocket-propelled grenade launchers or surface-to-air missiles.[53] Even so, where these basic capabilities exist, they may be negated by the superior side's own defensive capabilities. These considerations are extremely important in asymmetric urban armed conflicts, as one aspect of taking constant care of civilians is ensuring that they are given the chance to protect themselves.[54] Examples given by the ICRC of measures to facilitate this include giving notice by radio or pamphlets that particular objectives or categories of objective will be subject to attack.[55]

More recently, the Report of the UN Fact-Finding Mission on the Gaza Conflict[56] elucidates in greater detail the practical means of warning civilians and the form and degree of specificity required for warnings to be considered effective. First, warnings can be issued through various media, such as announcements on television, radio or public address systems, automated telephone calls and leaflets. Essentially, effective warnings are those which actually reach the civilians likely to be exposed to the attack. Second, warnings should be as clear as possible. They should specify the particular individuals or groups to whom the warning is addressed and "unless the circumstances do not permit", the warning should state the location and the approximate time of the impending attack. In this regard, general information about an upcoming attack will not generally constitute an effective warning, as civilians should not be left guessing its meaning.[57] Moreover, warning shots from light weapons cannot be considered effective advance warnings, as it is unclear whether they constitute a warning of an impending attack or the actual attack itself, and civilians cannot reasonably be expected to evacuate an area that they perceive to be already under attack. Third, warnings should give civilians sufficient time to react. Fourth, warnings should advise civilians on the steps they need to take to avoid harm. In particular, they should inform the persons concerned where they can and should seek safety so that the civilian population does not in fact flee in terror and confusion to areas that may be considered similarly unsafe. Where armed forces are capable of making detailed advance plans, the warnings will need to be part of comprehensive and joined-up contingency measures to evacuate the civilian population to areas that can be considered or have been designated by both sides as safe. Such a warning must include the location of emergency shelters and safe areas, as well as safe routes to get to them and the necessary precautions to take. Finally, the

53 Ibid., 2224.
54 Ibid., 2225.
55 Ibid., 2224–2225.
56 Goldstone Report, above n 35, 528–532.
57 Ibid.

warnings should be credible; that is, civilians must be in no doubt that they are intended to be acted upon.[58]

A former UN secretary-general has made the important point that modern technology can enable a major military power to exercise effective control over a territory even though it has no military presence on the ground.[59] Although this does not necessarily amount to a form of occupation,[60] it is submitted that the greater the means of an attacker, the more it must do to comply with the obligation to give advance warning, as suggested earlier, when confronted with an insurgency or resistance within and across urban areas that are under its effective control,[61] for in such circumstances inequality of arms and the availability of advanced ISR and weapons technologies have generally reduced the importance of the element of surprise as a necessity of war. Also, given that the risk of incidental loss or damage in densely populated urban areas is greater, the militarily superior side should in such circumstances operate on the basis that not giving an effective advance warning is likely to violate that precautionary rule of customary law, as civilians in close proximity to military objectives are then not given the chance to protect themselves.[62] This marks a progressive reconceptualisation in that it inserts proportionality calculations into this aspect of precautionary measures so that the consequences of not giving an effective advance warning should be considered part of *ex ante* proportionality assessments. In other words, the expected incidental loss of *not* giving an effective advance warning should not be excessive in relation to the concrete and definite advantage military advantage reasonably anticipated from a surprise attack.

Proportionality in urban warfare

The customary IHL principles of precaution and proportionality are closely interrelated and are of fundamental importance in situations of armed conflict in densely populated urban areas. Generally speaking, the normative functions underlying these rules are that parties to a conflict must keep civilians out of harm's way as far as possible[63] or, otherwise, that the danger and harm to which civilian populations are exposed must be 'reduced to a minimum'.[64] As will now

58 Ibid.

59 UNGA 'Situation of human rights in the Palestinian territories occupied since 1967: Note by the Secretary-General' (27 September 2006) UN Doc A/61/470, 7; see also Sylvain Vité, 'Typology of Armed Conflicts in International Humanitarian Law: Legal Concepts and Actual Situations' (2009) 91 (873) *International Review of the Red Cross* 83–85.

60 Vité, Ibid.

61 Nils Melzer, *Targeted Killing in International Law* (Oxford University Press, 2009) 365–366.

62 Goldstone Report, above n 35, 527.

63 *Commentary on the Additional Protocols*, above n 20, 1923.

64 Ibid., 1935.

be explored, the practical application of these rules will come under great strain in situations of asymmetric urban armed conflict.

Customary IHL requires *ex ante* proportionality assessments[65] to be carried out not only as part of the obligation to take all feasible precautions in attack, but, furthermore, even if all other conditions for a legitimate attack are fulfilled, 'incidental civilian losses and damages must not be excessive'.[66] In this respect customary IHL prohibits the actual launching of an attack 'which may be expected to cause incidental loss of civilian life, injury to civilians, damage to civilian objects, or a combination thereof, which would be excessive in relation to the concrete and direct military advantage anticipated'.[67] This requires that an assessment be made of what was known or ought to have been known to the party that made the targeting decisions being called into question. Launching such a disproportionate attack is to be considered a form of indiscriminate attack,[68] and may constitute a war crime under both international and domestic law.[69]

In this context, one of the key challenges to fixing the 'technical limits at which the necessities of war ought to yield to the requirements of humanity'[70] is that the test of proportionality is designed to be made *ex ante* and its practical application will be assessed *ex post facto*. In particular, for an indiscriminate attack to constitute a war crime, the prosecution must prove 'that the attack was launched wilfully and in knowledge of circumstances giving rise to the expectation of excessive civilian casualties'.[71] Thus, because proportionality is to be assessed according to a subjective *mens rea* standard, there is nothing *prima facie* that the law can do to prevent normative relativism, or, in other words, the phenomenon of military planners and decision makers assigning particularistic values to relative terms such as 'excessive' and 'military advantage' that are entirely in keeping with their own idiosyncratic military, social, cultural and historical perspectives and imperatives.

The challenge this creates with regard to ensuring the general protection of civilians, especially those caught up in urban armed conflicts, is that the practical application of this aspect of IHL not only requires 'complete good faith on the part of belligerents' but also 'the desire to conform with the general principle of

65 CIHL Study, above n 14, Rule 18.
66 *Commentary on the Additional Protocols*, above n 20, 1979.
67 CIHL Study, above n 14, Rule 14; API, above n 6, Article 51(5)(b).
68 API, above n 6, Article 51(5)(b); *Commentary on the Additional Protocols*, above n 20, 1967.
69 See, for instance UN General Assembly, Rome Statute of the International Criminal Court (last amended 2010), 17 July 1998, Article 8(2)(d) ('ICCS'), Article 8(2)(b)(iv).
70 Declaration Renouncing the Use, in Time of War, of Explosive Projectiles Under 400 Grammes Weight. Saint Petersburg, 29 November / 11 December 1868 (St Petersberg Declaration), Preamble.
71 *Prosecutor v Galić* (Trial Judgment) ICTY-98–29-T (5 December 2003), 59; API, above n 6, Article 85(3)(b); CIHL Study, above n 14, Rule 156.

respect for the civilian population'.[72] These are qualities which may be in short supply in asymmetric conflicts where pushing the rules of IHL to their vanishing points, or indeed their outright violation, is deemed justified by military necessity.

Calculating proportionality

Military objectives are defined in customary law as 'those objects which by their nature, location, purpose or use make an effective contribution to military action and whose partial or total destruction, capture or neutralisation, in the circumstances ruling at the time, offers a definite military advantage'.[73] Military planners and decision makers are responsible for assessing whether the expected incidental loss, injury or damage will be excessive in relation to the military advantage anticipated. As there is no accepted standard of comparison in this regard, there is a wide margin of discretion to assign greater weight or importance to the advantages anticipated by the destruction or neutralisation of particular military objectives than to the humanitarian consequences.[74] The 'difficult constraints of battle'[75] as well as political and military indoctrination may serve to skew this ' "balancing" or "equation" between the necessities of war and the requirements of humanity',[76] with the result that military commanders can easily refute claims of excessiveness in view of seemingly extensive, widespread and systematic collateral damage. State practice, as evidenced from reservations entered on ratifying API, indicates that an attack can be considered at a tactical or even a theatre level rather than at an operational level.[77] The consequences of such diverging interpretations are, first, that incidental damage resulting from an individual operation or 'isolated attack' may be balanced against the military advantage from an attack consisting of a number of discrete operations considered as a whole, and second, that states have adjusted their legal obligations to varying levels with the concomitant increased risk of humanitarian law being applied inconsistently.

This cumulative approach to calculating proportionality, whereby a number of discrete attacks are valued together to form an aggregate military advantage,

72 *Commentary on the Additional Protocols*, above n 20, 1978.

73 CIHL Study, above n 14, Rule 8; API, above n 6, Article 52(2).

74 Antonio Cassese, *The Human Dimension of International Law* (Oxford University Press, 2008) 246.

75 *Commentary on the Additional Protocols*, above n 20, 1981.

76 *Legality of the Threat or Use of Nuclear Weapons* (Advisory Opinion) [1996] ICJ Rep 226, Dissenting Opinion of Judge Higgins, 20.

77 See United Kingdom, Reservation of 28 January 2002: '. . . the military advantage anticipated from the attack is intended to refer to the advantage anticipated from the attack considered as a whole and not only from isolated or particular parts of the attack' available at: <www.icrc.org/ihl.nsf/NORM/0A9E03F0F2EE757CC1256402003FB6D2?OpenDocument> accessed 1 October 2013.

which is then balanced against net incidental loss, is one that can be distorted and used to conceal and justify isolated attacks that, arguably, from the perspective of 'public consciousness' and 'humanity' as opposed to purely legal and military perspectives, result in unacceptable levels of collateral damage. In such situations and on the basis of such an approach, the censure of such acts is unlikely because the military planners and decision makers responsible for applying the proportionality principle are to be judged solely according to 'the information reasonably available to them at the relevant time' and not according to 'information that has subsequently come to light'.[78] The principle of proportionality is designed to be applied *ex ante* and is concerned exclusively with a military commander's subjective appreciation of the quantum of risk and the military advantage at the time of making a decision.

The spatial and temporal scope of the proportionality principle

The concept of a military objective is broad in scope and means that 'dual-use' infrastructure, such as electricity power stations, may lose immunity from attack because they supply power for both civilian and military uses and can thus be deemed to be making an effective contribution to military action.[79] The approach of assessing the 'concrete and direct' military advantage anticipated from the attack as a whole does not similarly take into account any indirect incidental loss and damage caused 'as a whole', but merely the immediate and direct incidental loss caused by blast or fragmentation. Thus one of the limitations of the *lex lata* is that the 'cascading effects'[80] of attacks may be discounted from proportionality assessments; that is, even though attacks upon objectives such as electricity power stations may be justified on the basis that they make an effective contribution to military action by powering military communications and weapons systems, attacking them may cause civilian mortality rates to rise over time as they are also necessary for civilian health and survival by powering hospitals, sewage and water treatment systems.

It may be argued that from the point of view of military planners and decision makers, such information on the 'cascading effects' of attacks is generally not available within the 'fog' of battle and is thus outside their scope of appreciation. Hence, judging commanders on the information available to them at the time of an attack can only serve to limit the timeframe within which incidental loss can be

78 See Canada's Reservation of 20 November 1990, available at: <www.icrc.org/ihl.nsf/NORM/172FFEC04ADC80F2C1256402003FB314?OpenDocument>accessed 1 October 2013.

79 API, above n 6, Article 52 (2) which provides that '[a]ttacks shall be limited strictly to military objectives [which are] those objects which by their nature, location, purpose or use make an effective contribution to military action and whose total or partial destruction, capture or neutralization, in the circumstances ruling at the time, offers a definite military advantage'.

80 Schmitt, above n 43, 452.

calculated. The effect of such a restrictive interpretation is to render the rule of proportionality less effective as a protective measure. However, modern technology combined with advanced scientific knowledge and techniques allows the likely impact of destroying key dual-use infrastructure to be reasonably foreseeable – for instance, the declassified Defense Intelligence Agency memorandum on 'Iraq water treatment vulnerabilities' identified already in 1991 that a failure to secure supplies for water treatment 'could lead to increased incidences, if not epidemics, of disease and to certain pure-water-dependent industries becoming incapacitated, including (. . .) pharmaceuticals, food processing . . .'[81] It is submitted that where such predictions are possible and reasonably available, they should be taken into account as part of detailed advance target analysis and operational planning, as well as *ex post facto* assessments of proportionality. As will now be discussed, recent moves to strengthen the proportionality principle by forging an objective approach indicate that plausible deniability on the part of military and political decision makers of superior military forces is increasingly untenable.

The development of an objective approach to proportionality

The 'Final Report to the Prosecutor by the Committee Established to Review the NATO Bombing Campaign against the Federal Republic of Yugoslavia'[82] shows signs that the general approach to the principle of proportionality is changing in character. Such a change makes IHL stronger and able to protect civilians more effectively from the use of conventional high-intensity means and methods of warfare against forces concealed within urban areas. In seeking to further substantiate the concept of 'military advantage', the committee considered a number of questions. The first was (a) what are the relative values to be assigned to the military advantage gained, the injury to noncombatants and the damage to civilian objects, and (b) what is included or excluded in totalling the sums? Unlike the relative values assigned to chess pieces, the committee noted that in reality these issues cannot be definitively answered *in abstracto*. To date there exists no universal quantitative or qualitative standard of comparison, although in many cases a quantitative approach to comparing humanitarian and military considerations will be the most obvious and practical one for assessing excessiveness. The second was what is the standard of measurement in time or space? On the basis of the previous discussion, it is suggested that if military advantages can be defined very broadly, then the timescales for calculating the incidental damage should be construed in a similarly broad manner rather than being limited to the immediate

81 Defense Intelligence Agency, "Water treatment vulnerabilities", Washington DC, available at: <www.gulflink.osd.mil/declassdocs/dia/19950901/950901_511rept_91.html> accessed 1 October 2013; Joy Gordon, 'When Intent Makes All the Difference in the World: Economic Sanctions on Iraq and the Accusation of Genocide' (2002) 5 *Yale Human Rights and Development Law Journal* 70–74.

82 ICTY, 'Final Report to the Prosecutor by the Committee Established to Review the NATO Bombing Campaign Against the Federal Republic of Yugoslavia' (June 2000) 29 *ILM* 1257.

and direct effects of isolated attacks – especially in a paradigm where this can be reliably predicted and thus factored into projections. Third, the committee asked to what extent a military commander is obligated to expose his own forces to danger in order to limit civilian casualties or damage to civilian objects. It is suggested that limiting the risk to which materiel and combatants are exposed constitutes a concrete and definite military advantage, but within the emerging paradigm of unmanned surveillance systems and precision-weapon platforms, this issue should become obsolete as technological innovations lead to a greater coincidence of military and humanitarian interests.[83]

The crux of this discussion is the committee's statement that 'there will be many cases where reasonable military commanders will agree that the injury to noncombatants or the damage to civilian objects was clearly disproportionate to the military advantage gained'.[84] The approach of reasonableness in balancing the necessities of war with the requirements of humanity has been affirmed in *Galić*, where it was held that

> [i]n determining whether an attack was proportionate it is necessary to examine whether a reasonably well-informed person in the circumstances of the actual perpetrator, making reasonable use of the information available to him or her, could have expected excessive civilian casualties to result from the attack.[85]

Furthermore, the Appeals Chamber in *Galić* confirmed that the principle of proportionality 'does not mention any exceptions', and in particular that it 'does not contemplate derogating from this rule by invoking military necessity.'[86] This is a legal breakthrough, as it marks the development of a much-needed objective approach to proportionality which can determine on a case-by-case basis whether an attack was excessive in view of the evidence indicating the actual circumstances and consequences, rather than just the military planner's subjective appreciation. The ruling in *Galić* means that attacks which cause an apparently excessive level of loss, injury or damage, or a combination thereof, 'may give rise to the inference that civilians were actually the object of attack'.[87] Looking into the circumstances of the actual perpetrators and examining their ISR capabilities may allow for higher objective standards of reasonableness to be imposed on the basis that excessive incidental loss will generally be foreseeable and thus intended. For example, in *Dragomir Milošević* it was submitted that the accused was culpable of the 'deliberate, indiscriminate, and/or excessive and disproportionate' shelling of the civilian population residing within civilian areas

83 Ibid., 48–50.
84 Ibid., 50.
85 *Galić* (Trial Judgment), above n 71, 58.
86 *Prosecutor v Galić* (Appeals Chamber Judgment) ICTY-98–29-A (30 November 2006), 190–192.
87 Ibid., 60.

of Sarajevo as, 'given the inherent inability of modified airbombs to engage specific targets, their deployment could only have been intended to cause civilian casualties'.[88]

Obligations to ensure the survival of civilians and the civilian population

Even though parties may claim that hardship, suffering and loss among the civilian population are inevitable consequences of urban armed conflict,[89] it does not relieve them of their customary obligations to ensure the protection of objects indispensible to its survival, ensuring protection and care for wounded civilians and ensuring humanitarian relief for civilians in need.

Objects indispensable to the survival of the civilian population

During urban armed conflicts, objects indispensable to the survival of the civilian population are often under serious threat. To attack such objects will generally constitute a violation of the cardinal customary principle of distinction which prohibits attacks against civilian objects.[90] Thus, customary IHL generally prohibits 'attacking, destroying, removing or rendering useless objects indispensable to the survival of the civilian population'.[91] A list of such objects is to be found in Protocols I and II and includes foodstuffs, agricultural areas for the production of foodstuffs, crops, livestock, drinking water installations and supplies and irrigation works.[92] In spelling out the concept of 'objects indispensable to the survival of the civilian population', the use of the words 'such as' introducing that list shows that it is nonexhaustive and can thus include dual-use facilities that support drinking water installations, such as electricity power stations. The challenge in situations of asymmetric urban warfare is that the dual-use function of such objects, that is, that although serving civilian purposes, they are also being used 'in direct support of military action', may be cited as justification for attacks upon them.[93] Regardless of claims that the attack was carried out for a specific purpose other than denying sustenance to the civilian population, where attacks on dual-use infrastructure 'may be expected to leave the civilian population with such inadequate food or water as to cause its starvation or force its movement',[94] they will be impermissible.

88 *Prosecutor v Dragomir Milošević* (Prosecution's Submission of Amended Indictment Pursuant to Rule 50 and Trial Chamber's Decision dated 12 December 2006) ICTY-98-29/1-T (18 December 2006), 24–25.
89 Goldstone Report, above n 35, 1313.
90 CIHL Study, above n 14, Rule 7.
91 Ibid., Rule 54.
92 API, above n 6, Article 54 (2); APII, Article 14.
93 API, Ibid., Article 54(3)(b).
94 Ibid.

By recognising that 'starvation' does not only mean death due to deprivation of water and food but also malnutrition, sickness and disease resulting from deprivation of essential foodstuffs, medicines and commodities, the Preparatory Commission for the International Criminal Court made it clear that the scope of this customary rule is not as narrow as it would otherwise first appear.[95] In any case, when it comes to targeting decisions in asymmetric urban armed conflict, greater military capabilities and capacities will lead to higher standards of reasonableness vis-à-vis the obligation to choose military objectives which may be expected to cause the least danger to civilian lives,[96] as well as the most proportionate means and methods of attacking those objectives. [97] Indeed, for many modern armed forces that have the wherewithal to be discriminating, precautionary and proportionate in achieving their military objectives at operational and theatre levels, it must be considered unreasonable[98] to have recourse to forms of wholesale destruction that are unacceptably detrimental to food security and public health.[99]

95 Knut Dörmann, 'Preparatory Commission for the International Criminal Court: The Elements of War Crimes – Part II: Other Serious Violations of the Laws and Customs Applicable in International and Non-International Armed Conflicts' (2001) 83 (842) *International Review of the Red Cross* 475–476.
96 *Customary IHL Study*, above n 57, Rule 21.
97 Goldstone Report, above n 35, 1324–1325. 1223, 1246, 1257.
98 Ibid.
99 Ibid., 1330, 1331, 1335.

7 Weaponry law

Emerging approaches to the regulation of means of warfare and law enforcement

Introduction

The rationale for an examination of weaponry law in the context of this study is that growing urbanisation, combined with the increasing severity, magnitude and reach, of weaponry capabilities since the Second World War have increasingly exposed civilians to the destructive capacity of armed conflict.[1] General treaty-based IHL, namely the Additional Protocols to the Geneva Conventions, do not in themselves prohibit specific weapons per se but rather set out general principles that are to be applied on a case-by-case basis, including the prohibition of indiscriminate attacks such as those which employ a means of combat that cannot be directed at a specific military objective or that employ a means of combat the effects of which cannot be limited. The branch of IHL that provides weapons-specific prohibitions or regulation is referred to here as arms control law, and it will be suggested that the concepts and rules developed in this field may have import when it comes to interpreting progressively the general principles of precaution, proportionality and distinction.

All weapons can be considered to be inhumane – that is their very *raison d'être*. The regulatory issue becomes one of identifying and fixing where technical limits of warfare should concede to the demands of humanity. As will be discussed, this has not traditionally been a strictly logical or even a genuinely humanitarian-oriented area of regulation, but rather one driven by strategic and military policy considerations. Attempts to regulate weaponry at numerous diplomatic conferences indicate that this area of public international law

1 Malvern Lumsden, 'The UN Conference on Inhumane Weapons' (1979) 16 (4) *Journal of Peace Research* 289: 'The amount of munitions scattered over modern battlefields is enormous. With conventional munitions alone, the firepower of the front-line troops of the major powers has increased by more than 25 times since World War II. US forces in World War II delivered 1,100 kg for every enemy soldier killed, in Korea 5,600 kg, and in Viet Nam 17,800 kg. By 1968, a Soviet motorised rifle division could launch 53,000 kg of ammunition in a single salvo. At the same time, the range and area of coverage is increasing: this is one reason why the military in many countries are demanding larger training grounds, as in Larzac in France. At the same time, growing populations and increasing urbanization mean that modern war is more likely to involve civilian populations'.

has always been affected by overriding strategic and military considerations.[2] Indeed, Lumsden went as far as to suggest that '[t]he history of the struggle against cruel weapons provides a good example of how the inequitable distribution of political and military power in the world perverts the development of international law'.[3] In this way, the history of arms control indicates that states are unwilling to prohibit weapons that have a high degree of military utility and thus decisiveness,[4] despite the issue that they may be just as, if not more, inhumane and indiscriminate than those weapons subject to specific restrictions or prohibitions.[5] Accordingly, to a limited extent, the regulation and prohibition of specific means of warfare is achieved through arms control law, which Dekker describes as a legal and political process that seeks to 'limit or reduce certain categories of weapons or military operations' through a range of legally binding instruments, as well as through 'informal regimes' such as 'politically binding documents' that can serve as 'soft law'.[6]

McDonald notes that enhanced legal regulation of means and methods of warfare may occur in a gradual or incremental fashion[7] rather than taking place in 'sweeping gestures that are doomed to gather dust'.[8] Thus, whereas immediately entering into legally binding comprehensive bans or restrictions may suit some states, what is advantageous about mechanisms such as the Convention on Conventional Weapons is that states can sign up to the 'soft-law' aspects

2 Ibid.
3 Ibid.
4 Antonio Cassese, *The Human Dimension of International Law* (Oxford University Press, 2008) 235.
5 Lumsden, above n 1, 290.
6 Guido den Dekker, 'The Effectiveness of International Supervision in Arms Control Law' (2004) 9(3) *Journal of Conflict & Security Law* 316–320: An important feature of treaty-based arms control law is the establishment of mechanisms to supervise and ensure compliance. This may take place at the domestic level or the international level through the exchange of information between states or the establishment of independent international bodies to carry out inspections, monitoring, verification and dispute settlement. The Convention on Conventional Weapons (CCW) is important as it constitutes a legal framework that can regulate weapons 'that may be deemed to have indiscriminate effects'. It is an umbrella framework that has led to protocols such as Protocol I on non-detectable fragments, Protocol II and amended Protocol II on mines, booby traps and other devices, Protocol III on incendiary weapons and Protocol V on explosive remnants of war; Erwin Dahinden, 'The Future of Arms Control Law: Towards a New Regulatory Approach and New Regulatory Techniques' (2005) 10(2) *Journal of Conflict & Security Law* 270: Dahinden notes that unannounced on-site challenge inspections carried out by international organisations such as the International Atomic Energy Agency are still the exception as they are rarely, if ever, put into practice and in any case are not appropriate mechanisms for dealing with challenges to human security such as proliferation of small arms and terrorism.
7 Avril McDonald, Jann K Kleffner, and Brigit Toebes (eds), *Depleted Uranium Weapons and International Law: A Precautionary Approach* (TMC Asser Press, The Hague, 2008) 381.
8 N White, 'The Future of Arms Control Law: An Overview of the Workshop' (2004) 9(3) *Journal of Conflict and Security Law* 299, 303, 305.

of protocols that set out policy-based voluntary best practice.[9] Such 'soft-law' developments can be considered progress, as they may indicate emerging practice that can gradually become more widespread and consistent.[10] McDonald also notes that soft-law standards may be as important as legally binding standards and that the practical differences between these two types of standards may be minor, especially in cases where 'legally binding' standards have no real compliance mechanisms to enforce them.[11] Approaches to weaponry law vary in that the subject of regulation or prohibition may be identified according to its primary effects, its objective characteristics or its technical specifications. However, as will be discussed, these approaches can be seen to produce inconsistencies in regulation, in that specific prohibitions of a certain type of weapon due to recognition of its indiscriminate effects may not apply by analogy to similar types of weapons with similar effects.

Categories of weaponry

Lumsden noted seven broad categories of weapons based on their objective characteristics, namely, nuclear weapons, chemical and biological weapons, blast weapons, fragmentation weapons, incendiary devices, delayed action weapons such as antipersonnel mines and high-velocity small-calibre ammunition.[12] However, as a general regulatory category, the main basis for prohibition or restriction is the capacity of any given weapon to have *indiscriminate effects*, and such effects may occur over space and time. Lumsden broke down the notion of indiscriminate spatial effects into three main considerations. First, a weapon may be considered indiscriminate where its 'area of coverage' goes beyond military personnel into the 'risk zone' where no military advantage is to be sought or gained due to its civilian character. Second, a weapon may be considered indiscriminate where its effects spread beyond the user's control, and Lumsden notes that this is characteristic of nuclear, chemical, biological and incendiary weapons.[13] Third, a weapon may be considered indiscriminate due to the persistence of its effects, and this may be characteristic not only of nuclear, biological and chemical weapons, but potentially even more so with regard to conventional weaponry such as unexploded munitions and mines.[14] However, as discussed earlier, in the absence of a prohibition of a specific type of weapon, according to general targeting law, the issue of indiscriminateness is to be assessed on a case-by-case and *ex post facto*

9 Protocol on Explosive Remnants of War (Protocol V to the 1980 CCW Convention), 28 November 2003, Technical Annex (voluntary best practice); McDonald et al., above n 7, 381.
10 McDonald et al., Ibid., 383.
11 Ibid.
12 Lumsden, above n 1, 291.
13 Ibid.
14 Ibid.

basis. Therefore general rules do not amount to prohibitions of specific weapons per se.

Explosive violence

Explosive weaponry is used because of the utility of its blast or fragmentation effects against military objectives and because it can be deployed in a variety of ways: air to ground, ground to air or ground to ground. The kinetic effects of explosive weaponry are also capable of having blast or fragmentation effects in the area surrounding their detonation. Moreover, numerous munitions, such as cluster munitions, mortars and artillery shells, are designed precisely to have an area effect. This notion of 'explosive violence' is an important categorical term as it encompasses a variety of categories of explosive weapons and considers the contexts in which they are used. Accordingly, it provides a more comprehensive conceptual approach to the regulation of weaponry.[15]

It is suggested that the issue of the use of 'explosive violence' in urban areas with a high population density is one of the most pressing humanitarian challenges of our time, and it represents a major area for normative development and systemic integration given that it is an issue that cuts across the legal frameworks of humanitarian law, human rights law, arms control law and criminal law. There is growing recognition that the use of conventional weaponry poses long-term threats to civilians when used in civilian areas, for example, due to the problem of unexploded ordnance, caused by the high failure or 'dud' rates which can become a major problem, particularly when large numbers of munitions are deployed,[16] as well as the problem of the explosive remnants of war such as antipersonnel landmines which have potential to cause indiscriminate long-term harm postconflict because they are concealed and lie dormant, not because they are faulty, as may be the case with unexploded ordnance such as such as 'dud' cluster munitions, or where their self-detonating mechanisms do not work.

A former UN secretary-general noted that the use of explosive weaponry in 'densely populated environments . . . inevitably has an indiscriminate and severe humanitarian impact' because of the 'risk to civilians caught in the blast radius or killed or injured by damaged and collapsed buildings' and also because 'of damage to infrastructure vital to the well-being of the civilian population such as

15 Richard Moyes, 'Explosive Violence in Areas of Civilian Concentration: "Cities Are Not Targets!" Towards a Prohibition on the Use of Explosive Force in Populated Areas' (Presentation organized by 2020 Vision Campaign of Mayors for Peace Sponsored by the Mexican Mission to the United Nations) (28 October 2008).

16 Henry Dodd and Robert Perkins, *Monitoring Explosive Violence: the EVMP Dataset 2011* (Report) (Action on Armed Violence, 2012).

water and sanitation systems'.[17] Furthermore, a recent secretary-general report to the Security Council recommended that '[m]ember States, United Nations actors and international and non-governmental organizations [. . .] consider the issue of explosive weapons closely, including by supporting more systematic data collection and analysis of the human costs of their use' as '[t]his is essential to deepening the understanding of the humanitarian impact of such weapons and to informing the development of policy and practice that would strengthen the implementation of international humanitarian and human rights law'.[18] A plethora of research by international and nongovernmental organisations has noted the severe immediate and long-term effects of explosive violence upon civilian populations, particularly when used in urban areas where there will usually be a concentration of civilians unless civilians have either fled or been evacuated. Research also suggests that explosive violence disproportionately affects civilians as opposed to combatants or fighters.[19] Furthermore, research suggests that it

---

17 UNSC 'Report of the Secretary-General on the Protection of Civilians in Armed Conflict' (29 May 2009) UN Doc S/2009/277, 36; Jakob Kellenberger, 'Combien de morts faudra-t-il encore à Gaza!' (2 February 2009): 'Le recours aux armes lourdes dans une zone aussi dense que Gaza pose un sérieux problème . . . Même si vous avez la volonté de respecter ces deux dernières règles, c'est très difficile si vous utilisez des armes si lourdes dans une zone d'une telle densité de population'.

18 UNSC 'Report of the Secretary-General on the protection of civilians in armed conflict' (11 November 2010) UN Doc S/2010/579, 50–1; UN Doc S/2009/277, Ibid., 36 and 49.

19 See generally: Richard Moyes, *Explosive Violence: The Problem of Explosive Weapons* (Landmine Action, 2009) 24; Moyes, 'Cities are not targets!', above n 15; United Nations Institute for Disarmament Research, 'The Humanitarian Challenge of Explosive Weapons Use in Populated Areas' (Report of a residential symposium co-hosted by UNIDIR's Discourse on Explosive Weapons (DEW) project and The Geneva Forum Glion sur Montreux, 4–5 December 2010, January 2011) <www.inew.org/site/wp content/uploads/2011/07/UNIDIR-Report-of-the-Glion-symposium-Jan-2011.pdf> accessed 1 October 2013; United Nations Institute for Disarmament Research, 'Explosive Weapons Use in Populated Areas a Pressing Humanitarian Concern' (Report of the 2nd symposium of the Discourse on Explosive Weapons (DEW) project New York, 15 September 2010, October 2010) <www.unidir.org/files/medias/pdfs/summary-report-eng-0–293.pdf> accessed 1 October 2013; R Coupland and N Taback, 'Towards Collation and Modelling of The Global Cost of Armed Violence on Civilians' (2005) 21 (1) *Medicine, Conflict and Survival*; C Buhmann, 'The Direct and Indirect Costs of Explosive Violence: Recognition and Documentation Need to Translate into Policy Action and Political Support' (2009) 339 *British Medical Journal* 761; R Coupland and H Samnegaard, 'Effect of Type and Transfer of Conventional Weapons on Civilian Injuries: Retrospective Analysis of Prospective Data from Red Cross Hospitals' (1999) 319 *British Medical Journal* 410–412; Dodd and Perkins, above n 16; International Committee of the Red Cross, *Wound Ballistics: An Introduction for Health, Legal, Forensic, Military and Law Enforcement Professionals* (ICRC, June 2008); John Borrie and Maya Brehm, 'Enhancing Civilian protection from Use of Explosive Weapons in Populated Areas: Building a Policy and Research Agenda' (2011) 93 (883) *International Review of the Red Cross* 809; Madelyn Hsiao-Rei Hicks et al., 'The Weapons That Kill Civilians: Deaths of Children and Non-Combatants in Iraq, 2003–2008' (2009) 360 (16) *New England Journal of Medicine* 1585–1588.

is the 'explosive violence' of conventional 'explosive weaponry', rather than the categories of nuclear, biological and chemical weaponry, that in practice poses the gravest risks for civilians and civilian populations in contemporary conflicts.[20]

Progressive approaches to the regulation of weaponry

A major challenge in regulating weaponry has been to overcome disputes as to whether a weapon is indiscriminate per se, and thus ripe for prohibition, or whether it is indiscriminate when used under certain conditions, and thus its use should be restricted rather than prohibited.[21]

The general approach to have emerged in contemporary weaponry law embodies the latter approach by suggesting that particular weapons may be regarded as indiscriminate when used under certain circumstances and where they do not conform to certain technical specifications. For example, Article 2 of Protocol III to the Convention on Conventional Weapons is innovative in that it prohibits a specific weapons technology (incendiary weapons) in contexts where it is likely to cause indiscriminate effects, that is, where military objectives are located within 'a concentration of civilians'.[22]

It is suggested that, as with military doctrine on the obligation to consider possible second- and third-order effects of munitions when making *ex ante* assessments, contemporary arms control treaties demonstrate some important regulatory and conceptual approaches to particular forms of explosive weaponry that may serve to have broader import. In particular, they can be regarded as

20 Moyes, 'Cities Are Not Targets!', above n 15.

21 William Boothby, *Weapons and the Law of Armed Conflict* (Oxford University Press, 2009) 80–83; Consider also Article 8(2)(b)(xx) of ICCS (above n 140); *Legality of the Threat or Use of Nuclear Weapons* (Advisory Opinion) [1996] ICJ Rep 226, 95.

22 Protocol on Prohibitions or Restrictions on the Use of Incendiary Weapons (CCW Protocol III) Geneva, 10 October 1980, Article 2(2): 'It is prohibited in all circumstances to make any military objective located within a concentration of civilians the object of attack by air-delivered incendiary weapons'; Protocol Additional to the Geneva Conventions of 12 August 1949, and relating to the Protection of Victims of International Armed Conflicts (Protocol I), 8 June 1977 ('API'), Articles 51(5)(a): prohibition on attacks by 'bombardment by any methods or means which treats as a single military objective a number of clearly separated and distinct military objectives in a city, town, village or other area containing a similar concentration of civilians or civilian objects' and 58(b): 'avoid locating military objectives within or near densely populated area'; Protocol on Prohibitions or Restrictions on the Use of Incendiary Weapons (CCW Protocol III) Geneva, 10 October 1980, Article 4; CCW Protocol II (as amended 3 May 1996) ('Amended Protocol II to the Convention on Certain Conventional Weapons'), Article 3(9) and particularly Article 7(3): 'Without prejudice to the provisions of Article 3, it is prohibited to use weapons to which this Article applies in any city, town, village or other area containing a similar concentration of civilians in which combat between ground forces is not taking place or does not appear to be imminent, unless either: (a) they are placed on or in the close vicinity of a military objective; or (b) measures are taken to protect civilians from their effects, for example, the posting of warning sentries, the issuing of warnings or the provision of fences'.

embodying emerging benchmark standards that may be used to scrutinise other weapons that are similar in type and effect.[23] Furthermore, it is suggested that the regulatory approaches embodied within weaponry law may have a bearing on the interpretation of general targeting law under humanitarian law in the same way that general concepts such as indiscriminate harm have motivated the development of specific weapons prohibitions.[24] Indeed, generally speaking, it is suggested that recent trends in weaponry law are important in that they not only provide weapon-specific prohibitions, but also, they can be viewed as demonstrating a recognition and an acceptance amongst states, albeit to a limited extent, that the use of particular forms of explosive and incendiary weaponry in urban areas or areas where there is a 'concentration of civilians' is indiscriminate per se and thus unlawful, particularly when delivered by air power or artillery, and thus cooperation is needed to put into effect progressive legal regulation. Recent treaty developments embody recognition not only of the direct and immediate indiscriminate effects of explosive weaponry in a spatial sense, but also the indiscriminate, and purportedly unintended, effects over time.[25]

As discussed earlier, a central concern with an otherwise narrow interpretation of the principle of proportionality is that it discounts long-term collateral effects of conventional weaponry, particularly in the form of explosive remnants of war and unexploded ordnance on the basis they are not reasonably foreseeable to military commanders operating within the 'fog of war'. Approaches set out in weaponry law and military doctrine indicate that an understanding and consideration of second- and third-order effects of munitions is not only possible but required. Moreover, according to a narrow interpretation of the principle of proportionality, the long-term duration of effects can also be regarded as being irrelevant vis-à-vis the immediate military advantage sought in a given situation and the utility of a weapon in this regard.[26] However, contemporary arms control treaties embody a recognition that particular types of weaponry result in patterns of indiscriminate harm, particularly when used in urban areas or 'amongst concentrations of civilians'.[27]

For example, the protocols relating to explosive remnants of war introduce new conceptual approaches which can serve to factor in short- and long-term

23 Telephone Interview with Richard Moyes, Policy and Researcher Director, Landmine Action, and Co-Chair, CMC, in Exeter, UK (26 June 2008) cited in Bonnie Docherty, 'Breaking New Ground: The Convention on Cluster Munitions and the Evolution of International Humanitarian Law' (2009) 31 *Human Rights Quarterly* 948.

24 Guido den Dekker, 'The Law of Arms Control and Depleted Uranium Weapons', in McDonald et al., above n 7, 75, 78, 79.

25 Boothby, above n 21, 299.

26 Lumsden, above n 1, 290.

27 CCW Protocol II, above n 22, Article 1 which sets out a definition of a 'concentration of civilians' as 'any concentration of civilians, be it permanent or temporary, such as inhabited parts of cities, or inhabited towns or villages, or as in camps or columns of refugees or evacuees, or groups of nomads'.

effects of explosive weaponry on proportionality assessments.[28] The Preamble of Protocol V to the Convention on Conventional Weapons recognises 'the serious post-conflict humanitarian problems caused by explosive remnants of war'.[29] Article 3 paragraph (10) of Protocol II to the Convention on Conventional Weapons requires users to take 'all feasible precautions' which 'are practicable or practically possible taking into account all the circumstances ruling at the time' which includes *inter alia* consideration of 'the short- and long-term effect of mines upon the local civilian population for the duration of the minefield'.

The Ottawa Convention introduced a general prohibition on antipersonnel mines, and the rationale for this can be found in the preamble to the convention which states that

> [d]etermined to put an end to the suffering and casualties caused by anti-personnel mines, that kill or maim hundreds of people every week, mostly innocent and defenceless civilians and especially children, obstruct economic development and reconstruction, inhibit the repatriation of refugees and internally displaced persons, and have other severe consequences for years after emplacement.[30]

The 2008 Convention on Cluster Munitions expressly addresses the immediate as well as the mid- to long-term effects of cluster munitions by stating that they cause 'unacceptable harm to civilians'.[31] Indeed, the preamble of the convention expresses a determination 'to put an end for all time to the suffering and casualties caused by cluster munitions at the time of their use, when they fail to function as intended or when they are abandoned'.[32] The convention recognises and prohibits the 'unacceptable' area effects of cluster munitions and defines a 'cluster munition contaminated area' as 'an area known or suspected to contain cluster munition remnants'.[33] The convention also recognises the spatially and temporally indiscriminate effects that cluster munitions have had in practice by broadening the category of 'cluster munition victims' to comprise 'all persons who have been killed or suffered physical or psychological injury, economic loss,

28 Protocol V, above n 9; CCW Protocol II, Ibid.

29 Protocol V, ibid: Protocol V is important because at Article 2(1) it defines 'explosive ordnance' as 'conventional munitions containing explosives, with the exception of mines, booby-traps and other devices as defined in Protocol II to this Convention.' Protocol V defines 'unexploded ordnance' as 'explosive ordnance that has been primed, fused, armed, or otherwise prepared for use and used in an armed conflict. It may have been fired, dropped, launched or projected and should have exploded but failed to do so'. Article 3(1) imposes a duty to minimize postconflict effects of certain explosive weaponry by taking preventative as well as remedial measures.

30 Convention on the Prohibition of the Use, Stockpiling, Production and Transfer of Anti-Personnel Mines and on their Destruction, 18 September 1997 ('Ottawa Convention').

31 Convention on Cluster Munitions, 30 May 2008 ('CCM') Preamble.

32 Ibid.

33 Ibid., Article 2 (11).

social marginalisation or substantial impairment of the realisation of their rights caused by the use of cluster munitions' and importantly, this broadly includes 'those persons directly impacted by cluster munitions as well as their affected families and communities'. This indicates a recognition of the foreseeably broader and reverberating effects of a particular type of explosive weapon. The convention sets out technical criteria[34] to define and prohibit[35] certain effects of cluster munitions 'in order to avoid indiscriminate area effects and the risks posed by unexploded submunitions'.[36]

It is thus suggested that we can see the emergence and acceptance within treaty law that established patterns of indiscriminate harm have enough of a bearing on foreseeability of harm to warrant prohibitions. Furthermore, the approaches taken in treaty law may also have a bearing on the interpretation and application of treaty-based and customary humanitarian law to various forms of explosive weaponry deployed in urban areas, particularly when targets or areas are engaged by air power or artillery.[37] In this regard, the delegates of the High Contracting Parties to the Convention on Conventional Weapons themselves made a novel and striking synergy between arms control law and general principles of IHL in '[n]oting the foreseeable effects of explosive remnants of war on civilian

---

34 Ibid., Article 2(2): '"Cluster munition" means a conventional munition that is designed to disperse or release explosive submunitions each weighing less than 20 kilograms, and includes those explosive submunitions. It does not mean the following: (a) A munition or submunition designed to dispense flares, smoke, pyrotechnics or chaff; or a munition designed exclusively for an air defence role; (b) A munition or submunition designed to produce electrical or electronic effects; (c) A munition that, in order to avoid indiscriminate area effects and the risks posed by unexploded submunitions, has all of the following characteristics: (i) Each munition contains fewer than ten explosive submunitions; (ii) Each explosive submunition weighs more than four kilograms; (iii) Each explosive submunition is designed to detect and engage a single target object; (iv) Each explosive submunition is equipped with an electronic self-destruction mechanism; (v) Each explosive submunition is equipped with an electronic self-deactivating feature'.

35 Ibid., Article 1(1): 'Each State Party undertakes never under any circumstances to: (a) Use cluster munitions; (b) Develop, produce, otherwise acquire, stockpile, retain or transfer to anyone, directly or indirectly, cluster munitions; (c) Assist, encourage or induce anyone to engage in any activity prohibited to a State Party under this Convention'.

36 Brian Rappert and Richard Moyes, 'The Prohibition of Cluster Munitions: Setting International Precedents for Defining Inhumanity' (2009) 16 (2) *Nonproliferation Review* 236. However, given the detailed technical criteria, the CCM cannot be viewed as an absolute prohibition. The provisions of Article 2(2) do not catch cluster weapons that are designed to circumvent the technical criteria so as to avoid the indiscriminate effects defined in the chapeau of Article 2(2)(c). Nevertheless, the CCM essentially joins up specific technical criteria with unacceptable area effects to create a specific prohibition. Thus, in contrast with the approach to be taken under general principles of IHL, where it has to be demonstrated that a user deployed a weapon that is in fact indiscriminate or disproportionate, the CCM adopts the reverse approach, whereby cluster munitions are presumptively indiscriminate and thus unlawful unless the user can justify that their submuntion-based weapons are excluded or fall outside of the provisions of the CCM.

37 Guido den Dekker, above n 24, 75, 78, 79.

populations as a factor to be considered in applying the international humanitarian law rules on proportionality in attack and precautions in attack'.[38]

Such 'cross-fertilisation' may serve as a means to constrain the broad margin of appreciation that is available under the general principles of targeting law, particularly with regard to the use of explosive weaponry amongst concentrations of civilians. In particular, there are grounds for suggesting that where data suggest that the general effects of a weapon are delayed or persistent when used in a conventional fashion, then this may go towards a humanitarian law proportionality analysis in that the delayed or persistent effects do not confer a sufficiently direct or immediate military advantage.

Indeed, this broadening of the proportionality analysis to include mid- to long-term 'knock-on effects' appears logical given that, as discussed earlier, there is no adequate balance if the concept of military advantage may be construed very broadly, whereas the notion of expected or foreseeable incidental civilian casualties or damage may be construed very narrowly.[39] As discussed in Chapter 1, this is a notion that is reflected in contemporary military doctrine relating to unconventional military operations. An example of military doctrine relating to counterinsurgencies provides that military leaders '***must consider*** not only the [first-order], desired effects of a munition or action but also possible second- and third-order effects – including undesired ones' [emphasis added] when making *ex ante* proportionality assessments of what means and methods to employ so as to minimise collateral damage.[40] As the ICRC notes, 'the same scale has to be applied with regard to both the military advantage and the corresponding civilian casualties',[41] and it is suggested that this approach is implicitly embodied in the contemporary weaponry law developments discussed earlier.

It is suggested that the regulatory developments discussed previously indicate an awareness and understanding of the indiscriminate patterns of harm caused by certain types of weaponry and that this is contributing to the stigmatisation of explosive weaponry amongst concentrations of civilians. Moreover, in view of Article 31 paragraph (3) (c) of the Vienna Convention on the Law of Treaties, this treaty-based process of stigmatisation may not only lead to further doctrinal

38 Third Review Conference of The High Contracting Parties to the Convention on Prohibitions or Restrictions on the Use of Certain Conventional Weapons which may be Deemed to Be Excessively Injurious or to Have Indiscriminate Effects, 'Final Document, Part II: Final Declaration' (Geneva, 7–17 November 2006) CCW/CONF.III/11 (Part II), 4.

39 International Committee of the Red Cross, 'Report prepared by the ICRC for the 28th International Conference of the Red Cross and Red Crescent' (Geneva, September 2003), 12–14.

40 US Department of the Army (Training and Doctrine Command) Counterinsurgency (COIN) Field Manual (FM) 3–24 and Fleet Marine Force Manual (Final Draft) (Headquarters, Department of the Army, Washington, DC & Marine Corps Combat Development Command, Department of the Navy, Headquarters, United States Marine Corps, Washington, DC, 16 June 2006), 7–36.

41 ICRC (Report prepared by the ICRC for the 28th International Conference), above n 39.

and policy developments regarding the use of explosive violence amongst concentrations of civilians, but may also contribute to the progressive interpretation of international humanitarian law standards vis-à-vis distinction, proportionality and precautions as well as human rights law standards – Article 51 paragraph (4) (b) and (c) of API for example.[42] This process of stigmatisation may be furthered still by international and nongovernmental organisations which can continue to gather data suggesting that the use of certain conventional weapons in urban areas has effects similar to those weapons already subject to express prohibitions or restrictions, and so making them worthy of further specific treaty-based legal regulation.[43] As indicated earlier, the general way in which this has been achieved has been to link particular types of weaponry that belong to one of Lumsden's seven categories with a range of prohibited indiscriminate spatial and temporal effects that are capable of expression in general but clear objective criteria. Furthermore, contemporary treaty-based weaponry law indicates an emerging acceptance on the part of states that, because particular forms of explosive and incendiary weaponry cause unacceptable and disproportionate harm to civilians in the short, medium and long term, their use should be prohibited or at least restricted against use on military objectives within urban areas or a 'concentration of civilians'. Indeed, these developments in treaty-based law reflect the independent doctrinal and operational developments discussed in Chapter 1 to the effect that the use of conventional area weapons and indirect fire should be avoided in urban areas where military objectives are in close proximity to civilians[44] and may be used only under very limited conditions.[45] Indeed the tactical directives from

---

42 API, above n 30, Article 51(4): 'Indiscriminate attacks are prohibited. Indiscriminate attacks are: (a) those which are not directed at a specific military objective; (b) those which employ a method or means of combat which cannot be directed at a specific military objective; or (c) those which employ a method or means of combat the effects of which cannot be limited as required by this Protocol; and consequently, in each such case, are of a nature to strike military objectives and civilians or civilian objects without distinction'.

43 Moyes, 'Cities Are Not Targets!', above n 15;. Brian Rappert, *A Convention Beyond the Convention: Stigma, Humanitarian Standards and the Oslo Process* (Landmine Action, 2008), 19; *Prosecutor v Martić* (Rule 61 Decision) ICTY-95–11-R61 (March 8 1996), 23–31, cited in *Prosecutor v Galić* (Trial Judgment) ICTY-98–29-T (5 December 2003), 57: 'In the *Martić* Rule 61 proceedings, the Trial Chamber regarded the use of an Orkan rocket with a cluster bomb warhead as evidence of the intent of the accused to deliberately attack the civilian population. The Chamber concluded that "in respect of its accuracy and striking force, the use of the Orkan rocket in this case was not designed to hit military target but to terrorise the civilians of Zagreb. These attacks are therefore contrary to the rules of customary and conventional international law". The Trial Chamber based this finding on the fact that the rocket was inaccurate, it landed in an area with no military objectives nearby, it was used as an antipersonnel weapon launched against the city of Zagreb and the accused indicated he intended to attack the city'. See also US Department of Defense, *Law of War Manual* (12 June 2015), para 5.11.4 'attacks in areas in which civilians are present might be subject to greater restrictions'.

44 US FM 3–24, above n 40, 7–36.

45 NATO/International Security Assistance Force, 'Tactical Directive' (6 July 2009).

2007 to 2011 demonstrate the increasing prominence given to raising standards of civilian protection by ISAF and US forces in Afghanistan. The tactical directives were also important in linking the stringent rules on the use of air strikes and indirect fire on residential compounds to the wider strategic picture of minimising the type of civilian harm that was contributing to the growth of an insurgency, as well as weakening the legitimacy of the use of force and undermining the war effort in Afghanistan.[46]

What emerges from a discussion of arms control law is an underlying policy-based contradiction in that weaponry law recognises that the use of certain conventional weapons in urban areas causes 'unacceptable harm to civilians'.[47] However, as the technical criteria which set out the types of weapons covered by the restriction or prohibition are generally narrowly construed, this will serve to exclude weaponry with effects that are similarly unacceptable, but which have different objective or technical characteristics.[48] A way around this, it is suggested, is to use these treaty-based concepts and doctrinal developments concerning what constitutes 'unacceptable harm' to elucidate progressively general targeting and weaponry rules under humanitarian law so that it covers a broader range of explosive and incendiary weaponry, particularly when used in urban environments where there is a concentration of civilians. Furthermore, this approach may pave the way for the development of more specific treaty-based prohibitions and a general presumption against the use of explosive weaponry in urban areas that contain a concentration of civilians.

The import of human rights law to the regulation of weaponry: 'nonlethal' weapons

As discussed in Chapter 1, low-intensity conflicts bordering on or reaching the threshold of non-international armed conflict are the most prevalent form of conflict in our global strategic environment. Therefore, from a doctrinal point of view, in the contemporary operational environment where military forces can be seen to be taking on a broader range of tasks involving the use of force, particularly counterterrorism and counterinsurgency operations in urban areas amongst civilian populations, the escalation of nonlethal and lethal force involving the employment of nonlethal means and methods may be regarded as imperative.

---

46 Christopher Rogers, Rachel Reid & Chris Kolenda, The Strategic Costs of Civilian Harm – Applying Lessons from Afghanistan to Current and Future Conflicts (Report) (Open Society Foundations – Washington, DC June 2016), 23 and 31.

47 CCM, above n 31, Preamble; John Borrie, *Unacceptable Harm: A History of How the Treaty to Ban Cluster Munitions Was Won* (United Nations Institute for Disarmament Research, Geneva, 2009) 335; T di Ruzza, 'The Convention on Cluster Munitions: Towards a Balance between Humanitarian and Military Considerations?' (2008) 47 (3–4) *Military Law and the Law of War Review* 416–425.

48 Moyes, 'Cities Are Not Targets' above n 15; Rappert, above n 43, 19.

Furthermore, the use of 'nonlethal weapons' may be strategically advantageous in situations of extreme violence that do not reach the threshold of an armed conflict, as well as armed conflict itself.[49] Koplow argues that states such as the United States have recognised that the use of conventional weaponry may be 'too crude, too imprecise, too overwhelming' and may 'last too long and hurt too many people' to effectively achieve or advance strategic goals in a range of low-intensity conflicts.[50] As set out in Chapter 1, there is recognition in contemporary military doctrine itself that harm to civilian populations and civilian infrastructure may undermine the restoration and maintenance of civic security. In this way, as discussed in Chapter 1, the employment and escalation of nonlethal means and methods can be regarded as vital to ensuring postconflict transitions to peace in the midst of full-spectrum operations or even following international armed conflicts. Indeed, the use of nonlethals, such as chemical riot control agents or incapacitating agents, may be an effective way of responding to unconventional, irregular and asymmetrical threats that may be concealed and operating amongst concentrations of civilians. The development and use of nonlethal weapon technologies in such contexts would minimise the recourse to explosive weaponry, particularly where it is likely to cause unnecessary, indiscriminate or disproportionate harm.[51]

In this way, the material conditions of contemporary conflicts induce the pursuit of 'less devastating' weapons. The manifest desire to augment a conventional armoury with 'nonlethal' or 'less-than-lethal' weaponry purportedly arises 'not from a naïve desire to be nicer to enemy civilians (or even to enemy soldiers) but from a hard-headed desire to become even more effective in operating in today's complex and confusing battle environment'.[52] In this way, 'nonlethal' capabilities may allow engagement with lethal threats or hostile forces in situations where the use of conventional weaponry, especially explosive weaponry, may be counterproductive where it adversely affects a civilian population creating more antagonism

---

49 M van Creveld, *The Transformation of War* (The Free Press, 1991) 205; Squadron Leader C R Coles, *Air-Delivered Non-Lethal Weapons And The RAAF Weapons Inventory* (Geddes Papers, Australian Defence College, 2003) 70 <www.defence.gov.au/adc/publications/geddes_03.html> accessed 1 October 2013; David A Koplow, *Death by Moderation, The US Military's Quest for Useable Weapons*, (Cambridge University Press, 2010), 190, 223.

50 Koplow, Ibid., 14 and 18.

51 Van Creveld, above n 49, 205; Coles, above n 49, 70; Koplow, above n 49, 208.

52 Koplow, Ibid., 19; See also, National Institute of Justice, quoted in Lois Pilant, 'Crime and War: An Analysis of Non-Lethal Technologies and Weapons Development' (1998) 65 (6) *The Police Chief*, 55; David A Koplow, *Non-Lethal Weapons: The Law and Policy of Revolutionary Technologies for the Military and Law Enforcement* (Cambridge University Press, 2006) Preface; FM 3–24, above n 40: 'Sometimes, the More Force Is Used, the Less Effective It Is'; Neil Davidson, *'Non-Lethal' Weapons* (Palgrave Macmillan, 2009) Ch. 1; US Department of Defense, Nonlethal Weapons and Equipment Review: A Research Guide for Civil Law Enforcement and Corrections (US Army Nonlethal Weapons and Equipment) (US Department of Justice, Office of Justice Programs, National Institute of Justice, October 2004): US Army Non-lethal Weapons and Equipment.

and resistance.[53] Militaries of several countries are thus developing 'nonlethal' or 'less-than-lethal' weapons capabilities as a 'viable intermediate capacity'[54] with which to respond to the full-spectrum operational environment in a strategically effective manner.[55] General international humanitarian law and arms control do not explicitly refer to 'nonlethal' weapons and so this concept is a legal and conceptual enigma not expressly covered by these branches of law. In contrast, human rights law, with its emphasis on the escalation of nonlethal force and the use of lethal force only where absolutely necessary, can be viewed as having a role to play in the regulation of weaponry and the promotion of nonlethal means and methods of force.[56]

As stated earlier in this section, adopting an enhanced classification framework can assist with the identification of those contexts that objectively fall within the law enforcement paradigm and those which fall within the paradigm of armed conflict. This is significant, as according to Schmitt, the human rights law standard of necessity 'requires consideration of non-forceful measures as an alternative to forceful ones' and proportionality under human rights law generally 'requires consideration of non-forceful measures as a factor in reducing the degree and nature of forceful actions necessary'.[57] However, in the contemporary full-spectrum operational environment, human rights mechanisms are faced with

---

53 Davidson, Ibid., 84–85; Graham Allison and Paul Kelly, *Non-Lethal Weapons and Capabilities: Report of an Independent Task Force* (Report No 50 The Council on Foreign Relations, 2004) ISBN 0876093411; David Fidler, 'The meaning of Moscow: "Non-lethal" weapons and international law in the early 21st century' (2005) 87 (859) *International Review of the Red Cross*, 530.

54 Koplow, above n 49, 2.

55 Coles, above n 49, 70; Koplow, above n 52, 14; US Department of Defense, above n 52; US Department of Army, Headquarters, United States Army Training and Doctrine Command Fort Monroe, TRADOC Pamphlet 525–66, Military Operations.

56 *Isayeva v Russia* (Application No 57950/00) ECHR 24 February 2005, [189]–[201]: 'The Court regards it as evident that when the military considered the deployment of aviation equipped with heavy combat weapons within the boundaries of a populated area, they also should have considered the dangers that such methods invariably entail', and at [191]: '[t]he massive use of indiscriminate weapons. . . cannot be considered compatible with the standard of care prerequisite to an operation of this kind involving the use of lethal force by State agents' and the use of a highly explosive bomb by the air force 'is impossible to reconcile with the degree of caution expected from a law enforcement body in a democratic society'.

57 Michael Schmitt, 'Targeted Killings and International Law: Law Enforcement, Self-defense, and Armed Conflict' in R Arnold and N Quenivet (eds.), *International Humanitarian Law and Human Rights Law: Towards a New Merger in International Law* (Brill, Leiden/Boston, 2008) 535; *Güleç v Turkey* (Application No 21593/93) 28 EHRR 121, [71]–[73]: In this way, the absolute necessity standard indicates that where the circumstances permit, less lethal or even non-lethal means ought to be used before there can be a resort to lethal force. Accordingly, in *Güleç*, the European Court of Human Rights found that firing on a demonstration with a machine gun was not justified, as the authorities should have expected disturbances to arise and so they should have prepared to respond to crowd violence in a proportionate manner by having in place non-lethal or less-than-lethal means of force such as riot control equipment and agents such as batons and riot shields, water cannons, rubber bullets or tear gas.

dealing with complex issues of fact and law, and this is no less so in relation to issues of the use of weaponry where multiple legal frameworks are applicable. As alluded to earlier, this can be seen as a way to regulate the use of explosive weaponry amongst concentrations of civilians, but, as will now be discussed, nonlethal weaponry, in the form of chemical riot control agents or incapacitating agents, is legally and ethically problematic in situations of armed conflict.

Nonlethal or less-than lethal weapons?

In a 1996 directive, the US Department of Defense generally defined nonlethal weapons as '[w]eapons that are explicitly designed and primarily employed so as to incapacitate personnel or materiel, while minimizing fatalities, permanent injury to personnel, and undesired damage to property and the environment'.[58] In comparison with 'conventional lethal weapons that destroy their targets principally through blast, penetration and fragmentation', nonlethal weapons 'employ means other than gross physical destruction to prevent the target from functioning'[59] and to this end they may have 'relatively reversible effects on personnel or materiel'[60] or they may 'affect objects differently within their area of influence'.[61] Similarly NATO has described nonlethal weapons as those weapons 'which are explicitly designed and developed to incapacitate or repel personnel, with a low probability of fatality or permanent injury, or to disable equipment with minimal undesired damage or impact on the environment'.[62] Thus the utility of 'nonlethals' is that they are designed to reduce the 'probability of fatality' but not necessarily eliminate it altogether. This notion of 'reversibility' of disabling or incapacitating effects may, nevertheless, be difficult to achieve in practice. It has been suggested that the terms 'less-than-lethal', 'so-called nonlethal weapons' or 'sub-lethal' weapons are more apposite expressions given that such weapons may actually have lethal effects on individuals given their age, physical and medical condition or when used under certain conditions such as enclosed spaces.[63] Indeed, a report published by the US National Science Foundation in 1972 stated that 'nonlethal' is a 'relative term' and that

> [a]ll weapons, and a wide variety of objects that are not intended to serve as weapons, create some primary or secondary risk of death or permanent injury . . . [w]eapons not intended to kill or create permanent injury, if used with any degree of regularity, would undoubtedly cause some deaths because

58 US Department of Defense, *Directive No 3000.03E: Policy for Non-Lethal Weapons* (25 April 1996), 3.I.
59 Ibid.
60 Ibid., 3.1.2.1.
61 Ibid.
62 NATO, Policy on Non-Lethal Weapons (13 October 1999) <www.nato.int/docu/pr/1999/p991013e.htm> accessed 1 October 2013.
63 Koplow, above n 49, 9–10; Koplow, above n 52, 204.

> of physiological differences among those against whom they are employed, physical malfunctioning, improper utilization, and other circumstances.[64]

Three general effects sought from 'nonlethal' weapons are 'counterpersonnel' effects, 'countermateriel' effects and 'countercapability effects'.[65] With regard to 'counterpersonnel' usages, Davidson notes that 'nonlethals' may be used to 'control crowds; incapacitate individuals; deny area to personnel; and clear facilities, structures, or areas'.[66] Examples of 'nonlethal' weapon technologies include sticky and slippery foam; electric guns; pepper spray; acoustic rays; directed energy heat rays such as lasers, radio frequency, microwave and millimetre wave beams; chemical calmatives or incapacitants, malodorants and irritants; projectile netting; antimaterial biological and chemical agents;[67] and blunt impact projectiles, that is, low kinetic energy rubber bullets.[68]

Legal issues surrounding the use of 'nonlethal' weaponry: chemical agents as a substitute for explosive weaponry?

A specific 'nonlethal' weapons category does not exist, and so such weapons have to be regulated, depending on the context, by domestic rules and regulations, as well as general HRL, IHL and arms control law. The main example of arms control law regulating 'nonlethal' weapons is the Chemical Weapons Convention (CWC). Under the CWC, state parties are prohibited from using chemical weapons and using riot control agents as a method of warfare.[69] Article 2(2) CWC defines 'toxic chemical' as '[a]ny chemical which through its chemical action on life processes can cause death, temporary incapacitation or permanent harm to humans or animals'. Article 2(1) provides that a 'toxic chemical' becomes a 'chemical weapon' where it is (a) used for purposes prohibited under the CCW and where (b) it is included in 'munitions and devices, specifically designed to cause death or other harm through the toxic properties of those toxic chemicals . . . which would be released as a result of the employment of such munitions and devices'. Thus, under Article 2(1)(a) such 'toxic chemicals' are prohibited to the extent that they are 'intended for purposes not prohibited under this Convention' and 'as long as the types and quantities are consistent with such purposes'. What matters then is the intent behind the development, storage and use

64 US National Science Foundation, Less-than-Lethal Weapons Technology Report (1972), cited in M W Kroll and J D Holl (eds) *TASER Conducted Electrical Weapons: Physiology, Pathology, and Law* (Springer Science, 2009) 41.
65 Davidson, above n 52, 80.
66 Davidson, ibid; US Department of Defense, above n 52.
67 Koplow, above n 49, 12–24.
68 Davidson, above n 52, 78.
69 Convention on the prohibition of the development, production, stockpiling and use of chemical weapons and on their destruction, Paris 13 January 1993 ('CWC') 'General Obligations' Articles 1(1)(b) and 1(5).

of what may in fact be a toxic chemical. Under Article 2(9)(d), chemicals which are not prohibited as 'toxic chemicals' pursuant to the schedules of the CWC may be used for '[l]aw enforcement including domestic riot control purposes'.[70] Thus 'toxic chemicals', such as incapacitating chemical agents, may be used for law enforcement, as it is not a purpose prohibited under Article 2 of the CWC. However, if they are intended or are of a type or quantity for use in warfare, then the toxic chemical will constitute an unlawful 'chemical weapon'.[71]

Riot control agents (RCAs) can be used for 'law enforcement purposes'. RCAs are defined in Article 2(7) CWC as '[a]ny chemical not listed in a Schedule [to the CWC] which can produce rapidly in humans sensory irritation or disabling physical effects which disappear within a short time following termination of exposure'. Therefore, the CWC anticipates that chemicals such as riot control agents may be used lawfully in law enforcement operations, but not as a means of warfare, or, in other words, in combat operations connected to an armed conflict. The CWC does not clearly define what constitutes 'enforcement operations' as well as how to distinguish them from combat operations in the complex security conditions of full-spectrum operations. It is suggested therefore that the objective criteria discussed earlier in this section are the most appropriate basis for deciding the extent to which chemicals such as RCAs can be used for law enforcement purposes.

Finogenov v Russia: *discussion*[72]

As will now be discussed, despite the perceived advantages of purportedly 'non-lethal' weapons such as chemical incapacitating agents, their use is legally and ethically problematic in 'grey area' situations. These are situations that Koplow suggests represent a 'middle ground, containing aspects of both law enforcement and military counterterrorism operations, thereby illuminating the rainbow of legal and policy considerations at play'.[73]

Finogenov v Russia concerned a group of over forty terrorists belonging to the Chechen separatist movement who entered the Dubrovka Theatre in Moscow and held over 900 people hostage in what was described as 'an extreme law enforcement situation'.[74] The terrorists were armed with automatic weapons and

---

70 CWC, Ibid., Article 2(9)(d).

71 Another example of munitions that are prohibited in the context of armed conflict but permitted in law enforcement situations are expanding bullets on the basis that they generally cause unnecessary and superfluous injuries that are difficult to treat, but are useful and effective in extreme law enforcement situations as they can immediately kill a target that may represent an immediate lethal threat to those around them, whilst minimising the risk to civilians as they stop in the body of the target rather than passing through and killing innocent bystanders.

72 *Finogenov and Others v Russia* (Application Nos 18299/03 and 27311/03) ECHR (First Section) 20 December 2011.

73 Koplow, above n 52, 3.

74 Fidler, above n 53, 538.

explosive weaponry and had installed explosive devices in the theatre. Russian security forces used an undisclosed incapacitating chemical agent to sedate both the terrorists and hostages before retaking the theatre building and rescuing the hostages in a conventional assault. The chemical used was not identified and had not been registered under Article 3(1)(e) of the CWC. The gas used ended up killing approximately 15 per cent (125) of the hostages because it caused acute 'respiratory and cardiac deficiency'.[75] The Russian security forces killed most of the incapacitated terrorists as well as those who put up armed resistance, but this killing was not a material issue as part of the complaint brought by the families of the deceased hostages. The families of the deceased victims claimed that there had been a violation of Article 2 ECHR, and so the court had to consider whether the Russian government's use of force in this case was compatible with the requirements of Article 2 of the ECHR. The court viewed the assault as a law enforcement operation, noting that this hostage case 'exceeded everything known before and made that situation truly exceptional'. For this reason, the court adopted a deferential approach which granted the Russian government a wide margin of appreciation vis-à-vis the 'military and technical aspects of the operation'. The court's reasoning was that 'the hostage-taking came as a surprise' and so 'the military preparations for the storming had to be made very quickly and in full secrecy'. Additionally, 'the lives of several hundred hostages were at stake, the terrorists were heavily armed, well-trained and devoted to their cause'.[76]

Putting the facts of the case into their wider context, the court noted that 'terrorism by various separatist movements in the North Caucasus has been a major threat to national security and public safety in Russia for more than fifteen years, and fighting terrorism is a legitimate concern of the Russian authorities'.[77] On this basis, the court found that the use of force involving the incapacitating chemical agent did not violate the negative obligation under Article 2 per se.[78] However, the court gave 'closer scrutiny' to 'the subsequent phases of the operation . . . where no serious time constraints existed and the authorities were in control of the situation'.[79] In this way, the court adopted the methodological approach of applying 'different degrees of scrutiny to different aspects of the situation under examination'.[80] Thus the court confined itself to assessing whether the Russian security forces had taken 'all feasible precautions in the choice of means and methods of a security operation mounted against an opposing group with a view to avoiding and, in any event, minimising, incidental loss of civilian life'.[81] On this issue, the court found that there was a lack of precautionary measures in place to minimise the foreseeable risks associated with the use of the

75 *Finogenov and Others v Russia*, above n 72, 99.
76 Ibid., 213.
77 Ibid., 212.
78 Ibid., 226.
79 Ibid., 214.
80 Ibid., 216.
81 Ibid., 265.

gas. In particular, the court found that there had been a failure to ensure that the proceeding rescue operation was sufficiently prepared due to 'inadequate information exchange between various services, belated beginning of the evacuation, limited on-the-field coordination of various services, lack of appropriate medical treatment and equipment on the spot, and inadequate logistics', and on this basis the court found a violation of the positive obligation under Article 2 of the ECHR.[82] In response to the Russian government's admission that it had been impossible to foresee the effects of the gas and that some losses had been viewed as being unavoidable,[83] the court found that the gas used could not be considered harmless.[84] The court found that it was 'at best, potentially dangerous for an ordinary person, and potentially fatal for a weakened person'[85] and so considered it to be a 'dangerous substance'.[86]

Finogenov v Russia: *analysis*

Finogenov v Russia is an example of a human rights court assessing the legitimacy of the use of a 'nonlethal' chemical incapacitating agent. The way in which it effectively ruled that the Russian authority's use of an incapacitating agent was legitimate in these circumstances thus warrants close scrutiny. In its reasoning, the court observed that 'the legislative framework for the use of the gas in the present case remains unclear'.[87] Although this may have been so for domestic law, it is suggested that in assessing whether the Russian government had violated the right to life, consideration ought to have been given to Russia's compliance with the Chemical Weapons Convention.

Arguably, the CWC is a relevant source of law in assessing whether or not there had been compliance with Article 2, or put another way, whether Russia's use of the chemical incapacitating agent was legitimate. This case represented an opportunity for the ECHR to play an enhanced regulatory role in stating that lawfulness under the ECHR was connected to compliance with the CWC, and, furthermore, it represented an opportunity for human rights jurisprudence to offer some clarity with regard to the substantive lacunae within the CWC. Even if it is suggested that an assessment of Article 2 ECHR is in no way linked to the CWC, it is suggested that express reference to the CWC in its reasoning should have been made so as to ensure that the regulatory scheme of the CWC was in no way undermined through the 'exceptional' legitimisation of the use of an incapacitating agent under human rights law. In particular, given the apparent connections of the hostage crisis with surrounding terrorist acts and military operations, the court could have taken steps to ensure that the CWC

82 Ibid., 266.
83 Ibid., 194 and 201.
84 Ibid., 201.
85 Ibid., 202.
86 Ibid., 203.
87 Ibid., 229.

prohibition on toxic chemicals as a means of warfare was not undermined. In this regard, there is an evident risk, from a CWC perspective, that 'exceptional' usages of chemical incapacitating agents could spill over from lawful use in law enforcement operations to their use as a means of warfare in situations of armed conflict.[88]

The regulatory scheme under the CWC is a mechanism to ensure that chemical weapons development is kept under review in order to prevent any spillover into armed conflict. The ECtHR could have taken more steps to contextualise the use of the chemical incapacitating agent and ensure that it was not a 'chemical weapon' or used as 'method of warfare'. Moreover, it is suggested that the court could have taken greater steps to be assured that the agent used fell into the category of nonscheduled discrete organic chemical of a type and quantity consistent with law enforcement usage.[89] The court's language suggests it recognised that the incapacitating agent was dangerous in terms of nature and duration of effects, and this should have triggered reference to the CWC, as the lethal effect of the agent used raised the obvious question of whether it was of a 'type' consistent with law enforcement. Thus the court's finding that the 'legislative framework for the use of the gas in the present case remains unclear' was unsatisfactory.[90] In particular, in view of the applicable CWC regime, the court took an overly deferential approach in stating that it was 'prepared to admit that the gas was an *ad hoc* solution, not described in the regulations and manuals for law-enforcement officials' on the basis that because 'the exact formula of the gas was not revealed by the authorities' it was 'impossible . . . to establish whether or not the gas was a 'conventional weapon', and 'to identify the rules for its use'.[91]

Instead, the ECtHR should have asserted Russia's obligations under the CWC and pressed for details of the agent in order to ascertain whether the agent was declared as a riot control agent pursuant to Article 3(1)(e) of the CWC; whether the agent or its precursors were listed under Schedule 1 of the CWC as a chemical permissible 'research, medical, pharmaceutical or protective purposes' but not law enforcement;[92] or whether it was listed under Schedule 2 or 3 as a toxic chemical which may be used for law enforcement purposes, but not riot control.[93] Indeed, even in the absence of disclosure by the Russian authorities of the composition of the agent, the court could have ruled that agents consistent

88 Davidson, above n 52, 214.

89 Donald Neill, 'Riot Control and Incapacitating Chemical Agents Under the Chemical Weapons Convention' (Presentation to the OPCW Academic Forum, The Hague, September 2007) (Directorate of Strategic Analysis Defence R&D Canada, Centre for Operational Research and Analysis, Technical Memorandum TM 2007–22, June 2007), 12.

90 *Finogenov and Others v Russia*, above n 72, 229.

91 Ibid., 229.

92 Walter Krutzsch and Ralf Trapp, *A Commentary on the Chemical Weapons Convention*, (Martinus Nijhoff, The Hague, 1994) 418.

93 Neill, above n 89, 5.

with law enforcement usages in such circumstances may permissibly cause either 'temporary incapacitation' or 'disabling physical effects which disappear within a short time following termination of exposure'.[94] Thus a material aspect of the court's reasoning should have been an analysis of the nature and composition of the agent, or at least whether its effects were indeed temporary and whether they could be reversed with medical countermeasures. In this respect, the court could have either pressed for information of the 'therapeutic index' of the weapon or have drawn inferences as to its consistency with 'nonlethal' law enforcement usages. As discussed by Neill, the 'therapeutic index' is a medical term used to identify agents where the difference between the temporary incapacitating concentrations and lethal concentrations are too small for them to be administered without a foreseeable likelihood of fatality. In other words, where there is a small margin between safe and lethal dosages, the 'therapeutic index' is considered too high for it to be regarded as a safe agent for 'nonlethal' use, as it is not possible to avoid the foreseeable risk of an accidental overdose.[95] Also, the court should have enquired as to whether the agent used was produced and stored in such quantities so as to trigger the CWC's declaration, reporting, inspection and compliance mechanisms.[96]

Ultimately, the court granted the Russian authorities a large measure of discretion in responding to an exceptional situation, but did not consider whether there was such discretion to develop and store such a chemical agent as a signatory to the CWC in the time prior to the occurrence of this exceptional situation. Thus an analysis of whether the use of such chemical agents was legitimate could have been more broadly construed to take into account the CWC regime.[97] In other words, it is suggested the court should have gone beyond the simple approach of finding a violation of the positive obligation to ensure Article 2 in terms of putting into place sufficient precautionary measures and asserted Russia's negative obligations as arising from the CWC.

---

94 Abram Chayes and Matthew Meselson, 'Proposed Guidelines on the Status of Riot Control Agents and Other Toxic Chemicals under the Chemical Weapons Convention', *Chemical Weapons Convention Bulletin*, Issue 35, March 1997, p 17; Neill, above n 89, 12.

95 Neill, ibid; US Department of Army, Army Field Manual No 3–9: Potential Military Chemical/Biological Agents and Compounds (Department of the Army, Washington DC, 12 December 1990), 58–59 and 65–66; Lynn Klotz, Martin Furmanski and Mark Wheelis, 'Beware the Siren's Song: Why 'Non-Lethal' Incapacitating Chemical Agents Are Lethal' (March 2003) *Federation of American Scientists* <www.fas.org/bwc/papers/sirens_song.pdf> accessed 1 October 2013.

96 CWC, above n 69, Article VII.

97 Neill, above n 89, 8: Indeed, as Neill suggests, important issues were whether Russia used a toxic chemical that exceeded the parameters of a riot control agent for law enforcement purposes and whether it had unlawfully 'developed', 'produced', 'stockpiled', 'acquired' and 'retained' such a chemical agent as well. Although the court considered the sufficiency of *ex post facto* precautionary measures, it did not fully consider the whether the *ex ante* precautionary measures under the CWC applied and were complied with.

Conclusions: are chemical agents a viable substitute for conventional explosive weaponry?

In view of the direct and long-term harm caused by conventional explosive weaponry when used in urban areas amongst concentrations of civilians, it is suggested that nonlethal weapons may be strategically, legally and ethically preferable alternatives in that they help to separate and thus discriminate lawful objects of war from those that are protected and immune from attack; they may minimise the risk of collateral damage; they reduce the need to resort to lethal force; and they promote the strategically effective use of force.[98] Indeed, the US Department of Defense Non-Lethal Weapons Program has stated that nonlethal weapons 'provide tools for controlling force escalation preempting conflict where possible, deescalating tension, applying the right force at the right time and facilitating the return to peace'.[99] However, despite these potential advantages, in relation to chemical incapacitants and irritants, the CWC prohibits their use as a method of warfare, and so the question becomes whether the CWC should be modified in order to allow what may be considered a more ethical and strategically efficacious means of responding to asymmetric urban warfare.

As discussed earlier, the ECtHR in *Finogenev* found that the incapacitating agent or calmative gas in question was 'at best, potentially dangerous for an ordinary person, and potentially fatal for a weakened person'[100] and so considered it to be a 'dangerous substance'.[101] Thus at present, there is nothing to suggest that current scientific and technological developments in calmative gasses for law enforcement purposes have reduced the levels of foreseeable harm to satisfactory levels.[102] Nevertheless, the court also noted that the use of calmative gas in this case 'was not used "indiscriminately" as it left the hostages a high chance of survival'[103] but that the Russian authorities failed in their positive obligation to protect life by failing to ensure that a sufficient rescue operation was put in place in the aftermath of the incident once the immediate threat had been removed.[104] The court found that insufficient precautions had been taken 'to minimise the effects of the gas on the hostages, to evacuate them quickly and to provide them with necessary medical assistance'.[105]

According to the current state of the art, it is suggested that if nonlethals, such as calmative gasses, are used as a method of warfare in an operational context where it is not feasible to take such precautionary measures to ensure the safety of

98 Pauline Kaurin, 'With Fear and Trembling: An Ethical Framework for Non-Lethal Weapons' (2010) 9(1) *Journal of Military Ethics* 100.
99 US Department of Defense Non-Lethal Weapons Program 2007, cited in Kaurin, Ibid.
100 *Finogenov and Others v Russia*, above n 72, 202.
101 Ibid., 203.
102 Davidson, above n 52.
103 *Finogenov and Others v Russia*, above n 72, 232.
104 Ibid., 266.
105 Ibid., 237.

the civilian population, then it cannot be said that they are 'not used indiscriminately'. Thus, there is no plausible basis for stating that they should have a special permissible status under IHL in contrast to conventional explosive weaponry or that the CWC should be modified to allow for their use.

Thus, in view of Orbon's analysis, it is suggested that only in those circumstances where, first, nonlethal weapons are used for law enforcement purposes and, second, where they are used in an operational context where foreseeable health effects can be mitigated through precautionary measures, can the use of 'nonlethal weapons' be described as plausibly having a 'nonlethal' effect.[106] Indeed, as the US Council on Foreign Relations stated, 'to press for an amendment to the CWC or even to assert a right to use RCAs as a method of warfare risks impairing the legitimacy of all NLW' and also risks creating exactly what the CWC aims to prevent, namely compelling others 'to openly and legitimately conduct focused governmental R&D [research and development] that could more readily yield advanced lethal agents than improved nonlethal capabilities' for the purposes of warfare rather than law enforcement.[107]

However, the CWC allows for research and development of agents of a type and quantity for law enforcement purposes, and so the Organization for the Prohibition of Chemical Weapons and Human Rights Mechanisms may play a complementary and coordinated role in ensuring that developments and usages take place within the purview of established standards. In this way, it is suggested that the use of chemical calmatives and irritants may be used for law enforcement operations within the complex full-spectrum operational environment, such as that of belligerent occupation,[108] but that emerging human rights standards suggest that any such use is predicated upon precautionary measures so as to ensure the health and survival of individuals indirectly affected. Applying the objective criteria for the recognition of combat operations can indicate the circumstances where such precautionary measures are not to be reasonably practical or expected, and thus where their use is prohibited under the CWC and arguably, IHL, in that they may indiscriminately and disproportionately affect civilians. The high threshold of an armed conflict may ensure that in most circumstances, the presumptive human rights–oriented approach will apply and that the use of chemical agents for law enforcement purposes may be legitimately used in exceptional situations as an alternative or even to avoid altogether the use of conventional explosive weaponry.

---

106 Sjef Orbons, 'Non-Lethal Weapons: Peace Enablers or Troublesome Force? Assessing the Role of CS and Baton Rounds in the Northern Ireland Conflict' (2011) 22(3) *Small Wars & Insurgencies* 467–494.

107 The Council on Foreign Relations, above n 53, 32.

108 Neill, above n 89, 8: Examples given by Neill include: 'to enforce local laws, protect persons and property, and maintain public order; controlling prisoners of war; enforcing domestic law at the request of a host state during consensual peace-keeping operations; or when engaged in peacekeeping operations sanctioned by the United Nations pursuant to Chapter VII of the UN Charter'.

This argument comes at the expense of the potential of nonlethal weapons in armed conflicts to save more civilian lives in the long run. However, as Chris Mayer argues, despite this possible advantage, it is nevertheless the case that this risks noncombatants being deliberately or indiscriminately targeted for military, rather than law enforcement, purposes.[109] In this way, there is an incentive to set aside law enforcement restrictions on the use of force and use nonlethals on a wide spread and systematic basis according to IHL standards of precaution, proportionality and military advantage. As these standards are more permissive, where the HRL restrictions are set aside, then the perceived advantages of the use of nonlethals being a 'lesser evil' risk being undermined in that 'the excessive use of non-lethal weapons may result in no net improvement in rates of fatal injury when compared to lethal weapons in practice'.[110] It is suggested that the Moscow hostage crisis makes the intentional or indiscriminate use of nonlethal weapons in situations of conflict where the foreseeable effects of 'dangerous substances' cannot be controlled a major concern warranting continued restriction on the basis that their use may not confer any strategic or humanitarian advantage.[111] This is especially so where nonlethals are used as a 'force multiplier' or as a precursor to the use of lethal force, or, in other words, where groups are immobilised or incapacitated so as to separate lawful objectives from unlawful ones. Aside from the issue of killing fighters or combatants who are *hors de combat*, this risks rendering individuals incapable of defending or protecting themselves from the use of conventional weaponry around them.[112]

109 Chris Meyer (2007) cited in Kaurine, above n 98, 105.

110 S Sweetman, 'Report on the Attorney General's Conference on Less Than Lethal Weapons' (National Institute of Justice, Washington DC 1987), 26: 'If, for example, a less than lethal weapon is one-tenth as lethal as a handgun but is used ten times more frequently, an identical number of subjects will be fatally injured'.

111 Orbons, above n 106, 467–494.

112 Kaurine, above n 98, 106.

8 Regulating military operations abroad

The extraterritorial effect of human rights and the potential modalities of parallel application of the right to life under human rights law and international humanitarian law

Introduction

This section explores the jurisprudence relating to the extraterritorial application of human rights law with a focus on the right to life. In this way, the discussion attempts to overcome the theoretical and practical difficulties outlined in the critiques of the parallel applicability of humanitarian law and human rights law advanced by writers such as Modirzadeh and Dennis.[1] In this regard the purpose of the discussion here is to examine the ways in which the recent jurisprudence on this topic can further inform the discourse relating to the sequenced and parallel applicability of human rights law and humanitarian law in what has been described as the full-spectrum operational environment wherein military forces of states can be seen to pursue multiple 'lines of operations' including, *inter alia*, law enforcement and combat operations outside of their sovereign territory.[2]

---

1 Naz Modirzadeh, 'The Dark Sides of Convergence: A Pro-Civilian Critique of the Extraterritorial Application of Human Rights Law in Armed Conflict' in Raul Pedrozo (ed), *The War in Iraq: A Legal Analysis* (International Law Studies Series, Vol. 86, US Naval War College, 2010) 349–410; Michael Dennis, 'Application of Human Rights Treaties Extraterritorially in Times of Armed Conflict and Military Occupation (2005) 99 *American Journal of International Law* 119.

2 Nils Melzer 'Conceptual Distinction and Overlaps between Law Enforcement and the Conduct of Hostilities' in Terry Gill and Dieter Fleck, *The Handbook of the International Law of Military Operations* (Oxford University Press, 2010) 37 [3.02]: Melzer states that 'generic concept of hostilities refers to the resort to means and methods of warfare between parties to an armed conflict' and that the 'rules and principles of international law governing the conduct of hostilities form the legal paradigm of hostilities'. However, Melzer qualifies this by stating that, 'even in situations of armed conflict, not all forcible measures are necessarily part of the hostilities. On the contrary, a wide range of activities occurring in situations of armed conflict are governed exclusively by the law enforcement paradigm, such as the exercise of administrative, disciplinary, and judicial authority over occupied territory, the civilian population, and persons deprived of their liberty'. Thus, law enforcement operations are generally subject to basic principles of substantive human rights law, including, 'precautionary rules that require operations to be planned, prepared and conducted to minimize to the greatest extent possible the resort to lethal force'. Furthermore, operations to be carried out

As discussed earlier, a full-spectrum operational environment may be regarded as *status mixus* in that it may comprise a range of aspects such as international armed conflict, non-international armed conflict, belligerent occupation and extraterritorial military operations other than war such as peacekeeping. Indeed, as discussed earlier, the general concept of law enforcement can be described as 'all territorial and extraterritorial measures taken by a State or a collective entity to maintain or restore public security, law and order or to otherwise exercise its public power over individuals, objects, or territory'.[3] According to Melzer, the legal paradigm governing law enforcement operations is 'derived primarily from human rights law, and in times of armed conflict, also from international humanitarian law'. He goes on to say that '[a]lthough human rights law generally remains applicable during armed conflict, the precise content of the individual rights may have to be determined by reference to the *lex specialis* of international humanitarian law'.[4] However, it is suggested that the recent jurisprudence of international criminal tribunals discussed previously vis-à-vis situational status determination, as well as the jurisprudence of human rights mechanisms discussed later vis-à-vis the extraterritorial applicability of human rights, serve to elucidate further the modalities for the sequenced and parallel or simultaneous application of humanitarian and human rights law which is of major practical relevance for victims in *status mixus* situations of violence.

The extraterritorial applicability of human rights law is thus a hugely important area that has the potential to respond to the protection needs of individuals in unconventional or irregular operational environments with an international or transnational dimension that have in recent times seen much confusion and controversy surrounding the legality of 'targeted killing' or 'shoot-to-kill tactics', particularly when executed through what are often referred to as 'unmanned aerial vehicles' which are more commonly referred to as drones.[5] This section

in pursuit of legitimate aims, according to which lethal force may only be used for defined ends such as self-defence or defence of others against the imminent threat of death or serious injury, to prevent the perpetration of a particularly serious crime involving grave threat to life, to arrest a person presenting such a danger and resisting their authority or to prevent his or her escape. Generally, the IHRL principle of absolute or strict necessity according to which lethal force may be used against the target applies only when less extreme means are absolutely insufficient to achieve these objectives, and so the use of force must be proportionate to level and imminence of the threat. Thus, IHRL evaluates the use of force relative to the threat presented by an individual, rather than the status of an individual as per IHL.

3 Ibid.

4 Ibid., 36.

5 ECOSOC (UNCHR) 'Report of the Special Rapporteur, Philip Alston: extrajudicial, summary or arbitrary executions' (8 March 2006) UN Doc E/CN.4/2006/53, 46: This risk has been recognised by the UN Special Rapporteur on extrajudicial killings who noted that '[t]he use of shoot-to-kill tactics also imports, either consciously or otherwise, the language of international humanitarian law into situations which are essentially matters of law enforcement that international law requires be dealt with within the framework of human rights'. Furthermore, the UN Special Rapporteur argued that '[t]he notion that the law of armed conflict is an appropriate frame of reference for a Government seeking to deal with law enforcement issues is one that must be soundly rejected. To do otherwise is tantamount to

develops the previous discussion in relation to the import of the *Boškoski* guidelines for the sequencing of the paradigms of law enforcement and hostilities, or, in other words, providing guidance as to the point where there is a shift from a law-and-order paradigm to an armed conflict paradigm, particularly in relation to targeting by status as well as permissive standards on means and methods of force. This section explores the potential modalities and parameters of the extraterritorial applicability of the right to life in situations involving military operations inside and/or outside the conduct of hostilities, or, in other words, the interplay and complementarity between humanitarian law and human rights law in a full-spectrum operational environment.

Furthermore, this section explores the contemporary approaches taken to the extraterritorial application of the International Covenant on Civil and Political Rights, the American Declaration of the Rights of and Duties of Man, the American Convention on Human Rights and the European Convention on Human Rights, in particular by discussing how concepts of jurisdiction have been expanded from narrow territorial modes to personal modes of jurisdiction.

In contrast with writers such as Dennis,[6] it is suggested that a liberal approach to establishing a jurisdictional link on the basis of personal jurisdiction is a plausible approach to establishing subject matter jurisdiction and one which is necessary to fill gaps in protection that have become increasingly apparent in the course of unconventional or irregular situations of violence which may not reach the threshold of an armed conflict.

The International Covenant on Civil and Political Rights (ICCPR)

On the face of it, Article 2(1) limits the scope *ratione materiae* of the ICCPR by providing that each state party must 'respect and ensure' the convention rights to individuals who are 'within its territory *and* subject to its jurisdiction' [emphasis added]. Therefore, *prima facie*, the requirements of Article 2(1) are cumulative in that both elements must be satisfied before the ICCPR can be said to apply or, in other words, according to the plain and ordinary meaning of the text, state parties to this convention are not responsible for alleged violations that take place outside their territory and where they do not exercise effective control.[7]

The Human Rights Committee gave a broad interpretation of the applicability of the ICCPR in stating in its General Comment 31, which interpreted the conjunction 'and' to be a 'disjunctive conjunction' with the effect that jurisdiction may be established *ratione personae* or *ratione loci*. This means that a 'State Party must respect and ensure the rights laid down in the Covenant to anyone within the

---

allowing Governments to declare war simultaneously on a given group and on human rights in general'.

6 Dennis, above n 1, 461.

7 Ibid.

power or effective control of that State Party, even if not situated within the territory of the State Party'.[8] In stating that jurisdiction also refers 'to the relationship between the individual and the state in relation to a violation of any of the rights set forth in the Covenant, wherever they occurred', *Burgos v Uruguay*[9] affirmed this extraterritorial applicability of the ICCPR on the basis of '*de facto* personal jurisdiction'.[10] According to the Individual Opinion of Tomuschat, the rationale for broadly construing Article 2 paragraph (1) ICCPR was that to construe the words 'within its territory' according to their strict literal meaning would result in the absurd result of granting 'States parties unfettered discretionary power to carry out wilful and deliberate attacks against the freedom and personal integrity against their citizens living abroad'.[11] Thus, according to this interpretation, the legal obligations of states under the ICCPR could be invoked for the actions of their national forces acting as part of multinational peacekeeping or stabilisation forces involved in small-scale military operations even where they exercise no effective territorial control.[12]

Notwithstanding Dennis's criticisms of the reasoning[13] of the Human Rights Committee, as well as the authoritativeness[14] of its General Comment, it has been

---

8 UNHRC General Comment No 31, 'The nature of the general legal obligation imposed on States Parties to the Covenant' (26 May 2004) UN Doc. CCPR/C/21/Rev 1/Add 13, 10: 'State parties are required by Article 2, Paragraph 1, to respect and to ensure the Covenant rights to all persons who may be within their territory and to all persons subject to their jurisdiction. This means that a State Party must respect and ensure the rights laid down in the Covenant to anyone within the power or effective control of that State Party, even if not situated within the territory of the State Party . . . This principle also applies to those within the power or effective control of the forces of a State Party acting outside its territory, regardless of the circumstances in which such power or effective control was obtained, such as forces constituting a national contingent of a State Party assigned to an international peace-keeping or peace-enforcement operation'.

9 *Sergio Euben Lopez Burgos v Uruguay* (1981) UNHRC Communication No R.12/52, UN Doc Supp No 40 (A/36/40), 12.2.

10 Nils Melzer, *Targeted Killing in International Law* (Oxford University Press, 2009), 134.

11 *Burgos v Uruguay*, above n 9: Identical Individual Opinion of Tomuschat; See Melzer, Ibid., 125.

12 UNHRC General Comment No 31, above n 8; Dennis, above n 1, 471.

13 Ibid: According to Dennis, the *travaux préparatoires* of the ICCPR, the term of art, 'within its territory' under Article 2(1) was deemed to be such an important limitation on the scope of a state's obligations that proposals to delete it during its drafting stages were rejected. Accordingly, this undermines the interpretation that the conjunction 'and' in Article 2(1) is to be interpreted as a 'disjunctive conjunction'. At page 459 Dennis argues that '[t]he obligations assumed by states under the main international human rights instruments were never intended to apply extraterritorially during periods of armed conflicts. Nor were they intended to replace the *lex specialis* of international humanitarian law. Extending the protections provided under international human rights instruments to situations of international armed conflict and military occupation offers a dubious route toward increased state compliance with international norms'; See also Replies of the Government of the Netherlands to the Concerns Expressed by the Human Rights Committee, 19UN Doc CCPR/CO/72/NET/Add1 (2003) and Statement of Conrad Harper, Legal Adviser, Department of State, 20, UN Doc CCPR/C/ SR.1405 (1995).

14 Dennis, above n 1, 471; UNHRC, 'Summary Record of the 2380th Meeting on 18 July 2006: Consideration of Reports Under Article 40 of the Covenant' (27 July 2006) UN Doc CCPR/C/SR.2380: Under Article 5 paragraph (4) of the ICCPR, the HRC has the authority to 'forward its views to the State Party concerned and to the individual.' According

suggested that 'whilst there was no binding procedure for determining the correct interpretation of human rights under the ICCPR, [. . .] Article 40 gave the HRC the power to issue findings that nevertheless have 'considerable authoritative status'.[15] Furthermore, it is suggested that the HRC's 'grammatical re-interpretation' has gained more authoritative status given that it has been reflected in the decisions of the ICJ in its *Advisory Opinion in Legal Consequences of a Wall*[16] and *Democratic Republic of the Congo v Uganda*.[17]

It is suggested that the model of '*de facto* personal jurisdiction' that has emerged in the decisions of the Human Rights Committee represents an important development in the face of the protection needs of individuals within contemporary unconventional and irregular situations of violence, particularly with regard to the use of 'unmanned aerial combat vehicles' for the targeted killing in situations which may not reach the threshold criteria for an armed conflict. As noted by Marko Milanovic, despite the previous United States Department of Defense and Department of State legal stance in disputing the extraterritorial applicability of human rights treaties, the Fourth US ICCPR Report (in addition to its COIN manual) potentially indicates a shift towards accepting extraterritorial applicability of the ICCPR to relevant situations within full-spectrum operations.[18]

---

to a statement made to the HRC by Robert Harris, a legal advisor to the US Department of State, under Article 40 paragraph (4) of the ICCPR, the HRC merely has the power to 'study the reports submitted by the States Parties' and then 'transmit its reports, and such general comments as it may consider appropriate, to the States Parties'. He goes on to argue, '[i]n no way does this provision give the HRC the power to issue interpretations of the ICCPR that are legally binding upon States Parties in the sense that their legal obligations under the ICCPR can be affected or modified'.

15 UNHRC (UN Doc CCPR/C/SR.2380), ibid; Dennis, above n 1, 459.

16 *Legal Consequences of the Construction of a Wall in the Occupied Palestinian Territory* (Advisory Opinion) 2004 ICJ Rep 136, 108–111. The ICCPR 'is applicable in respect of acts done by a State in the exercise of its jurisdiction outside its own territory'.

17 *Armed Activities on the Territory of the Congo (Democratic Republic of the Congo v. Uganda)* (Judgment) [2005] ICJ Rep 168, 25 and 216.

18 John B Bellinger III, Legal Advisor, US Department of State, United States' Oral Responses to the Questions Asked by the Committee Against Torture (May 5, 2006) <www.state.gov/j/drl /rls/68561.htm> Marko Milanovic, 'US Fourth ICCPR Report' *EJIL-Talk!* (2012). 'With respect to the application of the Covenant and the international law of armed conflict (also referred to as international humanitarian law or "IHL"), the United States has not taken the position that the Covenant does not apply "in time of war." Indeed, a time of war does not suspend the operation of the Covenant to matters within its scope of application' (para 506); 'More complex issues arise with respect to the relevant body of law that determines whether a State's actions in the actual conduct of an armed conflict comport with international law. Under the doctrine of *lex specialis*, the applicable rules for the protection of individuals and conduct of hostilities in armed conflict are typically found in international humanitarian law, including the Geneva Conventions of 1949, the Hague Regulations of 1907, and other international humanitarian law instruments, as well as in the customary international law of armed conflict. In this context, it is important to bear in mind that international human rights law and the law of armed conflict are in many respects complementary and mutually reinforcing. These two bodies of law contain many similar protections. For example prohibitions on torture and cruel treatment exist in both, and the drafters in each area have drawn from the other in developing aspects of new instruments; the Commentaries

The American Declaration of the Rights of and Duties of Man and the American Convention on Human Rights

In a similar fashion to the approach taken by the United Nations Human Rights Committee, the extraterritorial applicability of human rights under the Inter-American system are not limited to jurisdictional links founded on territorial control, but rather '*de facto* personal jurisdiction' which will now be explained in more detail.[19] Article 1 of the American Convention on Human Rights states that '[t]he States Parties to this Convention undertake to respect the rights and freedoms recognized herein and to ensure to all persons subject to their jurisdiction the free and full exercise of those rights and freedoms, without any discrimination [. . .]'

It is suggested that Article 1 ACHR has been construed broadly so as to allow for the extraterritorial applicability of the nonderogable right to life on the basis of the exercise of state power or effective control over an individual. This is because according to a key resolution regarding the effect of the American Declaration on the Rights and Duties of Man adopted by the Organization of American States, the right to life is deemed to be a universal and inalienable right.[20] Accordingly, this resolution provides that 'the essential rights of man are not derived from the fact that he is a national of a certain State, but are based upon attributes of his personality' and are thus not limited territorially as there is no jurisdiction clause.[21] On the basis of Article 29 (d) of the ACHR which provides that the provisions of the convention shall not 'be interpreted as . . . excluding or limiting the effect that the American Declaration of the Rights and Duties of Man and other international acts of the same nature may have', it is suggested that this resolution serves to allow for a broad approach to subject matter jurisdiction under Article 1.[22] This is significant in the context of contemporary situations of vio-

---

to Additional Protocol II to the Geneva Conventions make clear that a number of provisions in the Protocol were modelled on comparable provisions in the ICCPR. Determining the international law rule that applies to a particular action taken by a government in the context of an armed conflict is a fact-specific determination, which cannot be easily generalized, and raises especially complex issues in the context of non-international armed conflicts occurring within a State's own territory' (para 507). Harold Koh, Legal Advisor, U.S. Department of State, Remarks at the Annual Meeting of the American Society of International Law: The Obama Administration and International Law (March 25, 2010) <www.state.gov/s/l/releases/remarks/139119.htm>.

19 *Salas and Others v United States* (Report No 31/93: US military action in Panama) Inter-American Commission on Human Rights, Case 10/573, OEA/Ser.L/V/II.85 Doc 9 rev at 312 (October 14 1993) 6; Melzer, above n 10, 126 & 128; Jann Kleffner, 'Human Rights and International Humanitarian Law: General Issues' in Gill and Fleck, above n 718, 71.

20 American Declaration of the Rights and Duties of Man, Organization of American States Resolution XXX, adopted by the Ninth International Conference of American States (1948), reprinted in Basic Documents Pertaining to Human Rights in the Inter-American System, OEA/Ser.L.V/II.82 doc 6 rev 1 at 17 (1992).

21 Ibid.

22 Melzer, above n 10, 126.

lence in that the Inter-American Commission on Human Rights, in its Report on Terrorism, asserted that 'a state's human rights obligations are not dependent upon a person's nationality or presence within a particular geographic area, but rather extend to all persons subject to that state's authority and control'.[23]

Indeed, in *Armando Alejandre et al. v Cuba*, the commission reasoned that '[b]ecause individual rights are inherent to the human being, all the American States are obligated to respect the protected rights of any person subject to their jurisdiction' which is to be broadly construed so as to include 'extraterritorial actions, when the person is present in the territory of a State but subject to the control of another State, generally through the actions of that State's agents abroad'.[24] Thus in *Alejandre* the commission found that the attack by agents of the Cuban state that led to the deaths of individuals in international airspace effectively constituted an 'exercise of power and authority' of the state over those individuals, and this constituted a jurisdictional link for the purposes of rendering applicable its human rights obligations.[25] Accordingly, this approach of establishing a jurisdictional link on the basis of the exercise of power and control over individuals can avoid lacunae in substantive protection and international oversight in situations where extraterritorial military operations do not reach the threshold for the application of international humanitarian law.

The European Convention on Human Rights

The remainder of this discussion will now focus on developments in the area of the extraterritorial applicability of human rights within the European regional system. Despite recent developments in this area, there remain important differences between the European and Inter-American regional systems of human rights protections, and so the discussion here not only argues for the further liberalisation of the emerging model of '*de facto* personal jurisdiction', but also uses

---

23 *Report on Terrorism and Human Rights*, Inter-American Commission on Human Rights, OEA/Ser.L/V/II.116 Doc 5 rev 1 corr (22 October 2002) 44.

24 *Armando Alejandre et al. v Cuba* (Report No 86/99) Inter-American Commission on Human Rights, Case 11/589 OAS/Ser.L/V/II.104 (29 September 1999) 23: '[a]lthough this usually refers to persons who are within the territory of a State, in certain instances it can refer to extraterritorial actions, when the person is present in the territory of a State but subject to the control of another State, generally through the actions of that State's agents abroad. In principle, the investigation refers not to the nationality of the alleged victim or his presence in a particular geographic area, but to whether, in those specific circumstances, the State observed the rights of a person subject to its authority and control'.

25 Ibid., 25: 'the victims died as a consequence of direct actions taken by agents of the Cuban State in international airspace. The fact that the events took place outside Cuban jurisdiction does not limit the Commission's competence *ratione loci*, because, as previously stated, when agents of a State, whether military or civilian, exercise power and authority over persons outside national territory, the State's obligation to respect human rights continues – in this case the rights enshrined in the American Declaration. The Commission finds conclusive evidence that agents of the Cuban State, although outside their territory, placed the civilian pilots of the "Brothers to the Rescue" organization under their authority'.

European human rights jurisprudence to explore further the degree to which the right to life may apply within an operational theatre involving hostilities, or, in other words, the degree to which the right to life can be 'divided and tailored' according to the particular conditions within a *status mixus* environment.

According to Article 1 of the ECHR, High Contracting Parties 'shall secure to everyone within their jurisdiction the rights and freedoms defined in Section I of [the] Convention'. In contrast with the previously mentioned approaches and until the recent decision in *Al-Skeini*, the European Court of Human Rights in *Banković* permitted the extraterritorial applicability of the convention only in exceptional circumstances, namely where a state had 'effective overall control' over an area outside its national territory as a consequence of lawful or unlawful military action.[26] In this way, the obligation to secure convention rights was seen to arise from 'effective overall control' over territory, as exercised directly through a state's armed forces, or even through a subordinate local administration.[27] Allowing for the extraterritorial application of the convention in the exceptional circumstance that a contracting party had effective control over the territory of another state was seen to be the only plausible type of situation where a state could be expected to ensure the implementation of its convention obligations and, conversely, where violations of convention rights could be rendered attributable to a state in a practical sense.[28] Thus, according to *Banković*, the convention could not be 'divided and tailored' according to the particular circumstances of each case because Article 1 entailed the obligation to secure all rights that exist under the convention and, practically speaking, this requires effective territorial control, the existence of which is to be assessed on a case-by-case basis.[29] Furthermore, the court in *Banković* viewed the convention's jurisdiction to be limited *ratione loci* for the reason that it is primarily 'an instrument of European public order' and 'a multi-lateral treaty operating, subject to Article 56 of the Convention, in an essentially regional context and notably in the legal space (*espace juridique)* of the Contracting States'.[30] On the basis of this narrow

26 *Banković and Others v Belgium and Others* (Application No 52207/99) ECHR (Grand Chamber) 2001-XII 890, [61] & [67]; *Soering v UK* (Application No 14038/88) (1989) Series A No 161, [86]; *Ilaşcu and Others v Moldova and Russia* (Application no 48787/99) ECHR 2004-VII, [312].

27 *Loizidou v Turkey* (Application No 15318/89) (Preliminary Objections) Series A 310 [1995] ECHR 10 [62]; *Cyprus v Turkey* (Application no 25781/94) (1996) DR 86-A, 13, [76] – [77].

28 *Loizidou v Turkey*, Ibid., [78]; *Banković v Belgium*, above n 26, [80]; *Al-Skeini and Others v UK* (Application No 55721/07) ECHR (Grand Chamber) 7 July 2005 [141]–[142]: the ECtHR has traditionally ruled that where the territory of contracting party to the ECHR is occupied by another contracting party, that occupying state should in principle be accountable for violations within the occupied territory so as to prevent a 'vacuum' of protection within the 'convention legal space'.

29 *Banković v Belgium*, above n 26; *Al-Skeini v UK*, Ibid., [131] and [132].

30 *Al-Skeini v UK*, Ibid., [109]; *Loizidou v Turkey*, above n 27, [75]; *Soering v UK*, above n 26, [86].

approach to jurisdiction, the court in *Banković* found the aerial bombardment of Belgrade by Council of Europe members of NATO to be an insufficient basis for the extraterritorial application of the ECHR.

The discussion now will turn to the court's judgments following *Banković* which, although indicating a relaxation of this strict territorial principle, also call into question whether *Banković* is still good law, albeit on its own or similar facts, that is, aerial attacks without any form of territorial control or exercise of public powers per se. Post-*Banković* jurisprudence shows the progressive development of the exercise of state agent authority and control over individuals or circumscribed areas and demonstrates that this is a plausible basis upon which convention obligations can be rendered applicable extraterritorially, even outside the conventional *espace juridique*. Examples include situations where diplomatic and consular agents exercise authority and control over individuals on foreign territory[31] and where an individual is taken into custody by a state's agents operating abroad and so can be deemed to be under the control of those agents and therefore under the authority and jurisdiction of a contracting party to the convention.[32]

Al-Skeini is an important decision as it provides an illustration of the modalities and parameters of the right to life in a full-spectrum operational environment and the complementarity between human rights law and international humanitarian law. It will be submitted that, at the very least, this is indicative of the

31 *Al-Skeini v UK*, Ibid., [134] ; *Banković and Others v Belgium and Others*, above n 26, [73]; See also, *X v Federal Republic of Germany* (Application No 1611/62) (1965) 8 Yearbook 158 (EComHR), [158] and [169].

32 *Al-Skeini v UK*, Ibid., [136]; *Öcalan v Turkey (*Application no 46221/99) ECHR 12 May 2005, [91]: In *Öcalan* the court found that 'directly after being handed over to the Turkish officials by the Kenyan officials, the applicant was effectively under Turkish authority and therefore within the "jurisdiction" of that State for the purposes of Article 1 of the Convention, even though in this instance Turkey exercised its authority outside its territory'; *Issa and Others v Turkey* (Application No 31821/96) ECHR (Second Section) 16 November 2004: in *Issa*, the court stated that had there been sufficient evidence that Turkish soldiers had taken the applicants' relatives into custody in Northern Iraq, taken them to a nearby cave and executed them, then the deceased would have been within Turkish jurisdiction by virtue of the soldiers' authority and control over them. In Al-Saadoon paras [86]–[89], we can observe an attenuated form of the spatial model of jurisdiction, as rather than requiring 'effective control' over an area, it permits a jurisdictional link to be established on the basis of effective control over a place; Marko Milanovic, 'European Court Decides Al-Skeini and Al-Jedda' [2011] *EJIL- Talk!* <www.ejiltalk.org/european-court-decides-al-skeini-and-al-jedda/> accessed 1 October 2013: according to Milanovic (EJIL Talk) the court has allowed for the base of effective control to become ever more attenuated or reduced. In this case, the court held that two Iraqi nationals detained in British-controlled military prisons in Iraq fell within the jurisdiction of the United Kingdom, because the United Kingdom exercised total and exclusive control over the prisons and the individuals detained in them; *Medvedyev and Others v France* (Application No 3394/03) ECHR (Grand Chamber) 29 March 2010, [67]: the court held that the applicants were within French jurisdiction due to the exercise by French agents of full and exclusive control over a ship and its crew from the time of its interception in international waters.

role that human rights mechanisms may play in ensuring the indirect application of humanitarian law within municipal legal systems.[33] The applicants in this case were relatives of the deceased victims, and they claimed that the procedural aspect of the right to life under Article 2 of the ECHR, namely the obligation to carry out effective investigations where there have been deprivations of life, was applicable because the victims were within the jurisdiction of the United Kingdom under Article 1 of the ECHR at the time of death.[34] The UK government responded that with the exception of the sixth applicant who was killed by British armed forces in a British military prison, the deaths of the other five applicants were related to acts that took place in the south of Iraq. In this regard, the UK government argued that it had no 'effective control' over this area at the time of the alleged violations, which in any case was not within the *espace juridique* of the convention.[35] Thus, relying on the decision in *Banković*, the UK government claimed that these five applicants were outside the United Kingdom's jurisdiction pursuant to Article 1 ECHR[36] because the shooting of the victims in the course of military security operations per se did not constitute a sufficient jurisdictional link as no 'distinction could be drawn in this respect between a death resulting from a bombing and one resulting from a shooting in the course of a ground operation'.[37] Moreover, the UK government claimed that international humanitarian law norms pertaining to the existence of a state of belligerent occupation as well as the obligations of an occupying power could not be used to interpret Article 1 ECHR and thus determine the extraterritorial applicability of the convention. In this way, the UK government submitted that 'legal authority' over the victims could not be derived *de jure* from Article 43 of the Hague Regulations to 'take all measures in [its] power to restore and ensure, as far as possible,

33 Common Article 1 to the Geneva Conventions 1949: IHL provides that 'High Contracting Parties undertake to respect and ensure respect' for the Geneva Conventions of 1949 'in all circumstances' such as by observing the duty under Article 146 GCIV 'to enact any legislation necessary to provide effective penal sanctions for . . . grave breaches' and 'to search for persons alleged to have committed, or to have ordered to be committed, such grave breaches, and shall bring such persons, regardless of their nationality, before its own courts'. Article 87(3) of API supplements these obligations by requiring 'High Contracting Parties and Parties to the conflict [to] require any commander who is aware that subordinates or other persons under his control are going to commit or have committed a breach of the Conventions or of this Protocol . . . to initiate disciplinary or penal action against violators thereof'.

34 *Al-Skeini v UK*, above n 28, 95.

35 Ibid., 112: The UK government and UK House of Lords, as it then was, argued that there was no 'effective control of an area' on which to base jurisdiction in this case as Iraq is not within the *espace juridique* of the ECHR and in any case, the United Kingdom did not have 'effective control' over any part of Iraq during the time of the alleged convention violations given that the size of the UK armed forces was small in relation to the size of the area and population in southeast Iraq and given the conditions of widespread criminal activity, terrorist attacks and tribal clashes prevalent at the time.

36 Ibid., 101.

37 Ibid., 116.

public order and safety, while respecting, unless absolutely prevented, the laws in force' in occupied Iraq, and, furthermore, that there was no coherent basis for determining the applicability of the convention upon 'the particular activity that a soldier was engaged in at the time of the alleged violation, whether street patrol, ground offensive or aerial bombardment'.[38]

The Grand Chamber in *Al-Skeini* systematically rejected the arguments put forward by the UK government. First, it rejected the argument that the convention can in no circumstances apply outside of the conventional *espace juridique* on the basis that its jurisprudence relating to 'overall territorial control' as well as 'State agent authority and control' has never categorically applied any such restriction.[39]

Second, the Grand Chamber qualified the UK government's reliance on a strict reading of the territorial principle in *Banković* not only by giving more weight to the jurisdictional link of 'state agent authority and control', but also by interpreting this particular line of authority in a novel fashion, namely by stating that it 'does not consider that jurisdiction [in the cases of *Öcalan*, *Issa*, *Al-Saadoon and Mufdhi*, and *Medvedyev*] arose solely from the control exercised by the Contracting State over the buildings, aircraft or ship in which the individuals were held'. Rather, the Grand Chamber reasoned that the 'decisive' issue in determining whether or not there had been an exercise of jurisdiction for the purposes of Article 1 in these cases was 'the exercise of physical power and control over the person in question'.[40] Accordingly, the Grand Chamber in *Al-Skeini* found 'a jurisdictional link between the deceased and the United Kingdom'[41] on the basis that the United Kingdom's armed forces 'engaged in security operations [and] exercised authority and control over individuals killed in the course of such security operations'.[42]

This decision is thus not to be equated with the pure model of functional or *de facto* personal jurisdiction as manifest in the previously mentioned case of

38 Ibid., 114, 117 and 119. The UK government argued, instead, that UK armed forces were regulated by IHL and thus soldiers were subject to UK domestic criminal law. In this way, the UK government and the HOL argued that under the law of occupation, namely the Hague Regulations, as an occupying power, it was not obliged to secure the rights under the ECHR to individuals in southeast Iraq as they were not laws in force there and, moreover, the Hague Regulations prevented the United Kingdom from changing Iraqi law so as to conform with the UK's domestic and international legal obligations. The UK's obligations under the Hague Regulations were to respect the laws in force in Iraq 'unless absolutely prevented'. The ICC also had jurisdiction to prosecute war crimes in the event that the UK government should be unable or unwilling to prosecute. In addition, there were remedies available in tort before the UK civil courts for victims and their relatives with respect to any injury or loss caused by UK agents or authorities abroad under the principles of private international law.

39 Ibid., 142.

40 Ibid., 136 and 137.

41 Ibid., 149.

42 Ibid., 150.

Alejandre. In contrast, the Grand Chamber further framed this 'jurisdictional link' as contingent, not on the UK government's 'effective control of an area' as *per Banković*, but rather on its exercise of 'public powers', which came in the form of its 'responsibility for the maintenance of security in South East Iraq', which further manifested itself in the form of 'security operations'.[43] Therefore, in *Al-Skeini* public powers were broadly construed to include the maintenance of security in support of the civil administration in Iraq. Thus, it is now questionable whether this extended approach to jurisdiction overrules the territorial principle in *Banković* in that, according to *Al-Skeini*, the use of force alone does not constitute a sufficient jurisdictional link unless (a) there is the exercise of some public powers which are normally exercised by the sovereign state or (b) the individual is taken into custody by the state agents.[44] Therefore this raises an important question concerning extraterritorial jurisdiction, namely, if the United Kingdom had conducted security operations without exercising any general 'public powers', would there have been a sufficient jurisdictional link on which to impose the positive obligation to ensure the right to life?[45] *Jaloud v The Netherlands* seems to suggest movements in this direction. In *Jaloud*, the ECtHR found that although Dutch troops were stationed in an area of southeastern Iraq where the forces were under the command of an officer from the United Kingdom, the Netherlands assumed responsibility for providing security in that area, to the exclusion of other participating states, and retained 'full command' over its contingent. This was deemed sufficient to comprise 'the exercise of some of the public powers normally to be exercised by a sovereign government'.[46] Importantly, Sari notes that *Jaloud* indicates that full command constitutes a sufficient link between the state and its armed forces operating in a multinational context so that the activities of national contingents do not fall outside the scope of Article 1 on the grounds that they act as part of a multinational force pursuant to foreign orders in pursuit of an international mandate.[47] As to the form that public powers took in this case, in contrast with *Al-Skeini* where it was found that the United Kingdom assumed authority for the maintenance of security in southeast Iraq and that individuals were killed in the course of security operations carried out by its troops pursuant

43 Ibid.

44 The decision in *Al-Skeini* is thus much broader than *Banković* (above n 26, [71]) which states that 'the case-law of the Court demonstrates that its recognition of the exercise of extraterritorial jurisdiction by a Contracting State is exceptional: it has done so when the respondent State, through the effective control of the relevant territory and its inhabitants abroad as a consequence of military occupation or through the consent, invitation or acquiescence of the Government of that territory, exercises all or some of the public powers normally to be exercised by that Government' [emphasis added].

45 *Al-Skeini v UK*, above n 28, [194]; Milanovic, above n 32.

46 *Jaloud v The Netherlands* (Application no. 47708/08) ECHR (Grand Chamber) 20 November 2014, paras 129–135 and 149.

47 Aurel Sari, 'Jaloud v Netherlands: New Directions in Extra-Territorial Military Operations' (2014) *EJIL: Talk!* <www.ejiltalk.org/jaloud-v-netherlands-new-directions-in-extra-territorial-military-operations/> accessed 27 June 2016.

to that assumption of authority, the court in *Jaloud* found that with the 'consent, invitation or acquiescence' of the Coalition Provisional Authority, it oversaw the Iraqi Civil Defence Corps at the checkpoint, and so asserted authority and control over persons passing through a checkpoint. This constituted a sufficient jurisdictional link between the Netherlands and the individual killed. In terms of exercising public powers, what mattered to the court was the practical position on the ground in terms of the powers which the Netherlands was actually purporting to exercise and not the mandate, legality or legal basis of its operations.[48] According to Sari, although this implies a welcome broadening of the personal rather than the geographical model of extraterritorial jurisdiction, the court does not yet admit a purely functional or 'cause and effect' notion of jurisdiction, and so the use of a weapon alone is still insufficient to bring the target within the jurisdiction of the state concerned. Nevertheless, Sari points out that this renders this jurisdictional basis 'fluid and uncertain' in that 'checkpoints do not have to be fixed or permanent . . . [t]hey can be mobile and set up at short notice' and he suggests that 'the Court will find a way to address these questions in a principled manner to avoid the drift towards "cause and effect" jurisdiction'.[49] Arguably, *Al-Skeini* and *Jaloud* can be seen as important but insufficient developments in subject matter jurisdiction given that it leaves unjustifiable gaps in legal protection.

Third, the decision in *Al-Skeini* suggests that the humanitarian law of occupation may not inform the general determination of the existence of jurisdictional links for the purposes of establishing the extraterritorial applicability of the right to life. In particular, the framing of 'public powers' to include basic security and public order operations on behalf of a transitional government suggests that this mode of jurisdiction is not predicated on the territory being 'actually placed under the authority of the hostile army' as per Article 42 of the Hague Regulations. This suggests that the conditions precedent for a state of occupation to exist under international humanitarian law and domestic military manuals may not preclude the application of human rights obligations that are relevant and appropriate to the particular exercise of state agent authority and control in question.[50] In other words, it is suggested that the Grand Chamber's framing

48 *Jaloud*, above n 46, 129.

49 Sari, above n 47.

50 UK Ministry of Defence, *The Manual of the Law of Armed Conflict* (Oxford University Press, 2005) 275–276: according to the UK *Manual of the Law of Armed Conflict*, a state of occupation exists where 'firstly, the former government must have been rendered incapable of publicly exercising its authority in that area; and secondly, the occupying power must be in a position to substitute its own authority for that of the former government'; *Prosecutor v Naletilić and Martinović* (Trial Judgment) ICTY-98-34-T (31 March 2003) 217 and 218: the Trial Chamber set out some guidelines for the existence of a state of occupation under Article 42 of the Hague Regulations based on the following indicia of an occupying power's authority as it extends to areas 'actually controlled' and thus which 'ceases to apply where the occupying power no longer exercises any actual authority over the occupied area': 'the occupying power must be in a position to substitute its own authority for that of the occupied authorities, which must have been rendered incapable of functioning publicly'; 'the

of 'public powers' may not be equated with 'exercising the functions of a Government' or even territorial or civil administration as provided for in Article 6 GC IV, or even the definition of occupation as provided for in Article 42 of the Hague Regulations. In this way, even though Article 6 GC IV extends the application of enumerated provisions of GCIV beyond 'the general close of military operations', this does not act as an obstacle to the extraterritorial applicability of the right to life.

The modalities of the extraterritorial applicability of the right to life will be discussed later, but for present purposes, it is suggested that the approach taken by the Grand Chamber in *Al-Skeini* was necessary, but not sufficient, when viewed against the dictum in *Naletilić and Martinović* that 'the law of occupation as it affects "individuals" as civilians protected under Geneva Convention IV does not require that the occupying power has actual authority' because otherwise 'civilians would be left, during an intermediate period, with less protection than that attached to them once occupation is established', and accordingly this protection 'becomes applicable to individuals, ie to the protected persons, as they fall into the hands of the Occupying Power'.[51] Thus the development of the doctrine of state agent authority and control in *Al-Skeini* marks a liberal expansion of human rights protections into full-spectrum operational environments, whilst also raising important questions that can serve to foster further normative progression in this field vis-à-vis the Grand Chamber's qualified appreciation of *de facto* personal jurisdiction, which, as indicated earlier, is not entirely consistent with the approaches taken in *Alejandre* as well as *Naletilić and Martinović*. Namely, as discussed, these approaches, respectively, provide for jurisdictional links where 'agents of a State, whether military or civilian, exercise power and authority over persons outside national territory' or where 'protected persons . . . fall into the hands of the Occupying Power'.

A major issue now is whether *Banković* is still good law. One way of looking at it may be that *Al-Skeini* can be distinguished from *Banković* and therefore does not overrule it. In this way, *Banković* would still apply in factual situations

---

enemy's forces have surrendered, been defeated or withdrawn. In this respect, battle areas may not be considered as occupied territory. However, sporadic local resistance, even successful, does not affect the reality of occupation'; 'the occupying power has a sufficient force present, or the capacity to send troops within a reasonable time to make the authority of the occupying power felt'; 'a temporary administration has been established over the territory'; 'the occupying power has issued and enforced directions to the civilian population'.

51 *Naletilić and Martinović* (Trial Judgment), Ibid., 219 and 221: On its reading of the Commentary to Geneva Convention IV, the Trial Chamber made clear that the application of the law of occupation under GC IV to the civilian population is broader than Article 42 of the Hague Regulations in that GC IV 'becomes applicable to individuals, i.e. to the protected persons, as they fall into the hands of the Occupying Power' and so '[t]here is no intermediate period between what might be termed the invasion phase and the inauguration of a stable regime of occupation'; Jean S Pictet (ed), *Geneva Convention relative to the Protection of Civilian Persons in Time of War* (International Committee of the Red Cross, Geneva 1958) ('Commentary IV') 60.

where there is just aerial bombardment, but no 'effective control of an area' or 'exercise of some public powers normally to be exercised by a sovereign government' – in other words, aerial bombardment or the use of air power alone would not constitute a sufficient 'jurisdictional link' between the persons affected by the bombardment and the contracting party carrying it out.[52] This would mean that aerial attacks by manned and unmanned aerial vehicles in countries such as Libya, Pakistan, Iraq and Afghanistan would not fall within the jurisdiction of the state carrying them out, and would therefore constitute a major gap in protection.[53]

However, for what it is worth, the judgment of Justice Leggatt in *Al-Sadoon v Secretary of State* contains a discussion from a UK High Court judge that *Banković* can no longer be relied upon as good law. At the time of writing, this issue has yet to be addressed by the European Court of Human Rights itself. Justice Leggatt approached the issue as a matter of principle and dismissed arguments that 'instantaneous extra-territorial' uses of force to kill are not sufficient to constitute a jurisdictional link per se for the applicability of Article 2 ECHR. In this way, and as understood by the UK Court of Appeal, Justice Leggatt appears to have suggested that the exercise state agent power and control, for example shooting someone dead without arresting them first, constitutes a free-standing basis for bringing that individual within the jurisdiction of the ECHR. However, it is suggested that Leggatt's reasoning did not unequivocally disentangle the issue of state agent authority and control from the connected issue of public powers, which appears to have formed a significant backdrop to his reasoning, and so the UK Court of Appeal read it to suggest that the negative obligation under Article 2 to refrain from unlawful killing could apply where an individual was not in a state's custody and where the state is not exercising any public powers in the territory, that is where a state exercises legal authority or, according to Leggatt, merely where it uses physical force abroad. This approach appears logically compelling. Why should there be a jurisdictional link and a finding of an Article 2 violation in cases where soldiers have arrested a person before proceeding to shoot them, but not in those cases where soldiers shoot someone before arresting them? The former approach to jurisdiction would appear to offer a perverse incentive to kill rather than arrest and capture, particularly in those situations that have not reached the threshold of a non-international armed conflict as outlined and discussed in Chapter 3. However, the UK Court of Appeal stated that had the Grand Chamber in *Al-Skeini* wished to lay down such a broad exception based on physical power and control, independent of the exercise of public powers, then it would have set this out as a clear alternative basis for finding jurisdiction. Instead, from an examination of the reasoning

52 Kleffner, above n 19, 70.

53 Milanovic, above n 32. Further compounding this interpretation is the issue that *Issa* and *Öcalan* concerned situations where the 'State through its agents exercises control and authority over an individual' in the form of custody. Custody alone was deemed to be such a 'decisive' 'exercise of physical power and control' that it may constitute a 'jurisdictional link' per se.

in *Al-Skeini*, the UK Court of Appeal found that it did not intend to base a jurisdictional link solely on the use of lethal force, as Leggatt's reasoning would appear to suggest, but rather that there should be an element of control over an individual prior to the use of lethal force.[54] Justice Leggatt reasoned that despite the lack of transparency in its reasoning, in recognising the exercise of physical power and control over an individual as a basis of jurisdiction, the Grand Chamber in *Al-Skeini* effectively departed from its previous decision in *Banković* which held that those killed by bombing alone are not capable of coming within a state's jurisdiction.[55] Leggatt held that the principle of physical power and control and the principle of effective territorial control were in direct contradiction with each other to the extent that *Al-Skeini* effectively overruled *Banković*.[56] Accordingly, the UK Court of Appeal took issue with this proposition by stating that it was a conclusion which could only be drawn by the European Court of Human Rights, and not by a national court.[57] However, on the issue of overruling *Banković*, Justice Leggatt stated that the principle of jurisdiction based on the physical power and control was derived from the UK Supreme Court in *Smith v The Ministry of Defence* which in turn was expressly based on the restated principle of control over individuals in *Al-Skeini*.[58] Accordingly, Justice Leggatt stated that the High Court was bound to follow the Supreme Court's adoption of this particular *Al-Skeini* principle, rather than the principles of effective territorial control and the 'indivisibility' of convention rights in *Banković*.

Nevertheless, at the time of writing, this contentious issue has been dealt with at the level of the UK Court of Appeal, and so it remains to be seen whether Leggatt's seemingly broad extension of extra-territorial jurisdiction will be explicitly accepted by the UK Supreme Court as well as the European Court of Human Rights. In reaching its decision, the UK Court of Appeal in *Al-Sadoon* noted the 'real and difficult problems as to how human rights law under the Convention can be accommodated to the realities of international peacekeeping and situations of armed conflict' as well as the policy considerations involved in seeking to restrict the territorial scope of the Convention so as to avoid floods of claims before UK courts in the event of overseas military operations.[59] The two main issues that come into conflict are firstly trying to establish a conceptual model of jurisdiction that is logical and principled, and secondly, trying to marry this with policy considerations that increasingly, at least in the UK, seek to restrict the extra-territorial applicability of the Convention to military operations

54 *Al-Sadoon and Others v Secretary of State for Defence* [2015] EWHC 715 (Admin), 101, 102, 103. *Al-Saadoon & Ors v Secretary of State for Defence* [2016] EWCA Civ 811, paras 59–69.

55 Ibid., 56, 57, 102.

56 Ibid., 102 and 103.

57 Ibid., 112 and 113.

58 *Smith & Ors v The Ministry of Defence* [2013] UKSC 41.

59 *Al-Sadoon*, above n 54, paras 55, 57, 58, 115 and 116. *Al-Saadoon & Ors v Secretary of State for Defence* [2016] EWCA Civ 811, para 70 and 72.

abroad, particularly on the basis that this serves to undermine the operational effectiveness of armed forces abroad and in the words of the current UK Prime Minister, Theresa May, results in 'vexatious' claims of human rights violations against members of the military. Indeed, in the case of *Al-Sadoon*, consideration has been given to the consequences of the breadth of Leggat's approach to jurisdiction. However, in trying to formulate appropriate and coherent jurisdictional links, it is suggested that international and domestic courts should not necessarily be constrained by extraneous policy considerations that seek to promote or encourage impunity and avoid the consequences of states involved in overseas military operations where they fail to provide adequate training, discipline and accountability. In particular, the issue of subject-matter jurisdiction should be given more prominence by international and domestic courts when trying to resolve some of the conceptual difficulties and extraneous policy controversies surrounding the personal or functional model of jurisdiction. Namely, it is suggested that the *Boškoski* classification criteria may be used to examine whether or not a situation is amenable to the framework of law enforcement, and if it is, then a personal or functional approach to jurisdiction should apply at least in relation to Article 2, as it would do in a state's own territory. To argue otherwise seemingly incentivises extra-judicial killing in the context of overseas military operations that do not amount to factual situations of armed conflict by creating a culture of impunity. Furthermore, an absence of regulation in this regard may lead to strategic failures as discussed in Chapter 1. Where a situation reaches the threshold of a non-international armed conflict in this regard, then that may be sufficient to act as a control mechanism on alien claims based on human rights law, thus addressing extraneous policy concerns about floods of claims before national and international courts.

Despite the potential widening of the state agent authority and control principle in *Jaloud*, Milanovic argues that the framing of jurisdiction for the purposes of Article 1 of the convention is still not plausible because

> [w]hile the power to kill *is* authority and control over the individual *if* the state has public powers, killing is *not* authority and control *if* the state is merely firing away missiles from an aircraft . . . [u]nder this reasoning, drone operations in Yemen or wherever would be just as excluded from the purview of human rights treaties as under *Banković* [emphases added].[60]

In view of the Inter-American and ICTY jurisprudence discussed earlier, as well as its own decision in *Pad v Turkey* and *Isaak*, this reasoning becomes compelling and suggests that the approach taken by the Grand Chamber in *Al-Skeini* is untenable. Instead, the court's decision in *Pad v Turkey* and *Isaak* indicates the existence of a separate and arguably more plausible jurisdictional link which could have been used to support a ruling that the use of force per se is a sufficient

60 Milanovic, above n 32, Ibid.

jurisdictional link for the purposes of Article 1 of the convention.[61] As discussed previously, Melzer refers to this as an emerging form of '*de facto* personal jurisdiction' that is independent of territorial considerations.[62]

It is suggested that it is the *de facto* exercise of control over an individual, or, in other words, the capacity and power of a state to deprive someone of their life, which constitutes the most appropriate form of jurisdictional link, or, to borrow a cogent expression from Sassoli, it should be the case that 'international forces have to respect the right to life of a person simply by omitting to attack that person as soon as those forces could affect that right by their attack.'[63] Similarly, Hampson describes 'personal jurisdiction' as arising where a state can 'control the infliction of the alleged violation and where it was or should have been foreseen that the victim would be adversely affected by the act or omission'.[64] In this way it is suggested that it is not plausible to require that a state have effective control over a territory or exercise some form of public powers in order to refrain from depriving an individual of their life and, to a certain extent, to carry out an investigation into the circumstances surrounding the deprivation of life due to the actions of state agents. The plausibility of this approach garners further support from Lord Justice Sedley's reasoning in *Al-Skeini* before the UK Court of Appeal, namely, 'the one thing British troops did have control over, even in the labile situation described in the evidence was their own use of lethal force'.[65] In this way, the model of *de facto* personal jurisdiction is plausible in that it is

---

61 *Pad v Turkey* (Application No 60167/00) (Admissibility Decision) ECHR (Third Section) 28 June 2007. *Pad* concerned Turkish helicopter gunships killing Iranians on the Turkish-Iranian border. The court in this case held that, '[i]t is not required to determine the exact location of the impugned events, given that the Government had already admitted that the fire discharged from the helicopters had caused the killing of the applicants' relatives [. . .] Accordingly, the Court finds that the victims of the impugned events were within the jurisdiction of Turkey at the material time'; *Al-Skeini v UK*, above n 28, [136] and [137]. Isaak (Application No. 44587/98, Judgment 28 September 2006). The deceased took part in a demonstration at the UN buffer zone between Cyprus and TRNC and was beaten to death by a mob, which included Turkish-Cypriot police officers. The Chamber referred to Issa and considered a state's authority and control through its agents to be a basis of extra-territorial jurisdiction. It concluded that "even if the acts complained of took place in the neutral UN buffer zone, the Court considers that the deceased was under the authority and/or effective control of the respondent State through its agents" and was therefore within the jurisdiction of Turkey.

62 Melzer, above n 10, 134 and 138; *Burgos v Uruguay*, above n 9, 12.2; *Alejandre et al. v Cuba*, above n 24, 23; *Coard et al. v United States* (Report No 109/99) Inter-American Commission on Human Rights, Case 10/951OEA/Ser.L/V/II.106 (29 September 1999), 37.

63 Marco Sassóli, 'The Role of Human Rights and International Humanitarian Law in New Types of Armed Conflicts' in Orna Ben-Naftali (ed), *International Humanitarian Law and International Human Rights Law* (Oxford University Press, 2011) 64–65.

64 Françoise J Hampson, 'The Relationship between International Humanitarian Law and Human Rights Law From the Perspective of a Human Rights Treaty Body' (2008) 90 (871) *International Review of the Red Cross* 89 and 92.

65 *Al-Skeini and others v Secretary of State for Defence* [2005] EWCA Civ 1609, 197 *per* Lord Justice Sedley.

functionally based on notions of spatial and causal proximity that are easily identifiable on a case-by-case basis subject to their ascertainability.

According to Melzer, the model of *de facto* personal jurisdiction implies that 'even marginal or punctual exercise of power may give rise to the extraterritorial "jurisdiction" of the acting State, albeit only with regard to the precise act and to the individuals affected'.[66] In this way, although states may plausibly contend that 'effective control' over territory is necessary to secure a range of derogable rights, for example, those relating to grounds and conditions of detention, as it may be considered as a precondition for the operation of executive, judicial and legislative institutions of governance and civil society, this should not be used to circumvent the application of fundamental nonderogable rights such as the right to life, particularly where states can claim the absence of 'effective control' or public powers on tenuous and spurious grounds, such as the alleged presence of an organised armed group,[67] but nevertheless proceed to use lethal force against individuals. In this way, it is argued that the existence of 'effective control of an area' or the 'exercise of public powers' are by no means necessary and sufficient conditions for the applicability of the right to life. The reason for this is that the 'exercise of public powers' can be regarded as being connected with the exercise of legislative, administrative, judicial or law enforcement functions aimed at ensuring public order and the protection of individual rights. In this regard, when viewed against the jurisprudence surrounding the admissibility criteria under Article 35 paragraph (1) of the convention, and subject to Article 15 discussed earlier in this study, it becomes clear that within the conventional *espace juridique*, individuals are not precluded from invoking their human rights before the ECtHR where they can demonstrate that domestic remedies are inadequate and ineffective in view of their personal circumstances[68] or that effective and adequate remedies are not available due to the general circumstances prevailing at the time, such as where national authorities are totally passive in the face of serious allegations of misconduct or infliction of harm by state agents – for example, by failing to undertake investigations or offer assistance, or where individuals face practical difficulties because law enforcement bodies are not functioning properly, which may be an acute problem in times of civil strife.[69] On this basis, it is suggested that if states cannot dispense from answering for their acts before an

66 Melzer, above n 10, 138.

67 Marco Sassòli and Laura Olson, 'The Relationship between International Humanitarian and Human Rights Law Where It Matters: Admissible Killing and Internment of Fighters in Non-International Armed Conflicts' (2008) 90 (871) *International Review of the Red* Cross 614.

68 *Selmouni v France* (Application No 25803/94) ECHR (Grand Chamber) 1999-V, [74]–[76].

69 *Akdivar v Turkey* (Application No 21893/93) (1997) 23 EHRR 143, [68]–[69]; *Isayeva v Russia* (Application No 57950/00) ECHR 24 February 2005, [152]–[153]; *Khashiyev and Akayeva v Russia* (Application Nos 57942/00, 57945/00) ECHR 24 February 2005, [116]–[117]; *Aksoy v Turkey* (Application No 21987/93) ECHR 1996-VI, [51]–[54].

international body in the context of domestic contexts where legal remedies are neither available nor sufficient due to the unstable and violent circumstances,[70] then there appears to be no valid reason why states should be able to dispense with answering for their use of force extraterritorially. Indeed, as noted earlier, this contradiction creates a state of affairs that is tantamount to granting states 'unfettered discretionary power to carry out wilful and deliberate attacks' against individuals abroad, but not on their own territory.[71] Accordingly, although focusing on alleged procedural violations of the right to life, it is suggested that the decision in *Al-Skeini* leaves open the possibility for the finding of substantive violations of the right to life arising from the extraterritorial use of force in military operations outside the conduct of hostilities.[72]

This approach is in keeping with the policy-based rationale of extraterritorial effect undergirding the decision in *Al-Skeini* as posited by Judge Giovanni Bonello, namely that 'those who export war ought to see to the parallel export of guarantees against the atrocities of war . . . [a]nd then, if necessary, bear with some fortitude the opprobrium of being labelled human rights imperialists'.[73]

---

70 *Selmouni v France*, above n 68.

71 Identical Individual Opinion of Tomuschat. See Melzer, above n 10, 125.

72 *Al-Skeini v UK*, above n 28, [161] and [162]: Although recognising that British armed forces were the target of many attacks and were operating in a context where there was a general breakdown of the Iraqi civilian infrastructure, including the systems of law enforcement and criminal justice, the Grand Chamber emphasised the need to ensure that the right to life under Article 2 was rendered practical and effective as no derogation is permitted, 'except in respect of deaths resulting from lawful acts of war'. Although the Grand Chamber restricted itself to examining whether there had been a violation of the procedural aspect of the right to life in this particular context, the court nevertheless juxtaposes its statements on the general principles concerning procedural obligations under Article 2 with an insertion of the *McCann* dicta concerning the associated substantive principle that '[a]ny use of force must be no more than "absolutely necessary" for the achievement of one or more of the purposes set out in sub-paragraphs (a) to (c)' of Article 2 (*McCann and Others v UK* (Application No 18984/91) (1995) Series A no 324, [146]–[148]); see also UNGA (HRC) 'Report of the Committee of independent experts in international humanitarian and human rights laws to monitor and assess any domestic, legal or other proceedings undertaken by both the Government of Israel and the Palestinian side, in the light of General Assembly resolution 64/254, including the independence, effectiveness, genuineness of these investigations and their conformity with international standards' (21 September 2010) UN Doc A/HRC/15/50, 18: 'International standards are derived from the duty to investigate under international humanitarian law (IHL) and international human rights law (IHRL). Because of the intensity of the clashes between the Israeli Defense Forces (IDF) and the armed Palestinian groups, "Operation Cast Lead" in the Gaza Strip constitutes an armed conflict governed by IHL. The Committee views this conflict as being of an international character, as do both Israel and the Palestinian side. Consequently, IHL was applicable to the conduct of hostilities in the Gaza Strip. The other violations alleged in the FFM report, such as those in the West Bank, did not take place within the context of an armed conflict. They must, therefore, be assessed by the yardstick of IHRL'.

73 *Al-Skeini v UK*, above n 28, Concurring Opinion of Judge Giovanni Bonello, 38.

Thus, as a corollary of this, if we have the 'export of guarantees against the atrocities of war', by which he means convention rights, then we must necessarily have the importation of individual petitions or even mass claims from 'alien' litigants invoking their human rights before our domestic courts and supervisory mechanisms, and then the European Court of Human Rights in the case that domestic remedies have been exhausted or are otherwise not available or effective.

Ultimately, to propose that a state's extraterritorial use of lethal force does not constitute a jurisdictional link where a state does not exercise 'public powers' is to create an unacceptable level of uncertainty, impunity and thus major normative lacunae in the context of contemporary unconventional military operations. Indeed, given that the Grand Chamber's watering down of the territorial principle in *Banković* has the effect of decoupling the issue of extraterritorial jurisdiction under Article 1 of the convention from the Hague and Geneva rules on occupation discussed earlier, it is unfortunate that it did not clearly spell out the form that interventions or activities should take as well as their extent so as to constitute an exercise of 'public powers' for the purposes of establishing a jurisdictional link.[74]

It is suggested that the Grand Chamber's reference to the exercise of authority and control over individuals during the course of security operations should have constituted a free-standing jurisdictional link so as to avoid uncertainty that may arise from this potentially arbitrary criterion. Otherwise, this bifurcated approach to jurisdiction comprising state agent authority and control and a much-relaxed form of the territorial principle not only serves to maintain an unwarranted lacuna in legal protections, but it could also serve to undermine existing protections under humanitarian law in that it potentially deters compliance with the laws of occupation relating to restoration and maintenance of public order and security where states wish to avoid the imposition of human rights obligations. This is because this bifurcated approach incentivises the strategic response of exercising physical power alone through the use of manned and unmanned air power so as to avoid obligations under humanitarian law as well as human rights law.

Conclusions: the modulation and parameters of the right to life in the full-spectrum operational environment

As discussed in Chapter 3, *Boškoski* can assist with the sequencing of obligations, or what *Banković* referred to as the unwarranted 'sliding scale' of obligations.[75] In this respect, *Al-Skeini* is significant in that it departs from this position in *Banković* that obligations cannot be 'divided and tailored'. In this way, rather than an 'all or

74 Adam Roberts, 'Transformative Military Occupation: Applying The Laws of War and Human Rights' (2006) 100 *American Journal of International Law* 580.

75 *Banković and Others v Belgium and Others*, above n 26, 75.

nothing' approach to extraterritorial jurisdiction whereby 'effective control' over foreign sovereign territory triggers a contracting party's obligation to secure all or most rights and freedoms under the convention, *Al-Skeini* demonstrates rights or protections can be 'divided and tailored' not only according to the particular degree of authority and control exercised over an individual in foreign territory, but also to the prevailing context at the time.[76] This raises the challenging practical task of determining the rights or protections that are 'relevant to the situation' of an individual.[77]

In Al-Skeini, patrols by British soldiers and military police constituted a sufficient form of authority and control over those directly and indirectly killed in armed clashes for the United Kingdom's procedural obligation under Article 2 to become applicable, namely to carry out an 'effective official investigation where individuals have been killed as a result of the use of force by agents of the State' in order to 'ensure the effective implementation of domestic laws safeguarding the right to life by effectively reviewing the lawfulness of the use of force and provide accountability for deaths occurring under the authority and control of State agents'.[78] Accordingly, the Grand Chamber held that it had the legal competence to decide on whether the United Kingdom had violated this procedural obligation under Article 2 as it continued to apply 'in difficult security conditions, including in the context of armed conflict'.[79]

In its submissions to the Grand Chamber, the UK government argued that Article 2 'should not be interpreted in such a way as to place an impossible or disproportionate burden on a Contracting State' and that

> [i]f the investigative duty were to apply extraterritorially, it had to take account of [the] circumstances, [that is, the United Kingdom lacked full control over the territory and legislative, administrative or judicial competence], and also of the very difficult security conditions in which British personnel were operating.[80]

---

76 *Al-Skeini v UK*, above n 28, 137: '. . . whenever the State through its agents exercises control and authority over an individual, and thus jurisdiction, the State is under an obligation under Article 1 to secure to that individual the rights and freedoms under Section 1 of the Convention that are relevant to the situation of that individual. In this sense, therefore, the Convention rights can be 'divided and tailored'.

77 Ibid., 137.

78 Ibid., 163; *Nachova v Bulgaria* (Application Nos 43577/98 and 43579/98) ECHR 2005-VII, 110.

79 *Al-Skeini* above n 28, [164]; *Güleç v Turkey* (Application No 21593/93) 28 EHRR 121, [81]; *Ergi v Turkey* (Application No 23818/94) ECHR 1998-IV, [79] and [82]; *Özkan and Others v Turkey* (Application no 21689/93) ECHR (Second Section) 6 April 2004, [85]–[90], [309]–[320], [326]–[330]; *Isayeva v Russia*, above n 69, [180] and [210]; *Georgia v Russia* (Application no. 38263/08) ECHR (Decision) 13 December 2011, [72].

80 *Al-Skeini*, Ibid., 152.

Accordingly, in terms of the parameters of the extraterritorial applicability of this procedural aspect of ensuring the right to life, the Grand Chamber took into account the UK government's concerns by stating that the ability to comply with the obligation to carry out effective investigations may be constrained or limited 'in circumstances of generalised violence, armed conflict or insurgency'.[81]

However, as a general rule, the Grand Chamber held that 'the obligation under Article 2 to safeguard life entails that, even in difficult security conditions, reasonable steps must be taken to ensure that an effective, independent investigation is conducted into alleged breaches of the right to life'.[82] According to the Grand Chamber, the extent of this obligation is that it should be

> broad enough to permit the investigating authorities to take into consideration not only the actions of the State agents who directly used lethal force but also all the surrounding circumstances, including such matters as the planning and control of the operations in question . . .[83]

The Grand Chamber also affirmed that investigations 'must be effective in the sense that it is capable of leading to a determination of whether the force used was or was not justified in the circumstances and to the identification and punishment of those responsible'. Characterising this as an obligation of means, the court held that

> the authorities must take the reasonable steps available to them to secure the evidence concerning the incident, including *inter alia* eye-witness testimony, forensic evidence and, where appropriate, an autopsy which provides a complete and accurate record of injury and an objective analysis of clinical findings, including the cause of death. Any deficiency in the investigation which undermines its ability to establish the cause of death or the person or persons responsible will risk falling foul of this standard.[84]

Additionally, the Grand Chamber ruled that '[f]or an investigation into alleged unlawful killing by State agents to be effective, it is necessary for the persons responsible for and carrying out the investigation to be independent from those implicated in the events'. This requires that there be no 'hierarchical or institutional

81 Ibid., 164; *Bazorkina v Russia* (Application No 69481/01) (2006) 46 EHRR 15, [121].

82 *Al-Skeini v UK*, above n 28, [164]; *Kaya v Turkey* (Application No 158/1996/777/978) ECHR 19 February 1998, [86]–[92]; *Ergi v Turkey*, above n 79, [82]–[85]; *Khashiyev v Russia*, above n 69, [156] [166]; *Isayeva* v Russia, above n 69, [215]–[224].

83 *McCann v UK*, above n 72, [150] [162]; *McKerr v UK* (Application No 28883/95) ECHR 2001-III, [143] [151]; *Finucane v UK* (Application No 29178/95) ECHR 2003-VIII, [77]–[78]; *Nachova v Bulgaria*, above n 78, [114]–[115].

84 *Al-Skeini v UK*, above n 28, [166]; *Özkan v Turkey*, above n 79, [312]; *Isayeva v Russia*, above n 69, [212].

connection' and also 'practical independence'.[85] Furthermore, the court went on to rule that 'there must be a sufficient element of public scrutiny of the investigation or its results to secure accountability in practice as well as in theory' and that the investigation must be commenced promptly and carried out with reasonable expedition.[86]

In the ways described in this discussion, *Al-Skeini* is important as, on the back of the issue of jurisdictional links for the purposes of extraterritorial effect of convention obligations, it further elucidates the potential modalities of the applicability of the right to life in full-spectrum operational conditions.[87] In particular, it suggests that the procedural aspect of the nonderogable right to life may apply in its procedural form 'in circumstances of generalised violence, armed conflict or insurgency'.[88] Thus, this makes a distinction between what Alston describes as 'the question of what rules govern the use of lethal force' and the 'question of investigating violations of these rules'.[89] Accordingly, 'the question of investigating violations' is related to the role that human rights mechanisms may play in ensuring that procedural safeguards are in place at the municipal and international levels so as to supervise indirectly the implementation of the relevant standards vis-à-vis

85 *Al-Skeini v UK*, Ibid., [167].

86 *Al-Skeini*, ibid; *Özkan v Turkey*, above n 79, [311]–[314]; *Isayeva v Russia*, above n 69, [211] and [214]; General Comment No 31, above n 8, 15: 'the general obligation to investigate allegations of violations promptly, thoroughly and effectively through independent and impartial bodies . . . A failure by a State Party to investigate allegations of violations could in and of itself give rise to a separate breach of the Covenant'; UNHRC 'CCPR General Comment No 29: Article 4: Derogations during a State of Emergency' (24 July 2001) UN Doc CCPR/C/21/Rev1/Add11, 15: 'It is inherent in the protection of rights explicitly recognized as non-derogable . . . that they must be secured by procedural guarantees . . . The provisions of the Covenant relating to procedural safeguards may never be made subject to measures that would circumvent the protection of non-derogable rights'; UNHRC, UN Doc A/HRC/15/50, above n 72, 21: 'The human rights treaties and soft law instruments rely on a range of criteria or standards, at times overlapping, to guide investigations. Most of the relevant pronouncements stem from the Human Rights Committee. Its jurisprudence runs largely parallel to the jurisprudence of the European Court of Human Rights and the Inter-American Court of Human Rights. The most common criteria – referred to in the FFM report as "universal principles" – are independence, impartiality, thoroughness, promptness and effectiveness'.

87 *McCann v UK*, above n 72, [86]; 'The obligation to protect the right to life under [article 2], read in conjunction with the State's general duty under Article 1 of the Convention to "secure to everyone within their jurisdiction the rights and freedoms defined in [the] Convention", requires by implication that there should be some form of effective investigation when individuals have been killed as a result of the use of force by, inter alia, agents of the state'.

88 *Al-Skeini v UK*, above n 28, [164]; *Bazorkina v Russia*, above n 81, [121]; Report of the Special Rapporteur (UN Doc E/CN.4/2006/53), above n 5, 36: The UN Special Rapporteur Alston stated that armed conflicts 'will never discharge the obligation to investigate' because 'this would eviscerate the non-derogable character of the right to life'; however, the circumstances of armed conflict 'may affect the modalities or particulars of the investigation' but nevertheless 'investigations must always be conducted as effectively as possible'.

89 Report of the Special Rapporteur (UN Doc E/CN.4/2006/53), above n 5, 42.

the use of force and to review institutional failings.[90] This is significant because, as Alston puts it, 'a State cannot determine whether a particular act was lawful without first investigating what occurred'.[91]

However, in view of the former UN Special Rapporteur's report stating 'it is of continuing concern that States often fail to comply with their obligation to effectively investigate, prosecute, and punish violations of the right to life in situations of armed conflict and occupation' which is often based on 'unjustifiable exceptions' to investigating deaths and failures to ensure that investigations are impartial and independent,[92] human rights mechanisms have an important role to play in finding procedural violations of the right to life in such cases. This is especially so given the Rapporteur's concerns that '[e]fforts at monitoring the consequences of choices of weapons and tactics on the incidental loss of civilian life generally remain *ad hoc*, leaving compliance with requirements of proportionality and precautionary measures under-examined'[93] and that such 'practices threaten to roll back 50 years of progress in subjecting armed conflict to the rule of law'.[94]

Where it is not feasible or mandated for a human rights mechanism to find or reasonably infer substantive violations of human rights law or humanitarian law in a situation of armed conflict, then it is suggested that they may nevertheless proceed to find procedural violations of the right to life, that is, by finding that there has been an absence of an effective investigation into alleged abuses. Although this may not be considered as having the same effect as the finding of a substantive violation as it affects the level of compensation and remedial measures and may not involve the level of scrutiny into the conduct of state agents as many victims would like to see, it nevertheless represents an important form of oversight for individuals, and may serve to encourage or indeed require further investigations or prosecutions at the domestic level.[95] However, this needs greater clarity.

90 Ibid., 41: 'The obligation to investigate is part and parcel of the obligation to ensure the right to life and, thus, entails more than the determination of criminal responsibility. States are also responsible for undertaking the systematic supervision and periodic investigation necessary to ensure that their institutions, policies, and practices ensure the right to life as effectively as possible. Canada's experience in Somalia illustrates the complementary roles of criminal and non-criminal investigation. Canada prosecuted and punished several soldiers for their actions in Somalia, but it also established a Commission of Inquiry to determine the institutional defects that allowed those abuses to occur. By identifying pervasive problems in how rules of engagement were drafted, were disseminated through the chain of command, and were taught to soldiers on the ground, Canada improved its institutional capacity to better ensure the right to life in the future. States must constantly monitor and investigate whether they are effectively ensuring human rights law and adopt all necessary measures to prevent the recurrence of a violation'.

91 Ibid., 42.

92 Ibid., 33.

93 Ibid.

94 Ibid., 34.

95 Philip Leach, Costas Paraskeva, and Gordana Uzelac, 'Human Rights Fact-Finding: The European Court of Human Rights at a Crossroads' (2010) 28 (1) *Netherlands Quarterly of Human Rights* 41–77, 2010, 48; UN HRC General Comment No 31, above n 8, 15: 'States Parties must ensure that individuals also have effective remedies to vindicate their rights' and that '[a] failure by a State Party to investigate allegations of violations could in and of itself give rise to

Al-Skeini concerned the extraterritorial effect of the procedural aspect of the right to life under Article 2 ECHR, namely the duty to carry out an effective investigation, vis-à-vis the United Kingdom during its time as an occupying power in Iraq. In examining the extraterritorial effect of this procedural obligation, as a starting point, the court took into account the practical problems associated with the fact that the United Kingdom was an occupying power in a foreign and hostile region in the immediate aftermath of invasion and war.[96] Thus *Al-Skeini* may be broadly construed as relating to the extraterritorial effect of the procedural aspect of Article 2 to foreign military operations, and this may include, but is not necessarily confined to, situations of belligerent occupation. Indeed, the court in *Al-Skeini* stated that this 'procedural obligation under Article 2 continues to apply in difficult security conditions, including in a context of armed conflict'.[97] Thus, although it primarily relates to the issue of the extraterritorial applicability of the procedural aspect of Article 2 ECHR to foreign military operations, it is suggested that this case may in the future have relevance to the separate question of the relationship between international human rights law and humanitarian law, although the court did not specifically deal with this issue. This second issue raises two problems: first, a potential horizontal clash with humanitarian law and, second, whether such an obligation is feasible in that it could place impossible investigative burdens on states in situations of international armed conflicts where there may be generalised violence and non-international armed conflicts where there has to be organised and high-intensity violence.

On the first issue, the rules of IHL relating to a requirement to carry out investigations are implicit in the four Geneva Conventions and API which apply to international armed conflicts. These treaty-based rules set out an obligation upon contracting states to search for persons alleged to have committed, or ordered to have committed, grave breaches and to try or extradite them.[98] Accordingly, civilian deaths that do not amount to grave breaches, for example, launching a disproportionate attack, may not fall within the scope of this obligation, and treaty-based rules applicable to non-international armed conflicts contain no such obligation. Nevertheless, the ICRC Customary Law study suggests that the obligation upon states to investigate war crimes committed by their nationals or armed forces or on their territory has customary status.[99] In contrast, *Al-Skeini*

a separate breach of the Covenant'. To this end, General Comment No 31 interprets Article 4 as setting 'a general obligation to investigate allegations of violations promptly, thoroughly and effectively through independent and impartial bodies'; see also ECOSOC Resolution 1989/65 (24 May 1989) Annex: 'Principles on the Effective Prevention and Investigation of Extra-legal, Arbitrary and Summary Executions' which sets out 'Principles on the Effective Prevention and Investigation of Extra-legal, Arbitrary and Summary Executions'.

96 *Al-Skeini*, above n 28, [168].

97 *Al-Skeini*, Ibid., [164].

98 First Geneva Convention, Article 49; Second Geneva Convention, Article 50; Third Geneva Convention, Article 129; Fourth Geneva Convention, Article 146; Articles 85 and 86 of Additional Protocol I.

99 Jean-Marie Henckaerts and Louise Doswald-Beck, *Customary International Humanitarian Law* (Volume 1: Rules, ICRC-Cambridge University Press, 2005) ('CIHL Study'), Rule 158.

indicates a far broader obligation under the ECHR in that 'there should be some form of effective official investigation when individuals have been killed as a result of the use of force by, inter alios, agents of the State'.[100] This seems a very broad and demanding obligation and it is doubtful whether the applicability of this procedural obligation is realistic in a conflict situation. Accordingly, one way of merging these two approaches in a situation of armed conflict would be that states are only required to investigate and prosecute where there is a suspicion that war crimes have been committed, and that a failure in this regard can amount to a procedural violation of the right to life. It is suggested that this process can serve to require the criminal investigation and trial of state agents at the domestic level.

However, this leads to the second issue of whether such an obligation is feasible in practice. In this respect, *Al-Skeini* recognises that 'obstacles may be placed in the way of investigators' and so summarises ECtHR jurisprudence in relation to what constitutes an effective investigation, but qualifies this by stating that these standards may be constrained or limited 'in circumstances of generalised violence, armed conflict or insurgency'. In stating that 'all reasonable steps must be taken to ensure that an effective, independent investigation is conducted into alleged breaches of the right to life', the court indicated that this is to be considered an obligation of means and thus is proportionate to the difficulties faced in all of the circumstances.[101] It is suggested that given the institutional limitations of humanitarian law with regard to accountability situations of armed conflict, the expanded reach of the European Court of Human Rights in response has resulted in progressive jurisprudence on the applicability of the right to life in situations involving armed conflict and occupation.[102] It is suggested that the general requirement that an investigation be 'broad enough to permit the investigating authorities to take into consideration not only the actions of the State agents who directly used lethal force but also all the surrounding circumstances . . .' is feasible even in situations where there is no territorial control as it may in such circumstances be limited to internal

100 *Al-Skeini*, above n 28, [163].

101 *Al-Skeini v UK*, Ibid., [164]; *Bazorkina v Russia*, above n 81, [121]; See also *McKerr v UK*, above n 83, [111]–[115].

102 Juliet Chevalier-Watts, 'Has Human Rights Law Become Lex Specialis for the European Court of Human Rights in Right to Life Cases Arising from Internal Armed Conflicts?' (2010) 14 (4) *The International Journal of Human Rights* 597; *Kaya v Turkey*, above n 82, [91]: '[the] loss of life is a tragic and frequent occurrence in view of the security situation in south-east Turkey [. . .]. However, neither the prevalence of violent armed clashes nor the high incidence of fatalities can displace the obligation under Article 2 to ensure that an effective, independent investigation is conducted into deaths arising out of clashes involving the security forces, more so in cases such as the present where the circumstances are in many respects unclear'; In this regard, at [108], the court went on to state that 'in the absence of any effective investigation into the circumstances of the death' which occurred in the context of numerous 'violent armed clashes' resulting in a 'high incidence of fatalities', the court was seemingly uncompromising in finding a violation of Article 13 in Kaya on the basis of the 'serious deficiencies in the autopsy and the forensic examination conducted at the scene and to consider seriously any alternative options which may have explained the death'; with regard to the latter, the court found that the authorities were not prepared to test the assumption that the deceased victim was a terrorist killed in an armed clash with security forces [sections II.A & II.B].

planning and control matters.[103] Accordingly this is an area where the frameworks of human rights and humanitarian law can be considered complementary in the sense of providing important guidance not only as to what is practical and feasible in terms of effective investigations, but what can be reasonably expected, so as to ensure that impossible or disproportionate burdens are not placed upon states in the challenging conditions of full-spectrum operational theatres.[104]

In this regard, because *Al-Skeini* does not provide guidance as to how reasonable expectations vis-à-vis the procedural aspect of the right to life can be correlated with the intensity of violence, conflict or insurgency,[105] it is suggested that a parallel be drawn with the feasibility of threat-based assessments and what can be reasonably expected from domestic authorities in terms of carrying out effective individual investigations.[106] In this regard, it is proposed that the *Boškoski* classification criteria that elucidate and grade the elements of organisation and intensity of collective violence may be employed in order to determine what can be reasonably expected in

---

103 *McCann v UK*, above n 72, [150] [162]; *McKerr v UK* above n 83, [143] [151]; *Finucane v UK* above n 83, [77] – [78]; *Nachova v Bulgaria*, above n 78, [114]–[115].

104 Michael Schmitt, 'Targeted Killings and International Law: Law Enforcement, Self-defense, and Armed Conflict' in R Arnold and N Quenivet (eds.), *International Humanitarian Law and Human Rights Law: Towards a New Merger in International Law* (Brill, Leiden/Boston, 2008) 552: Schmitt contends that investigations 'might be well-advised as a matter of policy during low-intensity conflict' whereas 'it would generally be impractical to conduct one into every strike executed in a high intensity armed conflict' and in such situations, 'IHL only requires investigations into possible war crimes'; *Public Committee Against Torture v The Government of Israel*, Israel, Supreme Court, Judgment of 14 December 2006, HCJ 769/02, 40: In contrast, the Israeli Supreme Court mandated that 'after an attack on a civilian suspected of taking an active part, at such time, in hostilities, a thorough investigation regarding the precision of the identification of the target and the circumstances of the attack upon him is to be performed (retroactively)'. In putting forward this proposition that retroactive review is required of the use of force upon civilians suspected of directly participating in hostilities, the Israeli Supreme Court itself referenced the ECtHR decisions in *McCann* and *McKerr* which indicates that this policy-based reasoning concerning *ex post facto* review is not confined to Israeli domestic law, but has parallels elsewhere. However, note Kenneth Watkin, 'Controlling the Use of Force: A Role for Human Rights Norms in Contemporary Armed Conflict' (2004) 98(1) *American Journal of International Law* 32: in situations of armed conflict, it may not be possible to 'Carry out an investigation into each and every loss of life given the scale and intensity of hostilities; Investigate and carry out criminal prosecutions of non-state actors and state actors carrying out combat operations in the field. In this regard, it may not be possible to call back soldiers and military commanders from front line duties; Gather evidence and carry out crime scene investigations in hostile territory or areas; Obtain access to sensitive information that could undermine military operations and national security'. For example, disclosing information on weapons capabilities, rules of engagement and strategy would enable adversaries to adopt counterstrategies. Furthermore, it may not be possible to ensure that there is no 'hierarchical or institutional connection', as primarily, under IHL, it is the responsibility of states, in particular, parties to a conflict, to ensure that there is satisfactory command and control over their forces in order to prevent and punish violations of IHL. Having a fully independent reviewing body could potentially undermine military operations, and is arguably why there is no such requirement under IHL.

105 *Al-Skeini v UK*, above n 28, [164]; *Bazorkina v. Russia*, above n 81, [121].

106 Zemach, above n 22, 111–112.

unconventional operational environments that contain mixed and fluid aspects of authority, control and collective violence. Accordingly, as described earlier, where hostilities can be considered so 'serious' that they exceed a state's capacity to carry out individualised threat assessments and employ law enforcement techniques, then the finding of procedural violations on the basis that, for example, the authorities did not 'secure the evidence concerning the incident, including *inter alia* eye-witness testimony, forensic evidence and, where appropriate, an autopsy which provides a complete and accurate record of injury and an objective analysis of clinical findings, including the cause of death',[107] may not be considered reasonable. Thus, as indicated by the former Special Rapporteur on extrajudicial, summary or arbitrary executions, international and regional human rights mechanisms strike an appropriate balance in recognising that states may utilise less effective measures of investigation in situations where there are concrete constraints, such as where hostile forces control the scene where individuals have allegedly been killed.[108]

107 *Al-Skeini v UK*, above n 28, [166]; *Özkan v Turkey*, above n 79, [312]; *Isayeva v Russia*, above n 69, [212].

108 Report of the Special Rapporteur (UN Doc E/CN.4/2006/53), above n 5, 36 and at 32: 'Nonetheless, there are constraints during armed conflict that do impede investigations. For example, not every death during an armed conflict can be effectively investigated. Similarly, the level of transparency expected of human rights investigations is not always achievable in situations of armed conflict, particularly as questions of national security often arise. The nature of hostilities might obstruct on-site investigations or make prompt medical examinations impossible. The conflict might have led to the destruction of evidence, and witnesses might be hard to locate or be engaged in conflict elsewhere. When the fighting is over, some of these constraints tend to lose their relevance'. Furthermore, '[o]n a case-by-case basis a State might utilize less effective measures of investigation in response to concrete constraints. For example, when hostile forces control the scene of a shooting, conducting an autopsy may prove impossible. Regardless of the circumstances, however, investigations must always be conducted as effectively as possible and never be reduced to mere formality'.

9 Conclusions

Grey zones of war and peace in our globally networked information environment

Overview of discussion

Chapter 3 noted that 'virtual theatres' in cyberspace can serve to undermine the spatial conception of a war zone by increasing the capacities of groups to instigate, plan and execute operations ranging from isolated 'lone wolf' attacks, to small-scale 'guerrilla' attacks, to widespread and coordinated conventional attacks. The globally networked reach of individuals and groups has increased, and this creates the risk that the conduct of hostilities paradigm can spill over and prevail outside of combat zones and also that the distinction between crime and war, as well as our response to it, becomes increasingly blurred. Individuals may be geographically remote from a war zone, but that does not stop them from being virtually 'in theatre', for example, by providing intelligence, logistics and finance for specific military operations. Chapter 1 of this study noted that civilians are at major risk in contemporary crisis and conflict situations that take place in urban locations, especially where means and methods of conventional warfare are used. The application of conventional military means and methods to such situations may be permitted under IHL, but there is the risk that this is being applied to what are situations of crisis rather than conflict. This study has noted that in these situations it is very difficult to know what rules apply, how they apply and what those rules mean. In part, this is because there has been uncertainty in how to categorise a state of affairs in pragmatic terms, that is, when is violence so dangerous and intense that it exceeds the capacity of law enforcement methods and thus law enforcement regulation? This is a problem faced by state militaries and law enforcement agencies, as well as UN treaty and charter mechanisms and regional human rights mechanisms. Accordingly, state military doctrine and the authoritative decisions of a range of international human rights bodies demonstrate similar approaches and interests, but also are useful in demonstrating how different rules can be interpreted and applied in a progressive way so that they are fit for the uncertainties and complexities of contemporary unconventional and irregular crises/conflicts: for example, counterinsurgency, counterterrorism, and large-scale organised crime. Furthermore, this study has suggested that international and regional mechanisms of international civil society have become increasingly relevant in providing a range of oversight and review functions. It has been suggested that this has arisen in response to the weaknesses in the institutional framework for the implementation of humanitarian law. It is suggested that the individual complaints and reporting procedures generally available within human rights mechanisms represent important interpretative dynamos for the progressive realisation of existing standards.

This study has made some bold proposals: first, that human rights approaches and humanitarian law approaches may apply in the same operational environment; second, that higher standards of reasonableness ought to apply vis-à-vis the use of force in certain grey zone crises/conflicts; and third, that the jurisprudence of international criminal tribunals greatly assists with clarifying the general transition from the paradigm of law enforcement to that of armed conflict, and thus where Hague permissive and prohibitive rules on lethal force can be used, that is, with regard to the former, where targeting may occur on the basis of status in the context of targeted or planned operations. In addition, the threshold criteria for a basic armed conflict as elucidated by international criminal tribunals may be used by human rights bodies to identify those situations where human rights standards on the use of force are no longer practicable or feasible. This study has taken issue with the position of writers who argue that this can only occur at the threshold of an APII NIAC by contending that the threshold criteria for a CA3 NIAC as indicated by *Boškoski* actually require high-intensity hostilities and a large degree of organisation on the part of organised armed groups; however, writers such as Hampson accept this general principle but challenge the extent of the *Boškoski* guidelines. The fourth proposal is that military doctrine and authoritative pronouncements of international civil society actors demonstrate what may be referred to as common policy preferences in terms of higher standards of reasonableness and the interoperability of law enforcement approaches and combat approaches in the same operational theatre. It is suggested that these common policy preferences can influence further legal development in a plausible way – that is, they interpret and apply existing rules so that they are fit for regulating force and protecting civilians in a sensible and appropriate way in contemporary situations.

This study is important, because, in the words of Hampson, 'the 'fog of war' has become the 'fog of law'.[1] In other words, complex legal frameworks have emerged during the course of the twentieth and twenty-first centuries, and from legal and military perspectives there is a high degree of controversy in relation to their scope, meaning and interoperability. In particular, this discussion has attempted to provide a general basis for more coherent systemic integration of these legal frameworks so that they provide clear protection and are capable of being applied by primary duty bearers affected by binding legal rules and associated policy considerations. As noted in this study, this is a complicated issue, because in 1949 we only had the Geneva Conventions, and in 1977 there was

1 Françoise Hampson, 'The Relationship between International Humanitarian Law and Human Rights Law', in Scott Sheeran and Sir Nigel Rodley (eds), *The Routledge Handbook of International Human Rights Law* (Routledge, 2013) 209.

recognition that these needed to be updated, so Additional Protocols I and II were drafted, but there were still uncertainties on important issues such as the parameters of civilian immunity from attack. Since then we have had a massive increase in human rights law and associated bodies, as well as international criminal law and associated bodies. This study has argued that 'authoritative decisions' of these judicial and quasi-judicial bodies can be used to interpret the treaty-based and customary Hague rules in a more progressive fashion, so that they are fit for contemporary protection needs.

In relation to the use of force, this study has identified ways in which the paradigm of law enforcement and hostilities can be interoperable both generally and in relation to specific incidents. It is important as it has addressed these practical problems: first, it shows that the lessons that have been learned from the past two decades of unconventional/low-intensity conflicts (that is, higher standards of reasonableness in civilianised operational theatres, and the coordination of law enforcement and combat operations) and it suggests that these can lead to the plausible development of IHL, as well as its interaction with other related branches of law such as human rights law and international criminal law. Second, this study has examined and proposed new guidelines for assessing when a crisis becomes a conflict, and thus where permissive and prohibitive Hague rules on the conduct of hostilities can be applied. On this issue, the concern is that many crises are being approached as if they were conflicts, and therefore the permissive rules of IHL are being applied as if they were the norm rather than the exception. This helps us apply the rules/expectations that are most protective to people in contemporary situations of conflict and other situations of violence. In particular, the approach proposed in this study actually seeks to confine such permissive standards to a very high threshold and give further clarity as to when this threshold is met: this gives further clarity as to when military/IHL approaches to targeting and weaponry can be lawfully used. Third, this study has argued that in many contexts law enforcement approaches/regulations are sufficient and ought to be applied in the first instance. Indeed, this study has also sought to clarify when human rights approaches/regulations should apply to the use of force in a foreign country, that is, where there is no armed conflict, any time a state/state agents have the power to kill someone or in the context of an armed conflict, there is a procedural duty to investigate the deprivation of life to the highest standards feasible. Fourth, in clarifying the exceptional circumstances where military approaches/permissive regulation apply, this study has sought to demonstrate that there are increasing restrictions on the use of high-explosive conventional means of force (missiles, mortars, artillery, mines) in the context of unconventional/irregular conflicts that take place in urban areas: in this sense higher standards of reasonableness are required (for example, distinction: positively identifying lethal threats; precautions: verifying on the basis of good intelligence/giving effective warnings; proportionality: considering second- and third-order effects of attacks, rather than just their immediate impact (that is, mid- to long-term impact of attacks). Given the risks of 'conventional' weapons, this study has explored whether 'nonlethals' may be used in urban conflicts.

This study has argued that the use of chemical calmatives/relaxants is too risky in urban warfare as people may suffocate if they do not get medical treatment quickly enough. This study has noted that greater restraints have been increasingly imposed on forces operating in civilianised and urbanised environments in order to avoid the strategic costs associated with incidental harm and collateral damage. Fifth, this research has attempted to make an important contribution by taking the concepts and approaches relating to participation and perpetration used by *international* criminal law and extrapolating them to notions that IHL has consistently struggled to define in clear and analytic terms, namely direct participation in hostilities and membership in organised armed groups. This, it is suggested, would form part of precautionary measures which are increasingly feasible in our information environment. In such an environment, heightened precautionary measures are important to avoid the strategic costs associated with misidentification of civilians as fighters or positive identification errors. Finally, and more broadly, this study has explored the complex *status mixus* operational environment of contemporary hostilities, which can involve multiple layers of organised violence that can be represented on a continuum of violence. Different aspects of this continuum may be interconnected and fluid in terms of their level of organisation and intensity over time. Some of the key trends to occur within *status mixus* milieux include asymmetric tactics and irregular forms of organisation which means that the contemporary battle space is most often civilianised and urbanised. In this context, civilians are at greater risk and thus so are the strategic objectives behind the use of force. Accordingly, it can be observed from contemporary doctrinal responses that there is a greater coincidence of military and humanitarian considerations, which takes the form of a correlation between the continuum of violence and the continuum of force. With regard to the modalities for the application of a continuum of force in unconventional operational environments, it can be observed that humanitarian considerations are integral to doctrinal calculations of advantage at all levels of conflict. This compels greater restraints on the use of force, or, in other words, greater standards of reasonableness in unconventional operational environments where there is a concentration of civilians, and thus, it is argued, a presumption in favour of civilian protection. This manifests itself in the form of the sequenced and parallel application of the law enforcement and combat operations or, in other words, the sequenced and parallel application of escalation of nonlethal and lethal force doctrines. This has been referred to as population-centric approaches to unconventional and irregular operational environments that are in essence presumptively oriented towards the human rights–based model of law enforcement.

Given that contemporary doctrinal responses to the unconventional operational environments outlined in Chapter 1 correlate the continuum of violence with the continuum of force, it is suggested that this forms the basis for a reflexive relationship with normativity; that is, what has been learned and thus implemented in doctrine and policy can and should lead to progressive legal interpretation of existing standards.

Namely, the doctrinal responses outlined in Chapter 1 provide the conditions and practice that can undergird the reconceptualisation and restructuring of relevant legal frameworks, not only so that they are fit for the prevalent full-spectrum milieux, but also so that they can effectively guide the force continuum at tactical, operational and strategic levels of intervention. Rather than suggesting that the ideas presented in this study represent the actual development of the law, this study has aimed to identify trends, possibilities and opportunities for potential development, or, in other words, a proximal zone of development into which legal frameworks relative to the regulation of means and methods of force can progress in a plausible fashion.

Postscript: transforming a king's bounty into law

The 'progress of civilisation' compels an adaptive interplay between the changing character of conflict and parties to it, advancing technologies and progressive 'usages established among civilised peoples', 'laws of humanity' and 'dictates of the public conscience'.[2] Emerging from this dialectical process are higher standards of reasonableness. The examination of contemporary military doctrine and international civil society discourse discussed in this study reveals a trend towards the greater coincidence of military and humanitarian interests. This is gradually manifesting itself in the form of doctrinal and normative population-centric approaches to the most prevalent type of operational theatre in our global strategic environment, namely unconventional conflict situations that contain a full spectrum of violence. However, there is the constant danger that the tide will turn and important lessons vis-à-vis the effective use of force and how to respond appropriately to political conflicts will be forgotten as states have to respond to multiple and overlapping challenges, crises and unconventional conflicts. There is the danger of a retrenchment from the international norms and institutions that expanded and developed towards the end of the twentieth century and the beginning of the twenty-first as the world became increasingly polarised and violent.

In this context, a defining feature of this form of unconventional war is that only where their weaker opponent fights on their terms are conventional armed forces most likely to prevail through their superior capabilities at the operational and theatre levels. This can be seen from the empirical survey by Arreguín-Toft of 202 asymmetric conflicts that took place between 1816 and 2003. It shows that where asymmetric adversaries use diametrically opposed military strategies – for instance, where a weaker side adopts the means and methods of guerrilla warfare as a counterstrategy to a militarily superior side's conventional offensive, the

2 Hague Convention (IV) respecting the Laws and Customs of War on Land and its annex: Regulations concerning the Laws and Customs of War on Land, The Hague, 18 October 1907, Preamble.

weaker side is almost three times more likely to prevail over the stronger side than if it were to fight using the same means and methods of warfare as the stronger opponent.[3] The survey also shows that in the period 1950–1999, militarily strong adversaries were defeated in 51.2 per cent of all asymmetric conflicts.[4] Arreguín-Toft's findings suggest that weaker adversaries generally prevail in asymmetric conflicts because they adopt unconventional counterstrategies that transform the hostilities into protracted wars of attrition, which become politically costly and unsustainable for the stronger side. In such situations, a stronger side may attempt to employ similarly unconventional and indirect strategies to defeat its weaker opponent. However, the historical case studies analysed by Arreguín-Toft, such as the Battle of Algiers in 1957 and Operation Rolling Thunder during the 1965–1975 Vietnam War, indicate that 'barbarism' is a self-defeating strategy, especially if the long-term goals are to achieve a political outcome such as peace and security or regime change, because it serves to increase political and military resistance.[5] As indicated in Chapter 1, this notion is recognised in contemporary military doctrine relating to unconventional and low-intensity conflict situations and so serves to influence the interpretation of existing treaty-based and customary standards of humanitarian law. Moreover, as argued by Walzer, the strategic pitfall for militarily stronger sides is that asymmetric conflicts have a tendency to escalate into wars not only among but also against entire civilian populations – in this sense there is a danger that 'barbarism' may become an inevitable outcome of asymmetric urban armed conflict.[6]

International and internal asymmetric urban armed conflicts are 'a mere continuation of policy by other means',[7] and for this reason, until the frameworks of international humanitarian and human rights law are further developed or reformed to ensure the universal application of satisfactory humanitarian protections, it is a strategic imperative that progressive interpretations of treaty-based and customary IHL be identified and sequenced with human rights standards that presumptively apply in the absence of objective indicators of hostility, which are then further integrated into basic military doctrine and practice and so in turn become part of a broader political and economic strategy towards achieving legitimate aims.

What the Lieber Code, the first modern codification of the laws of war, told the armies of the United States of 1863 was as wise a praxis then as it is now: 'military necessity does not include any act of hostility which makes the return to

3 Ivan Arreguín-Toft, *How the Weak Win Wars: A Theory of Asymmetric Conflict* (Cambridge University Press, 2008) 205.
4 Ibid., 4.
5 Ibid., 211–213, 220–227.
6 Michael Walzer, *Just and Unjust Wars: A Moral Argument with Historical Illustrations* (rev 7th edn Basic Books, New York, 2007) 187.
7 Clausewitz, *On War* (Wordsworth Classics of World Literature, 1997).

peace unnecessarily difficult'.[8] Thus, as outlined earlier, a failure to be reasonable does not create the conditions in which the use of superior force can be beneficial at the strategic level, namely to facilitate peace, justice and security; it may, on the contrary, create and intensify internal and internationalised armed conflicts, as adversaries are forced into adopting more and more unconventional means and methods of warfare in order to counter conventional military superiority. If there is anything to be learned from the hostilities in cities, towns and villages in Vietnam, Chechnya, Lebanon, Iraq, Afghanistan, the West Bank and Gaza, it is that asymmetric urban warfare is seldom decisive, and, furthermore, that failure to adopt a population-centric approach to urban warfare can undermine the utility of force by making the return to peace unnecessarily difficult. The sequenced application of human rights law and progressive elucidations of customary IHL can but serve to increase the utility of force in modern conflicts when viewed from a strategic perspective, in that aside from ideological differences, all parties to any armed conflict have a fundamental interest in peace, justice and security and that unbridled military force alone cannot achieve these ends.[9]

This study has taken stock of some of the fresh and population-centric elucidations of the substance and ordering of existing treaty-based and customary standards of humanitarian and human rights law that have emerged out of a range of contemporary military operations within full-spectrum operational environments during the last decade of the twentieth century and the first decade of the twenty-first. This study has attempted to reconceptualise and restructure human rights law and humanitarian law so that they can be applied to complex situations of violence with increased clarity and certainty. As discussed in this study, contemporary situations of violence are complex because they increasingly take place within urban settings containing high concentrations of civilians and because they increasingly take place within a global information environment. The proposals contained within this study are primarily for the benefit of states and are intended as ways of guiding the effective use of force in unconventional operational theatres in the second decade of the twenty-first century and beyond.

8 Instructions for the Government of Armies of the United States in the Field (Lieber Code), 24 April 1863, Article 16.

9 Rupert Smith, *The Utility of Force: The Art of War in the Modern World* (Allen Lane, London 2006) part III.

Index

For Product Safety Concerns and Information please contact our EU
representative GPSR@taylorandfrancis.com
Taylor & Francis Verlag GmbH, Kaufingerstraße 24, 80331 München, Germany

www.ingramcontent.com/pod-product-compliance
Ingram Content Group UK Ltd.
Pitfield, Milton Keynes, MK11 3LW, UK
UKHW020020200926
475702UK00014B/1986

* 9 7 8 0 3 6 7 0 2 5 1 0 6 *